SITE ANALYSIS

SITE ANALYSIS

Linking Program and Concept in Land Planning and Design

James A. LaGro, Jr.

University of Wisconsin–Madison

JOHN WILEY & SONS, INC.

New York • Chichester • Weinheim • Brisbane • Singapore • Toronto

To Rosi and David.

This book is printed on acid-free paper. ♾

Published simultaneously in Canada.

Library of Congress Cataloging-in-Publication Data:

LaGro, James A.
Site analysis : linking program and concept in land planning and design / James A. LaGro, Jr.
p. cm.
Includes bibliographical references (p.).
ISBN 0-471-34412-5 (cloth : alk. paper)
1. Building sites—Planning. 2. Building sites—Environmental aspects. I. Title.

NA2540.5 .L34 2001
720'.28—dc21

00-043854

Printed in the United States of America.
10 9 8 7 6 5 4 3 2 1

Contents

Preface

CONTEXT

The built environment is the result of decisions made by individuals and intitutions within both the private and public sectors. In the United States, the subdivision of large tracts of land into smaller parcels is a significant step in the land development process. The individual land parcel is the spatial unit for which most land development projects are designed and implemented. This book is concerned with the land planning and design process that occurs at the site, or individual land parcel, scale.

Private sector land development projects include single-use developments such as office buildings or shopping centers, as well as mixed-use developments combining retail, commercial, residential, and other uses within individual projects. Although land development in the United States is largely a private sector enterprise, significant land use changes are also initiated within the public sector. Local, state, and federal governments provide a wide range of public services requiring buildings and other physical infrastructure. Public sector projects range from interstate highways and national parks to neighborhood parks and playgrounds. Highways, greenways, and public recreational trails occupy long linear corridors, and these projects require the acquisition of many contiguous land parcels. The length of these corridors may stretch from a few to several hundred kilometers. In contrast, public schools and parks are built on individual land parcels, making these similar in many ways to private sector projects.

Protecting ecosystem structure and function and maintaining a site's "sense of place" are laudable development goals. This implicitly requires, however, a sound understanding of the site and its biophysical and cultural context. The arrangement of buildings, the organization of pedestrian and vehicle circulation systems, and the management of stormwater are a few of the many land use decisions that require a comprehensive understanding of local site conditions.

In many cases, a well-designed project—supported by a thorough analysis of the site and its surrounding context—is not any more expensive to build than a poorly designed project. Moreover, site planning and design excellence can yield significant economic and social benefits (Bookout, 1994). The linkages between design quality, location, and real estate value are a fundamental concern within the land development industry. For example, in a panel discussion convened by *Architectural Record,* Dennis Carmichael, a landscape architect with EDAW, Inc., asserted (Dean, 1997, p.49):

> ...developers have learned that a good design equals return on investment. Rather than bulldozing a site into submission, they now try to celebrate its intrinsic qualities.

The careful analysis of sites — and the surrounding context — can lead to better development proposals and, ultimately, to higher-quality built environments.

Adapting development to the unique conditions of a site is also good business. Proposals for carefully sited projects may receive faster approvals and permitting, improved marketability, and rent and sales premiums (Bookout, 1994). A contextual approach to land development also helps protect public health, safety, and welfare. By avoiding inherent site problems, or constraints, and by capitalizing on inherent site assets, or opportunities, developers can limit long-term maintenance costs and, more important, reduce the risks to life and property from natural hazards.

ORGANIZATION OF THE BOOK

This book is divided into four parts. Part I contains Chapter 1 (Land and Society) and Chapter 2 (Spatial Information and Mapping). The first chapter summarizes the land planning and design process, and places land planning and design in the broader context of land use decision making. The second chapter summarizes the major principles and processes of collecting, organizing, and mapping site attribute data within a geographic information system (GIS).

Part II has two chapters. Chapter 3 (Site Selection) examines methods of identifying and evaluating alternative sites. Chapter 4 (Programming) focuses on programming methods such as user surveys, focus groups, and market analyses. Part III (Site Inventory and Analysis) is the core of the book. Chapter 5 (Site Inventory: Physical Attributes) and Chapter 6 (Site Inventory: Biological Attributes) cover a wide array of physical and biological attributes that, depending on the unique features of the site and the program, may be analyzed during the land planning and design process. Chapter 7 (Site Inventory: Cultural Attributes) concentrates on documenting relevant cultural and historic attributes. Chapter 8 (Site Analysis: Integration and Synthesis) describes how site opportunities and constraints for specific project programs are identified and graphically communicated to clients and other stakeholders.

The last two chapters of the book are in Part IV. Chapter 9 (Concept Development) addresses alternative approaches to spatially organizing site land uses and associated infrastructure. Chapter 10 (Design Development and Implementation), the last chapter of the book, addresses several key principles of site planning and construction documentation. The chapter also examines the role that local government — and citizen boards and commissions — play in reviewing land planning and design proposals. The book concludes with an Appendix and a Glossary. The Appendix lists both commercial and government sources of data and other information that can be potentially useful in land planning and design.

EDUCATIONAL USES

Practitioners from several professions are involved in the land planning and development process. Depending on the project's size, location, and complexity, the planning and development team may include architects, engineers, landscape architects, planners, economists, environmental specialists, bankers, builders, developers, or realtors. Landscape architecture is a profession that is integrally involved in the analysis and planning of the land.

However, professional trade magazines in landscape architecture and other allied fields routinely include articles about the *product* — rather than the process — of design. That is, the articles focus on the buildings and outdoor spaces created or modified by designers. These articles may be accompanied by attractively rendered site plans, sections and elevations, aerial perspectives, and glossy photographs of the recently completed projects. However, relatively little attention — and usually no graphic documentation — is devoted to explaining the factors that influenced the designs. In fact, many articles virtually ignore the site's context, as well as other design determinants, and focus exclusively on the artifacts of design (i.e., the edifice complex). What, if anything, would convince a potential client — or a colleague — that these attractively illustrated designs are appropriate for each particular site? What evidence is there to justify the design decisions portrayed in the photographs? More important, from an educator's perspective, what values and priorities do these articles convey to students in professional design programs?

A task analysis of the profession of landscape architecture in North America was conducted in 1998 by the Council of Landscape Architectural Registration Boards (CLARB). One goal of the survey was to document the types of work performed by practicing landscape architects. The respondents were asked to identify their work tasks, and rank them in terms of each activity's perceived contribution to the protection of public health, safety, and welfare. This is a relevant question, because state licensing laws for landscape architects, engineers, architects, and many other professions are specifically intended to protect public health, safety, and welfare. Completed surveys were received from a randomly selected sample of more than 2,000 landscape architects. Six of the fifteen most important tasks listed in the CLARB survey — including two of the top three — involve either site selection or site analysis (Table 1).

TABLE 1 Partial results of a survey of over 2,000 landscape architects. Self-assessment of work tasks, by rank, that affect public health, safety, and welfare.

Rank	*Task*
2	Identify relevant laws, rules, and regulations governing the project.
3	Evaluate natural site conditions and ecosystems (e.g., slopes, wetlands, soils, vegetation, climate).
6	Identify required regulatory approvals.
10	Evaluate the capability of the site and the existing infrastructure to support the program requirements.
11	Elicit user's intentions and determine needs.
15	Determine the opportunities and constraints of the site.

Source: CLARB, 1998, p. 7.

I hope this book contributes to the evolution of rigorous — and defensible — land planning and development methods. It should be useful to practitioners, educators, and students in several fields. In the academic arena, it can be used in at least four types of college-level courses. It can serve as a required text in site planning courses taught in architecture, civil engineering, landscape architecture, planning, and urban design programs. By focusing on the planning and design process, this book should complement other textbooks that emphasize the products of that process, such as the individual elements that comprise a developed site (e.g., buildings, walkways, vegetation). Second, the book also may serve as either a primary or supplementary text for site analysis courses in landscape architecture. Third, this book can be used as a supplementary text in graphic communication courses in architecture and landscape architecture. Although most design students in these programs are proficient at illustrating final design proposals, far fewer are proficient at graphically communicating information that supports, and justifies, the results of the planning and design process.

Finally, this book should serve as a general reference for courses in both urban planning and real estate development programs. Real estate students — as future clients of multi-disciplinary planning and design teams — should understand what services can be expected from land planning and design consultants. This book can help current and future real estate developers become better-informed consumers of professional land planning and design services. Additionally, many public sector planners are involved in the administration of zoning codes, subdivision ordinances, and a broad array of other land use regulations. These planners also may be involved in design review of development proposals. My hope is that this book will encourage them to seek, from consultants who submit these proposals for review and approval, explicit — and defensible — evidence that supports their land planning and design decisions.

Acknowledgments

Teaching is a very creative and, of course, challenging endeavor. Many of the ideas presented in this book have originated, or have been influenced, by the questions, comments, and occasional quizzical looks of students I've taught in the Department of Landscape Architecture and the Department of Urban and Regional Planning at the University of Wisconsin–Madison. I certainly appreciate the opportunity to help educate past, present, and future planning and design professionals.

The book's production was facilitated by a variety of people and firms. The following individuals (and land planning firms) generously provided maps and other graphic materials: Paul Kissinger (Edward D. Stone, Jr. and Associates), Jim Fetterman (Helmuth, Obata + Kassabaum), Jack Scholl (Environmental Planning & Design), Fran Hegeler (Wallace, Roberts & Todd), Meg Connolley (Land Design), and Bob Thorpe (R.J. Thorpe and Associates). I particularly appreciate the terrific selection of digital images provided by Jim Fetterman, of the HO+K Planning Group in St. Louis. In anticipation that a second edition of this book will be published someday, I would like to issue an invitation to firms and students engaged in land planning and design. If you have graphic materials that would be appropriate for a revised edition of this book, please contact me (my e-mail address is jalagro@facstaff.wisc.edu).

Several educators provided insightful reviews of an early outline and synopsis of this book. Constructive critiques were received from Jack Ahern (University of Massachusetts), Gary Clay (California Polytechnic State University–San Luis Obispo), Randy Gimblett (Arizona State University), Paul Hsu (Oklahoma State University), David Hulse (University of Oregon), Nate Perkins (University of Guelph), Rob Ribe (University of Oregon), and Peter Trowbridge (Cornell University).

Margaret Cummins, acquisitions editor at John Wiley & Sons, helped guide the book's growth and development from an initial proposal through the final production process. Also providing valuable help along the way were Jennifer Mazurkie, James Harper, and Kim Aleski.

David LaGro, my son, provided extensive assistance with word processing. His willingness to make corrections to edited drafts—and then do it again a few days later—was invaluable. He also converted my pencil sketches to publishable digital line art. But my greatest debt of gratitude is owed to my wife, Rosi LaGro. Throughout this long and time-consuming process, she has provided unwavering support and astute counsel.

PROCESS AND TOOLS

P A R T I

PROCESS AND TOOLS

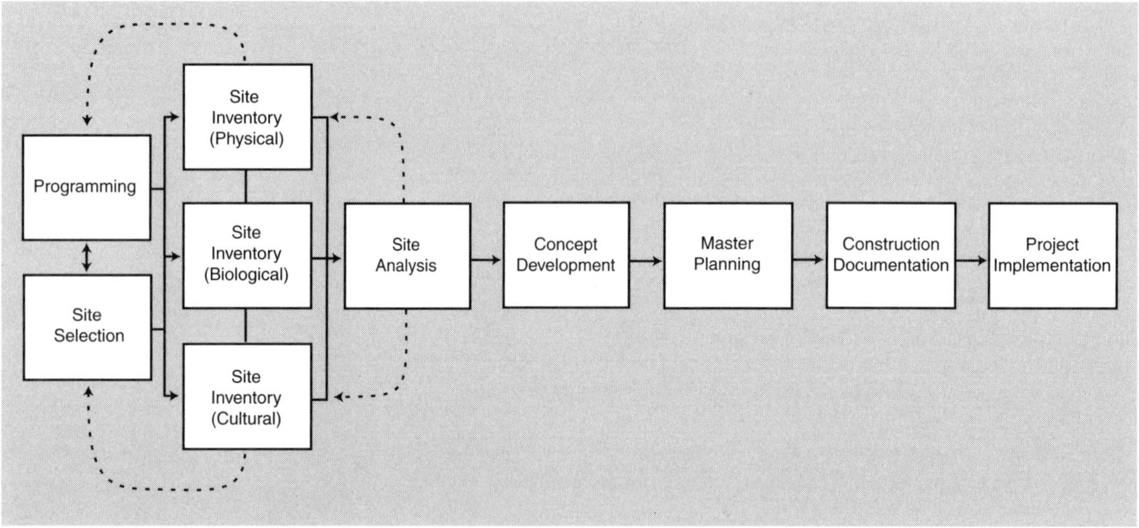

Land planning and design take place within a biophysical and social context. One purpose of land planning and design is to accommodate human needs and aspirations. Especially in market-driven economies like that of the United States, this includes the creation of income and wealth. As human populations increase, however, impacts on the earth's ecosystems also increase. Contemporary land development should encompass, therefore, not only the protection of intrinsic environmental systems and the development of areas best suited for construction, but also the restoration of degraded systems.

Part I of this book contains Chapters 1 and 2. The first chapter provides a summary of the land planning and design process. The second chapter addresses the tools needed for mapping and analysis.

CHAPTER

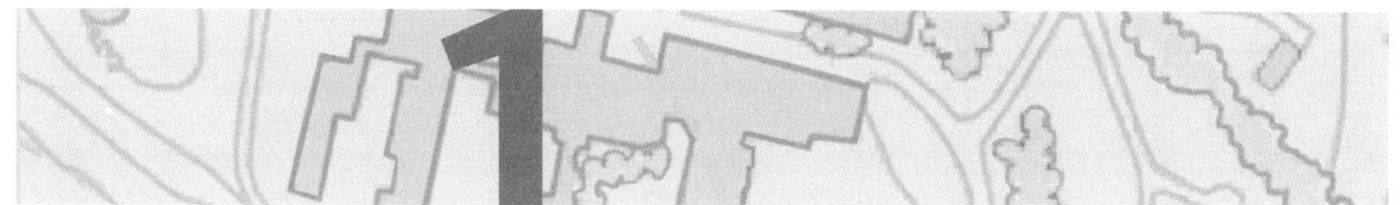

Land and Society

INTRODUCTION

Overview

When viewed from an airplane, landscapes with a long history of human settlement typically appear as mosaics of land covered by patches and corridors. These patterns usually result from a complex array of legal, economic, technological, and biophysical factors. For example, advances in telecommunications technologies, combined with highly developed transportation systems, now allow the spatial diffusion of formerly "urban" land uses into the rural landscape. This enhanced connectivity—and reduced "friction of distance"—has facilitated, for many adults, greater separation between home and the workplace.

> Economic constraints on locational behavior are relaxing rapidly, and as they do, the geography of necessity gives way to a geography of choice. Transportation costs, markets, and raw materials no longer determine the location of economic activities. We have developed an information-based economy in which dominant economic activities and the people engaged in them enjoy unparalleled locational flexibility. In this spatial context, amenity and ecological considerations are more important locational factors than in the past. Cities located in amenity regions of North America are growing more rapidly than others, and such trends will intensify as society becomes more footloose (Abler et al., 1975, p. 301).

TABLE 1-1 Landscapes encompass natural environmental systems that directly benefit humans.

Function	*Good or Service*
Production	Oxygen
	Water
	Food and fiber
	Fuel and energy
	Medicinal resources
Regulation	Storage and recycling of organic matter
	Decomposition and recycling of human waste
	Regulation of local and global climate
Carrier	Space for settlements
	Space for agriculture
	Space for recreation
Information	Aesthetic resources
	Historic (heritage) information
	Scientific and educational information

Source: Adapted from deGroot, 1992, Table 2.0-1.

Human societies have dramatically changed landscapes and, in fact, human activities now have a pervasive influence on the earth's ecosystems. Landscape changes have resulted from both individual and collective efforts to provide military defense, create shelter, and produce food and fiber. The organization of land uses and built structures within landscapes has a profound effect on the integrity of local ecosystems as well as on our own quality of life. Unfortunately, our ability to alter the earth's atmosphere, oceans, and landscapes has exceeded our current capacity to fully understand — or mitigate — the ecological impacts of those changes.

The earth's environmental systems perform a variety of functions that are essential to human health and welfare. The Dutch scientist deGroot (1992) developed a typology of environmental functions of direct benefit to humans. These four categories of functions are summarized in Table 1-1.

Landscapes have long been settled, cultivated, and in many other ways modified by humans. Quality of life is a function of many factors, including: our safety, sense of security, and individual freedom, our physical and mental health, leisure and recreation, and opportunities for self-expression as individuals (Kaplan and Kivy-Rosenberg, 1973). Most, if not all, of these factors are affected by the spatial organization and articulation of the built environment. For example, a landscape's ecological infrastructure helps protect the quality of the air we breathe and the water we drink, and it can reduce our vulnerability to floods and other natural hazards.

Land use planning decisions often involve choices about the locations of new roads, buildings, and recreation areas. These decisions may also involve choices about the management of forests and woodlands, prairies and savannas, and lakes and rivers (Figure 1-1). Development in areas that are unsuitable for the intended uses usually is accompanied by a set of costs — some internalized and some externalized. Off-site externalities, such as flooding, erosion, and nonpoint source pollution of local water resources, are increasingly the concern of local land use regulations.

Hurricanes, earthquakes, and other natural hazards continually threaten human health, safety, and welfare. According to the National Science Foundation (NSF), since 1989 natural hazards have accounted for an average of about $1 billion in losses per week in the United States. These losses are heavily subsidized by public disaster relief funding. Yet many disasters causing the loss of life and property can be prevented, or

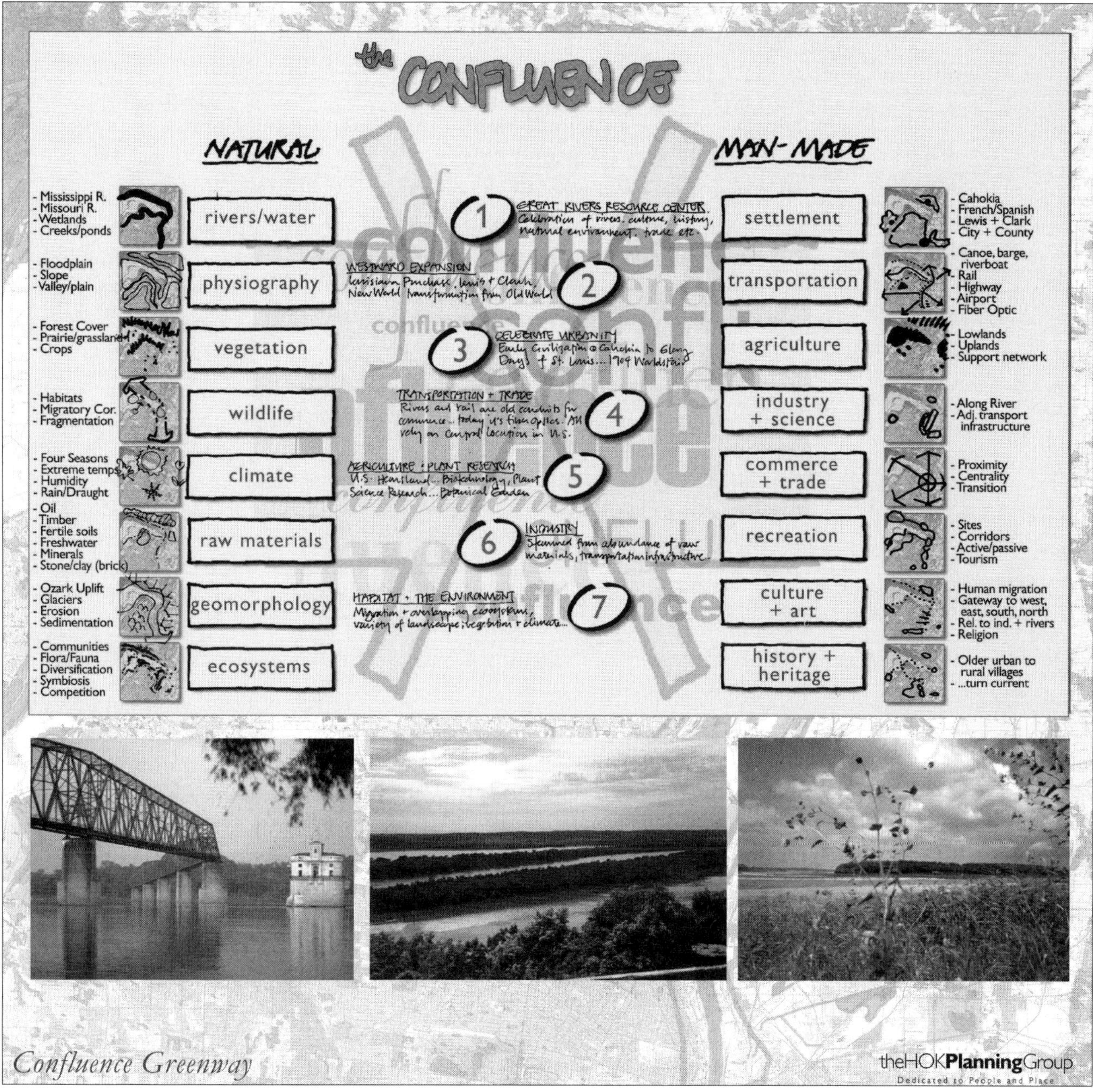

Figure 1-1 Natural and man-made factors influencing a greenway planning project along the Mississippi River in St. Louis, Missouri, USA. *Source:* The HOK Planning Group.

at least mitigated, by decisions to reduce these risks proactively (H. John Heinz III Center for Science, Economics and the Environment, 2000). This is possible because the risks from natural hazards are not uniformly distributed across landscapes. Building on land that is inherently unsuitable for development can have serious, and costly, consequences. Dennis Mileti (1999), who led the NSF study team of 132 experts, concludes:

> The really big catastrophes are getting large and will continue to get larger, partly because of things we've done in the past to reduce risk.... Many of the accepted methods for coping with hazards have been based on the idea that people can use technology to control nature to make them safe.

Land planning and development that respects, rather than discounts, inherent environmental hazards can prevent many of these costly mistakes.

Population growth and increasing human mobility heighten the need for careful land use planning. In a recent Lincoln Institute of Land Policy report, ten land use initiatives were proposed to improve the health and well-being of America's communities. Agenda Item #9 (Diamond and Noonan, 1996, p. xix), in particular, calls for new partnerships and recognition of a broad set of valuable resources:

> A constituency for better land use is needed based on new partnerships that reach beyond traditional alliances to bring together conservationists, social justice advocates, and economic development interests. These partnerships can be mobilized around natural and cultural resources that people value.

Decisions made by different individuals and institutions influence land use patterns over a broad range of spatial scales (Figure 1-2). Each level of government has a role in protecting public health, safety, and welfare, but the government units most closely involved in land use planning typically are at the "local" level. Local government plays a significant role in "project planning" through development permitting processes. The focus of this book is the influence of the site on land development decision making. An understanding of the site, within its biophysical and cultural context, is crucial to the land development activities of a constellation of allied professions (Figure 1-3). This chapter examines the land development process from the perspective of the land planning and design professional.

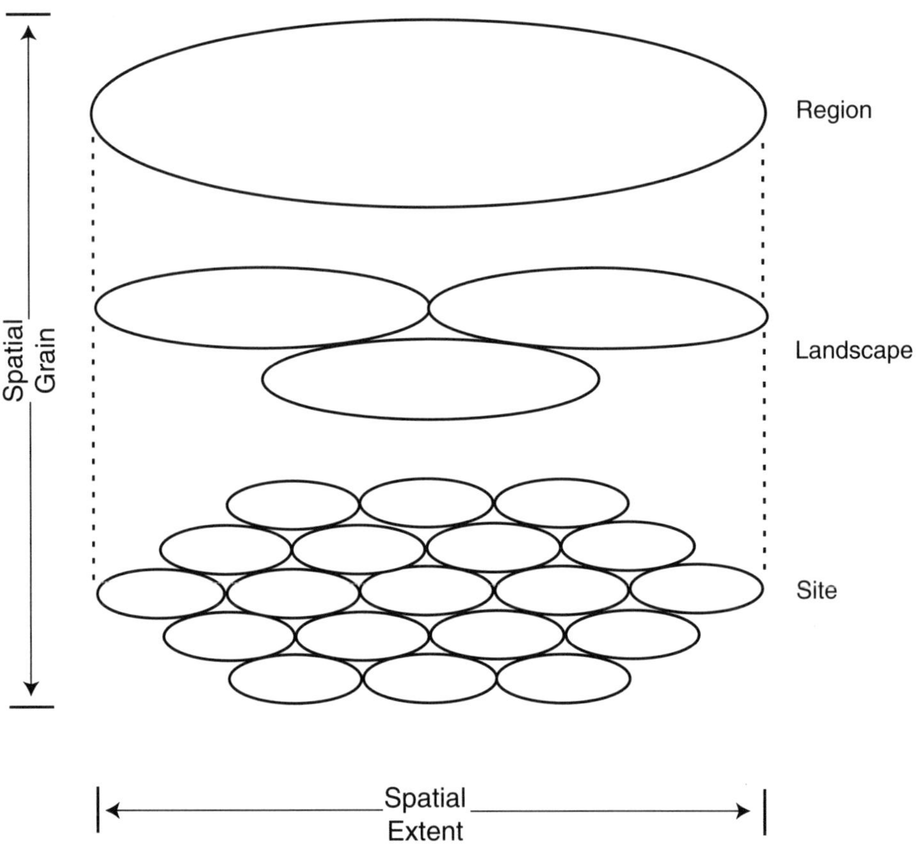

Figure 1-2 Spatial hierarchy—regions, landscapes, sites.

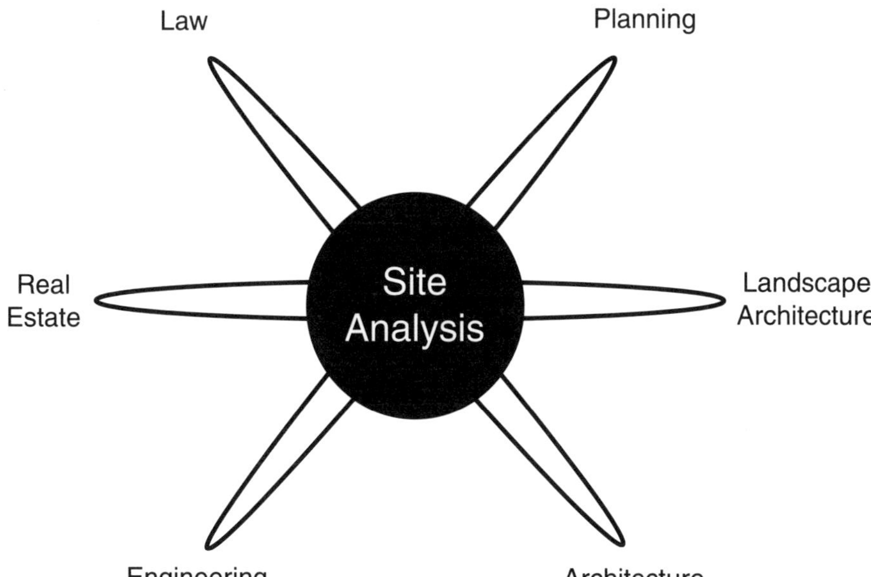

Figure 1-3 Information from the site analysis is utilized by many professions engaged in the land development process.

Land, or site, planning and design occur over a broad range of spatial scales (the words "land" and "site" are used interchangeably throughout this book). Site planning—as defined by Kevin Lynch (1971, pp.3–4)—is very much a topic of this book:

> Site planning is the art of arranging the external physical environment to support human behavior. It lies along the boundaries of architecture, engineering, landscape architecture, and city planning, and it is practiced by members of all these professions. Site plans locate structures and activities in three-dimensional space and, when appropriate, in time.

Site planning decisions are made for individual land parcels, under a single ownership. Landowners may be private individuals or partnerships, business corporations, nonprofit organizations, or federal, state, or local governments. Land planning projects vary not only in parcel area and prospective land uses, but also in location within the urban-rural continuum. This complexity requires a systematic decision-making process.

The land planning and design process is a systematic, and often iterative, sequence of steps (Figure 1-4). The client for a project may be an individual, a corporation, or a department of local, state, or federal government. Variations in this process can be expected among different types and locations of projects. Some projects might involve the construction of roads, buildings, or other infrastructure. Other projects might not have any new construction, but result instead in the conservation, restoration, and management of natural and cultural resources.

There are many reasons to follow a rigorous planning and design process when making land development decisions. Development that is responsive to site opportunities and constraints reduces construction costs, protects inherent natural amenities, and allows the continuation of critical environmental processes. Careful design of the physical environment can also play a prominent role in enhancing employee satisfaction and productivity, and, of course, business profitability (Russell, 1997; Stein,

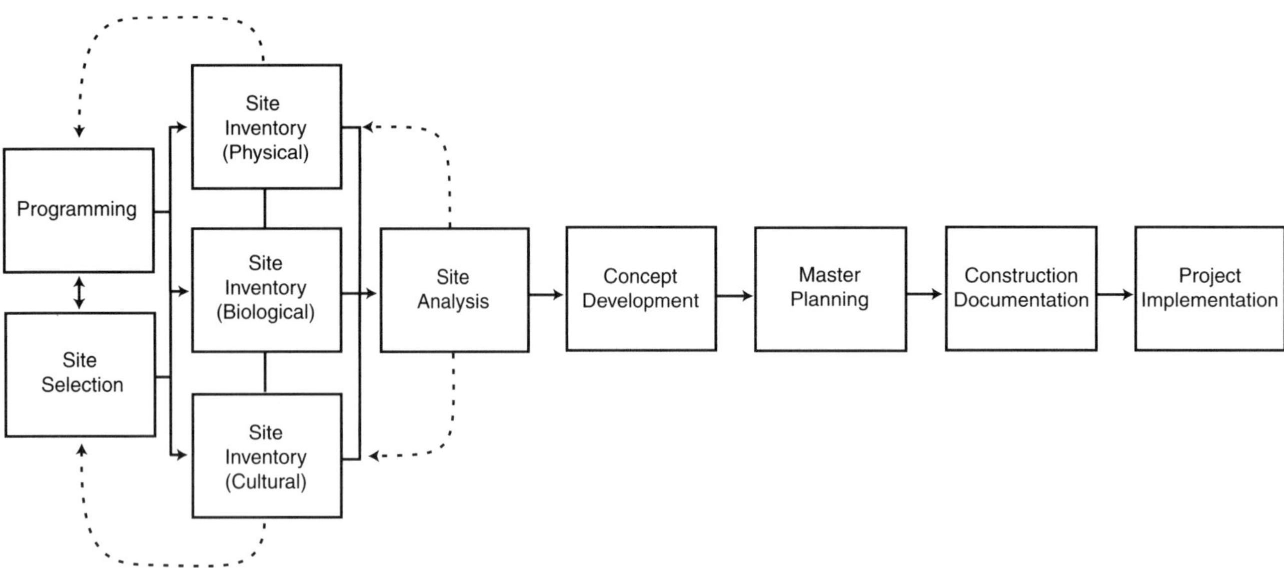

Figure 1-4 Land planning and design process.

1997). Documenting efforts to protect public health, safety, and welfare can also expedite the permitting and approval process. This process can benefit the developer, the future site users, and the surrounding community.

Graphic Communication

The land planning and design process is a series of activities requiring the visualization of diverse site information. Graphic and verbal communication can help clients, consultants, and other individuals understand—and participate in—the various phases of the land planning and design process. The site's constraints, for example, must be understood in order to evaluate the merits of a conceptual land use plan or a more specific design proposal. The form in which maps, plans, and other illustrative material are presented typically plays an important role in the effectiveness of graphic communication.

In land planning and design, symbols are used alone and in combination to convey information about the characteristics of the site and the spatial organization and articulation of the proposed development. Qualities of specific attributes also can be expressed graphically. Diagramming is an effective way to simplify and communicate important project information. These graphics can also provide tangible evidence of the logic behind a land use proposal. Without this supporting evidence—particularly as development regulations become increasingly stringent—why should government staff and affected stakeholders believe that a land development proposal is *appropriate* for the site? Equally important, how can they offer constructive suggestions for possible improvements to the land development plan? Edward T. White (1983, p.1) comments:

> We designers are often more comfortable and skilled at drawing plans, elevations, sections and perspectives than at diagraming project needs, issues and requirements. We sometimes seem overly anxious to draw the architectural answers to ill-defined project questions and reluctant to invest in graphic techniques that help us better understand the project needs and that stimulate responsive and creative design concepts.

Several kinds of information can be represented diagrammatically. Important features of a site and its surroundings can be depicted graphically as either points, lines, or polygons. In some instances, individual elements are portrayed by a combination of two or more symbols. Whether drawn by hand or by computer, symbols convey information about the functions and qualities of both existing and proposed site elements. Diagrams, including, of course, text, may also convey information about the existing and desired relationships among these elements.

Graphics can convey information about site nuisances, hazards, and other constraints. They are also used to identify site amenities. Effective diagrams and other graphics can simplify reality, and reveal significant patterns and processes. These diagrams can help stakeholders effectively participate in the land use planning and design process. When preparing to convey project information graphically, these five factors should be considered: message, medium, audience, time, and setting (Wester, 1990).

Message

Efforts to communicate graphically may have one of three results: (a) the message is received as sent, (b) the message is not received, or (c) a message is received, but the intended message is not received as sent. Of course, the message will vary from one phase of the land planning and design process to the next, and from one site to the next. During the site inventory phase, for example, essential information may include maps of key site attributes such as topographic slopes, depth to bedrock, and vegetation communities. In the concept development phase, however, the information to convey might include the locations of proposed structures and paved spaces, and the physical as well as visual relationships between these elements. The steps that will be taken to mitigate negative impacts of proposed land use changes also could be communicated.

Medium

Because the message varies as the planning and design process progresses, the techniques for communicating this information also vary. Construction drawings, for example, are not only technical, but legal, documents that comprise, in part, the contract for a project's implementation. These drawings must be precisely drafted—whether by hand or with computer. In contrast, conceptual land use plans may be shown as "bubble" diagrams. These drawings are relatively informal and drawn—not drafted—in a generally "loose" graphic style (Linn, 1993). Because the land use concept plan conveys the spatial organization of future uses of the site, drafting this information in meticulous detail is unnecessary. In fact, too much precision may subtly convey to project stakeholders, or others reviewing the drawing, that the land use plan is already "etched in stone." Consequently, a highly refined concept plan may inhibit participation by stakeholders and limit constructive dialogue on ways to improve the plan.

Audience

Graphic communication in land planning and design is often intended for multiple audiences. An audience's expertise and familiarity with the planning process determines what—and how—project information should be conveyed. On many projects, the intended audience includes the client, the design team, government staff, and stakeholders within the general public. Effective graphic communication emphasizes the most important information, and deemphasizes, or omits, the least important information. Project graphics, after all, should help orient and inform the audience.

Setting

The setting for a presentation should be considered when planning to prepare and organize project information. If a presentation will occur in an auditorium or a large public meeting room, the illustrations might be photographed for projection as slides. If the illustrations are created with a computer, or if photographs of the illustrations are digitally scanned, the information may be presented with a laptop computer and video projector. In a smaller setting, like a conference room, drawings mounted on foam-core presentation boards may be most appropriate. Displaying the full array of drawings, rather than one at a time, may facilitate a more dynamic dialogue with the audience.

Time

The amount of time available for the preparation and presentation of graphic materials determines, in part, which graphic techniques to employ. A "quick and dirty" tracing paper presentation may be appropriate for discussing alternative land use concepts with the client and other members of the design team. Whether or not the images will be left with the audience for subsequent review is also a consideration. If they will be left with the audience, additional detailed project information can be conveyed with accompanying labels, notes, tables, and graphs.

LAND PLANNING AND DESIGN

Site Selection

Land development typically occurs in one of two ways: clients have a site and need a program, or clients have a program and need a site. Land parcels vary greatly in size, shape, and context. Across the urban–rural continuum, land parcels tend to be small in urban areas and much larger in rural areas. The land planning and design process begins, therefore, with identifying and evaluating alternative sites.

Development parcels differ in many ways. Some sites are hilly and others are nearly flat. Sites may be heavily forested or have no trees at all. The site may be small or large, linear or more compact. These attributes — and many others — account for the variability among development sites. But there may be other factors, beyond the site boundaries, that are crucial to an understanding of the site's context within the landscape. This holds true whether the site is within an urban, suburban, or rural landscape. A site's context is a function of many different physical, biological, and cultural attributes. These include adjacent land uses, access to public infrastructure, approval and permitting requirements, costs of land and construction, microclimate, and ecological patterns and processes. Community resource inventories map the locations of significant physical, biological, and cultural resources. The following are nine basic resources that may be documented at the community level (Arendt, 1999):

- Wetlands and wetland buffers
- Floodways and floodplains
- Moderate and steep slopes
- Groundwater resources and aquifer recharge areas
- Woodlands

- Productive farmland
- Significant wildlife habitats
- Historic, archaeological, and cultural features
- Scenic viewsheds from public roads

All of these are potential concerns in land planning at both the community and site scales.

Programming

The project program is a description of the intended uses of one or more parcels of land. General project objectives may include land development, restoration, or management. The program also usually includes specific information about the intended uses of the site. For example, the program for a multifamily residential project could include the number of housing units that will be constructed at different densities. The program may be developed by the client, or by consultants with programming expertise. The programming phase may involve visiting the site, inspecting aerial photographs, performing market analyses or user demand studies, and reviewing other available site and user information.

Site Inventory

The site inventory is the next phase in the land planning and design process. The project program, in conjunction with the physical, biological, and cultural features of a site, determines which data should be collected. For example, consider a partially wooded and hilly site along a small but navigable river. Several site attributes could be mapped (Table 1-2), but not all of these attributes may be relevant to this particular project. A map showing the site's range of slope percentages (e.g., 0–5%, 5–20%) is potentially useful, because some land uses are better suited for gentle slopes, and other uses are better suited for steeper slopes. The site's suitability for future development or restoration depends, however, upon the land use program under consideration. The site attributes relevant to a proposed nature conservation area, for example, may differ significantly from the site attributes relevant to a proposed development consisting of fifty condominium units, six tennis courts, and an outdoor swimming pool. The nature conservation program would place a high priority on diversity of wildlife habitats—from dry, upland, south-facing slopes to lowland marshes and bogs. In contrast, the condominium project might place a high priority on nearly flat to gently sloping areas without development constraints like shallow bedrock, a shallow water table, or federally protected endangered species.

Ecologists, hydrologists, anthropologists, and other experts may participate in collecting, mapping, and analyzing site attribute data. Yet for any given program and site, there always will be attributes that can be ignored. Land planning projects in mountainous regions, for example, invariably require data on topographic slope, elevation, and aspect. In more gently rolling to nearly level terrain, slope and aspect may have an insignificant effect on land planning and design decisions. Site elevation, in contrast, is an important attribute on most projects, because even slight variations in elevation affect site drainage patterns.

Simply mapping a site's physical, biological, and cultural attributes is not, however, a site analysis. The inventory maps, alone, simply describe various biophysical and

TABLE 1-2 Examples of physical, biological, and cultural attributes that may be mapped at the site scale.

Category	*Sub-Category*	*Attribute*
Physical	Soils	Bearing capacity
		Porosity
		Stability
		Erodibility
		Fertility
		Acidity (pH)
	Topography	Elevation
		Slope
		Aspect
	Hydrology	Surface drainage
		Water chemistry (e.g., salinity, nitrates, phosphates)
		Depth to seasonal water table
		Aquifer recharge areas
		Seeps and springs
	Geology	Landforms
		Seismic hazards
		Depth to bedrock
	Climate	Solar access
		Winds (i.e., prevailing, winter)
		Fog pockets
Biological	Vegetation	Plant communities
		Specimen trees
		Exotic invasive species
	Wildlife	Endangered or threatened species habitats
Cultural	Land use	Prior land use
		Land use on adjoining properties
	Legal	Political boundaries
		Land ownership
		Land use regulations
		Easements and deed restrictions
	Utilities	Sanitary sewer
		Storm sewer
		Electric
		Gas
		Water
		Telecommunications
	Circulation	Street function (e.g., arterial, collector)
		Traffic volume
	Historic	Buildings and landmarks
		Archaeological sites
	Sensory	Visibility
		Visual quality
		Noise
		Odors

cultural attributes of the site and surroundings. An inventory map of vegetation, for example, shows the existing site conditions for a single attribute—vegetation. This map, like other inventory maps, is valid for any land use that might be considered for that site. Consequently, the vegetation map remains the same whether the proposed uses of the site include intensive development or no development at all. The fate of the existing vegetation depends, of course, on the decisions made in subsequent phases of the land planning and design process. In contrast to the inventory, a site analysis identifies — in a spatially explicit form — the site's opportunities and constraints for a *specific* land use program. The inventory maps provide data needed for the site analysis.

Site Analysis

The site analysis may entail several different kinds of evaluations. Information contained in a site's physical, biological, and cultural attribute maps might be synthesized, for example, to create maps of the site's suitability for residential, commercial, or other land uses. Attribute mapping and analysis are particularly well suited for applications of geographic information systems. Not all land uses have the same site requirements, so assessing the suitability of a site for multiple land uses typically requires data for several site attributes.

A variety of physical, biological, and cultural attributes can influence the suitability of a site for the proposed uses (Figure 1-5). The scope of the inventory and analysis is narrowed by considering the assets and liabilities — or opportunities and constraints — that the site poses for a specific development program. The liabilities (constraints) associated with a site reduce the site's suitability for one or more of the pro-

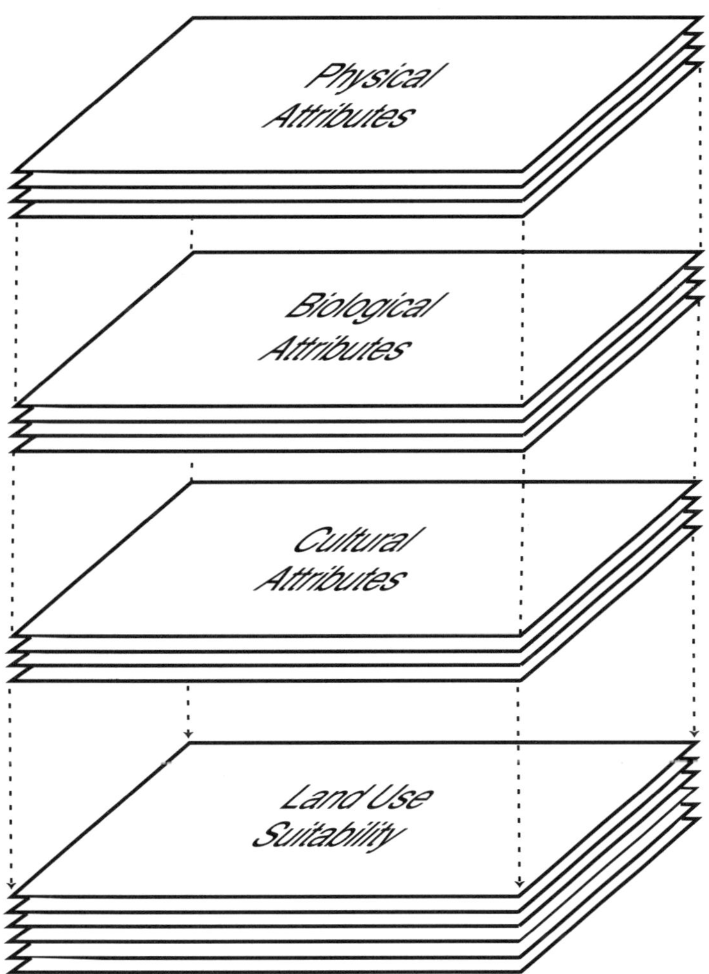

Figure 1-5 Relationship between attribute mapping and land use suitability analysis.

posed uses. Conversely, the assets (opportunities) associated with a site increase its suitability for other uses. These site assets may be unique or valuable resources that warrant protection from development. These assets may increase the site's visual quality and create a sense of place that links the site to its local and regional context.

A site analysis may be a single map that identifies significant opportunities and constraints for the program under consideration. Identifying a site's opportunities and constraints for a specific land use program is crucial to sound — and defensible — land planning and design. For example, the Western Australian Government Sustainable Cities Initiative recently published *Liveable Neighborhoods,* a proposed set of policy guidelines for subdivision and neighborhood design. In contrast to more conventional approaches to land planning and design, this proposal seeks "a more thorough analysis of the site and its context to inform subdivision design and graphically explain the basis of the design" (Western Australia Planning Commission, 2000, p. 2). Yet only the information that is relevant to that program needs mapping. Consequently, analyses of a single site — and multiple programs — can yield markedly different conclusions.

Concept Development

The site analysis summarizes the site's suitability for programmed uses, while also identifying the site's positive and negative features. Concept development, the process of adapting the program to the unique features of the site, occurs after the site analysis. Concept plans spatially organize proposed site activities and improvements on the site. If the development program is unrealistic, the concept plan will reveal those deficiencies. In some cases, the program must be revised.

More than one concept plan is often developed from a single site analysis (Figure 1-6). Creating two or more concept plans is particularly useful, in public sector proj-

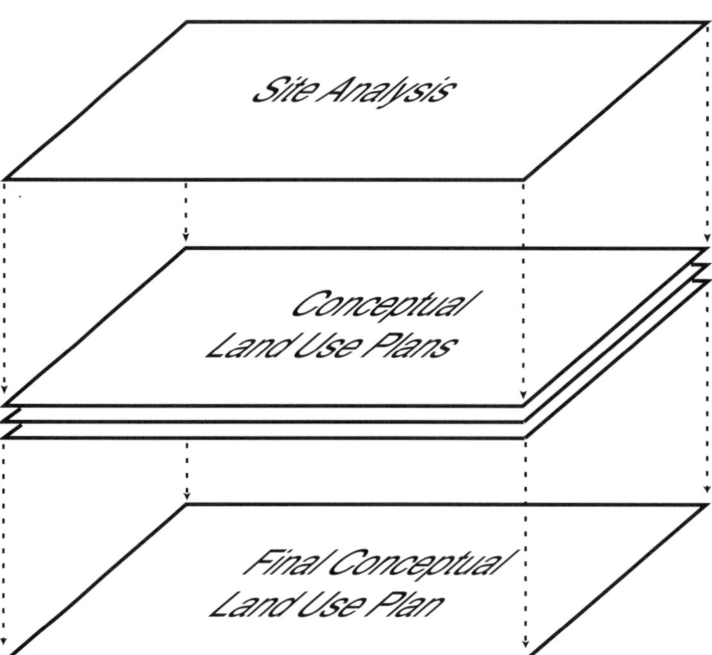

Figure 1-6 Relationship between land use suitability analysis, site analysis, and concept development.

ects, when seeking consensus from a diverse set of stakeholders. This shows clients and stakeholders that a range of potentially viable land use options were considered. If one concept plan is clearly superior to the others, then the argument for that alternative is made more persuasive by comparing it to feasible, but less desirable, alternatives. However, an optimal concept plan may be created by merging two or more different concepts.

Design Development and Implementation

Also known as schematic design or master planning, design development is a process of determining how the conceptual land use plan will be articulated. Design development drawings convey a variety of detailed information that does not appear on the concept plan. Proposed buildings and other improvements, such as roads, parking lots, and walkways, are portrayed realistically on the master plan or site plan. On a concept plan, in contrast, these elements may be drawn diagrammatically as "arrows" or "bubbles." Regardless of the program under consideration, implementing the plan involves documenting—with plans and sections, primarily—how the various built components of the plan should be constructed (Figure 1-7).

But not all land planning projects result in new construction. In addition to the construction of buildings, roads, walkways, or various other site structures, project implementation could also involve the restoration of a degraded wetland, or the bioengineering of an eroded streambank. The plans, elevations, details, and sections, together with the written specifications, comprise the construction documents. Once this documentation is complete, and necessary financing and approvals have been acquired, the plan can be implemented. Depending on the location and scope of the project, approvals and permits may be required from government agencies at the local, state or provincial, and national levels.

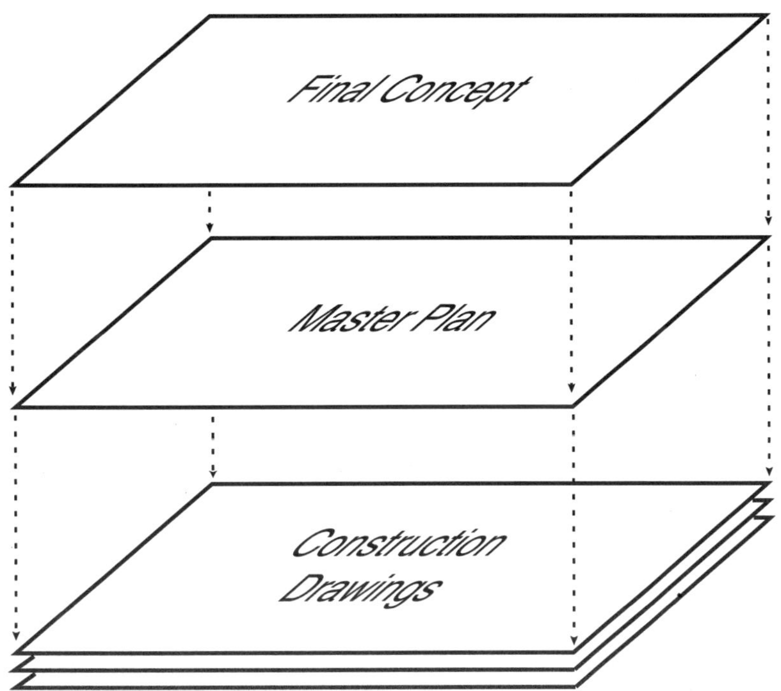

Figure 1-7 Relationship between concept development and design development.

SUMMARY

Land planning and development typically result in the design and construction of buildings, roads, pathways, and other site structures. A good "fit" between the plan and the site requires a compreshensive understanding of the site and its surrounding context. If the site's existing conditions are poorly understood, the planned uses of the site may create a variety of detrimental ecological, social, and economic impacts.

Each site has a unique set of physical, biological, and cultural attributes. Some of these attributes substantially limit the site's suitability for development (Table 1-3). The land planning and design process is a systematic, multiphased, and often multidisciplined effort to utilize land in ways that are efficient, aesthetically pleasing, and ecologically benign.

TABLE 1-3 Examples of hazards, constraints, or nuisances that may influence site selection and development.

Category	*Hazard*	*Constraint*	*Nuisance*
Physical	Flooding	Shallow bedrock	
	Storm surge	Shallow water table	
	Hurricane	Erosion susceptibility	
	Earthquake	Hardpan soils	
	Landslide	Expansive clay soils	
	Volcano	Open water	
	Avalanche	Wetlands	
		Aquifer recharge areas	
		Springs and seeps	
		Steep slopes	
Biological	Wildfire	Endangered Species	Insects
Cultural	Toxic waste	Wellheads	Harsh views
	Unstable fill	Historic sites	Odors
		Archaeological sites	Noise

CHAPTER

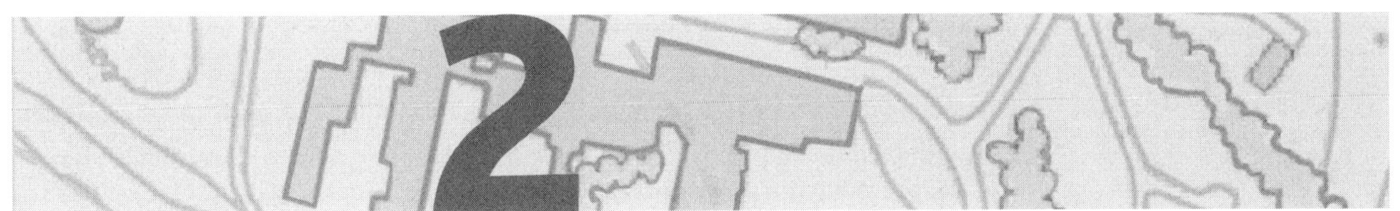

2

Spatial Information and Mapping

INTRODUCTION

Analyzing the site and its context within the surrounding landscape is an important step in land planning and development. A selected subset of the site's physical, biological, and cultural attributes must be analyzed to adapt the development program to the unique conditions of the site. This chapter summarizes several key principles of cartography—or mapmaking. Putting site data into a spatially explicit form (i.e., map) is an essential part of the land planning and design process. Sources of site data, including aerial photographs, satellite-borne multispectral digital images, and global positioning systems (GPS) are also discussed. Finally, this chapter describes the components of a geographic information system (GIS), and explores some of the ways this spatial information technology can facilitate the land planning process.

MAPPING FUNDAMENTALS

What Is a Map?

A map is a graphic representation, or model, of a geographic setting (Robinson et al., 1995). Maps are efficient tools for conveying information about a site and its surroundings. Jenks (1976, p. 19) states:

> Maps are created to provide information about spatial relationships. No other medium communicates distance, directional and areal pattern relationships as well.

Maps can depict the physical, biological, and cultural attributes of a site and the surrounding landscape, and maps can show important spatial (or temporal) relationships among these different attributes. To make a map, three basic elements must be known (Fisher, 1982, p. 5):

- the study space
- the information or values to be displayed
- the locations, within the space, to which the information applies

Throughout human history, maps have been drawn or printed on cloth, paper, mylar, and other surfaces. Today, land planning is supported by computer-generated digital maps—or hard-copy maps plotted from digital data. Regardless of the medium on which a map is conveyed, several basic mapping concepts, or principles, apply.

Map Scale

Map scale defines the spatial relationship between the dimensions of the map features and the dimensions of features the map represents. Therefore, map scale is the ratio of the distance on the map to the distance on the surface portrayed by the map. Map scale is typically expressed as a reduction ratio (e.g., 1:24,000). A map of the world, for example, would have a very large ratio (e.g., 1:12,000,000), whereas a map of a city would have a much smaller ratio (e.g., 1:5,000). The larger the ratio, the smaller the map scale. Map accuracy is fundamentally related to map scale (see Box 2-1).

Site plans—a specialized form of reference map—typically express map scale as an equation (e.g., 1 inch = 200 feet, 1 meter = 100 meters). Converting a ratio to an equation is straightforward (Table 2-1). Converting between English and metric scales may also be necessary (Table 2-2).

Georeferencing

Maps are georeferenced to coordinate systems, or mathematical projections. According to Fisher (1982, p. 20):

> A map projection is the transformation of coordinates measured on the earth surface (spherical coordinates, or latitude and longitude) to coordinates measured on a flat surface (planar, or x,y coordinates).

TABLE 2-1 **Two common ways of expressing a map's scale.**

Ratio	*Equation*
1:24,000	1 inch = 24,000 inches, or 1 inch = 2,000 feet
1:10,000	1 centimeter = 10,000 centimeters, or 1 centimeter = 10 meters

TABLE 2-2 Conversion of length and area between metric and English units of measurement.

Measure	*Unit (English)*	*Unit (Metric)*
Length	1 foot = 12 inches	0.3048 meter
	1 yard = 3 feet	0.914 meter
	1 mile = 1,760 yards	1.61 kilometers
	0.39 inches	1 centimeter
	3.28 feet = 1.09 yards	1 meter = 100 centimeters
	0.62 miles	1 kilometer = 1,000 meters
Area	1 square yard	0.84 square meters
	1 acre = 43,560 square feet	0.40 hectares
	1 square mile	2.59 square kilometers
	1.20 square yards	1 square meter
	2.47 acres	1 hectare = 10,000 square meters
	0.39 square miles	1 square kilometer

Many different coordinate systems are used in mapmaking. An in-depth review of coordinate systems is beyond the scope of this book, but a few of the more widely adopted systems will be briefly summarized. Among the coordinate systems used in the United States, the Universal Transverse Mercator (UTM) grid system is widely used for topographic maps, natural resource maps, and satellite imagery. The UTM grid system divides the area of the earth between 84 degrees north and 80 degrees south latitude into cells that are 6 degrees of longitude (east–west dimension) and 8 degrees of latitude (north–south dimension). Each 6-degree-by-8-degree cell, or quadrilateral, is divided into a nested system of squares. The sizes of these square grid cells (e.g., 10,000 meters, 1,000 meters) depend on the scale of the map.

Other coordinate systems that are widely used in United States, and in similar forms in other countries, are the State Plane Coordinate (SPC) system and the Public Land Survey System (PLSS). The State Plane Coordinate system, a rectangular grid structure linked to locations within the national geodetic survey system, has four times the accuracy of the UTM system (Robinson et al., 1995). A very different, and old, coordinate system is the Public Land Survey System (PLSS). First implemented in 1785, this grid structure was used to map about three-fourths of the land area of the United States (Robinson et al., 1995). The primary units of this nested grid system are townships (six-by-six-mile squares), sections (one-by-one-mile squares), and quarter-sections (160 acres).

Map Types

Maps can be classified by scale, function, or subject matter (Robinson et al., 1995). As a rule of thumb, large-scale maps have reduction ratios of 1:50,000 or less; small-scale maps have reduction ratios of 1:500,000 or more (Robinson et al., 1995). Three basic map types, by function or purpose, are:

- reference maps
- thematic maps
- charts

TABLE 2-3 Examples of reference maps, thematic maps, and navigational charts.

Class	*Information Conveyed*
Reference maps	Topography Flooding hazards Bathymetry
Thematic maps	Elevation ranges Land use types Vegetation communities Soil suitability for building construction
Charts	Aeronautical routes and airports Nautical routes and hazards Streets and highways

Maps of each type can be useful in the land planning and design process (Table 2-3). Yet the distinctions between these map types are not clear-cut. Each type of map, for example, may have features that occur in another map type.

Reference Maps

Reference maps are widely used in land planning and design. A planimetric map is a reference map that portrays features in two-dimensional space. A plat map (Figure 2-1), for example, shows land ownership boundaries and the land parcels delimited by those boundaries. Old reference maps can be a good source of information about the historic uses of a site. Historic maps can be particularly useful when a site's prior land uses suggest that potential risks of hazardous waste contamination may exist on the site (American Society of Civil Engineers, 1996). Sanborn maps of cities in the United States were created for fire insurance purposes between 1867 and the early 1950s (American Society of Civil Engineers, 1996). These maps are available at most university libraries and major public libraries, and at the U.S. Library of Congress.

Topographic maps are another common form of reference map. Topographic maps use isolines or contours to link points of equal elevation. Landforms are graphically portrayed with contours, and on some topographic maps, also by shading and color. These maps also typically show buildings, utility corridors, and roads. Other types of potentially useful reference maps include flood hazard maps, bathymetric maps, and wetlands maps (see Appendix). A project base map provides the framework for each phase of the land planning and design process. Providing a common frame of reference, the base map contains crucial project information (e.g., locations of property boundaries, utility lines, and roads).

Thematic Maps

Thematic maps express information about a single attribute, although additional information is usually included on a thematic map to help the user understand the context of the mapped area. Site attributes can be portrayed with two different types of thematic maps:

- chloropleth maps
- isopleth maps

A chloropleth map is a type of thematic map that expresses attribute data as discrete categories. The classification, a form of generalization or spatial aggregation, is

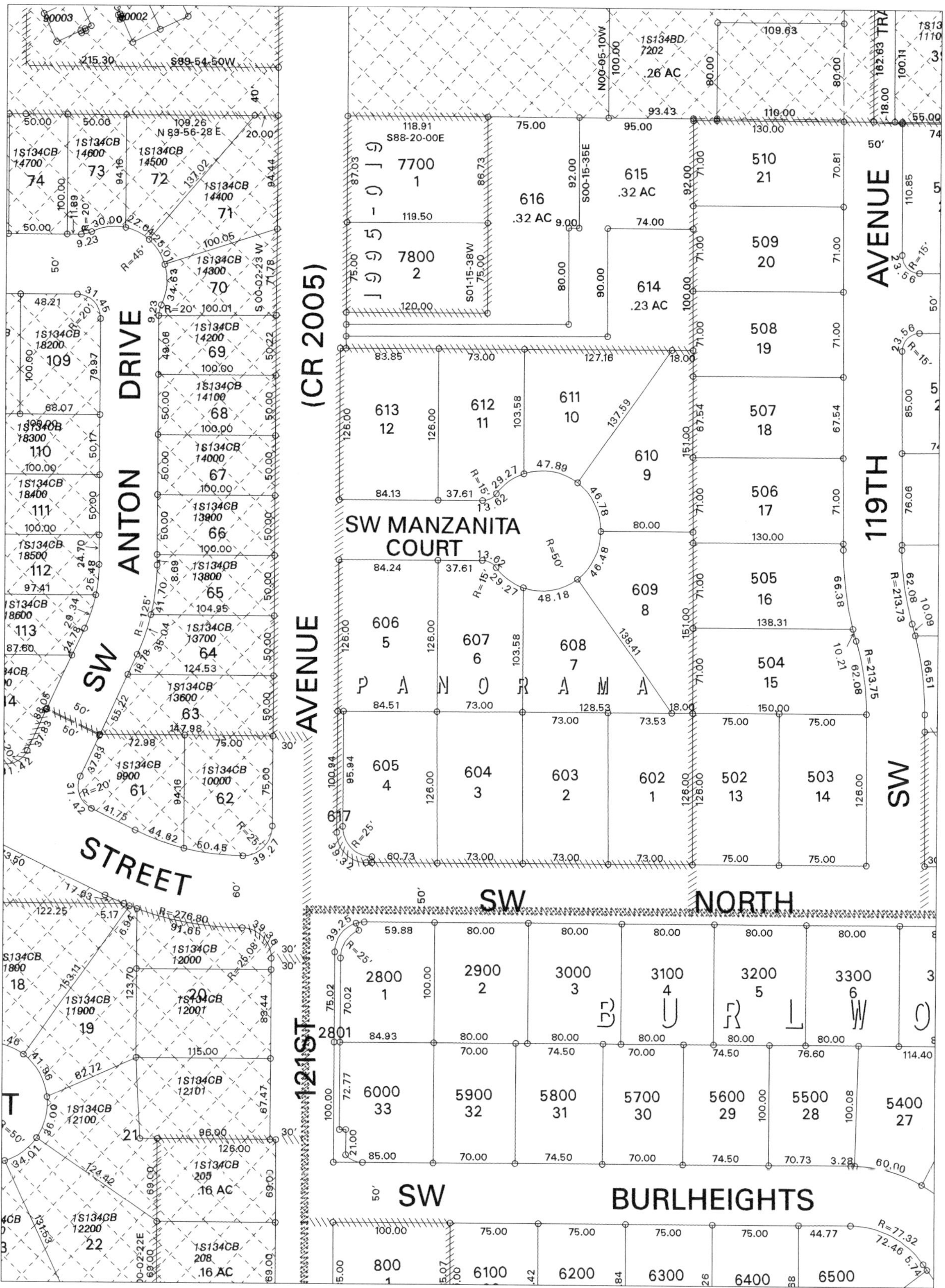

Figure 2-1 Parcel map for Washington County, Washington. *Source:* Roger Livingston, Washington County, Washington.

accomplished by partitioning the range of data values into intervals. Each of these intervals, or classes, is represented on the chloropleth map by a single color or texture (Muller, 1976). A land use map is one example of a chloropleth map. Land use — a cultural attribute — can be classified with many different categories. A major land use classification system developed by the U.S. Geological Survey (Anderson et al., 1976) has three levels of classification. Categories in each level are arranged in a nested hierarchy, ranging from the general (Level I) to the specific (Level III). For example, the "urban" class is a Level I land use category. Level II subcategories of the urban class include residential, commercial, and industrial uses.

An isopleth map, in contrast to a chloropleth map, displays the locations of numerical values of a single attribute. For example, an isopleth map of elevation partitions the entire range of elevations within the mapped area into equal increments. An isopleth map of elevation might show several elevation classes, each of which represents the surface area where elevations fall within equal increments (e.g., 10 meters). Therefore, each elevation class is simply a subset of all the elevations within the mapped area.

An important decision in thematic mapping is choosing the number of classes to map. Research on human cognition suggests that seven (plus or minus two) is the maximum number of objects that an individual can compare without becoming confused (Miller, 1956; Saaty and Vargas, 1982). Therefore, the number of map classes within a theme should be kept as small as practicable (Figure 2-2).

Charts

A chart is a type of map created to aid transportation. Charts include road maps, aeronautical charts, and navigation charts. Charts can be useful, particularly early in the land planning process, when a general understanding of the site's context is still being formulated.

Measurement Scales

Many spatially distributed phenomena, including site attributes, can be expressed as thematic maps. Attribute values may be displayed as either absolute or derived values, but these values are typically expressed in one of four measurement scales (Table 2-4):

- nominal
- ordinal
- interval
- ratio

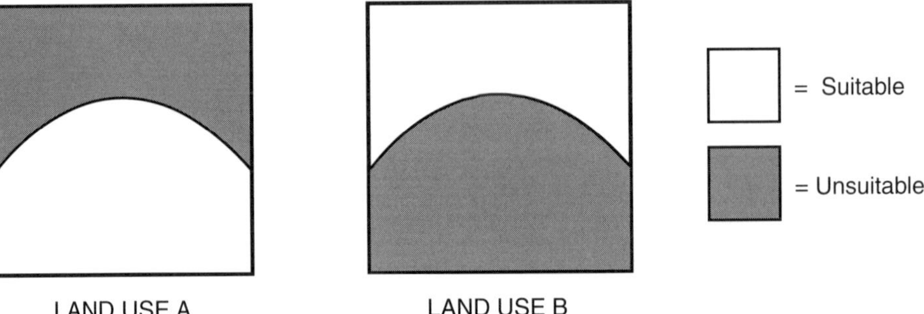

Figure 2-2 Schematic examples of a two-class chloropleth map of a site's suitability for two different land uses.

TABLE 2-4 Common measurement scales and examples of site attributes expressed in each scale.

Scale	*Site Attributes*
Nominal	Land use Plant communities Slope aspect
Ordinal	Soil drainage capability Visual quality
Interval	Terrain elevation
Ratio	Slope gradient

Each of these scales of measurement can be useful in the site inventory and analysis.

Nominal Scale

Attributes values that do not imply rank or order fall within the nominal category. Land use, for example, is an attribute that is expressed on a nominal measurement scale. Land use classes include residential, commercial, and industrial uses. Although these are very different types of uses, land use itself is not an attribute that implies rank or quantity. Yet land use could be displayed in many ways. A thematic map of development intensity—measured by the percentage of parcel area covered by buildings and other imperious surfaces—could be expressed on an ordinal scale.

Ordinal Scale

The ordinal scale of measurement conveys a gradation or ranking of elements. For example, the U.S. Natural Resources Conservation Service (NRCS) ranks soils by the limitations they present to various types of agriculture, recreation, and construction. Site limitations for building foundations range from no significant constraints at one end of the gradient to severe constraints at the other end.

Interval Scale

The interval scale of measurement applies to attributes with continuous spatial distributions. Elevation is an example of a land attribute, with a continuous distribution, that is measured on an interval scale. This measurement scale has equal increments between units, but zero does not have to be included within the range of interval values.

Ratio Scale

The ratio scale of measurement is derived by dividing one attribute value by another attribute value. An example of a land attribute measured on the ratio scale is topographic slope. Gradient values are computed by dividing the slope's vertical change in elevation by the slope's horizontal length. Slope values may be expressed as either a ratio (e.g., 3:1) or a percentage (e.g., 33 percent). Ratio values are commonly used in the building industry to quantify roof slopes, or pitches. Percentage values are typically used to quantify the slope gradient of land forms and unpaved site surfaces. The percentage value of a slope is the angle of the slope relative to a flat, or horizontal, surface.

Graphic Communication

Hierarchy

Graphic communication in land planning and design employs three basic symbols—points, lines, and polygons—which are used individually and in combination. Each of these symbols represents information about the physical or aesthetic characteristics of a site or a proposed plan. Hierarchies play an important organizing role in graphic and nongraphic communication. In writing, for example, symbols (the alphabet) are combined to form words that are organized into sentences and paragraphs. Paragraphs in a book may be organized into sections. Hierarchies organize information to clearly convey the significance, or importance, of individual components. Placing greater emphasis on certain information helps convey the entire set of information more efficiently and effectively.

Communication effectiveness can be strengthened by emphasizing one or more attributes. For example, value is the darkness of points, lines, and areas. As any one of these elements is made darker, in relation to other elements on a drawing or map, they take on greater importance. The placement of these symbols on a map or other presentation medium can also help to accentuate the most important information.

Graphs and Tables

Graphic communication in land planning and design conveys relevant information about the site, its context, and the proposed changes to the site. In each phase of the land planning and design process, it may be appropriate to communicate statistics about the program, the existing site, or the proposed plan. Graphs and tables are efficient ways of summarizing relatively large quantities of data. The area of land allocated to different proposed uses, for example, can be easily conveyed in either a table or graph.

Titles, Labels, and Notes

Information hierarchies are created by carefully laying out each sheet, including the titles, labels, and notes. The most important information can be accentuated by emphasizing the size, font, placement, darkness, or color of relevant text. Titles and subtitles serve as visual signposts that facilitate "way finding" among the information conveyed on a set of project illustrative materials.

A title "block" is a common feature of construction drawings. Examples of construction drawings include layout plans, grading plans, and planting plans. These technical drawings are an essential part of the construction contract. The drawings created earlier in the planning and design process usually have a more informal appearance. A site analysis map or a conceptual land use plan, for example, may be drawn freehand. Because of the preliminary nature of these drawings, a "hard line" drafting style is unnecessary. Effective labeling is concise, accurate, and informative. Rather than full sentences, labels may be in "bullet" form, a type of shorthand that conveys essential information succinctly yet clearly. Labels are meant to supplement information contained in a diagram, plan, or other illustrative drawing. Labels and notes must be legible, of course, and they should be located where they will be readily associated with the feature addressed by the label (Figure 2-3). Not all of the information on a map or drawing deserves equal weight, and a text hierarchy helps draw attention to the more important site and project information.

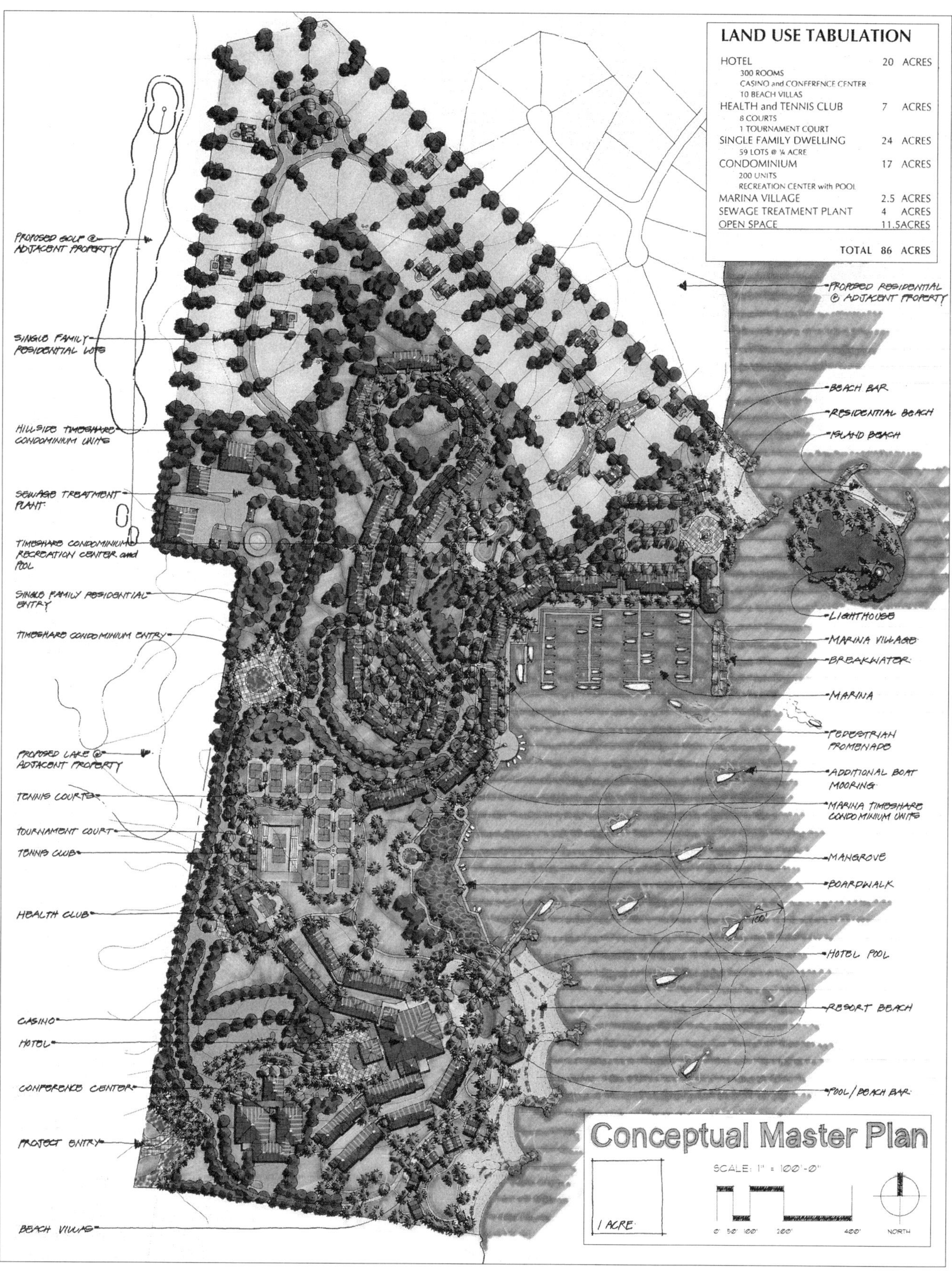

Figure 2-3 Title, north arrow, and scale are essential map information. Land use information is summarized effectively with a table.
Source: Edward D. Stone, Jr., and Associates.

Sheet Size

A wide variety of sheet sizes can be used to present project information. The size and orientation of presentation media depend largely on the size and shape of the site, the complexity of the program, and the importance of off-site factors. If the site is an unusual shape, then fitting a site base map on a single sheet may require unconventional sheet dimensions. Ideally, a single size and orientation is used consistently for each element in the set of illustrative materials. The placement of elements on the sheet, or other two-dimensional medium, affects the clarity of the intended message. The size and proportions of the presentation medium influence the arrangement of the elements on that medium. A common approach is to divide the presentation into sections equivalent to simple fractions, such as halves, thirds, or quarters. Balance can be achieved with either symmetric or asymmetric arrangement of the components.

REMOTE SENSING

Remote sensing is the process of collecting and analyzing data about the earth's environment from a distance, typically from an aircraft or satellite. Remote sensing facilitates inventories of land use, land cover, and other landscape attributes. Aerial photography, perhaps the most common form of remote sensing, is particularly useful in land planning.

Aerial Photography

Military reconnaissance was one of the earliest applications for aerial photographs. Aerial photographs have also been used in the assessment of land suitability for agriculture. Most agricultural areas in the United States were photographed, or "flown," in the 1930s and subsequently at various intervals by the U.S. Department of Agriculture (USDA). These photographs, in conjunction with soils data acquired through field sampling, facilitated the mapping of soils throughout most of the United States.

Cameras

Airborne cameras capture either oblique or vertical images of the earth's surface. Oblique photographs can provide synoptic views of the site from a low viewing angle. Oblique photographs are often acquired to get an overall sense of the site that cannot be attained from the ground. Vertical photos are taken with the surface of the camera lens parallel to the earth's surface. These can be very useful in analyzing a site, but vertical photographs are not maps. These aerial photographs have both vertical and horizontal distortion that, unless corrected, preclude accurate measurements of surface distance directly from the photos.

Horizontal distortion results from the physical properties of the camera lens. The horizontal scale of an uncorrected aerial photograph actually varies over the photo's surface. At the edges of the photograph, the distance depicted on the photo is greater than the same distance depicted nearer to the photo's center. Horizontal distortion can be corrected through digital photogrammetry, using specialized software and a rectification process called "rubber sheeting."

In contrast to horizontal distortion, variation in the distance between the camera and the earth's surface causes vertical distortion. Vertical distortion is especially significant in photographs of landscapes with large elevation changes, as in hilly or mountainous terrain. Vertical distortion is not a significant problem in photographs of terrain where there is relatively little variation in elevation.

Three basic types of film are commonly used in aerial photography for land planning purposes. These films are:

- color
- black and white (panchromatic)
- color infrared

Color infrared film is sensitive to visible light and to portions of the electromagnetic spectrum that are invisible to the human eye. Sensitive to near-infrared light, this film is particularly useful in monitoring vegetation growth and vigor. Color infrared photographs are regularly used to detect the spread of oak wilt blight, the progression of gypsy moth dispersal and damage, and other tree diseases and insect infestations.

Multispectral Scanning

Digital sensors aboard airplanes and satellites record both visible and invisible electromagnetic energy reflected from the earth's surface. The major commercial satellite-based sensors record data in several wavelength bands. Multiple sensors, with different spectral sensitivities, facilitate image analysis using different combinations of remotely sensed data. These digital images support research and monitoring in geology, engineering, agriculture, and many other fields.

Many land planning and design projects are for sites that are small enough to make aerial photography the most practical choice among available remote sensing data. Aerial photos can be used for land use and land cover classification, and to gain a synoptic view of the site within its environmental and cultural context. On very large sites, and for community-wide planning, satellite imagery can prove useful. One advantage of digital satellite imagery is that these data are easily incorporated within a geographic information system. As the spatial resolution of commercially available images increases, these data should become more commonly used for site inventory and analysis.

GLOBAL POSITIONING SYSTEMS (GPS)

The global positioning system (GPS) is a worldwide navigation and positioning system created for both military and civilian use. Developed by the U.S. Department of Defense, a network of 24 satellites serve as spatial reference points, enabling receivers on the ground to compute their geographic position. The GPS identifies geographic position in three basic steps (Hurn, 1993, pp.7–9):

STEP 1: SATELLITES ARE THE REFERENCE POINTS

The orbital motion — and exact positions — of 24 GPS satellites are continuously monitored by ground tracking stations.

STEP 2: SIGNAL TRAVEL TIME GIVES DISTANCE

Specially coded messages, or signals, are regularly transmitted by each satellite. A receiver on the ground calculates its distance to the satellite by multiplying the signal travel time by the speed of light.

STEP 3: THREE DISTANCES GIVE POSITION

Using trigonometry, the ground receiver uses the distances to the three satellites to "triangulate," or locate the receiver's position on the earth's surface.

The global positioning system is particularly useful in the site inventory and analysis phases of the land planning and design process. Handheld GPS receivers can be used to map wetlands and other vegetation communities, individual specimen trees, and many other site features.

GEOGRAPHIC INFORMATION SYSTEMS (GIS)

A geographic information system (GIS) consists of computer hardware and software, data on locations and attributes, and data about the data—or metadata. Rapid advances in computer hardware and software have vastly improved the mapping and spatial analysis capabilities of commercially available GIS technology. Improvements in software interfaces have made GIS less intimidating and easier to use. Formerly tedious mapping and spatial analysis tasks have been made accessible for a broad spectrum of applications.

Advances in information technology during the last two decades have made geographic information systems (GIS) powerful and cost-effective tools for land analysis, planning, and management. Using GIS, analysts can more efficiently identify significant opportunities and constraints for proposed land uses. The advantages of using a digital GIS include (Arlinghaus, 1994):

- ease and speed of map revision and map scale changes
- inexpensive production of short-run special purpose maps
- potentially greater mapping accuracy
- changes in the database are immediately reflected in digital maps
- spatial analysis

Digital spatial data are available in two forms: raster or vector. Raster data are grid-cell surfaces composed of hundreds, thousands, or—with large data sets—millions of cells. Vector data, in contrast, consist of arcs, nodes, and polygons. Both types of spatial data are linked to tabular databases that store attribute information about the locations delineated by each grid cell or arc, node, and polygon. The choice of GIS data models, or forms, depends on the intended purpose of the data.

Raster data are widely used for environmental modeling and natural resource management. Site gradients, such as elevation, are effectively expressed in a raster format. Vector data, in contrast, are well-suited for mapping cultural features such as roads and land parcel boundaries.

Massachusetts GIS (MassGIS) is a state-level government initiative that creates a central source for large-scale georeferenced data. These digital data are potentially useful for land use planning applications at both the municipality and individual parcel scale. Digital orthophotos for the entire state are available on CD or by downloading through the Internet (www.state.ma.us/mgis). These digital black and white orthophotos are available in four resolutions (0.5, 1.0, 2.0, and 5.0 meters). Also available are digital terrain models (DTMs) with 3-meter contours. These images meet or exceed the

National Map Accuracy Standards (Box 2-1). Other vector data layers that either are, or will be, available in the MassGIS library include:

- Administrative boundaries (e.g., municipal zoning, regional planning agencies)
- Infrastructure (e.g., state roads, transmission lines, rail trails)
- Topography and physical resources (e.g., surficial geology, soils)
- Water-related features (e.g., wetlands and streams, aquifers, barrier beaches)
- Cultural resources (e.g., state register of historic places, landmarks)
- Regulated areas (e.g., underground storage tanks, wellhead protection areas)

The accuracy of maps and associated spatial data must be considered when used for land planning purposes. The source of the data, the scale of the data, and how and when it was collected can affect data accuracy and, of course, the reliability of analyses based on these data. Even though GIS data can be displayed at any scale, disregarding the scale of the source material can create problems when attempting to register (or overlay) multiple data layers. Therefore, the accuracy at which the data was developed should determine the maximum scale at which the data are displayed and overlayed.

SUMMARY

Advances in geographic information systems, combined with the proliferation of commercially available digital data, have substantially broadened the analytical capabilities of site analysts engaged in the land planning and design process. The role of spatial information technologies in land planning and design will surely expand substantially in the future.

BOX 2-1

United States National Map Accuracy Standards

With a view to the utmost economy and expedition in producing maps that fulfill not only the broad needs for standard or principal maps, but also the reasonable particular needs of individual agencies, standards of accuracy for published maps are defined as follows:

1. Horizontal accuracy. For maps on publication scales larger than 1:20,000, not more than 10 percent of the points tested shall be in error by more than 1/30 inch, measured on the publication scale; for maps on publication scales of 1:20,000 or smaller, 1/50 inch. These limits of accuracy shall apply in all cases to positions of well-defined points only. Well-defined points are those that are easily visible or recoverable on the ground, such as the following: monuments or markers, such as bench marks and property boundary monuments; intersections of roads, railroads, etc.; corners of large buildings or structures (or center points of small buildings); etc. In general, what is well defined will be determined by what is plottable on the scale of the map within 1/100 inch. Thus, whereas the intersection of two road or property lines meeting at right angles would come within a sensible interpretation, identification of the intersection of such lines meeting at an acute angle would obviously not be practicable within 1/100 inch. Similarly, features not identifiable upon the ground within close limits are not to be considered as test points within the limits quoted, even though their positions may be scaled closely upon the map. In this class would come timber lines, soil boundaries, etc.

BOX 2-1 (continued)

2. Vertical accuracy, as applied to contour maps on all publication scales, shall be such that not more than 10 percent of the elevations tested shall be in error more than one-half the contour interval. In checking elevations taken from the map, the apparent vertical error may be decreased by assuming a horizontal displacement within the permissible horizontal error for a map of that scale.

3. The accuracy of any map may be tested by comparing the positions of points whose locations or elevations are shown upon it with corresponding positions as determined by surveys of a higher accuracy. Tests shall be made by the producing agency, which shall also determine which of its maps are to be tested and the extent of the testing.

4. Published maps meeting these accuracy requirements shall note this fact on their legends, as follows: "This map complies with National Map Accuracy Standards."

5. Published maps whose errors exceed those stated above shall omit from their legends all mention of standard accuracy.

6. When a published map is a considerable enlargement of a map drawing (manuscript) or of a published map, that fact shall be stated in the legend. For example, "This map is an enlargement of a 1:20,000-scale map drawing," or "This map is an enlargement of a 1:24,000-scale published map."

7. To facilitate ready interchange and use of basic information for map construction among all federal mapmaking agencies, manuscript maps and published maps, wherever economically feasible and consistent with the uses to which the map is to be put, shall conform to latitude and longitude boundaries, being 15 minutes of latitude and longitude, or 7.5 minutes, or $3\frac{3}{4}$ minutes in size.

Issued June 10, 1941 U.S. BUREAU OF THE BUDGET
Revised April 26, 1943 and June 17, 1947

SITE SELECTION AND PROGRAMMING

PART II

SITE SELECTION AND PROGRAMMING

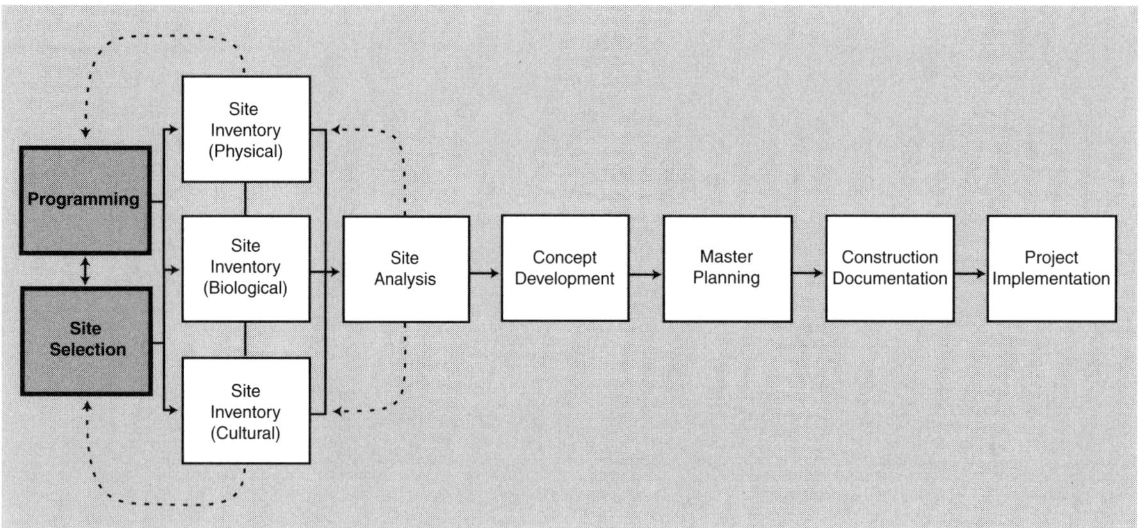

The next two chapters address site selection and programming—two integrally related phases of the land planning and design process. The order of these chapters reflects the sequence in which these two phases might occur in an "ideal" project. That is, a site is selected and then the land use program is developed for that site. In many cases, however, a land use program is first identified, and then a search is made for the site that best meets those objectives. Regardless of the sequence of these steps (programming, then site selection; or site selection, then programming), the land planner's task is ultimately to adapt the program to the site.

CHAPTER

3 Site Selection

INTRODUCTION

Location, location, location — as the old adage goes — are the three most important factors in real estate. A wide array of factors collectively make up the "location" of a site. From a geographic perspective, location is a product of three factors: space, time, and attributes (Johnston, 1980). Site selection involves the comparative analysis of potential sites. Each site is evaluated and selected, or rejected, on the basis of its attributes and spatial relationships to the attributes of its surroundings. The winnowing process spans a range of spatial scales, and can involve analysis at the national, regional, community, and site levels.

The expertise of several different professions may be enlisted in a search for potential development sites. The International Development Research Council (IDRC), for example, includes a wide array of professions among its corporate real estate and facility planning executives (Table 3-1). In the economic development and corporate real estate fields, site selection may involve several different scales of analysis. A national search for a large manufacturing facility, for example, might require the analysis of community-level statistics on crime, taxes, cost of living, and skilled workforce. These data could be collected for communities in several states and regions of the country. Site selection firms specialize in making this information available to companies and developers in search of sites. Community databases, and site selection locator services, are also available on the Internet.

TABLE 3-1 Selected real estate services provided by associate member firms of the International Development Research Council (IDRC).

Service	*Percentage of Firms*
Location analysis	60
Economic development	45
Project management	39
Real estate development	31
Brokerage	30
Strategic planning	29
Corporate real estate management	26
Construction	25
Property management	25
Financial services	24
Land use planning	22
Management consulting	20
Architectural design	19
Engineering	15
Appraisal	14
Environment assessment	11
Legal	4
Title	1

Source: Site Selection (1999, Jan., p.1122).

When a small number of potentially suitable communities has been identified, additional data must be collected on available sites within each community. Key attributes to consider in this initial site reconnaissance include:

- legally protected natural or cultural resources
- natural or man-made hazards
- visual quality on- and off-site
- physical impediments to excavation and construction
- potential linkages to existing circulation systems
- site drainage patterns

Consequently, documentation for potential sites should, at a minimum, include ground-level photographs of views on- and off-site, an aerial photograph of the site and the surrounding area, a local street or highway map with the site location identified, and—if available—a site survey showing topography, major trees, and buildings or other site structures.

The attractiveness of cities as places to work and live has much to do with the physical environment. Various publications annually select the best places to live in the United States, and the livability of cities depends on a broad array of attributes. The criteria used to evaluate communities include proximity to jobs, schools, shopping, and recreational opportunities. Other factors, such as crime, air quality, medical services, and property taxes, may also influence prospective residents' locational preferences. Site selection decisions at the national or regional scale are beyond the scope of this book. This chapter focuses instead on the site selection process at the local level.

LAND VALUATION

Taxation of property value is the basis for local government revenue in communities throughout the United States. Property taxes support local public services, such as fire and police protection, which directly benefit property owners. Property assessments are also typically required by lending institutions before financing is disbursed for land or land improvements. Land accrues economic value due to a variety of factors. Property assessors consider the attributes of the site itself, and the improvements made to the site. Common improvements to property include buildings and other site structures.

Real estate appraisal attempts to predict the probable selling price of a property by modeling, as closely as possible, the influence of various factors on buyers' and sellers' decisions.

> In general, appraisal theory approaches the concept of value by synthesizing three different models of economic behavior. In appraisal, these three models are called *approaches to value* and are referred to as the cost approach, the sales comparison approach, and the income approach. (Castle, 1998, p. 87).

These methods of property assessment estimate value based on the "highest and best use" of the property. Highest and best use reflects the property owner's objectives — not the community's. Therefore, externalities, or costs that are not internalized to the property, are not factored into the assessment. For example, projects with high economic returns but significant environmental impacts will compare more favorably in highest and best use analyses that ignore these externalities.

Cultural and biophysical amenities are not evenly distributed over the landscape, and land parcels vary widely in the quality and quantity of these amenities. Moreover, these assets influence the site's suitability for different uses. Scenic views of lakes, rivers, or other environmental amenities may contribute significantly to the site's desirability for residential and some commercial uses. These amenities, in addition to built amenities like parks, golf courses, tennis courts, or other recreational facilities, also enhance property values. The influence of amenities on property value is clearly demonstrated in the price disparity among housing lots in resort communities. Beachfront lots, for example, sell at a premium in comparison to nearby, and otherwise comparable, lots that are not adjacent to this open-space amenity. If the same site were used for industrial uses, these scenic waterfront views would play little or no role in the value of the products manufactured at this site. The "highest and best use" concept suggests, therefore, that the character of a site and its surroundings should determine, in part, how the site is used.

SITE SELECTION CONTEXT

In some cases, a site is already owned by a client, and the future uses of the site have yet to be determined. In other cases, the program has been tentatively determined, but a site must be found to accommodate the intended uses. Sites that could satisfy a particular set of project objectives may be widely dispersed across the world, or they might all be located within one large, contiguous parcel. These alternatives comprise a typology of site selection scenarios.

Stand-Alone Sites

Site selection may occur at several spatial scales. Depending on the intended uses of the site, the scope of the selection process may require the evaluation of attributes associated with the site, community, region, or nation. A parcel of land — or perhaps two or more contiguous parcels of land — may be selected to accommodate a specific land use program. Or — especially in the United States — it may be selected for speculative purposes. That is, a development site may be acquired and then sold in the future, when the location has become more attractive for development — and the property's value has significantly increased.

Site Within a Site

Site selection may also involve the selection of a site from a larger contiguous parcel or several noncontiguous parcels that are under a single ownership. This process commonly occurs with projects initiated by public or private institutions that have relatively large land holdings. Colleges and universities, for example, are often faced with renovating and, in many cases, expanding their campus facilities (see Box 3-1). Campuses are complex built environments that carry out many of the same functions as small cities. Creating new spaces for classrooms, laboratories, and other instructional facilities are common reasons for new construction. Campus expansion or redevelopment may also involve the construction of administrative buildings, parking lots and garages, pedestrian circulation systems, and new facilities for recreational and intercollegiate athletics.

College and university campuses may be several hundred acres or hectares in area, and a variety of potential building sites may be available for any given project. Yet two different sites on a campus could be dramatically different in their suitability for the proposed site uses. On a hilly site, for example, development constraints might include the area's high susceptibility to erosion or the site's poor accessibility. On a relatively flat site, in contrast, constraints might include the area's susceptibility to flooding. These and many other site attributes could potentially influence the design — and ultimately the function — of any new facility.

LAND DEVELOPMENT COSTS

Site selection is a process of weighing many disparate factors. Some of these are more easily quantified than others. Site and contextual attributes that can be measured in monetary terms, for example, are easily compared. Inevitably, however, most site selection decisions come down to weighing economic, social, environmental — and even ethical — factors.

Acquisition and Holding Costs

Large multi-national corporations may conduct national or even global searches for sites where new facilities will be located. Selecting a site for any new facility involves the application of a set of selection criteria. The criteria used to identify and evaluate potential sites depends on the nature of the proposed activities. Different sets of selection criteria are appropriate for various industries and, within a single industry, for various site purposes (see Corporate Site Seekers Center website: http://www.siteseeker.org). The selection of the site — in some cases from among a regional, national, or even global set of alternatives — can impact many facets of a company's operations. The location of a corporate headquarters will affect the corporation's ability to attract and retain skilled human resources. The location may also help define the organization's image — as it is perceived by current or prospective clients, investors, and employees, as well as by the general public. Therefore, the location of the headquarters can significantly impact a company's operational efficiency and profitability.

Land acquisition costs include fees for site evaluation and selection. Particularly for sites with a history of previous commercial or industrial uses, significant time and effort can be devoted to gaining information about a site before it is purchased. For example, ASTM standards for a Transaction Screen Analysis and a Phase One Environmental Site Assessment (ESA) involve an extensive set of tests and standardized reporting (American Society of Civil Engineers, 1996). After a site is purchased, land holding costs accrue as the development process continues.

Design and Permitting Costs

Research on land development patterns in the United States suggests that land parcels "passed over during the first wave of development tend to be developed later, at higher densities" (Peiser, 1992, p. 48). These leftover parcels may be particularly attractive for development because the sites are well served by existing public infrastructure, and they are often located in areas convenient to shopping, public transportation, and cultural and educational facilities. These sites may have remained undeveloped for a variety of reasons. A landowner may have simply held on to the land for speculative purposes, in anticipation that the property would increase in value. In other cases, however, these sites are undeveloped because they have significant development constraints. Rugged topography, unstable soils, and shallow bedrock are just a few of the physiographic attributes that could have deterred development on these sites.

The complexity of the land planning and design process — including approvals and permitting — is largely determined at the site selection phase. Difficult sites are more costly to develop for a variety of reasons. Development proposals for sites near environmentally sensitive areas often receive close scrutiny by public authorities, neighboring property owners, and other interested stakeholders. In some cases, public concern — or uncertainty — about potential development impacts can slow, or prevent, a project from being implemented. A difficult site usually requires a well-documented justification of any development proposal.

From the developer's perspective, greater scrutiny of development proposals may seem arbitrary and unfair. Peiser (1992, p. 48) writes:

> Historically, developers assumed that they had the right to develop land as long as they met the restrictions imposed by zoning and other land use regulations. This presumption of "development rights" is rapidly dissolving. Even where developers' projects conform to existing zoning, development rights may be subject to reduction, depending on the attitudes of neighboring homeowners and the political environment.

But modern building technologies and site engineering enable the construction of buildings and related infrastructure on environmentally sensitive sites. This capability comes with potential costs. Site development on difficult sites, particularly if the site constraints are not avoided or the impacts are not mitigated, can have significant on-site and off-site consequences. These potential impacts include higher public infrastructure costs, degradation of terrestrial and aquatic ecosystems, and potential life safety risks to future residents. Selection of these sites also may substantially increase the complexity and costs of the permitting and approval process.

Development impacts in the United States are increasingly mitigated through "exactions." These are payments, or contributions of land in lieu of money. On residential subdivision projects, for example, exactions may include payments for the installation of streets, lighting, sidewalks, and utilities. The completion of this work is typically required before any lots can be sold. Exactions also compensate communities for the increased costs of providing public services for new development (Altshuler and Gomez-Ibanez, 1993).

Construction Costs

Land development or restoration involves both labor and materials. These costs include site preparation and grading, stormwater management, installation of site utilities, excavation and building construction, and planting. Site constraints increase site preparation costs substantially, particularly if development is planned for areas that are not inherently well suited for construction. Difficult sites might increase costs for clearing vegetation, excavation and regrading, and designing and constructing complex building foundations. These sites may also increase the costs of constructing vehicle and pedestrian circulation systems and managing stormwater. The time elapsed from the selection of the site to the completion of construction also is likely to be greater for development proposals on less-suited areas. Development of poorly suited sites, or development of unsuitable areas on otherwise suitable sites, can significantly increase project construction costs.

Marketing Costs

Real estate value of residential and commercial properties, especially, is influenced by the quality of the site's buildings and other improvements, but also by the location of the site. Rental and sales prices within an area are also influenced by the quality and quantity of competing commercial and residential real estate. These factors influence not only the value but the marketability of this real estate (Castle, 1998). Preferences for residential locations vary widely among different segments of society. Different clientele, or "markets," for specific kinds of housing can be traced to variation in the population's age, occupation, education level, income, and family status. Housing preferences often vary with the different stages in the human life cycle. For example, customer demand for housing may be influenced by the proximity and quality of primary and secondary schools, public health and human services, or outdoor recreational opportunities. Quality-of-life issues play a substantial role in shaping consumer preferences and determining real estate value.

Management and Maintenance Costs

Project maintenance and management costs are also influenced, to some extent, by the site's location and attributes. Sites that are subject to natural hazards, for example, require additional carrying costs, such as hazard insurance.

SITE SELECTION FACTORS

Project Objectives

Potential problems that the site could pose for the intended uses should be identified before the site is purchased. Many different physical, biological, and cultural constraints can limit the area of a site that is suitable for development. The initial site assessment should consider both constraints and opportunities for the expected program. Small-scale land development, typically on sites of less than 50 acres (20 hectares), are most likely to involve four types of real estate product: single-family residential subdivisions, planned unit subdivisions, mixed-use subdivisions, and industrial/office parks (Peiser, 1992).

Market studies can provide information that is useful in the site selection process. These studies provide information on the competition for selling or renting comparable properties. Market studies can also reveal consumer preferences for site and building features or amenities.

Site selection is a specialized field. This is a type of spatial analysis that lends itself to applications of geographic information system technology (Castle, 1998). In choosing a location for a new manufacturing facility, for example, the analysis may occur at multiple spatial scales (Table 3-2). Site location can significantly influence a facility's costs of production. For a heavy-manufacturing facility, proximity to sources of essential raw materials may be the most important criterion in the site selection decision. This is particularly true if the raw materials are bulky and require expensive surface transportation. In contrast, for a firm that manufactures precision instruments, a location near an available supply of skilled labor—such as tool and die makers—would be critically important.

TABLE 3-2 Examples of locational factors that might influence the selection of a site for a manufacturing facility.

Scale	*Factor*
Nation	Taxes (e.g., corporate income tax) Raw materials (e.g., costs of water, energy) Market area and competition
Community	Transportation (e.g., rail, air, highway) Labor (e.g., skills, knowledge, work ethic) Quality of life (e.g., crime rate, quality of public schools, cultural and recreational opportunities, housing costs) Land use regulation (e.g., zoning) Development incentives (e.g., off-site improvements, tax abatements, low-interest loans)
Site	Parcel size and shape Property costs (e.g, land costs) Development costs (e.g., site preparation, permitting, construction) Operating costs (e.g., property taxes, energy costs) Accessibility (e.g., vehicle access, mass transit) Utilities (e.g., sanitary sewer, water, telecommunications) Biophysical conditions (e.g., topography, surficial geology, hazards) Protective services (e.g., fire protection, police)

The proposed uses of the site determine which site selection criteria are appropriate. For example, general criteria for selecting prison sites in the United States include (Ammons et al., 1992):

- proximity to the communities from which most inmates come
- areas capable of providing or attracting qualified professional staff of racial and ethnic origins compatible with the inmate population
- areas with adequate social services, hospitals, schools, universities, and employment opportunities to support the correctional goals<ENDLB>

Additional selection criteria typically address the site's physiographic constraints and capacity to provide needed utility services (Krasnow, 1998). Other, less common criteria include the site's visibility from adjacent roads and highways, and the ease with which views to a new prison can be screened.

The criteria used in selecting sites for other intended uses must, of course, be tailored to those intended uses. Consequently, some sites are particularly well suited for specific uses. For example, the American Society of Golf Course Architects (2000) suggests that a site for a golf course should have:

- a visually interesting landscape (e.g., rolling hills, mature vegetation), which will minimize earthmoving operations and reduce construction costs
- adequate soil drainage and quality topsoil, which is essential for growing fine turf
- sufficient utility availability (e.g., electricity and potable water)
- convenient access to transportation infrastructure, which is necessary to attract golfers at various skill levels

Other considerations that might influence the selection of a golf course site include demographic trends in the area and potential competition from other nearby existing or proposed golf courses.

Sites that will be used for retail or office uses have other sets of preferred criteria. For retail uses, in particular, sites must provide efficient customer access. High visibility from major streets and highways is another common site attribute. Particularly in metropolitan areas with relatively large populations, mixed-use development in transit corridors and near transit stations is becoming more common.

Yet privacy, rather than high visibility, is generally preferred for residential sites. Also, residential sites should, if possible, be free of nuisances such as bright lights, loud noises, unpleasant odors, and heavy vehicle traffic (Table 3-3).

Land Use Regulations and Incentives

Land use regulations typically have a significant influence on both public and private sector land development decisions. Local zoning ordinances, for example, limit the types of land uses that can occur at different locations within a municipality's jurisdiction. Zoning ordinances and other local codes may also dictate permitted land use densities and spatial configurations.

Land use controls, therefore, influence the location, pace, and character of development (Platt, 1996). Yet rigid zoning codes have been the target of much criticism (Kunstler, 1993, 1998), and there is now a growing trend in the United States to allow greater flexibility in development proposals. One approach is to include the site within a planned unit development (PUD) or planned development district (PDD). If

TABLE 3-3 Examples of factors that may influence the selection of sites for residential and mixed-use subdivisions.

Category	*Attribute*
Context	Market area and competition Land use regulations and development review process Accessibility Utility service Visibility (e.g., to and from the site) Adjoining land ownership and land uses
Site	Size and shape Easements and deed restrictions Land costs Topography and surficial geology Vegetation (e.g., mature trees, wetlands) Current and prior land uses Nuisances (e.g., noise, traffic)

Source: Adapted from Peiser, 1992, p. 51, table 3-2.

allowed under the local zoning code, PUDs or PDDs allow for land development patterns that depart from rigid single-use zoning requirements.

In the United States, the nation's Constitution gives landowners substantial clout in land use disputes. Land use controls, to be legally upheld — or deemed Constitutional — must protect public health, safety, morals, and welfare. Permitting and approval processes in the United States typically allow for public review and comment on major development proposals. Attitudes toward new development vary among municipalities, and the selected site can make a substantial difference in whether or not a development proposal is supported by community leaders and residents. Objections to development or redevelopment proposals typically hinge on concerns about the projects' off-site impacts. These impacts may affect local environmental quality, the community's fiscal health, and neighboring residents' quality of life. Logically, then, the site selection process should consider these potential development impacts.

Development incentives may also play a significant role in the site selection process. State and local incentives include tax abatements, fee waivers, low-interest loans, and off-site improvements to the public infrastructure (Haresign, 1999). These development subsidies are usually based on the expected economic impact of the new facility. Economic impact is typically measured by the number of jobs created, the expected payroll, or the revenue generated by selling a publicly owned facility (Moore, 1999). Business development incentives, such as Tax Increment Financing (TIF) districts, can stimulate economic development in neighborhoods with relatively high levels of unemployment. Property assessments — which determine property taxes in most communities — may be temporarily frozen at predevelopment levels in TIF districts.

Site Attributes

Parcel Size and Shape

Land area, of course, is a fundamental constraint on development capacity. If all other factors are equal, larger sites can accommodate more development, but larger sites also offer greater flexibility in the spatial arrangements of those uses on the site. The shape of the parcel can also affect property value, the potential uses of the site, in addition to the site's opportunities and constraints for future development. For example, long and linear properties have a much higher edge-to-interior ratio than properties that are more square in shape (Figure 3-1). This greater "exposure" to the surrounding landscape reduces the site's ability to buffer negative off-site impacts. However, if the adjacent areas are natural or cultural amenities, a parcel with a relatively high edge-to-interior ratio can be an asset—particularly if these amenities are in public ownership and are likely to persist well into the near future (Figure 3-2).

In combination, the size and shape of a parcel can have a significant impact on the potential uses of a site. A small site may have a relatively large percentage of the total site area dedicated to required building setbacks from property lines. Therefore, the influence of adjacent uses may be especially pronounced with linear sites. If proposed site uses are sensitive to setting, as are residential uses, for example, then the site's immediate surroundings are a primary concern in the site selection process.

Easements and Deed Restrictions

Easements and other deed restrictions also limit how a parcel of land can be used. Easements may provide access to a site from adjacent properties or for other purposes, such as utility system maintenance. Conservation easements, in contrast, reduce the parcel's development potential.

Natural Hazards

Sites on the edges of water, wetlands, and other scenic natural areas are often attractive properties for real estate development. Yet the cost of damage and destruction attributable to natural hazards in the United States has been estimated at an average of $1 billion per week (Mileti, 1999). The Federal Emergency Management Agency's (FEMA) flood insurance program compensates the insured for their losses of buildings in floodplains and other hazardous areas. Until very recently, the federal government routinely facilitated reconstruction of destroyed buildings on sites that were repeatedly struck by natural disasters.

The Year 2000 Building Code marks a substantial shift in public policy regarding construction in areas prone to natural hazards. Government buyout programs have been implemented in an attempt to reduce continued rebuilding in floodplains and other hazardous areas. In addition, the U.S. Geological Survey has created a series of maps that inventory the risks of various natural hazards in the United States.

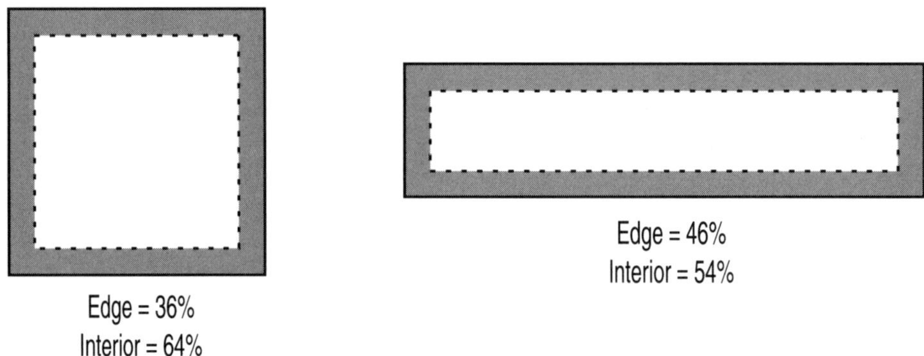

Figure 3-1 Relationship between parcel shape and edge-to-interior ratio for two parcels of equal area.

Figure 3-2 Water is an amenity with a significant influence on the value of waterfront real estate.

Chemical Hazards

The lack of environmental regulation in the United States prior to the 1960s allowed the indiscriminate disposal of chemical wastes in urban, suburban, and rural areas. Commercial sites were often used as dumping grounds for a variety of toxic wastes. Consequently, former gasoline stations, printing presses, dry cleaners, and other commercial sites may still be contaminated by a variety of toxic substances. Heavy metals and other highly toxic chemicals pose substantial health risks, particularly to children.

The toxic chemicals found oozing out of the ground within a residential development in Love Canal, New York, was a major event in the development of hazardous waste policy in the United States. Federal legislation was subsequently adopted to redress the nation's toxic waste problems. The national Environmental Protection Agency (EPA) was charged with administering the resulting Superfund Program. Although created to clean up contaminated sites, this program had dramatic yet unintended consequences. Liability for the cleanup costs of contaminated sites could be assigned to new landowners who were not responsible for—or even aware of—the original pollution. In addition, Superfund regulations held these sites' owners liable for the remediation costs of restoring the sites to precontamination conditions. The enormous costs of even small toxic waste cleanups had a chilling effect on the redevelopment of many commercial and industrial sites, which are common in large, older cities. The significant legal and financial risks of purchasing and attempting to develop these contaminated, or "brownfield," sites effectively redirected new development to "greenfield" sites on the urban periphery. Especially in central city areas, these vacant brownfield sites inhibited economic investment in the surrounding areas, thereby worsening the economic and social impacts of the environmental contamination.

During the 1990s, a radical shift in public policy began eliminating disincentives, and creating new incentives, for the redevelopment of contaminated "brownfield" sites. In the state of Wisconsin, for example, a "Land Recycling Law" (WiscAct 453) had two major objectives:

- encourage local governments to take title to environmentally contaminated land and restore the sites to productive use
- exempt municipalities from responsibility for remedial action if the property is acquired through a tax delinquency proceeding or by order of a bankruptcy court

These types of redevelopment programs reduce developers' risks (e.g., liability) and allow remediation — in certain situations — to conditions that are less than pristine. Instead of requiring complete waste removal on every contaminated site, certain types and quantities of wastes are allowed to remain underground. Permanent deed restrictions may be required to ensure that the remaining contaminated areas are sealed from infiltrating stormwater. When infiltration of these soils is prevented by impervious (clay) caps or by other means, leaching and the resulting movement of contaminants into the groundwater can be prevented.

Former commercial and industrial sites, as well as former agricultural lands, should be carefully assessed prior to development. When considering these sites for development, an essential step in the site selection process is an ASTM Phase One Environmental Site Assessment (ESA). This report summarizes the site's ownership and land use history, in addition to current soil and groundwater conditions. Analysis of soil and groundwater samples are included in Phase One ESA documentation. All buildings and other structures on the site are also evaluated and mapped. The cost of an ASTM Phase-One site assessment in the late 1990s ranged from $60,000 to $200,000, depending on the size of the parcel, the complexity of the existing site structures, and the types of contaminants found on the site (Talarico, 1998).

A detailed environmental assessment requires the services of both legal and environmental experts. Assistance with regulatory compliance and project permitting are services offered by firms specializing in brownfield redevelopment. Yet federal, state, and local financial incentives are increasingly available to encourage redevelopment of brownfield sites, particularly those sites in economically depressed areas. Urban sites may present complications for development, but these sites may also offer good investment opportunities. Brownfield sites, especially in cities, typically have very good access to a full range of public services and utilities. Brownfield sites also may be eligible for financial subsidies from multiple economic development programs. Brownfield redevelopment can create new job opportunities in economically depressed neighborhoods and improve the visual quality of formerly "blighted" areas. These efforts also can boost civic pride and reduce pressure for urban fringe development.

Drainage

Site drainage is influenced by topography as well as by soil and subsoil conditions. Depth to groundwater and depth to bedrock are attributes that are often addressed in the site selection process. The primary site selection criterion for a development of single-family detached homes in an unsewered area may be the suitability of the soil for on-site wastewater treatment systems.

Archaeological Remnants

Archaeological finds, or discoveries, in the United States can have a significant impact on project planning and implementation. According to Talarico (1998, p. 250):

> Rules governing finds vary according to the locality, the size of the site, and who is involved in the project. If the property is private, finds can be bulldozed, except where there's legislation that says otherwise. If there are ties to the federal government, even if the project is only partially funded by a federal agency, the site falls under the National Historic Preservation Act, administered by the Department of the Interior. The property must then undergo a phase-one archaeological analysis, during which test pits are dug. If anything of value is found, the act requires a more extensive phase-two dig. A phase-three dig is a full-blown excavation.

Endangered and Threatened Species

The National Environmental Protection Act and other legislation at the federal and state levels provide legal protection for endangered and threatened species in the United States. Similar legal protections also exist in other countries. Information on the presence of endangered and threatened species can be obtained from government agencies (e.g., U.S. Fish and Wildlife Service) and from local environmental consultants.

Visibility and Visual Quality

Visual access to a site from adjacent highways or other off-site locations may be an asset or a liability, depending on the purposes for which the site will be used. Scenic views, mature trees, water, and other environmental amenities can significantly enhance real estate value. The importance of these amenities in the site selection process depends on the proposed uses of the site. Yet these amenities may also influence the uses that can be programmed for the site.

Infrastructure

Although telecommunication technologies have broadened the range of suitable locations for most land uses, physical connectivity through road networks remains an important site selection criterion. Depending on the program and the site's context, physical access to a site may occur by several different modes of transportation. Access by pedestrians and bicyclists, as well as by private vehicles and public transportation, may be desirable. Public infrastructure in urbanized areas also includes the delivery of potable water and the collection and treatment of wastewater. In less urban areas, these and other public services are typically more limited.

COMPARING SITE ALTERNATIVES

Many disparate social, economic, and environmental factors may influence a project's success. Yet not all of these factors are important in selecting the vast majority of sites. A systematic approach is therefore necessary to identify the site selection criteria that are relevant for each set of circumstances. For some site selection decisions, a multi-scaled selection process may be necessary (see Box 3-1). Analysis of site and contextual factors is always helpful in identifying and comparing site alternatives (Figure 3-3). These analyses may involve market data, such as demographic and household economic characteristics, for areas within a specified distance of each potential site. Typically, one or two criteria have a disproportionately large influence on the site selection decision. These criteria are essential site or contextual attributes that, if absent, exclude a site from further consideration.

Figure 3-3 Oblique aerial photograph with potential project sites delineated. *Source:* Wallace, Roberts & Todd, LLC.

Suppose, for example, you are responsible for selecting a site for a new restaurant. Two essential site selection criteria may be: (1) a location near a sufficient number of potential customers, and (2) a site where customers can conveniently arrive at the restaurant, and enter it. If these two essential criteria are met, the site evaluation process can then proceed to consider other selection criteria.

Yet many land development programs include more than one proposed land use (Figure 3-4). Complicating the site selection process further, different land uses may require different types of sites. One approach to the evaluation of alternative sites is to prioritize the proposed land uses, then solve first for the most important land use. When a subset of sites that satisfy the primary land use criterion has been identified, then the process can proceed to the next most important land use, and so on. Another approach is to attempt to optimize for all land uses simultaneously.

The weighted matrix method involves the assignment of weights, or values, to each site selection criterion. Values are assigned on the basis of each attribute's importance to the proposed uses of the site. Of course, a critical step in this process is the selection of weight values. The scheme for weighting the selection criteria can dramatically influence the results of the site selection process. Therefore, the weighting values for each criterion should be made in consultation with the client and other stakeholders.

Theoretically, site selection data can be reduced to a single suitability index. Although this approach is attractive for its simplicity, condensing an array of diverse data can ignore potentially useful information. An intermediate approach is to calculate indices for different categories of selection criteria, then subjectively compare these different indices. Rather than relying on a single index to summarize the complex effects of multiple site factors on multiple site uses, the site selection decision is based on the evaluation of suitability values for each attribute category. These site selection criteria may include, for example:

- visibility and visual quality
- access to public infrastructure
- acquisition and development costs
- development regulations and incentives
- management and maintenance costs

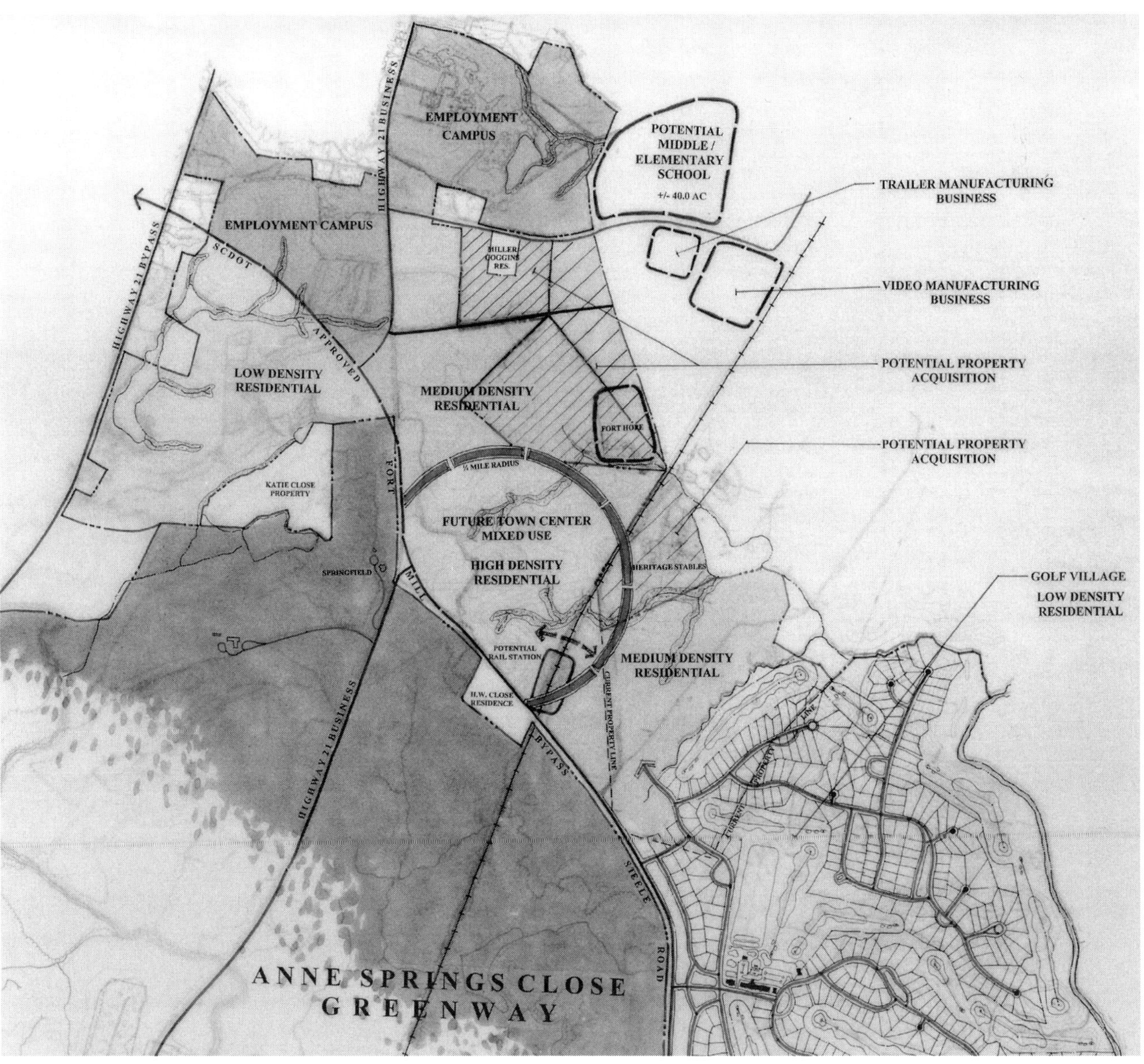

Figure 3-4 Conceptual land use plan showing a potential site for a new elementary school and two other locations of potential property acquisition. *Source:* Land Design.

BOX 3-1 In Practice

SUMMARY OF A NATIONAL-SCALE SITE SELECTION PROCESS FOR LOCATING A NEW BUSINESS FACILITY

1. Pre-project Planning
   a) Form a site selection team (skills needed include finance, marketing, manufacturing operations, human resources, transportation/distribution, engineering, law, and environment).
   b) Identify goals and objectives of the new facility (e.g., lowering operating costs, entering new markets).
   c) Develop a budget and analyze the feasibility of building a new facility (e.g., design and engineering concepts, facility requirements, market research, and financial feasibility).
   d) Identify critical site evaluation criteria (e.g., quality and quantity of the workforce, transportation and utilities, and site and building characteristics).
   e) Determine which site evaluation factors are necessities and which are desirable but less critical.
   f) Collect and analyze data for these factors (if available from national sources); identify a geographical area for the site search (typically between five and ten states).

2. Narrowing the Search
   a) Collect more detailed data on the communities (typically between fifteen and twenty) that are being considered. State and local development organizations can usually provide needed data (e.g., higher education resources, payroll costs, average salaries, transportation, quality of life).
   b) Using the community data and the site evaluation criteria, narrow the number of potential sites to five or six.

3. Community Fieldwork and Site Visits
   a) Visit each community to meet with major employers and local leaders, and to collect additional community information (e.g., labor costs and availability, transportation and utility service capacity, neighborhood and housing conditions).
   b) Visit each site and any accompanying buildings to collect additional information (e.g., available site utilities, utility service capacity, construction date of buildings).
   c) Using the additional community and site data, narrow the number of remaining sites to two or three.
   d) Prepare a report on the results of the work for review by company management. Identify, for each site, the projected facility costs (e.g., land costs, site development costs, utility extension costs, construction costs). Also identify available community financial assistance or development incentives.
   e) Once the best site is selected, additional site data should be collected to identify potential sources of unusual development costs (e.g., severe soil conditions, hazardous contamination).

(*Source:* www.siteseekers.org).

SUMMARY

A site's location has a fundamental influence on the complexity and cost of the project planning, approval, and implementation processes. Therefore, site selection typically involves the collection and analysis of a wide array of both site and contextual data. Land use regulations, local real estate markets, and cultural and physiographic attributes all influence, to varying degrees, the ability of a site to successfully accommodate a particular development or conservation program. Ian McHarg's (1969) credo, "design with nature," remains a compelling land use objective. Designing with nature can reduce a development's impact on the complex web of biophysical systems that functionally link land, water, and biota. Moreover, the conservation of a site's natural — and cultural — resources can make the developed site a more desirable place to reside, work, or play.

BOX 3-2 In Practice

Site Selection Study

Evansville State Hospital
Evansville, Illinois, USA

Consultants
Hellmuth, Obata + Kassabaum, Inc., St. Louis, Missouri, USA

Overview
The new Evansville State Hospital will be a 228-bed replacement facility. The hospital is a mental health center for the state of Illinois. This new facility will be located in a parklike setting on property adjacent to the existing hospital (Figures B3-1 and B3-2). It will provide housing and treatment facilities that meet current standards for the care of patients and the efficient use of staff.

Selection Process
The HOK Planning Group created a series of illustrations that graphically document the factors that were considered in selecting the site for the new hospital building. Two potential sites were identified. Both sites, east and west, were near the old hospital on a single large parcel of land owned by the state of Illinois. Site selection criteria for this project included: potential site development costs, and site accessibility (Figure B3-3), and proximity to existing facilities (Figure B3-4). Other criteria included access to existing utilities (Figure B3-5) and existing drainage patterns (Figure B3-6) The evaluation of these criteria is summarized in a site selection matrix (Figure B3-7).

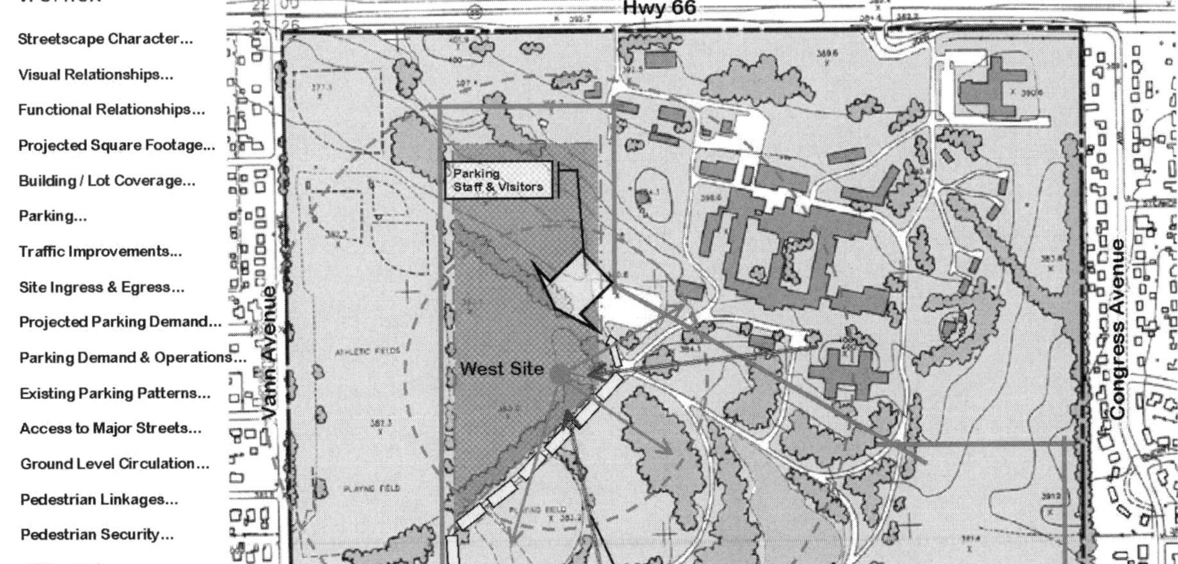

Figure B3-1 Potential site (west) for the new medical building. *Source:* The HOK Planning Group.

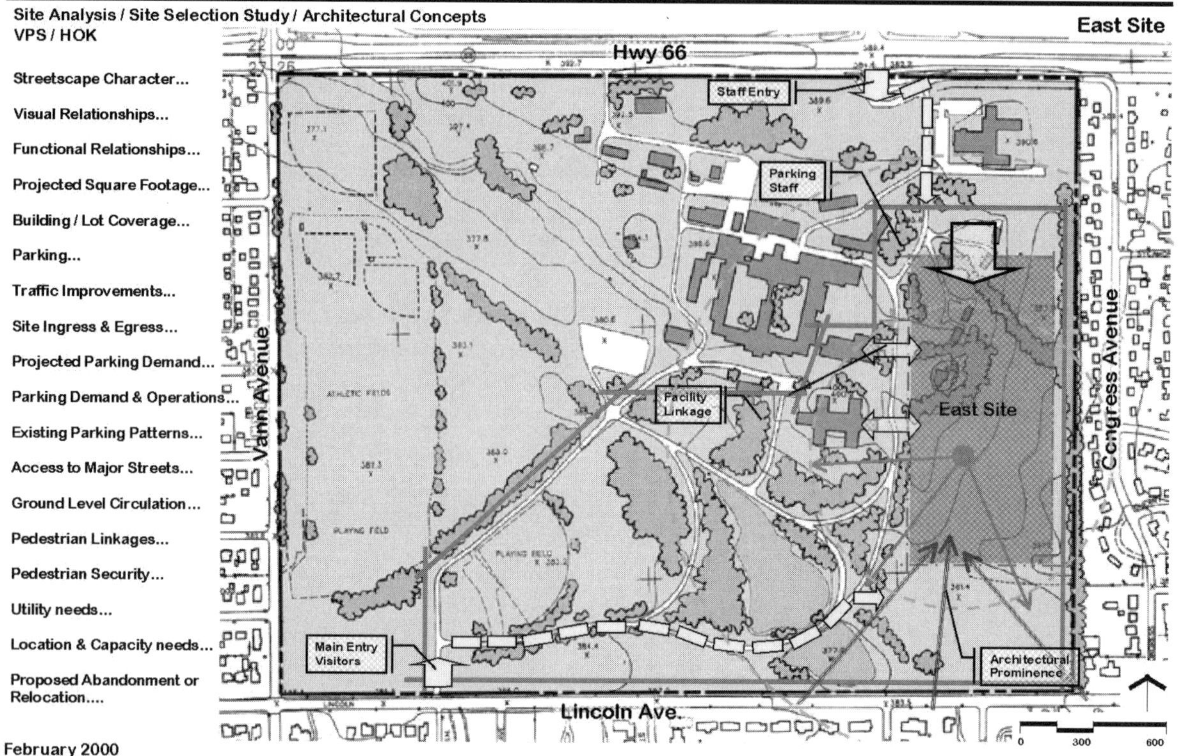

Figure B3-2 Potential site (east) for the new medical building. *Source:* The HOK Planning Group.

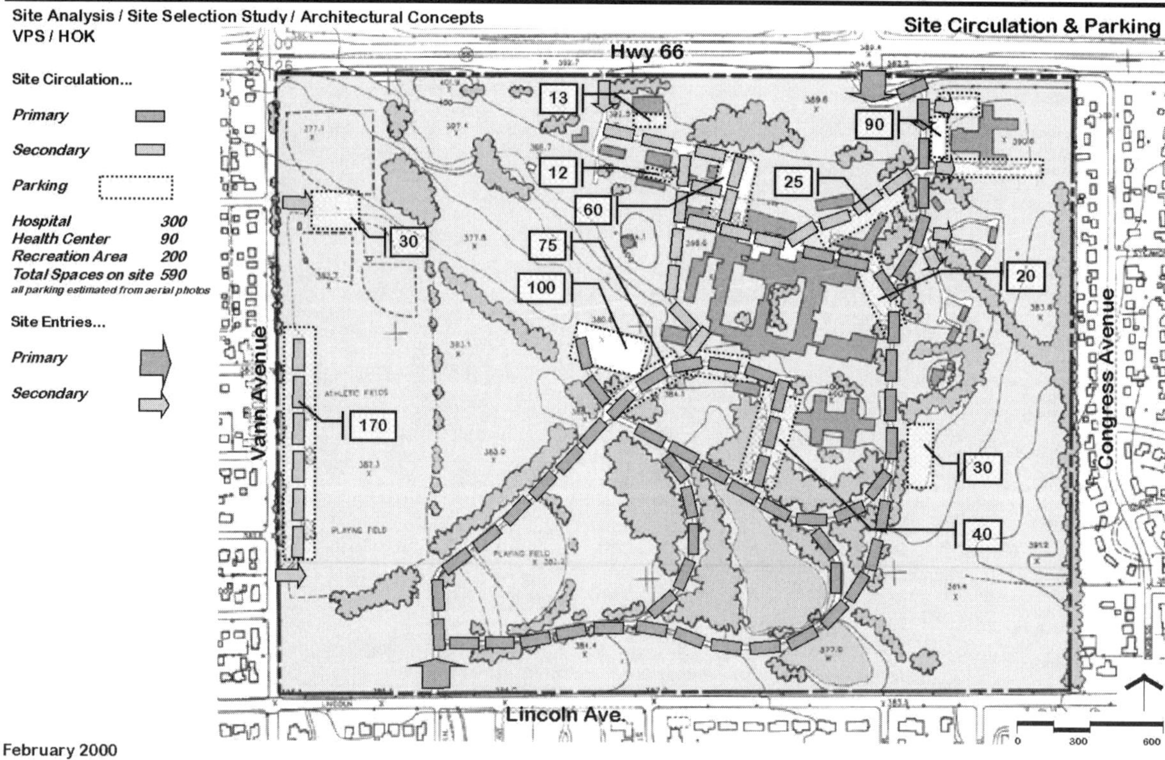

Figure B3-3 Existing vehicle circulation and parking. *Source:* The HOK Planning Group.

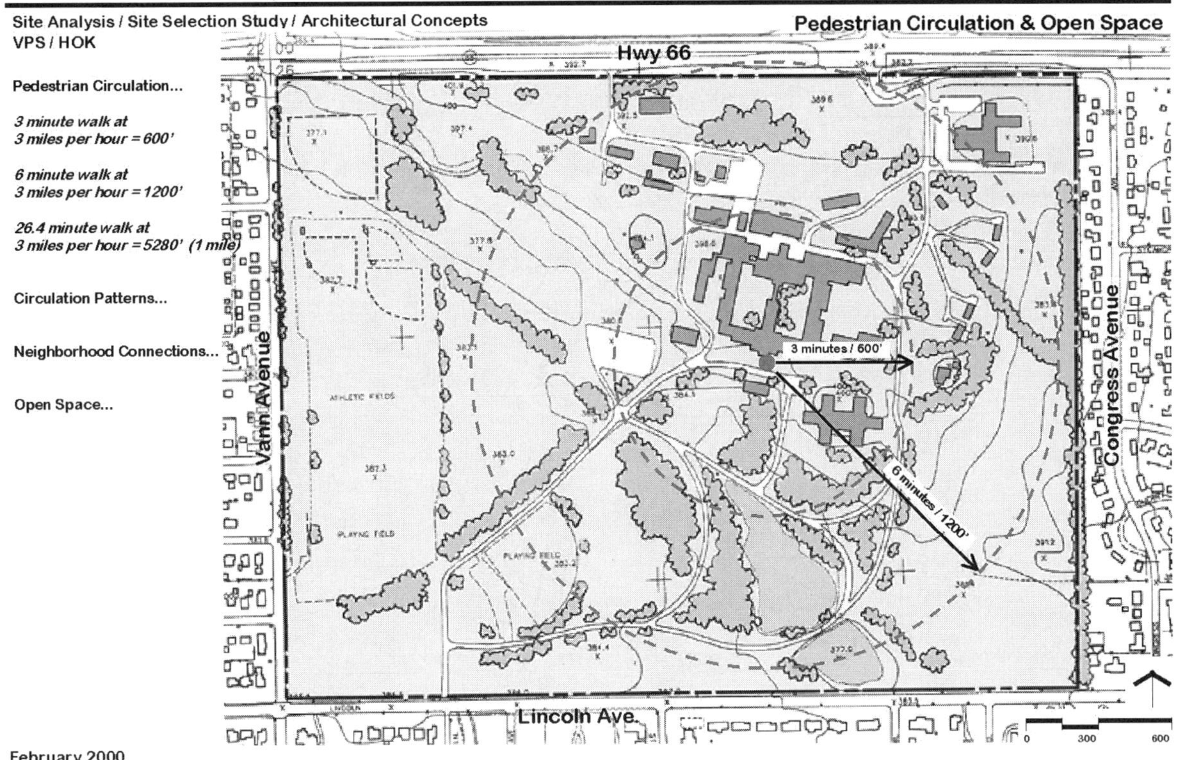

Figure B3-4 Existing pedestrian circulation. *Source:* The HOK Planning Group

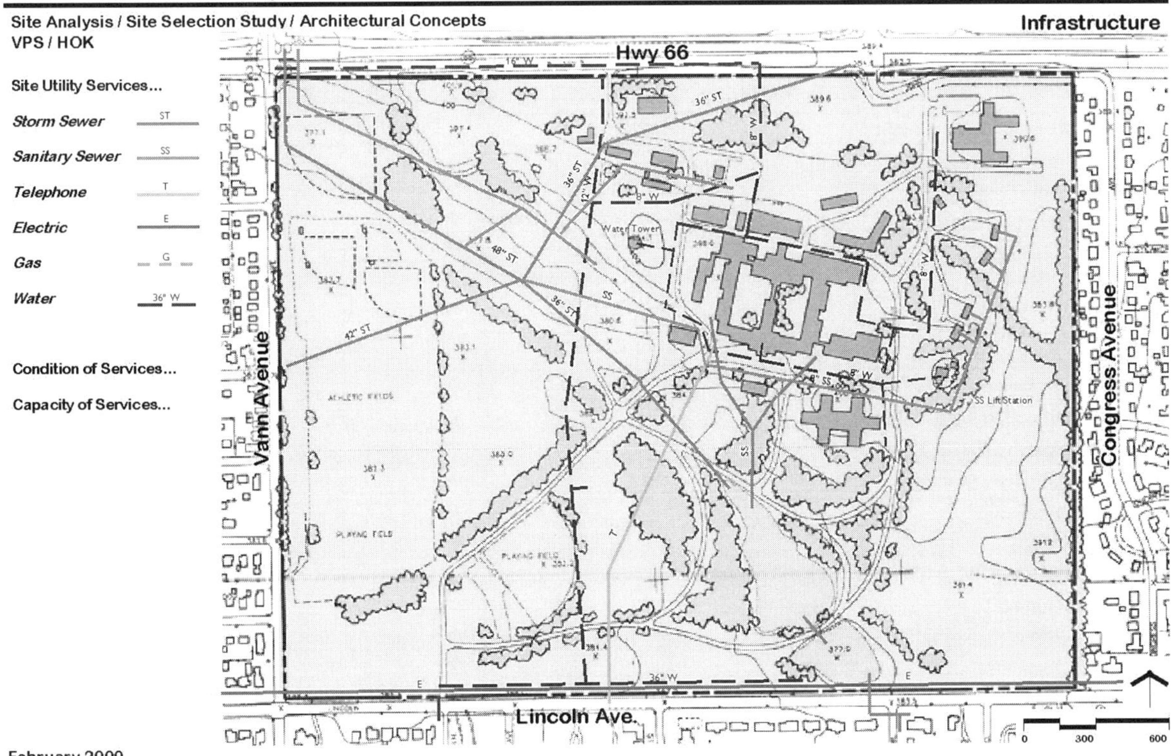

Figure B3-5 Existing utility systems. *Source:* The HOK Planning Group.

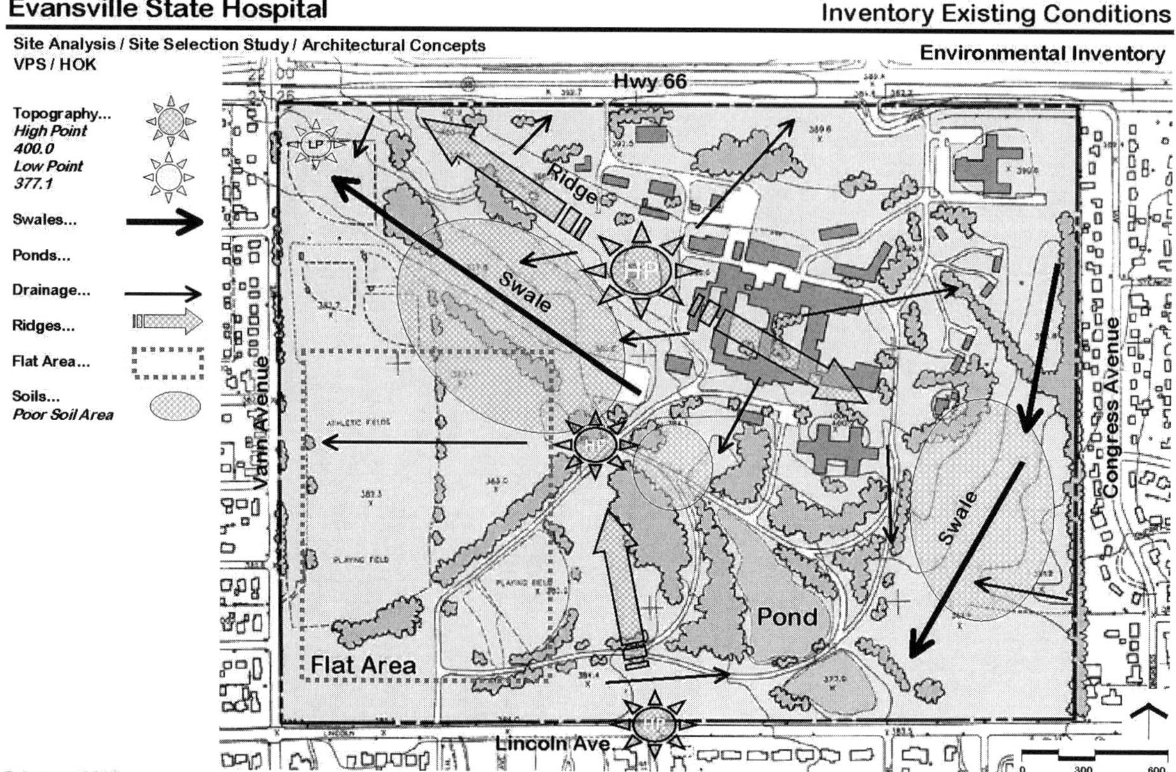

Figure B3-6 Inventory of existing environmental conditions. *Source:* The HOK Planning Group.

Evansville State Hospital — **Site Selection Criteria**

Site Analysis / Site Selection Study / Architectural Concepts
VPS / HOK

Issue	West	East
1. Cost of Site Development		
A. Topography (Leveling the Site)		
B. Soils		
C. Sewer Connection	+	✓
D. Utilities	✓	✓
- Water - Gas - Telephone - Electric	✓	✓
E. Demolition	+	—
2. Construction Area of Site	✓	☆
3. Proximity to Existing Facilities	—	☆
4. Existing Tree Damage	—	☆
5. Site Access		
A. Public	+	+
B. Service	✓	+
6. Site Buffers		
A. Street	+	+
B. Neighbors	+	—
C. Existing Buildings	+	+ —

☆ Very Good   + Good   ✓ Acceptable   — Negative

February 2000

Figure B3-7 Site selection matrix comparing criteria ratings for the two alternative sites. *Source:* The HOK Planning Group.

CHAPTER 4

Programming

INTRODUCTION

Once a site is selected for development, the future uses of the site must be identified. This preliminary development program is revised and refined as more information is acquired about the site and the future users' needs and preferences. These requirements are typically expressed in terms of the quantity and quality of spaces needed to meet anticipated future needs. But programming is not a rigid sequence of steps that can be repeated identically for each and every project.

Programmers must help clients set project priorities and sometimes make difficult choices among conflicting program options. According to Tusler et al. (1993, p. 233), a successful programmer:

- communicates the proposed process to all involved
- does not lock in preconceived solutions
- reconciles subcomponent needs with overall organizational goals and resources
- frequently tests and reviews design concepts as functional and space models are explored

Programming for new buildings, in particular, has developed into a recognized professional specialization, separate from the field of architecture. These specialists are particularly active in programming for hospitals, schools, prisons, and other similar facilities, which have a clearly defined public purpose.

Tusler et al. (1993) identify four reasons for the development of a programming profession whose members do not necessarily have formal educations in architecture. In their opinion, a major reason for this separation stems from contemporary expectations for professional architectural services.

Clients for a project may be single individuals or large institutions. Client objectives vary widely, of course, within the private corporate sector, the private nonprofit sector, and the public sector. Moreover, clients may not associate project programming with the architectural profession. Other reasons for the separation involve the culture of the architecture profession itself. According to Tusler et al. (1993, p. 228–229), these factors include:

- perceived conflicts of interest in defining the scope of work and also providing subsequent professional design services
- bias in the professional design schools against specialization
- limited education of designers in psychology, communications, finance, statistics, and other skills necessary for effective programming

Advances in technology impact all of the professions engaged in planning, designing, or constructing the built environment. Professional competence in any of these endeavors requires an expanding combination of knowledge and skills. Programming, for example, requires a set of knowledge and skills that is more often taught in business schools or planning programs than in architectural, landscape architectural, or engineering programs. Whether or not designers should be responsible for both programming and design is an issue on which there are widely differing opinions. However, there does seem to be consensus on the importance of programming in the land and facilities development process.

Land planning and design is a problem-solving process, and for each and every project planners and designers are faced with a set of problems to solve. These problems may not be explicitly articulated, but they nevertheless influence the scope and direction of the subsequent inventory, analysis, and design phases. Programming for land planning projects is currently a less institutionalized process than programming for public buildings and other similar facilities. But as the legal and environmental context for land planning becomes more complex, development programming may emerge as a viable specialization.

Increasingly, land planning and design has become a multidisciplinary team effort. The fragmentation of knowledge and skills among many allied professions is perhaps responsible for recent trends in how professional services are delivered. Architects, engineers, and landscape architects provide not only programming, analysis, and design services, but they also advise clients during the administration of the contracts for project construction. However, a team leader must coordinate communication among all involved parties, and ensure that the information generated by each team member is not only considered but adequately synthesized. Maxwell and Brown (1993, p. 260) comment on this role of the programmer:

> The programmer must be expert not only at synthesizing disparate—and often seemingly unrelated—user data, but also at translating these data into practical, "designer-friendly" information.

The process of synthesizing a diverse array of data, and communicating information in a spatially explicit form, requires training. Programming specialists may not be designers, but programming in isolation from the designers can potentially overlook important project opportunities and constraints. Commenting on trends in health care architecture, Tusler et al. (1993, p. 242) conclude:

> What is necessary is for both disciplines, design and progamming, to be involved simultaneously in the very early, formative stages of project conception. There also needs to be mutual respect for each other's specialization and a close working relationship as an integrated team.

There are potential advantages to the client, however, when the project designers are not also responsible for programming. The separation of programming and design responsibility reduces the potential for biased program analysis and prevents inappropriate design solutions caused by preconceptions or misconceptions about the design problem to be solved (Brown and Scarborough, 1993).

PROGRAMMING METHODS

Goal Setting

Project programming entails four basic steps (Goldman and Peatross, 1993):

1. initiate the project
2. develop the project mission and objectives
3. determine the project's operational and physical requirements
4. document and present the program to the client

Establishing a list of program goals and objectives is an important step in the land planning and design process (Figure 4-1). In addition to determining the project's operational and physical requirements, programmers — in consultation with the client and other stakeholders — must clarify quality-level expectations.

Data Collection

The program is a function of several related factors, including client goals, market demand, legal context, project budget, and existing site conditions. Appropriate responses to these different factors require the analysis of a diverse set of data. Based on a survey of 74 professional programmers, Preiser (1985, p.11) found that the most common methods of gathering program data were, by rank:

1. interviews
2. surveys
3. document analysis
4. behavioral observation
5. visiting a state-of-the-art project
6. literature search
7. other (e.g., interactive group techniques such as charettes, workshops, and discussions)

These data-gathering activities have three broad targets: site context, user needs, and design precedents.

Goals and Objectives

1. Preserve and ensure the security, tranquility and sanctity of the Stella Maris monastery and grounds...
2. Promote the religious, historic and social attributes of Stella Maris and Mount Carmel...
3. Celebrate the rich history and significance of the Carmelite Order in the Holy Land...
4. Enhance Stella Maris as a pilgrimage destination and prolong visitors' experiences...
5. Preserve historic profile of Mount Carmel...
6. Nurture environmental features of Mount Carmel and protect its natural beauty...
7. Create a plan that enables certain parcels to be developed for economic return...
8. Maximize return on investment for the Carmelite Fathers to ensure the perpetual operation of Stella Maris...
9. Enhance existing facilities with restoration and expansion...
10. Provide for expanded program needs of Stella Maris to enhance spiritual outreach of Carmelite Fathers...
11. Formulate a concept that will support Stella Maris as well as stimulate economic development in Haifa...
12. Develop a program and plan that is sensitive to the diverse culture and interests within Haifa...
13. Develop a plan that is implementable and phaseable over a reasonable time frame...
14. Create a plan that is flexible to adapt to changes in the market...
15. Create a plan that is economically feasible...
16. Produce a plan that is sustainable and enduring...

Program Elements

Religious Zone	Residential Zone	Hospitality Zone	Mixed Use Zone	Commercial Zone	Open Space Zone	Archaeological Zone
Handicapped / elderly access	Multi-family	Hotel / hospice	Tourism	Retail	Playground	Preserve features
Buffer zone	Luxury condos	Meeting space	Entertainment (appropriate / sensitive)	Convenience shops	Promenade	Wayfinding / trails
Closed zone	Rental apartments	Spa	Retail	Office	Trails/linkages	Signage / story
Amphitheater (1,000) people	Hotel	Lush green space	Theater	Neighborhood support shops	Gardens	Educational exhibits
First aid	Hostel / retreat dormitory	Retail	Cafes		Landscape	Lighting
Parking	Villas	Restaurants	Shops		Art/sculpture	
Way of the Cross Restoration	Elderly care	Luxury hotel	Restauants		Lighting	
Learning Center		Villas	Antique shops		Water / stream / falls/ spring	
Cemetery		Hillside Bungalow	Ancient village		Plantation	
Chapels (3,5)			Water/spring		Recreation	
Gardens / plantation					Linkages ..to beach ..to town ..to neighbor-hoods ..to Stella Maris	
Art/sculpture					Memorials / dedications	
Recreation					Devotions / shrines	
Meeting rooms (3)						
Open space zone						

Figure 4-1 Project goals, objectives, and program elements conveyed graphically and verbally in a clearly organized poster format. Note that each goal begins with an action verb. *Source:* The HOK Planning Group.

Site Context

Site visits in the programming phase provide information about the physical, biological, and cultural attributes that are most likely to either facilitate or hinder the desired uses of the site (Figure 4-2). The initial site reconnaissance can provide a good understanding of the site attributes that should be inventoried and analyzed as the planning and design process continues. A client may have unrealistic expectations for the development of a site, and the potential site limitations should be addressed early in the process. The attributes, when considered in the context of program objectives, allow an initial evaluation of the site's opportunities and constraints.

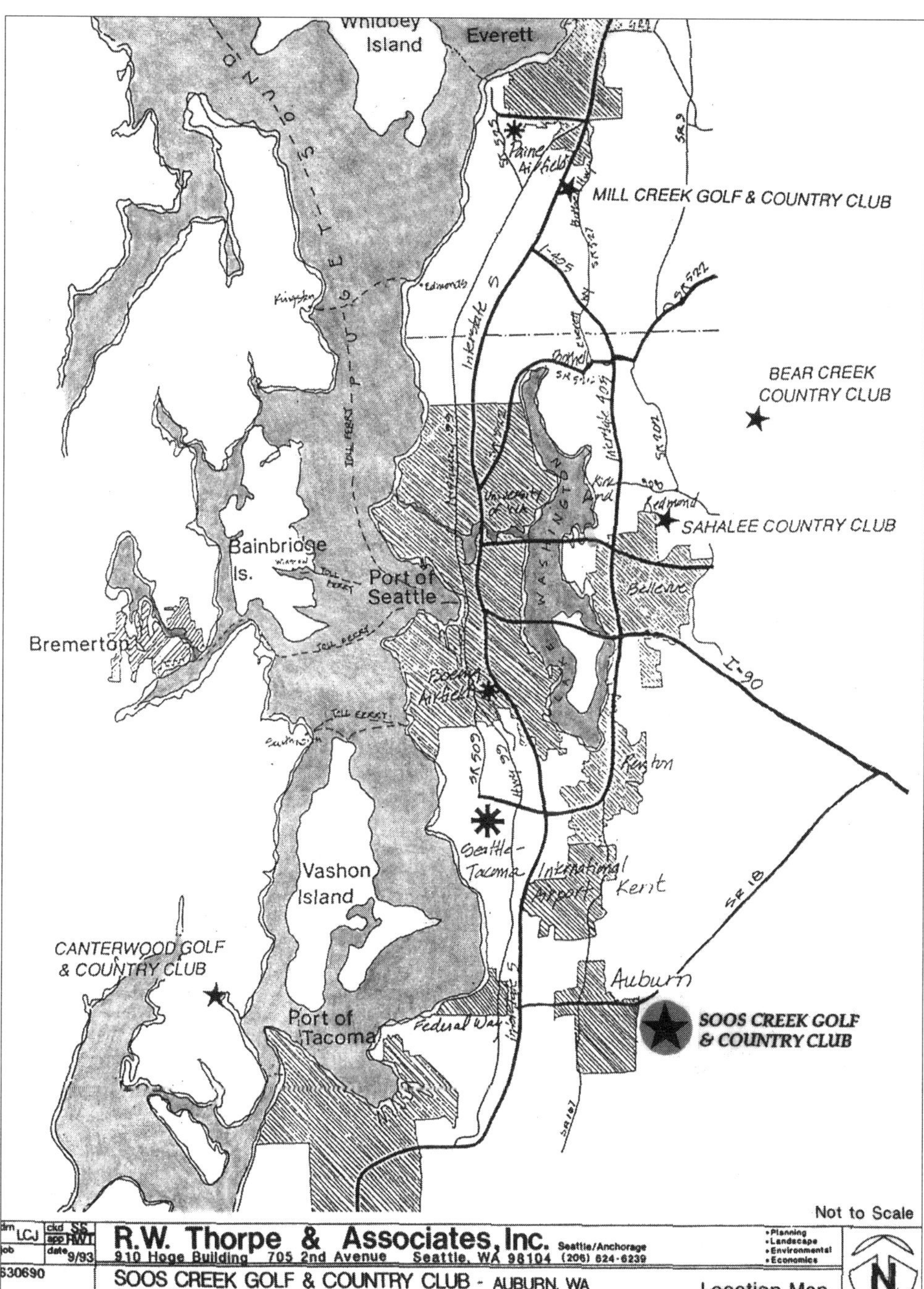

Figure 4-2 Programming considers market context for commercial projects. This map shows the locations of other major golf courses in the vicinity of a proposed golf course community (Soos Creek) near Seattle, Washington. *Source:* R. W. Thorpe and Associates.

The site reconnaissance should be aided by any readily available information about the site. Information collected and analyzed may differ markedly between land planning programs. Relevant supporting information may include:

- historic and current aerial photographs
- zoning maps
- road maps
- county soil survey maps
- flood hazard maps
- tax assessment maps

Some of these documents are readily available from local and state governments (see Appendix). Although the scale of these maps is generally too coarse to support detailed site planning decisions, these documents can provide information that is useful in narrowing the scope of the subsequent site inventory and analysis. More detailed site maps may be available from the property owner.

User Needs

Post-occupancy evaluations are on-site investigations of both the structure and function of the built environment. Post-occupancy evaluations of buildings are relatively common. Preiser et al. (1988, p. 3) define this activity:

> Post-occupancy evaluation is the process of evaluating buildings in a systematic and rigorous manner after they have been built and occupied for some time. POEs focus on building occupants and their needs, and thus they provide insights into the consequences of past design decisions and the resulting building performance. This knowledge forms a sound basis for creating better buildings in the future.

Post-occupancy evaluations of outdoor spaces such as parks, plazas, and campuses are less common, but they are equally important. This type of analysis is an important, but still underutilized, method of advancing land planning and design practice, and ultimately improving the quality of the built environment. The built environment, if carefully analyzed, can demonstrate how well — or how poorly — projects with similar programs and/or sites are designed and implemented. Systematic and carefully planned post-occupancy evaluations can yield important information about a myriad of issues relevant to land planning and design. Zube (quoted in Miller, 1997, p.68) comments:

> We do not invest an adequate amount of resources studying our design/planning successes and failures form an aesthetic, ecological, and functional perspective. We could learn much of benefit to both teaching and practice.

Nivola (1999) suggests that one major difference between European and American cities is the vast amount of space that is available in the United States compared to Europe. The use of space in the United States may be efficient from an economic perspective, but it certainly has led to the development of cities and suburbs that are inhospitable environments for pedestrians and bicyclists. Post-occupancy evaluations can identify opportunities for eliminating pedestrian-vehicle conflicts and otherwise improving the quality of the built environment.

Behavioral observation is an important part of post-occupancy evaluation. Human behavior at outdoor sites varies significantly with changes in the day of the week, the time of day, the weather, and other factors such as scheduled activities or special events

(Whyte, 1980). These factors can dramatically alter the use of a site over the course of a day, a week, or a year. The behavior of site users may also vary considerably with differences in age, gender, and other demographic factors.

One of the primary goals of programming is to reach a consensus, with the client and other stakeholders, about the expectations for the project. One of the first steps in programming is to identify the decision makers and to define the decision-making process (Goldman and Peatross, 1993). Public sector projects, such as affordable housing or a new park, typically involve a large and diverse group of stakeholders. These may include (Goldman and Peatross, 1993, p. 362) the following:

- elected officials
- appointed officials
- facility operators
- funding managers and analysts
- public works and building maintenance staff
- citizen groups representing taxpayers

Not only is there a diverse array of stakeholders, there may also be multiple levels of decision makers that must be consulted directly, or indirectly through their representatives, before important programming decisions can be finalized. To make the process most efficient, the programming team might want to establish two committees: "a policy committee composed of upper-level administrators and officials and a working committee composed of managers and operators" (Goldman and Peatross, 1993, p. 363).

Collaborative decision making involves stakeholders in the resolution of controversial, and potentially contentious, public sector decisions. Transportation planning is an area where citizen participation is relatively common. A modified Multiattribute Utility Analysis (MUA) is one approach that has been used to reach consensus on highway construction projects in California (Schwartz and Eichhorn, 1997). The nine-step process used in the modified MUA is as follows:

1. select stakeholder group
2. agree on problem or need
3. identify issues and concerns
4. develop evaluation criteria
5. develop alternatives
6. select and collect impact data for each alternative
7. weight evaluation criteria
8. measure evaluation criteria
9. rank alternatives and conduct sensitivity analysis

With private-sector projects, surveys, focus groups, and other means of soliciting consumer preferences can help a developer meet the demands of specific market sectors. These sectors, or demographic groups, include young single professionals, families with school-aged children, older couples whose children no longer reside with them (e.g., empty nesters), and the retired elderly. Learning more about consumer preferences prior to construction and marketing can help programmers make appropriate choices. In the housing area, for example, preferred dimensions of living rooms and bedrooms, or accompanying residential amenities, are the types of programming information that can be acquired through market analysis. By soliciting consumer preferences, market analysts can gain valuable insights concerning important project attributes that should be considered in the programming and site selection process. Survey research on residential preferences reveals a variety of locational factors that influence consumers' decisions in selecting their dwelling locations. Depending on the demographic profile of the individual, preferences may include:

- quality of nearby schools
- neighborhood safety
- proximity to restaurants, grocery stores, and other shopping opportunities
- nearby recreational facilities

These factors may not all be important to every household, but collectively they reflect the concerns of a substantial market segment.

Design Precedents

High population densities, long periods of intensive urban development, and a strong public policy interest in the design of the built environment make European countries living laboratories for architects, landscape architects, and urban designers. For decades, North American architects and landscape architects have traveled abroad to enrich their understanding of urban design and to supplement their formal design training (Fabos et al., 1968; Schulze, 1994). European cathedrals, plazas, parks, and waterfronts continue to be among the special places sought out by foreign educated designers. This process of expanding and refining one's design vocabulary through travel is enhanced by careful observation—often by keeping a sketchbook. This becomes an assemblage of notes and drawings, including perspective sketches, sections, elevations, and design details. Perhaps the most important reason to keep a sketchbook, at least early in one's design training, is that this activity nurtures critical observation—or the ability to "read" one's environment. Once acquired, every environment—pristine, gaudy, or mundane—can be assessed with a discerning eye.

Post-occupancy evaluations can improve land planning and design practice by identifying successful models that can be adapted to local circumstances. These analyses can also reveal design mistakes, or missed opportunities, that should be avoided in future projects. For example, the analysis of built projects can provide information on the durability of construction details, the vigor of new plant cultivars, or the capacity of bioretention areas to retain and infiltrate stormwater. A now classic book, *Learning from Las Vegas* (Venturi et al., 1972), is a post-occupancy evaluation of the Las Vegas "Strip" during the 1960s. The authors analyze the architectural and spatial qualities along this highway corridor. This ability to interpret and evaluate existing built environments is an invaluable skill in designing and evaluating land development proposals.

Books, articles in both journals and trade magazines, and government agency reports can yield useful information about planning and design precedents. The literature review process also can help inform important programming and design decisions. Information can be collected on current standards for programmed space requirements, environmental protection and restoration techniques, and needs of special user groups (e.g., children, the chronically ill, the elderly). Case studies of completed projects may provide models that can be reinterpreted and adapted to solve design problems involving a different combination of site and program. A contemporary example of historical precedents influencing site and community design is the New Urbanism movement's reliance on earlier, more traditional forms of development. New

Urbanism, or traditional neighborhood development (TND), advocates a return to mixed-use, human-scale development. This important design paradigm is firmly rooted in the past.

PROGRAM DOCUMENTATION

Project Objectives

A program may specify the amount of space required for the proposed activities, the desired adjacency relationships among the activities, and the phasing of future development (Figure 4-3). The program may also specify the expected quality of the spaces and structures within the project. These program expectations can be expressed on several levels. Programmers must initially identify the general types of land uses, activities, or facilities that will occur on the site. But there are many possibilities, and the best mix of uses depends on the client's goals as well as on the size, character, and location of the site. Once the types of uses or facilities have been identified, the quantity and qual-

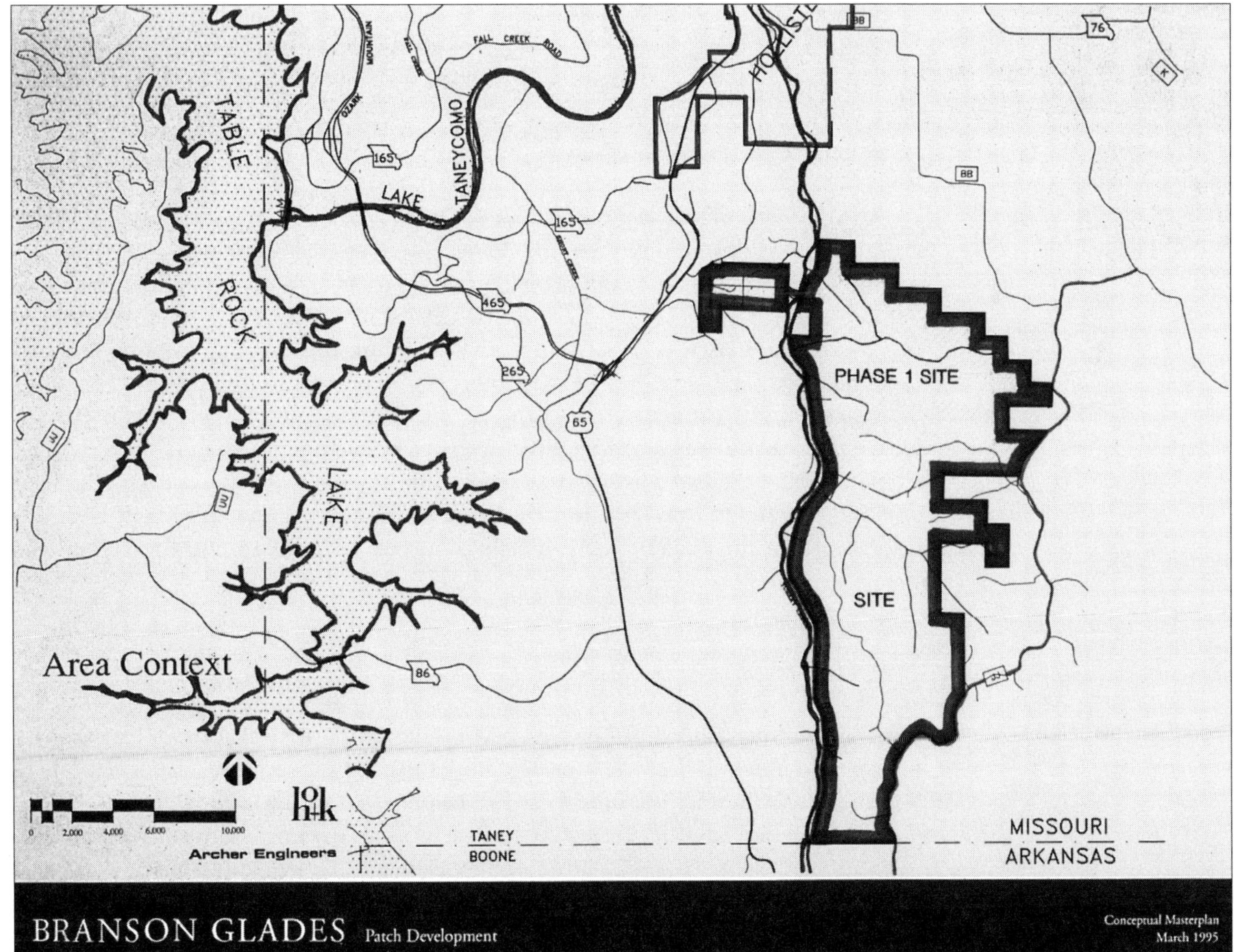

Figure 4-3 Programming may also involve phasing of future development activities. *Source:* The HOK Planning Group.

ity of these can be determined. For example, one of the land uses included in a development program might be multifamily housing. But additional information concerning the quantity and quality of this programmed use must be determined. This information includes the desired number of dwelling units, in addition to the number and size of rooms, the surface finishings, and the amenities to be included in each unit.

Open space should also be considered a program element. Open space facilitates groundwater infiltration, provides visual and recreational amenities, and protects wildlife habitats. The benefits of open space are compounded, in most cases, when the open spaces comprise a network with linkages to open space community systems.

Spatial Relationships

Development programs may include activities or uses that are relatively incompatible. Community facilities for wastewater treatment, for example, are typically considered incompatible with residential and commercial uses. Consequently, these incompatible land uses are typically separated spatially. Conversely, other site activities or uses may need to be physically adjacent to one another.

The desired spatial relationships among programmed uses may be determined from client surveys, reviews of the literature, and other sources. These spatial relationships fall into one of four categories:

- adjacency is essential
- adjacency is desirable but not essential
- adjacency is unimportant
- adjacency should be avoided

An adjacency matrix is a useful tool for summarizing and evaluating the desired spatial relationships among program elements. But spatial relationships among programmed uses entails more than simple physical proximity. Adjacent land uses may be connected functionally (e.g., pedestrian circulation), or visually, or both. Whether or not adjacent uses are functionally and/or visually linked is often an important design issue that should be identified in the programming phase.

When project programs are complex, the assessment of spatial relationships among program elements can be difficult to interpret from an adjacency matrix. This problem can be alleviated, somewhat, by creating adjacency diagrams. Each plan-view "bubble" diagram portrays the desired spatial relationships between a single land use, at the center of the diagram, and the adjacent uses arranged around this central element.

Design Guidelines

The programming process can go well beyond the simple compilation of lists describing expected uses and the land area or facilities needed for each use. The development of design guidelines, for example, is an extension of the programming process. Design guidelines are not site-specific solutions to a project's design problems. Yet they typically portray the desired qualities of program elements. Design guidelines may address a variety of site components that have significant effects on a project's economic success and environmental impact. These include: stormwater drainage and infiltration

TABLE 4-1 Subdivision regulations and other local ordinances may establish design requirements that have a significant influence on the spatial character of the built environment.

Site Element	*Attribute (minimum and/or maximum typically specified)*
Streets	Width Turning radius (for emergency vehicles) Cul-de-sac length
Lots (parcels)	Area Width Depth
Buildings	Number of dwelling units per building Building coverage (percentage of lot area) Building height Building placement (i.e., front yard, side yard, back yard setbacks)
Parking areas	Number of parking spaces per dwelling unit Location of parking spaces Location of driveways
Plantings	Number, size, and species of street trees Parking lot screening

techniques, street dimensions and parking lot configurations, building proportions and setbacks, and site furniture and signage.

Municipalities may use a design review process, in conjunction with design guidelines, to enhance or maintain the visual quality of neighborhoods, business districts, and other areas (Table 4-1). Design guidelines can be communicated with text and numbers, but graphic representations are the most effective. Guidelines may specify desired building facade articulation along a commercial block of a downtown redevelopment district, for example, or the preferred sizes, colors, and styles of benches or light fixtures along the district's streetscapes.

Large public institutions and corporations are especially sensitive to physical design issues. Creating or maintaining a particular "image" is typically a high-priority issue. Design guidelines can help ensure that new development is appropriate for the site's physical and social context. Zeisel and Maxwell (1993, p.168) see the need for explicit guidelines:

> In order to translate a facilities program into a physical environment for a workplace, designers need more than numbers and diagrams. They need planning and design principles that respond to the organization's style — its culture.

This is especially important on university campuses and other large sites where development will be implemented in phases, by different designers and builders.

Although visual quality is an important concern of design guidelines, this is not the only objective. The maintenance and replacement of worn-out or damaged site furniture, for example, is more expensive if there is not consistency in the types and manufacturers of furniture installed on a site. A visually unified built environment can be achieved through the repetition of design elements. Repeating similar colors, shapes, and textures, for example, can create a harmonious, or visually unified, environment. This design principle is frequently overlooked in some campus settings, where decades of incremental growth and redevelopment lead to a hodgepodge of paving materials, site furniture, and other site elements.

SUMMARY

Programming is an integral part of any land planning and design project. The programming process requires information about user needs, the site and its context, and both successful and unsuccessful design precedents. Depending on project objectives and site conditions, programs may vary in specificity. A project program may be simply a list of desired project elements, but the expected qualities of programmed uses are usually articulated — often in the form of design guidelines.

PART III

SITE INVENTORY AND ANALYSIS

PART III

SITE INVENTORY AND ANALYSIS

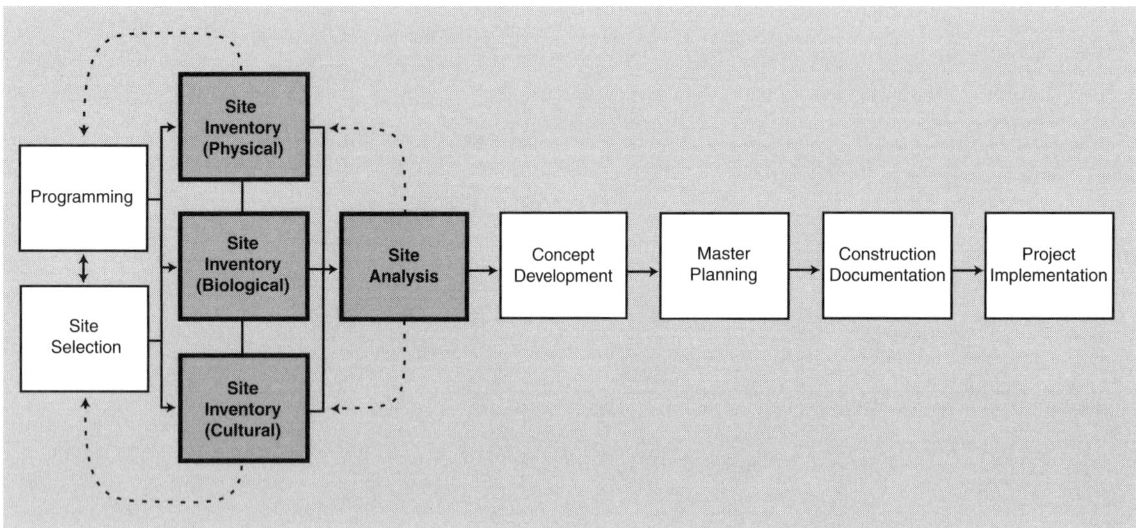

Allocating proposed uses or activities on a site may require the analysis of data for several site attributes. One set of attribute data may be needed in siting a particular activity or land use, whereas a different set of attributes may be needed in siting other uses. In some cases, a single site attribute will determine the suitability—or feasibility—of a site for a particular use. Deciding which attributes to map and analyze, and which attributes to ignore, requires consideration of at least four factors:

- proposed site uses (e.g., project program)
- existing on-site and off-site conditions
- requirements for permitting and approvals
- costs of data collection and analysis

Collectively, these four factors dictate the scope of the site inventory and analysis.

CHAPTER

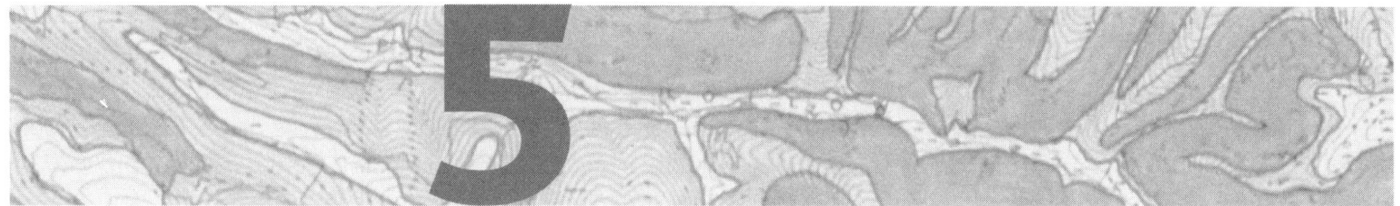

Site Inventory: Physical Attributes

INTRODUCTION

Every site is embedded within a larger landscape. The site inventory is an essential step in understanding the character of the site and the physical, biological, and cultural linkages between the site and the surrounding landscape. Land development, restoration, and management require a broad knowledge of, and appreciation for, environmental and cultural systems. Both basic and applied research have contributed to our understanding of physical, biological, and cultural phenomena. This knowledge base is the foundation for land planning, design, and management theory.

The *American Heritage Dictionary of the English Language* (3rd edition) defines theory as:

1. a system of assumptions, accepted principles, and rules of procedure devised to analyze, predict, or otherwise explain the nature or behavior of a specified set of phenomena
2. a belief that guides action or assists comprehension or judgment

The field of medicine is a good example of the synergistic relationship between theory and application, or—put another way—between research and practice. Research on heart function, blood chemistry, and many other aspects of human physiology support health care by medical practitioners (e.g., surgeons, cardiologists, nurses). The natural and social sciences similarly provide the theoretical underpinnings of efforts to modify, restore, and manage land.

Decisions to develop or restore a parcel of land require an understanding of the site as well as the surrounding landscape. Because land planning and design involve decisions about future uses of land, an understanding of human behavior, attitudes, and preferences is also necessary. However, the site inventory should be a focused process of collecting and mapping essential attribute data. It is not a "fishing expedition," or an open-ended investigation of all biophysical or cultural phenomena that occur on or near the site. The purpose of collecting data about a site, and its surrounding context, is to gather the information needed in the subsequent steps of the land planning and design process. If this data-gathering activity is not well-focused, the site inventory can consume vast amounts of time, money, and professional expertise. The goals of the data collection effort must be predefined, therefore, to narrow the scope of the inventory. The program, although subject to further revision, helps focus the inventory.

The site inventory may be completed in stages by a team of specialists. The first stage of any inventory involves site reconnaissance. The purpose of this relatively quick site assessment is to identify potentially significant site assets and liabilities. After the initial reconnaissance, one of the first tasks is to develop a base map. The base map serves as the template for attribute mapping and analysis, as well as for subsequent land planning and design (see Chapter 2). If a topographic survey of the site is available, the base map could include project boundaries and other key site information (Table 5-1). If the site reconnaissance includes an aerial inspection, oblique aerial photos of the site can provide useful contextual information (Figure 5-1).

Most site attributes are not uniformly distributed over the landscape. However, some attributes, such as average seasonal temperatures and precipitation, show very little variation at the site scale. Attributes such as temperature and precipitation can vary dramatically, of course, throughout the year. This temporal variation may substantially influence the uses of the site from season to season. Consequently, it may be appropriate that site inventory maps document the spatial distribution of a particular attribute at more than one time of the year. Site attributes that vary seasonally include wildlife distributions, wind direction and speed, and seasonal high water table.

TABLE 5-1 Site data that may be conveyed on a topopgraphic survey.

Category	*Locational Data*
Legal	Property lines (angles and distances) Easements and building setback lines Site area
Topography	Elevation contours Spot elevations for high points and low points
Vegetation	Wooded areas Isolated trees (species and diameter at breast height)
Soils/Geology	Boreholes
Hydrology	Surface water Wetlands 100-year floodways and flood fringe
Utilities	Type (e.g., sanitary sewer, electric, gas, telephone) Size of line Manholes, hydrants, and other fixtures
Structures	Buildings
Circulation	Streets and rights-of-way Curbs and gutters Parking areas

Figure 5-1 Vertical aerial photograph with project boundaries superimposed. *Source:* The HOK Planning Group.

TOPOGRAPHY

Topography is an important factor in most land planning decisions. Consequently, having a topographic survey of the site is essential. The U.S. Geological Survey (USGS) makes topographic maps at several scales (e.g., 1:250,000, 1:24,000). These maps provide important information on the biophysical and cultural context of a community or region. Site topographic surveys, in contrast, are much larger in scale, and are usually completed by a licensed land surveyor in accordance with specifications tailored to the program and the site. Three key attribute maps can be derived from a topographic survey. These maps graphically depict three fundamental landform components: elevation, slope, and aspect.

Elevation

Spatial variation in elevation produces slopes that have both a gradient and an orientation—or aspect. Each of these three attributes can have a substantial influence on land planning and design decisions. Site elevations, for example, affect both drainage patterns and visibility. Variation of elevation on a site and the surrounding landscape determines the size and spatial configuration of local viewsheds. Visible areas may encompass portions of the site, or the entire site, and they may extend into the surrounding landscape.

Mapping. Elevation data are typically portrayed as contour lines on topographic maps. For land planning purposes, however, an effective way to visualize topographic relief is to create a chloropleth map of elevation. To limit the visual complexity of the

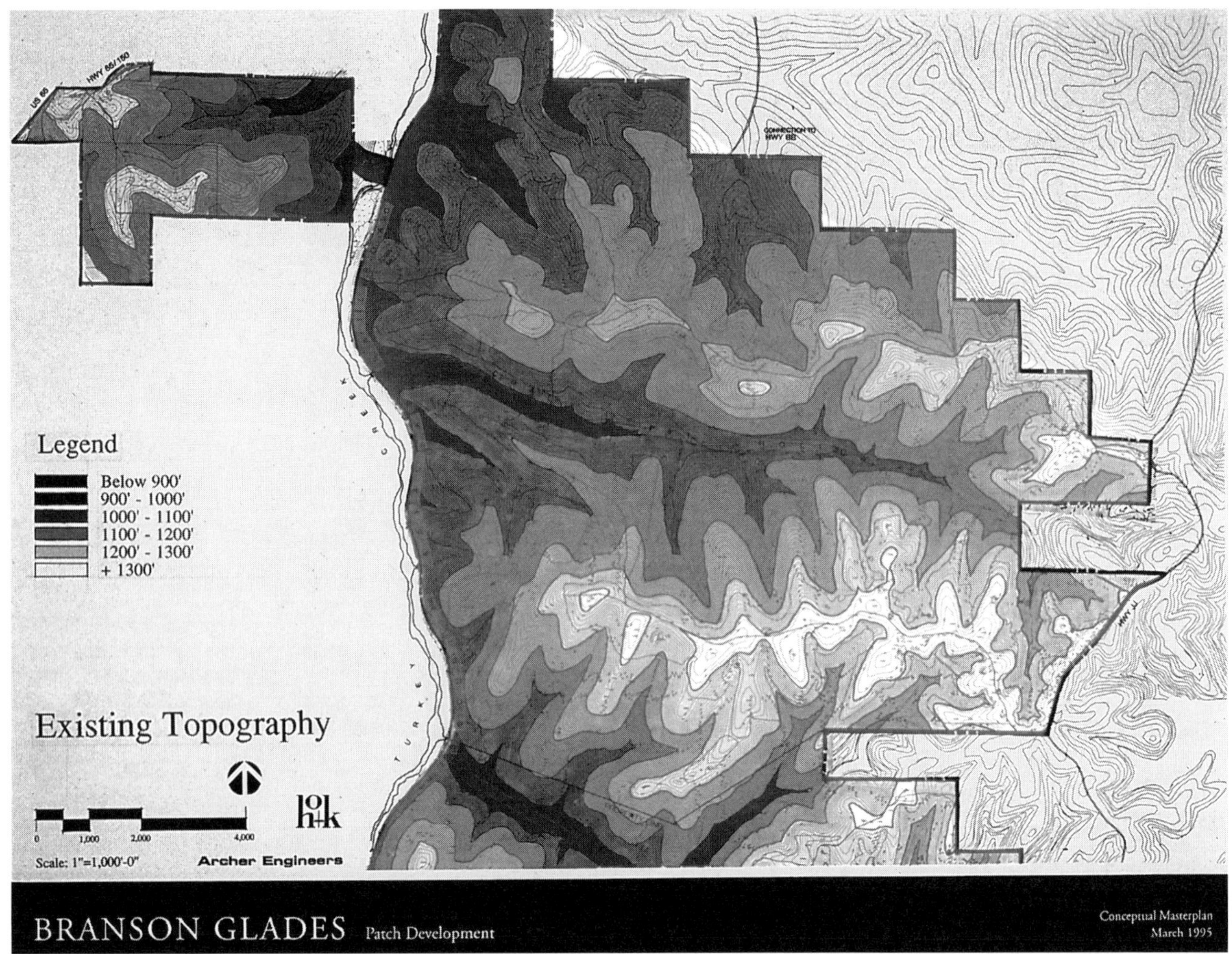

Figure 5-2 Chloropleth map showing six elevation classes. Each class represents a range of one hundred feet of elevation change. *Source:* The HOK Planning Group.

map and make it easy to understand, these maps should have seven (plus or minus two) classes of elevation. The range of existing elevations on and adjacent to a site determines the number and range of each elevation class. For example, if the highest elevation on the site is 827 feet above a local benchmark, and the lowest elevation is 532 feet, the map must show a range of elevation of at least 295 feet (827 – 532 = 295). To limit the map's visual complexity, 295 can be divided by 7 classes for a result of 42.1 feet. To create elevation classes of equal increments, 42.1 can be rounded up to 50. Each "layer" is then shaded or colored — typically with a spectrum ranging from cool colors (low elevations) to warm colors (high elevations) — to enhance the map's effectiveness (Figure 5-2).

Slope

The slopes of undeveloped sites reflect the local area's surficial geology, climate, and soils. Differences in parent materials and weathering account for different landforms, or landscape "signatures." Landforms, and, therefore, slopes, are the result of constructional processes (e.g., deposition) and destructional processes (e.g., erosion) acting on geologic structures (Bloom, 1978).

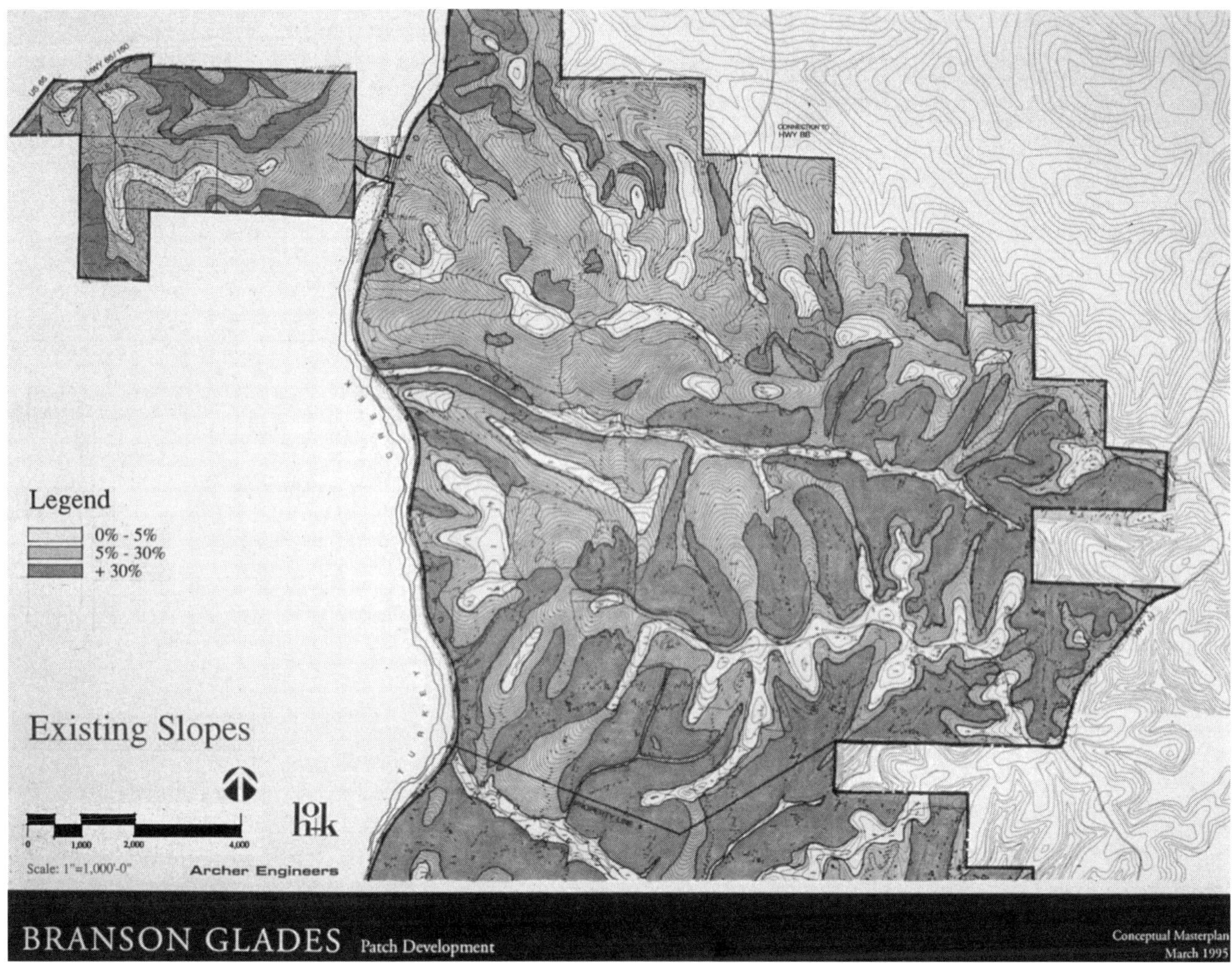

Figure 5-3 Chloropleth map of slope gradient. *Source:* The HOK Planning Group

A site's suitability for roads, walkways, buildings, and other structures is, in part, a function of the existing slopes on the site. In Hong Kong and San Francisco, for example, development frequently occurs on sites with steep slopes. But these cities are in locations with relatively warm climates. In locations with freezing winter temperatures, steep slopes are a significant safety concern when designing vehicle and pedestrian circulation systems. Gradients should be relatively low to prevent accidents such as slipping on icy surfaces.

Mapping. Slopes can be computed with most GIS and CAD software. Color or texture are typically used to identify slopes that exceed a minimum percentage (Figure 5-3). Five percent, 12 percent, and 20 percent slopes are common thresholds.

Aspect

A slope's orientation, or aspect, is simply the direction the slope faces. Aspect is typically identified, therefore, by compass direction (e.g., north, northeast). Variation in slope and aspect influence the amount of solar radiation received by the site on a daily and seasonal basis. For example, in the Northern Hemisphere, north-facing, ten-degree

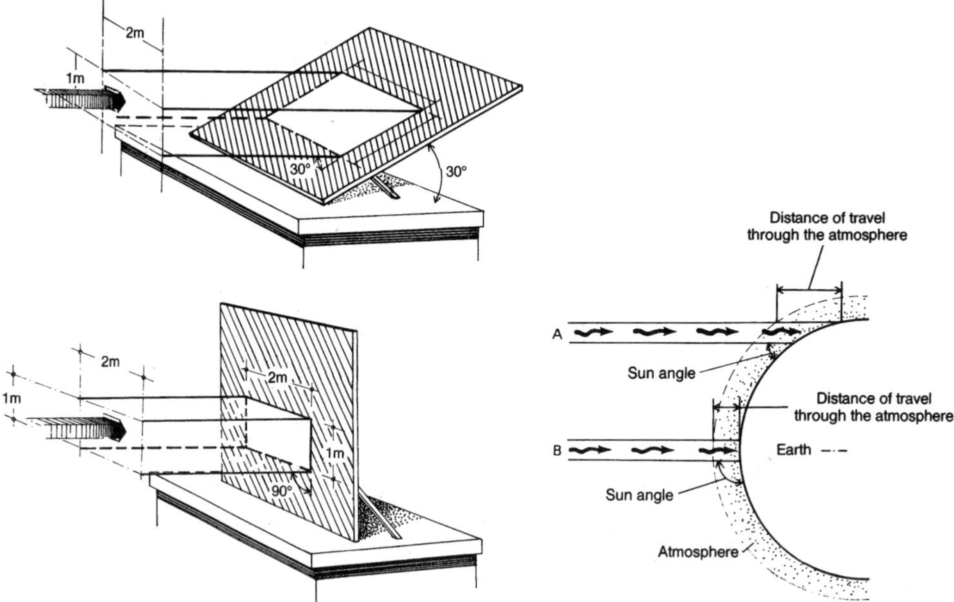

Figure 5-4 Influence of slope aspect on the intensity of solar radiation striking the slope surface. *Source:* Marsh, *Landscape Planning,* Third Ed., copyright © 1998, p. 289, Figure 15.1. Reprinted by permission of John Wiley & Sons, Inc.

slopes will receive less solar radiation than south-facing slopes of the same gradient. In the winter, the sun's highest point above the horizon is an acute angle. The north-facing slopes, when exposed to direct sunlight, receive less solar radiation per unit surface area than do the south-facing slopes. Because the slope faces away from the sun, the solar radiation striking a north-facing slope hits the surface at a shallow, or acute, angle. Consequently, sunlight strikes the slope in a more diffuse pattern, delivering to the surface less solar energy per unit area (Figure 5-4).

As with other site attributes, the importance of aspect to a project depends on the proposed land uses. Aspect influences microclimate by affecting the level of solar radiation that strikes the site. A project that involves siting downhill skiing slopes will certainly consider slope, elevation, and aspect. A north-facing slope may be imperative for ski trail development, in areas with relatively mild winters, to limit the melting of snow from direct solar radiation.

Mapping. Slope aspect, like slope gradient, can be mapped manually or with commercially available GIS software. Typically, aspect is classified using eight categories: north, northeast, east, southeast, south, southwest, west, and northwest. These are portrayed graphically by shading or color. More shaded northern slopes (in the Northern Hemisphere) are rendered with cooler colors or heavier hatching than are the areas with greater solar exposure.

GEOLOGY

Elevation and slope are good examples of quantitatively expressed landform attributes. Landform classification describes significant physiographic features of terrestrial, riparian, and aquatic environments. For example, eskers, kames, and moraines are the distinct signatures of prior glaciation. Landform classification is useful in site or regional inventories and analyses, particularly for characterizing difficult-to-quantify attributes like scenic beauty, sense of place, and landscape character. Landforms, in conjunction with vegetation, define view sheds, or visibility on a site, and can create visual interest. Landforms also influence microclimate, stormwater runoff and infiltration, and the distribution of plant and animal species.

Surficial geology is concerned with the structure, composition, and stability of the materials beneath—and in some locations at—the earth's surface. In some landscapes, bedrock is buried hundreds of feet below the ground surface. Bedrock geology has a persistent effect on landforms, due to the different rates of weathering that occur on the soil parent materials. Soil formation, soil erosion, and soil deposition are natural processes that involve rock fragmentation and weathering. Weathering occurs unevenly because of variations in the chemical composition and structure of bedrock.

An important attribute of surficial geology is the depth to bedrock. If excavation is planned for building foundations or for other site structures, the depth to bedrock should be determined. If excavation is planned for a site with shallow bedrock or glacial eratics (boulders), blasting or other special methods of removal may be necessary. The costs of excavating a cubic yard or meter of rock is many times greater than the costs of excavating the same volume of soil. Consequently, these difficult subsurface conditions can significantly increase the costs of construction.

Mapping. A geologic map shows the age and distribution of rock layers and other geologic materials. These attributes influence a site's suitability for excavation and grading, wastewater disposal, groundwater supply, pond construction, and other common land development objectives (Way, 1978). Geologic maps also show locations that are susceptible to earthquakes, landslides, and other hazards.

A geologic map usually includes information on topography and cultural elements, such as roads, to help orient the map user. Colors and letter symbols identify each kind of geologic unit at, or near, the Earth's surface. A volume of rock of a specific type and age range is considered a geologic unit. Therefore, a sandstone of one age might be shown as one color, for example, while a sandstone of a different age might be shown as a different color. Examples of geologic maps can be downloaded through the Internet (http://www2.nature.nps.gov/grd/usgsnps/gmap/).

A searchable catalog of paper and digital geologic maps is available on the Internet through the United States Geological Survey (http://ngmsvr.wr.usgs.gov/). Several map themes in the database are potentially useful in land planning and design (Table 5-2).

TABLE 5-2 Selected map themes of the National Geologic Map Database.

Category	*Theme*
Geology	General (e.g., rocks and sediment at or near the Earth's surface) Structure (e.g., thickness of buried rock units) Engineering (e.g., engineering properties of soils) Coastal (e.g., areas of coastal zone erosion or sedimentation)
Natural Resources	Nonmetallic resources (e.g., sand and gravel) Water (e.g., groundwater aquifers, water quality) Other (e.g., geothermal resources)
Hazards	Earthquake hazards (e.g., faults, earthquake zones) Volcano hazards (e.g., eruption history) Landslides (e.g, existing landslides, landslide potential)

Source: United States Geological Survey, 2000.

In addition to the more generalized maps, which are available from public sources, detailed site-scale data are usually required for land planning and design. In this case, a site's subsurface conditions are typically assessed in conjunction with the topographic survey. Data on depth to bedrock are typically collected by drilling core holes with a mechanical driller. These cores provide information about the site's soil and surficial geology (Joyce, 1982). The spacing and number of bore-holes depends on the conditions of the site and the purposes of the investigation. Sites with great variability in soil and geologic conditions may require more intensive subsurface investigation. Similarly, when large buildings will be constructed on a site, the area and depth of the subsurface investigation will be greater than if the project did not include these structures. A subsurface investigation for land planning and design usually requires the services of a geotechnical engineer.

The Earth's geology is far from stable, and volcanic activity and earthquakes are relatively common events. These and other land cover disturbances are potentially devastating hazards that new development should avoid. In some landscapes, especially those impacted by deforestation, landslides are also common. The locations of these and other natural hazards should be identified and documented in the site inventory (Figure 5-5).

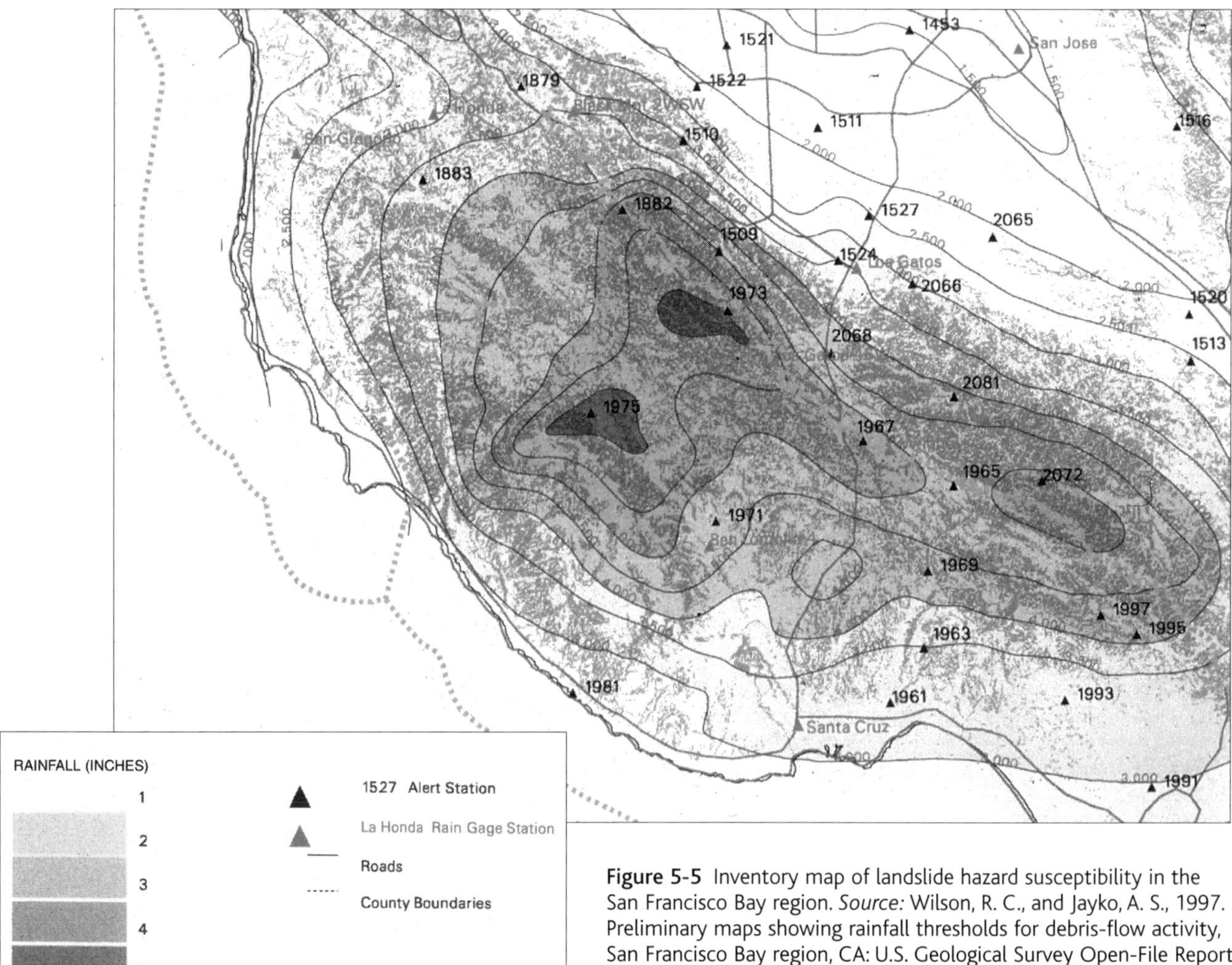

Figure 5-5 Inventory map of landslide hazard susceptibility in the San Francisco Bay region. *Source:* Wilson, R. C., and Jayko, A. S., 1997. Preliminary maps showing rainfall thresholds for debris-flow activity, San Francisco Bay region, CA: U.S. Geological Survey Open-File Report 97-945 F, *in* Ramsey and others, 1999. Landslide hazard susceptibility maps for the San Francisco Bay region: Tools for emergency planning during the 1997–98 El Niño: ESRI Map Book, v. 14, p. 18–19.

HYDROLOGY

Water circulates in the Earth's environment through precipitation, overland flow, infiltration, storage, and evapotranspiration. Groundwater moves by capillary action through the porous spaces between unconsolidated sand, gravel, and rock, and between the fractures and faults in the underlying bedrock. The surface of the saturated area, the water table, generally mirrors the surface terrain. In landscapes where groundwater is the source of local or municipal wells, groundwater pumping can have substantial impacts on the depth of the water table.

Topographic relief creates drainage patterns, which in turn influence vegetation associations and distributions. The spatial correlation between vegetation associations and site drainage patterns is particularly strong in arid and semiarid landscapes where water is often the primary limiting factor on plant growth and distribution. Although the groundwater–vegetation linkage is more subtle in less arid environments, the continuous — or seasonal — saturation of soils creates suitable conditions for wetland vegetation. Other hydrological conditions may also influence vegetation patterns in other landscapes as well. In coastal environments, for example, brackish or saline groundwater results in the development of distinct vegetation communities.

Urban development can have significant impacts on local and regional hydrology. Without mitigation, hydrologic impacts include (United States Environmental Protection Agency, 1993):

- increased volumes and rates of runoff discharges
- reduced time needed for runoff to reach surface waters
- increased frequency and severity of flooding
- reduced streamflow during prolonged periods of dry weather

Water quality also may be affected by land uses and by associated land cover changes. Pollution of both groundwater and surface water is a common problem in urbanizing landscapes. Contamination may result from erosion and sedimentation, from chemicals, or from microorganisms. Surface water pollution associated with stormwater runoff in urbanizing landscapes can negatively impact ecosystems and reduce the aesthetic and recreational value of rivers, lakes, and other water bodies. Groundwater pollution from septic tank effluent can also limit an area's suitability for wells.

Land development usually involves the construction of buildings and paved surfaces that are impervious or nearly impervious. Without mitigation, new construction and other site-disturbing activities can increase the risks of flooding, erosion, and other ecological impacts to properties "downstream." For this reason, stormwater management is an increasingly regulated component of the land development process. Like earthquakes and other geologic hazards, weather-related events can also present risks to human life and property. Floods, and especially storm surges, are hazards that are localized. Avalanches, although much less common, are also predictable in terms of where — if not when — they will occur.

When local groundwater is the source of a community's potable water, efforts must be made to ensure that on-site wastewater treatment systems and stormwater runoff do not contaminate local wells (Figure 5-6). For the past few decades, siting requirements for on-site wastewater treatment systems have used soil conditions as the primary siting criterion. As treatment technologies continue to evolve, more highly engineered on-site wastewater treatment systems are being constructed in many formerly unsuit-

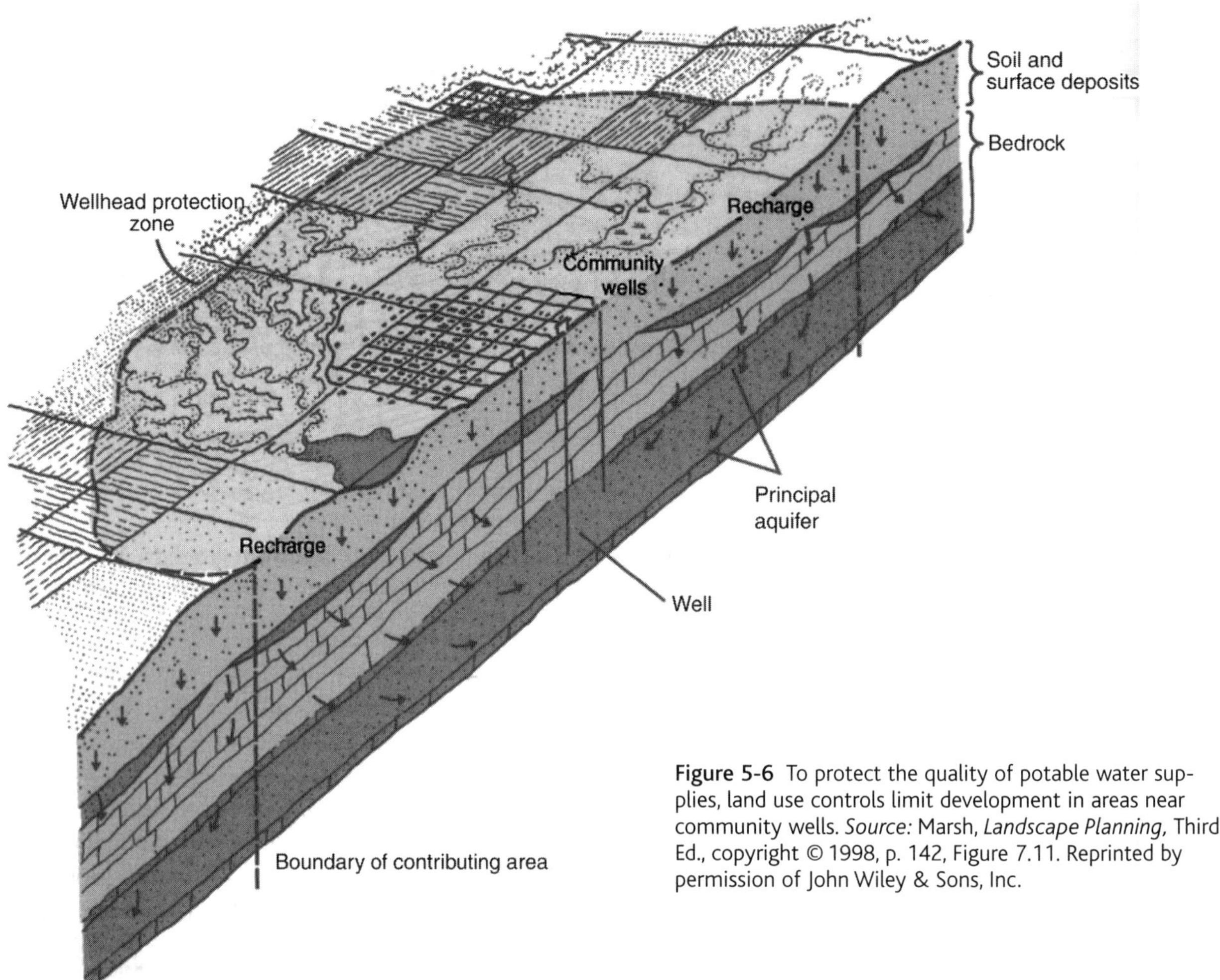

Figure 5-6 To protect the quality of potable water supplies, land use controls limit development in areas near community wells. *Source:* Marsh, *Landscape Planning*, Third Ed., copyright © 1998, p. 142, Figure 7.11. Reprinted by permission of John Wiley & Sons, Inc.

able locations (LaGro, 1996). These include areas with bedrock and/or water table as shallow as 20cm below the ground surface.

Mapping. Water movement, infiltration, storage, and discharge at a site should be considered in the inventory of physical attributes. This assessment of hydrologic conditions requires consideration of the site's surface and subsurface features. Characterizing surface conditions involves the analysis of topography, vegetation, surface water distribution, land use, climate, and soil-forming processes and deposits (Kolm, 1996). Characterizing the three-dimensional subsurface geologic structure involves the analysis of stratigraphy, lithology, and structural and geomorphologic discontinuities (Kolm, 1996). Maps that depict stormwater runoff patterns, surface storage, and locations of aquifer recharge can help guide land planning decisions. Hydrologic maps may also locate the primary paths of groundwater flow and the locations of groundwater discharge to the surface. Assessments of these attributes, in addition to aquifer permeability, thickness, and discontinuities, are usually completed by hydrologists or geological engineers.

Maps of groundwater and local geological conditions are particularly important in land use planning for rural and urban fringe areas (Figure 5-7). Detailed site data can be acquired by hydrologists or geological engineers to determine an area's potential sources of potable groundwater (Figure 5-8). Surface drainage also should be mapped (Figure 5-9). Depending on the site's context, this may include the identification and mapping of flood hazard areas (Figure 5-10).

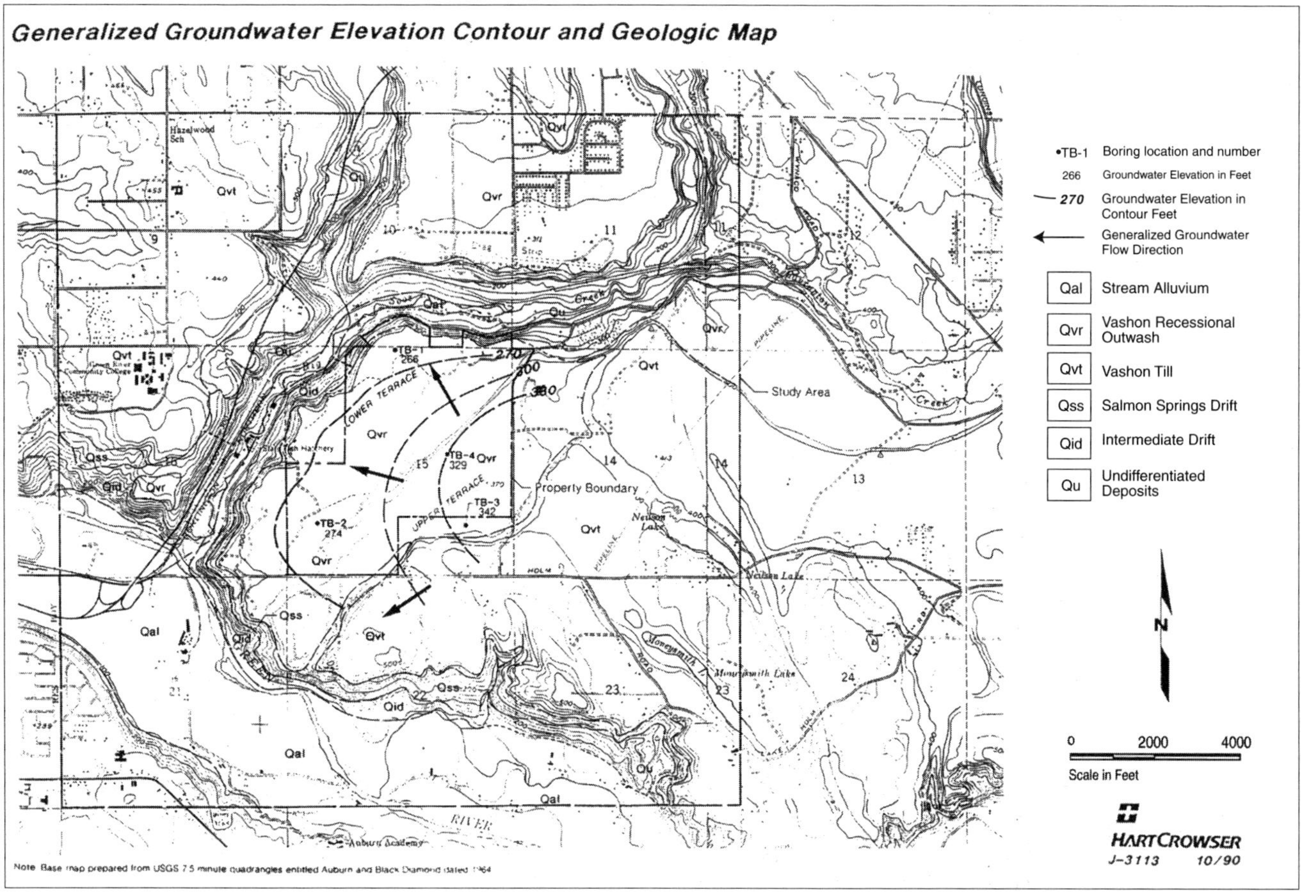

Generalized Groundwater Elevation Contour and Geologic Map

•TB-1 Boring location and number
266 Groundwater Elevation in Feet
270 Groundwater Elevation in Contour Feet
Generalized Groundwater Flow Direction
Qal Stream Alluvium
Qvr Vashon Recessional Outwash
Qvt Vashon Till
Qss Salmon Springs Drift
Qid Intermediate Drift
Qu Undifferentiated Deposits

Study Area
Property Boundary
LOWER TERRACE
UPPER TERRACE
TB-1 266
TB-4 329
TB-3 342
TB-2 274
N
0 2000 4000
Scale in Feet
HARTCROWSER
J-3113 10/90

Note Base map prepared from USGS 7.5 minute quadrangles entitled Auburn and Black Diamond dated 1964

Figure 5-7 Map of groundwater elevation and surficial geology. Source: R. W. Thorpe and Associates.

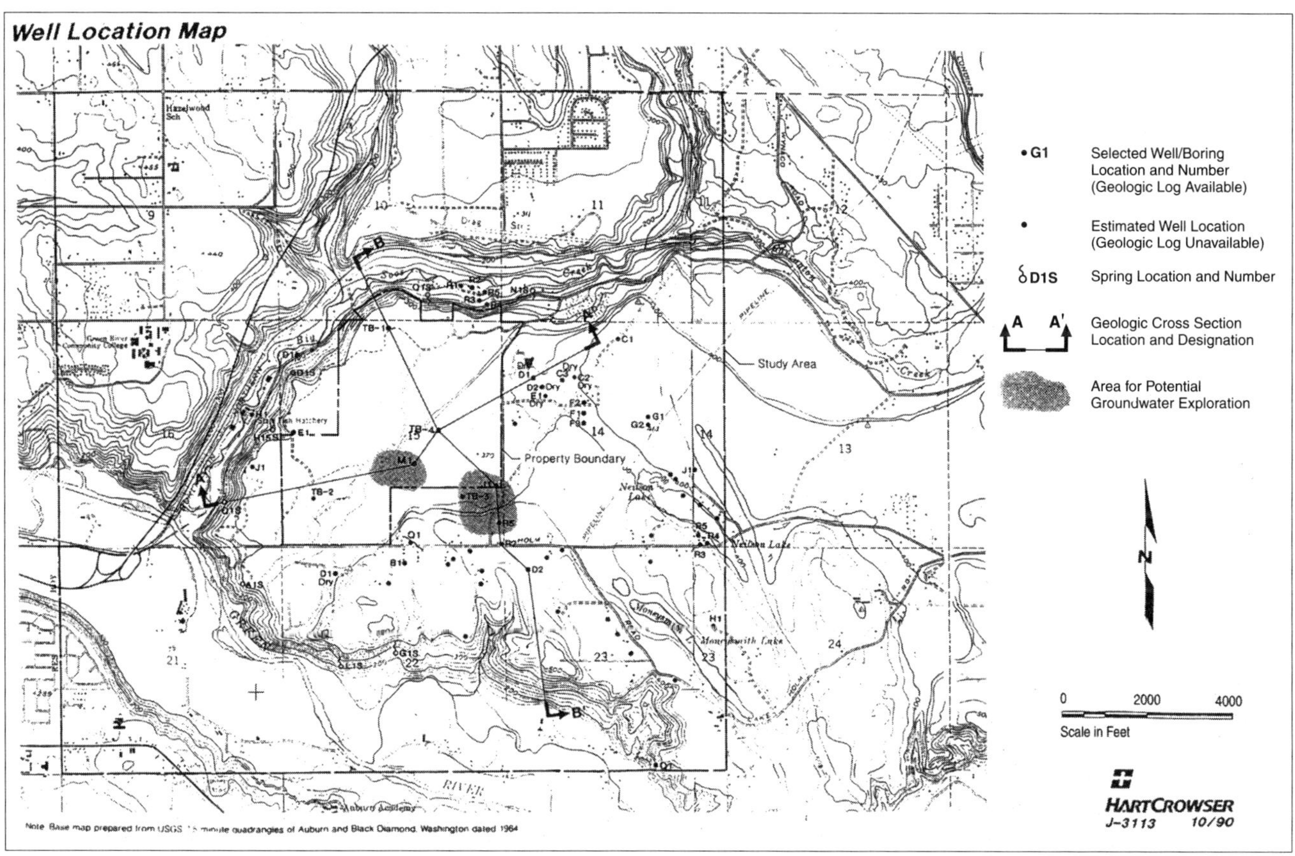

Figure 5-8 Map of potential well locations. *Source:* R. W. Thorpe and Associates.

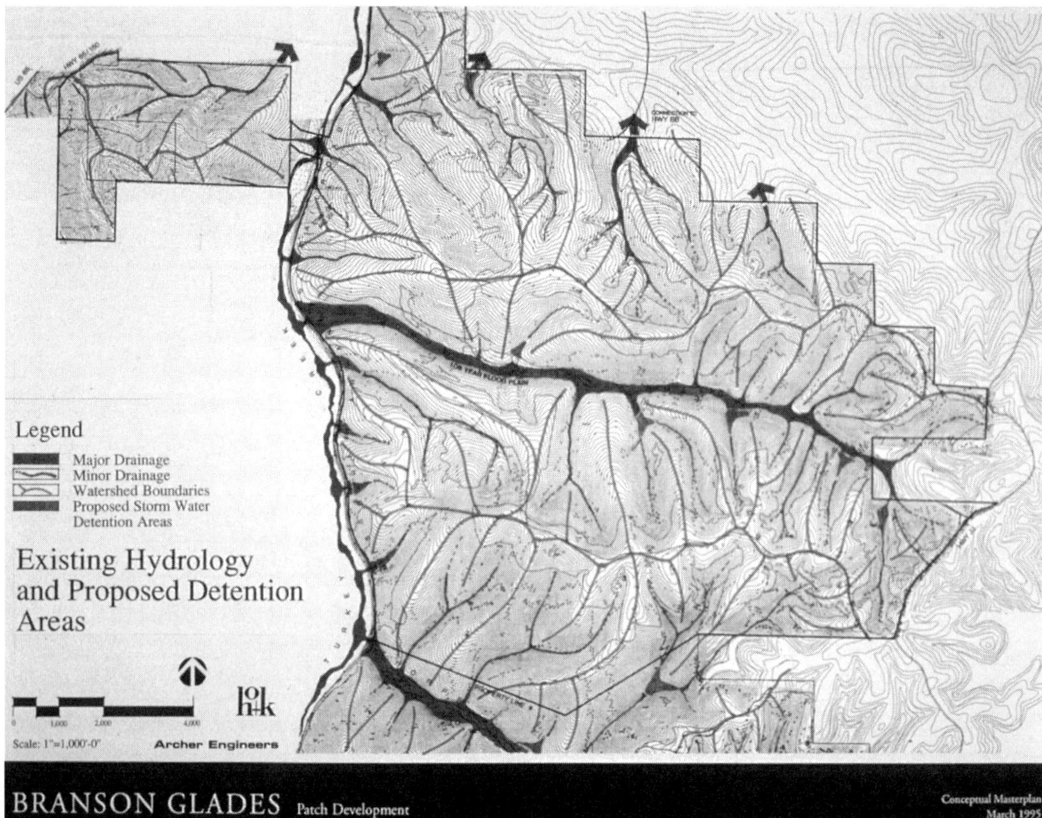

Figure 5-9 Inventory map showing watershed boundaries (ridges) and major drainage patterns (valleys). *Source:* The HOK Planning Group.

Figure 5-10 Map showing floodway and 100-year flood zone along a river in the Midwest. *Source:* The HOK Planning Group

SOILS

Physical, biological, and often cultural factors influence soil genesis and morphology. Climate, parent material, and landform position are key physical factors. Biological factors include the growth, death, and decomposition of vegetation, microorganisms, and other biota living above ground or within the soil itself. Soil properties are also affected by previous land use (Ferguson, 1999).

Attributes of soils that an inventory may consider, depending on the site's location and the intended program, include:

- acidity/alkalinity (pH)
- permeability
- erosion potential
- depth to seasonally high water table
- depth to bedrock

Buildings and other structures require foundations that must be constructed to a depth below the lowest frost level. For small structures in northern climates, this depth is between three and four feet below the ground surface. Large multistory buildings require larger foundations for adequate structural support. For these buildings, foundations may be constructed to much greater depths. Difficult subsurface conditions affect not only the complexity of excavation and construction, but also the design of new structures. A new building or structure must be designed and constructed to ensure that the integrity of the structure is not compromised.

Soils vary widely in texture, fertility, permeability, and other attributes that influence plant growth and development. Topsoil is a valuable natural resource that promotes the growth of healthy vegetation. A soil medium favorable for plant health reduces the impact of pests and diseases. Topsoil losses from prior agricultural activities, for example, can increase the costs of reestablishing vegetation on a site after construction. Erosion frequently occurs when vegetation cover is removed or substantially damaged during site clearing and construction.

Where on-site wastewater treatment systems will be installed, soils must be evaluated for their capacity to remove chemical and pathogen contaminants from wastewater effluent. This treatment function is performed by bacteria and other microbes that are naturally present in the soil. Very rapidly draining soils, typically those with high sand and gravel content, may be poorly suited for on-site wastewater treatment. Impervious soils, such as hardpan, are constraints that should be identified. Sites with a history of previous industrial or commercial activities may be contaminated with a variety of hazardous substances. If hazardous wastes are present on the site, the costs of remediation can be significant. Consequently, investigation of a site's subsurface conditions is warranted.

Mapping. In the United States, most landscapes outside of urbanized areas have had soils inventoried and mapped. The U.S. Department of Agriculture's Soil Survey maps general soil classes and finer-level soil types. Soil Survey maps are spatially coarse (e.g., 1:15,840 scale), and are generally inappropriate for making detailed site planning decisions. These maps do not capture the fine-scale variability that occurs in important soil conditions such as depth to bedrock, depth to water table, and permeability. The suitability of different soil types for the proposed site uses must be interpreted during the subsequent analysis phase of the land planning process. Soil factors that determine an area's suitability for different land uses can be portrayed with chloropleth maps (Figure 5-11).

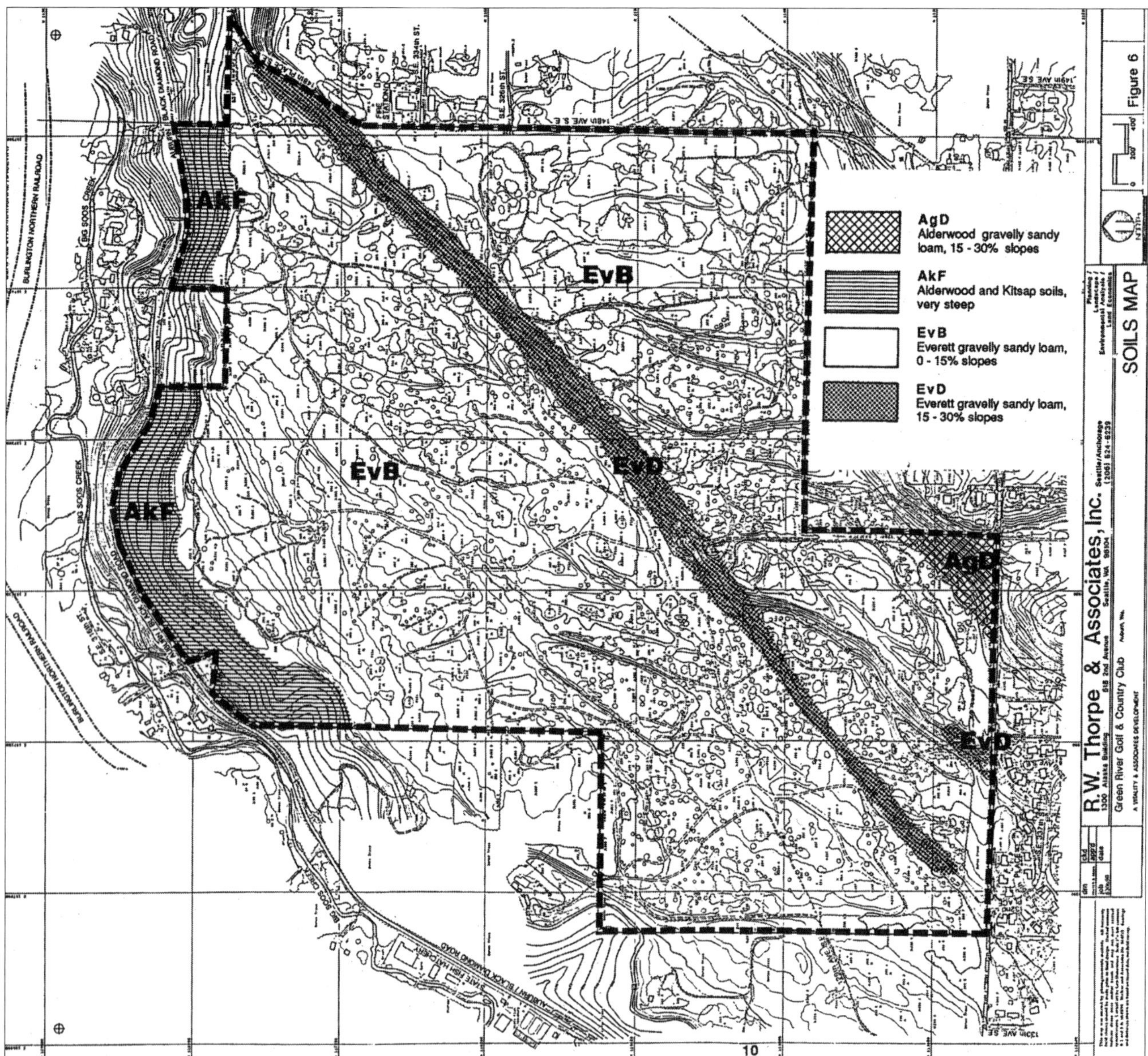

Figure 5-11 Chloropleth map showing four classes based on soil texture, slope, and erosion potential. *Source:* R. W.Thorpe and Associates.

CLIMATE

Atmospheric conditions that may influence land planning and design decisions include precipitation, air temperature, humidity, cloudiness, solar incidence, wind direction, and wind speed. These attributes vary annually, seasonally, and daily. Seasonal and monthly climate data are available from national weather services (e.g., in Australia, at http://www.bom.gov.au/climate). Local weather records can provide additional information about the daily weather conditions that can be expected each season. Collectively, these data include:

- temperature (maximum, minimum, and day-night temperature variation)
- humidity (high, low, and averages)
- wind (maximum, average velocity and direction)

TABLE 5-3 Plant hardiness zones, average annual minimum temperature ranges, and representative cities or States in each climatic zone of North America.

Zone	*Temperature Range*	*City or State*
1	Below -50 F (-45.6 C)	Fairbanks, Alaska
2a	-50 to -45 F (-45.5 to -42.8 C)	Flin Flon, Manitoba (Canada)
2b	-45 to -40 F (-42.7 to -40.0 C)	Unalakleet, Alaska
3a	-40 to -35 F (-39.9 to -37.3 C)	International Falls, Minnesota
3b	-35 to -30 F (-37.2 to -34.5 C)	Tomahawk, Wisconsin
4a	-30 to -25 F (-34.4 to -31.7 C)	Minneapolis/St.Paul, Minnesota
4b	-25 to -20 F (-31.6 to -28.9 C)	Nebraska
5a	-20 to -15 F (-28.8 to -26.2 C)	Illinois
5b	-15 to -10 F (-26.1 to -23.4 C)	Mansfield, Pennsylvania
6a	-10 to -5 F (-23.3 to -20.6 C)	St. Louis, Missouri
6b	-5 to 0 F (-20.5 to -17.8 C)	McMinnville, Tennessee
7a	0 to 5 F (-17.7 to -15.0 C)	Oklahoma City, Oklahoma
7b	5 to 10 F (-14.9 to -12.3 C)	Griffin, Georgia
8a	10 to 15 F (-12.2 to -9.5 C)	Dallas, Texas
8b	15 to 20 F (-9.4 to -6.7 C)	Gainesville, Florida
9a	20 to 25 F (-6.6 to -3.9 C)	Houston, Texas
9b	25 to 30 F (-3.8 to -1.2 C)	Fort Pierce, Florida
10a	30 to 35 F (-1.1 to 1.6 C)	Barstow, California
10b	35 to 40 F (4.4 to 1.7 C)	Miami, Florida
11	above 40 F (above 4.5 C)	Mazatlán (Mexico)

Source: United States Department of Agriculture, 1990.

- rainfall (monthly total, maximum for any one day)
- snowfall (monthly total, maximum for any one day)
- solar radiation (monthly average)
- potential natural hazards

Little can be done to control the forces of hurricanes, tornadoes, and other potentially destructive weather events. In the case of hurricanes, however, the most practical solution is to avoid development of sites that are most at risk.

The USDA Plant Hardiness Zone map shows the locations where different average annual minimum temperatures can be expected each year in the United States, Canada, and Mexico. Climate changes have led to the revision of the map that was previously published in 1960 and revised in 1965. The United States National Arboretum "web version" of the map depicts eleven zones (Table 5-3), each of which represents a different set of winter conditions for plants (United States Department of Agriculture, 1990). This map provides a guide to regional climatic conditions, but it cannot account for local variations in microclimate within each zone.

Vegetation modifies microclimate in several ways. Shade trees, for example, intercept the solar radiation that would otherwise strike pavement, rooftops, and other inorganic surfaces. These surfaces, especially if they are dark in color, absorb and subsequently re-radiate more heat energy than does vegetation. Leaves of plants also tend to cool air temperatures through evapotranspiration. In addition to moderating air temperature and humidity, plants can improve air quality by removing certain chemical pollutants and, as a result of photosynthesis, add oxygen to the atmosphere. Depending on the height of the tree, or any other vertical element, shadows of varying

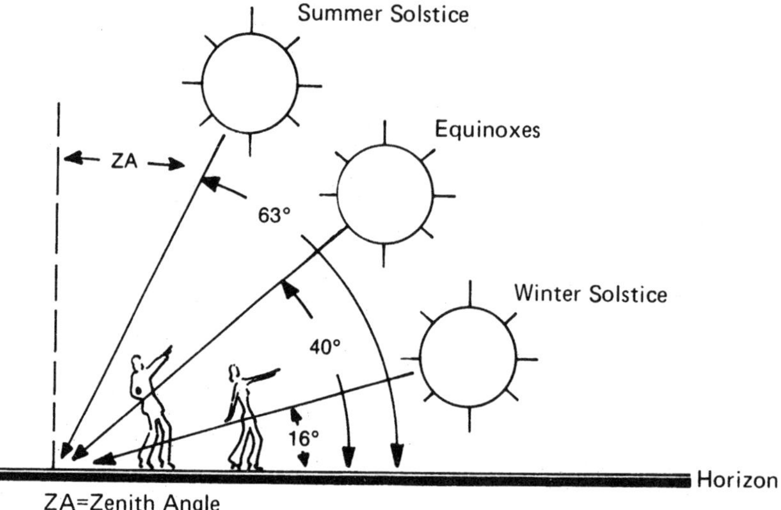

Figure 5-12 Diagram of seasonal changes in the maximum daily sun angle for a mid-latitude location in the Northern Hemisphere. *Source:* Marsh, *Landscape Planning*, Third Ed., copyright © 1998, p. 290, Figure 15.3. Reprinted by permission of John Wiley & Sons, Inc.

lengths will be cast during the course of a day. Shadow length also varies due to seasonal variations in the earth's relationship to the sun (Figure 5-12). Slope and aspect also influence the incidence of solar radiation striking the site's surface. The effect of slope and aspect on surface temperatures can be substantial.

Microclimate has a particularly important effect on two aspects of the built environment: (1) energy consumption for the heating and cooling of buildings, and (2) the comfort of people in outdoor settings. Both energy consumption and microclimate are influenced, however, by the spatial organization and orientation of buildings, structures, and outdoor spaces. Energy consumption for heating and cooling buildings can be reduced through both passive and active solar designs. Greater energy efficiency can be achieved by moderating the solar radiation striking and entering a building, and by moderating winds and breezes near the building. Winter winds can be buffered somewhat with windbreaks, and land uses can be arranged to reduce the negative effects of winds on human activities. In environments where winds are strong and persistent, significant modifications of building forms and spatial relationships may be necessary. Because wind is highly variable in both speed and direction, it is graphically depicted with "wind roses." These diagrams show the frequency distribution of the wind direction, velocity, and duration at a specific location.

A person is thermally comfortable when there is a balance between the body's heat losses and heat gains. Metabolic energy (generated within the body) and radiation (from the sun and from the earth) are the main sources of energy available to heat a person. Energy can be lost from a person's body mainly through evaporation of perspiration, convection from wind, and radiation. In outdoor environments, solar radiation and wind are the microclimatic factors that can be most easily modified by design (Brown and Gillespie, 1995).

Ambient air temperatures in outdoor areas depend, in part, on whether or not the space is exposed to full sunshine. Air temperatures are also affected by the surface materials and vegetation within the space. Paving materials like brick and stone absorb solar radiation, re-radiate the energy as heat, and thereby raise the air temperature immediately above the paved surfaces. Direct sunlight also warms people when it hits their clothing or skin. The heat index is an estimate of "apparent temperature"—the temperature that one feels because of the interaction between air temperature and relative humidity. Direct sunlight can raise heat index values by as much as 15 degrees Fahrenheit (United States National Oceanic and Atmospheric Agency, 2000). Buildings, trees, walls, and other vertical elements cast shadows that influence site microclimate. Understanding sun and shade patterns adjacent to both existing and proposed construction is essential in site planning and design for urban sites especially (Figure 5-13).

In a classic study of the relationships between environment and human behavior, William H. Whyte (1980) used time-lapse photography to document the locations of people in Seagram's Plaza in New York City. The rooftop of an adjacent building was his vantage point for viewing the plaza below. On a relatively cool spring day, plaza users sat or stood in locations that were exposed to direct sunlight. As shadows swept across this outdoor plaza, people came and went, but the majority of users at any one time were in the sun. In effect, the users moved across the space in synchronization with the movement of the area exposed to full sunlight.

Mapping. Microclimate can vary greatly over short distances and over short time spans. Therefore, mapping site microclimate is not a trivial matter. Brown and Gillespie (1995) recommend a process that identifies the site's exposure to both solar radiation and wind. A solar radiation map, which could be a digital layer in a GIS, can be created by overlaying and combining three attribute layers: (1) slope gradient, (2) slope aspect, and (3) vegetation (deciduous and coniferous trees, primarily). There are many possible combinations of slope, aspect, and tree cover, so the resulting map can be very complex. One possible map class, for example, would represent all site areas with less than 10 percent south-facing slopes and no tree cover. Another class would represent all areas with greater than 10 percent north-facing slopes and coniferous tree cover. In the northern latitudes, these two areas would receive markedly different levels of solar radiation during the winter months.

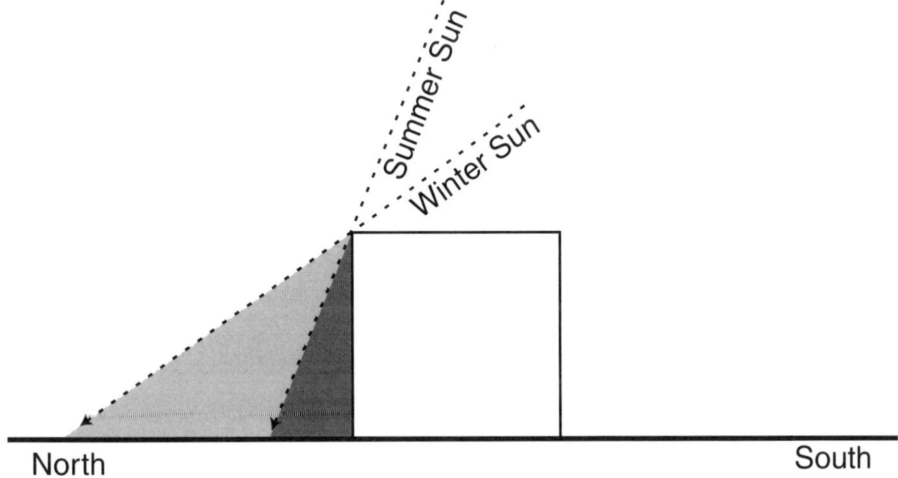

Figure 5-13 Schematic diagram of the seasonal variation in shade cast by a building in the northern hemisphere. Solar exposure in outdoor spaces near a building varies not only with weather conditions, but also with time of day, day of year, and location of the space in relation to both the building and the sun.

The complexity of the solar radiation map depends on the number of classes in each input layer. If each of these three layers has several classes, the potential number of combinations would be relatively high. For example, the slope gradient map could have three classes (0–10 percent, 10–20 percent, and greater than 20 percent); the slope aspect map could have eight classes (for the eight compass points); and the tree cover map could have four classes (no tree cover, deciduous trees, coniferous trees, and mixed deciduous/coniferous trees). If these three layers were combined, the resulting map of all slope, aspect, and tree cover combinations could have 96 classes (3 classes × 8 classes × 4 classes). Although useful as an intermediate layer, this map would be difficult to interpret. Within a GIS, however, this map could be reclassified, or recoded, to yield a much smaller number of classes that more clearly convey the site's microclimate. One possibility would be to aggregate each of the various slope, aspect, and vegetation combinations into one of four classes (Beer, 1990):

- very warm areas
- warm areas
- cool areas
- very cool areas

This recoding would have to consider the site's exposure to solar radiation and seasonal winds. These two factors will depend, of course, on the regional climate (e.g., hot-arid, warm-humid). They will also depend on the site's terrain and vegetation patterns.

Prevailing summer breezes and winter winds are typically shown as arrows on a site inventory map. Solar access is another important microclimatic factor that warrants documentation. Particularly in urban settings, where buildings may be either immediately adjacent to the site or on the site itself, shade diagrams should be evaluated. Because the position of the sun above the horizon changes daily from sunrise to sunset, these diagrams are typically created for several times of the day. Combined with seasonal changes in the position of the sun above the horizon, a variety of sun and shade patterns can occur on the site. When the development program includes outdoor spaces for seating, eating, and other activities, then several shade diagrams should be evaluated. These diagrams should coincide with the times of day and year when the programmed outdoor spaces (such as plazas and terraces) are most likely to be occupied with people. Shade diagrams may be appropriate, for example, for these four times of the day:

- midmorning (ten A.M.)
- noon (twelve A.M.)
- midafternoon (two P.M.)
- late afternoon (four P.M.)

Variation in solar access—and shadows—during the course of the year depends largely on the latitude of the site. In higher latitudes, especially in areas where cold winter temperatures are the norm, the use of outdoor space is strongly influenced by microclimate. Shade diagrams are typically prepared for these days of the year:

- midsummer (summer solstice)
- midwinter (winter solstice)
- equinox (vernal or autumnal)

The summer and winter solstices occur about June 21 and about December 22. The equinox occurs each year about March 21 and September 22. Day and night are of equal length on the equinox.

SUMMARY

The inventory of a site's physical attributes is driven by the project program and the characteristics of the site itself. Physical attributes on a site can have a broad impact on how a site is developed (Table 5-4). Potential data sources include aerial photographs, subsurface borings, and a wide variety of reference maps. Visiting a prospective site at different times of the day is useful in developing an understanding of a site's microclimate. Although not always possible due to budgetary constraints, visiting a site at different times of the year also can yield a much more comprehensive understanding of local site conditions, especially drainage patterns, wind patterns, and solar exposure.

TABLE 5-4 Selected physical factors to consider in land use planning.

Category	*Attribute*	*Land Use Significance*
Hydrology	Depth to water table	Excavations for building foundations On-site sewage treatment systems
	Drainage patterns	Flooding hazards Stormwater management
Geology	Depth to bedrock	Excavations for building foundations On-site sewage treatment systems
	Fault lines	Earthquake hazards Landslide hazards
Topography	Slope gradient	Circulation system safety Building design and construction complexity Erosion potential Site drainage and stormwater management
	Slope aspect	Microclimate
	Elevation	Visibility and visual quality Drainage patterns
Climate	Wind direction	Placement of outdoor seating Planting design
	Solar access	Building design and placement Placement of outdoor seating

CHAPTER

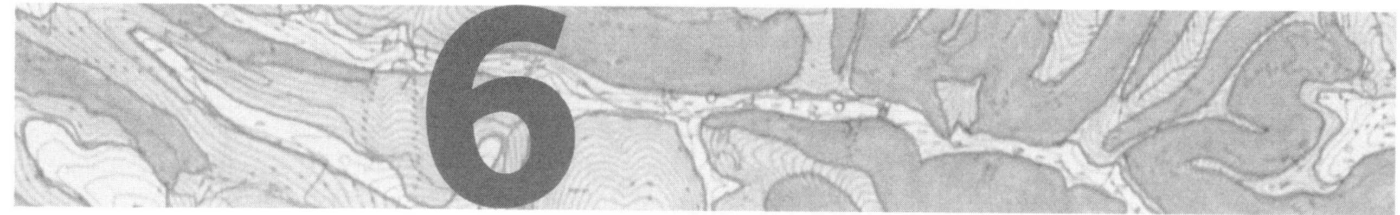

6

Site Inventory: Biological Attributes

INTRODUCTION

For the sake of clarity, the site inventory process is divided into three parts, each covered in a separate chapter. In land planning and design practice, distinctions between these three facets of the site inventory process are often less pronounced. The separation of physical and biological attributes into two different chapters in this book is a useful, but artificial, division. Ecosystems have both biotic and abiotic components, and the structure and function of ecosystems are influenced by the complex interplay of biological and physical factors. Moreover, ecosystems on every continent, and essentially on every landscape, have been influenced to varying degrees by human (cultural) activities.

A wide range of physical, biological, and cultural attributes influence landscape biotic and abiotic processes — or landscape function. For example, corridors of physical, biological, or cultural origin may be barriers to the movement of ground-dwelling animals, or serve as conduits for pathogens and invasive exotic species. Landscape barriers — whether roads, utility corridors, or other linear features — can isolate endemic, yet unsustainable populations of plant and animal species. Invasive exotic species may further compound the long-term threats to biodiversity and ecosystem function. Landscape ecology, a cross-disciplinary science, provides a useful framework for studying landscapes and making environmental planning, restoration, and management decisions (Naveh and Lieberman, 1984; Forman and Godron, 1986).

Large, contiguous natural areas should be given the highest priority for protection from future development. But simply leaving natural areas untouched may not be enough to ensure their continued viability. Isolated, small patches of forest, for example, may lose resident native species because of the barriers created by surrounding development. Many animal species need more than one habitat type for the completion of life cycle stages such as reproduction and dispersal. Daily or seasonal activities also may be inhibited by a habitat's context.

VEGETATION

Wetlands

Since the beginning of European settlement in the early 1600s, the area that is now the coterminous United States has lost—through agriculture, urban development, and other land uses—more than half the area's original wetland acreage (Dahl, 1990). In the United States, the federal agencies involved in wetland regulation define wetlands on the basis of hydrology, vegetation, and soils. Most states have also developed regulatory definitions of wetlands, but these definitions are generally broader than the federal definitions. The state definitions tend to emphasize the presence of certain vegetation, rather than the area's soils and hydrology. Wetlands classified on the basis of plant and soil conditions generally fall into one of three categories (Tiner, 1997; United States Fish and Wildlife Service, 2000).

- areas with hydrophytes and hydric soils (marshes, swamps, and bogs)
- areas without soils but with hydrophytes (aquatic beds and seaweed-covered rocky shores)
- areas without soil and without hydrophytes (gravel beaches and tidal flats) that are periodically flooded

The federal Fish and Wildlife Service's wetland classification scheme has five general classes and several subclasses (Cowardin et al., 1979):

- Marine (open ocean and its associated coastline)
- Estuarine (tidal waters of coastal rivers and embayments, salty tidal marshes, mangrove swamps, and tidal flats)
- Riverine (rivers and streams)
- Lacustrine (lakes, reservoirs, and large ponds)
- Palustrine (marshes, wet meadows, fens, playas, potholes, pocosins, bogs, swamps, and small shallow ponds)

A large majority of the wetlands in the United States are in the palustrine system; most of the remaining wetlands are in the estuarine system.

Wetlands perform a myriad of important functions that directly benefit humans. Coastal wetlands, for example, are nursery grounds for shellfish and other commercial sport fish. Other species, such as migratory birds, spend stages of their life cycle in these habitats. Wetlands buffer stormwater runoff and facilitate aquifer recharge. Wetlands are essential components of many landscapes' "plumbing" systems. They serve as the storage areas for large volumes of water, and are the interface for water movement above and below ground. This movement may occur in either direction—that is, from above to below (aquifer recharge), or from below to above (springs).

Wetland restoration and "banking" are allowed in some jurisdictions for mitigation purposes. Consequently, new wetlands are created in anticipation that existing wetlands will be destroyed. Yet this practice is not without criticism. Wetlands banking suffers from our inability, with current knowledge and technology, to create wetlands that structurally and functionally replicate natural wetlands. Constructed wetlands do not typically have the biodiversity of natural wetlands, in which biota have had decades to develop. Another concern involves the location of both the destroyed and created wetlands. Unless the new wetlands are near the destroyed wetlands, wetland banking can substantially alter drainage regimes and contribute to local flooding.

Mapping. The National Wetlands Inventory (NWI), administered by the U.S. Fish and Wildlife Service, includes information about the extent, characteristics, and status of wetlands in the United States. The NWI is in the process of producing a digital wetlands database for the entire United States. These maps, although relatively coarse in scale, provide an important source of land planning data. Yet these mapping programs are not intended to record the location of small and ephemeral wetlands. Ephemeral wetlands are those in which soils are saturated for a relatively brief period each year or, in more arid landscapes, even less frequently. These wetlands can be critical habitats for some species of migratory birds. Field assessments may be needed to identify and map all significant site wetlands (Figure 6-1).

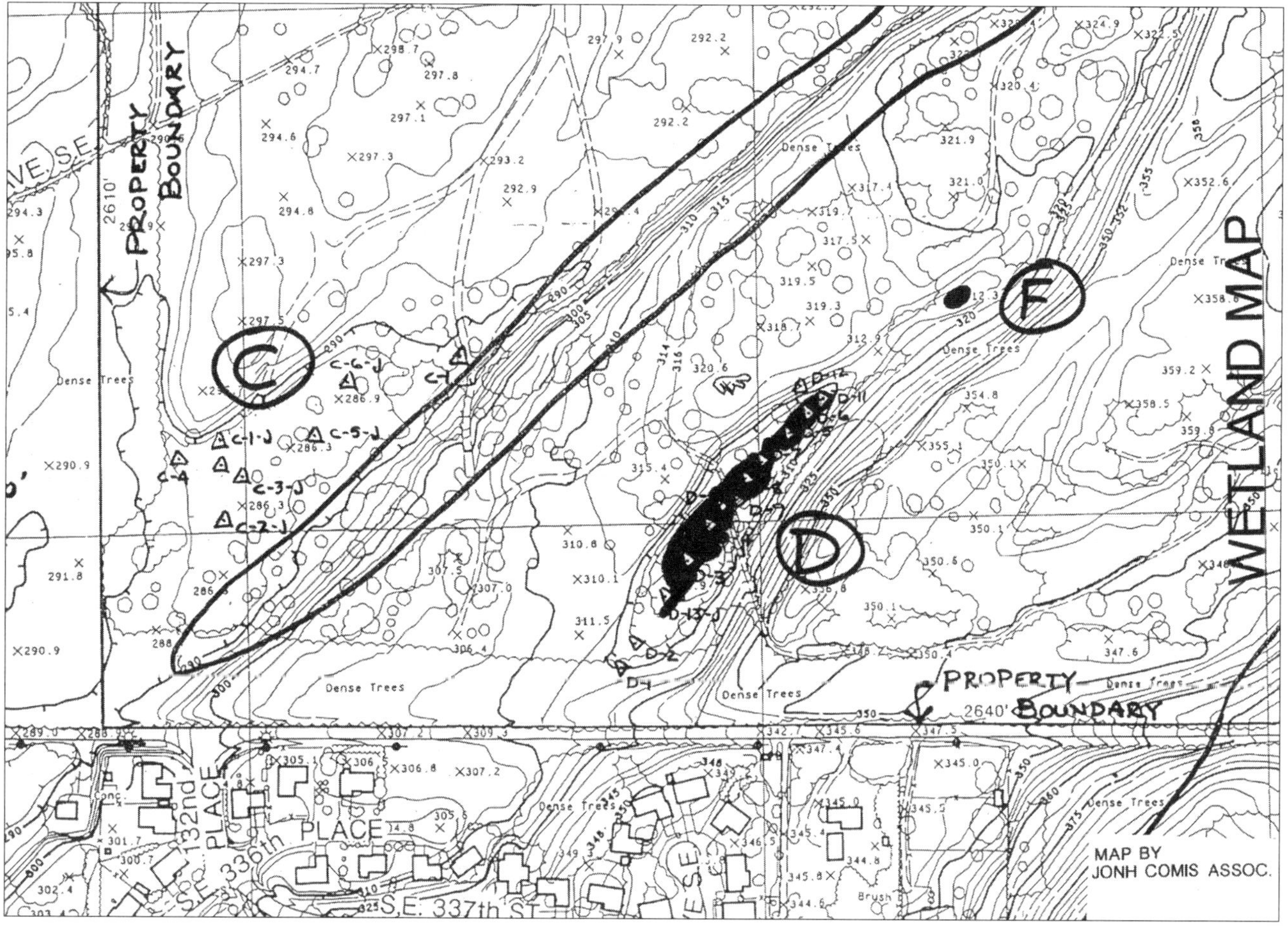

Figure 6-1 Wetland inventory map prepared in planning a land development project in the state of Washington. *Source:* R. W. Thorpe and Associates.

Native and Exotic Species

For hundreds of years, plant species have been adapting to habitats altered by human activities. Coincident with European settlement of North America, many introduced species became naturalized. Centuries of global trade and migration have introduced thousands of exotic — and sometimes invasive — species to new environments. These exotic species include megafauna, like horses and pigs. They also include megaflora, like the eucalyptus and melaleuca trees. Examples of other exotic plants include vines (kudzu) and shrubs (Brazilian pepper).

An estimated 50,000 species of exotic plants, animals, and microbes cause significant ecological changes in both managed and natural ecosystems within the United States (Myers, 1979; Pimentel et al., 2000). For example, nearly half of the species listed as threatened or endangered under the federal Endangered Species Act are at risk primarily because of predation by, or competition with, non-native species (Wilcove et al., 1998). Invasive exotic species also have substantial economic impacts. Annual expenditures for the control of nonindigenous species are estimated to exceed $6 billion per year in the United States alone (Pimentel et al., 2000).

Exotic species were often transported unintentionally to new habitats. Carried by ships, trucks, and airplanes, both large and small species have been introduced into new habitats. Exotic species are particularly successful colonizers when the new habitats present minimal constraints to their growth and reproduction. Typically, these competitive controls limit the populations of each species in their home territories. One type of competitive control is predation. A potentially invasive species may be limited in its native habitat by grazing (in the case of plants) or predation (in the case of animals). Other species may compete for the same resources, such as food and space. Competition for the same ecological "niche" helps hold in check the populations of the competing species. William E. Odum (1959), in the classic *Fundamentals of Ecology,* writes:

> The habitat of an organism is the place where it lives, or the place where one would go to find it. The ecological niche, on the other hand, is the position or status of an organism within its community and ecosystem resulting from the organism's structural adaptations, physiological responses and specific behavior (inherited and/or learned.) The ecological niche of an organism depends not only on where it lives but also on what it does. By analogy, it may be said that the habitat is the organisms's "address," and the niche is its "profession," biologically speaking.

Many exotic species also have been intentionally transported to — and, in fact, distributed within — new habitats. For example, the Melaleuca tree, now one of the most invasive tree species in the Florida Everglades, was seeded by airplane in the mid–twentieth century. Without understanding the potential impacts of the plant on the Everglades ecology, the seeds were dispersed in an effort to dry the wetlands and create new land for development. Similarly, the eucalyptus tree was imported to California from Australia and planted widely as a new source of timber. In the amenable California climate, and with little competition and no significant natural controls, the eucalyptus tree subsequently colonized native oak forests and savannas in the state.

There are many practical reasons to protect the remaining native habitats. In addition to the intrinsic ecological benefits of biodiversity (Wilson, 1988), these places often function as a landscape's hydrological infrastructure. These places also serve important cultural functions, such as providing outdoor areas for natural science education at all levels of instruction.

Figure 6-2 Analyst assessing vegetation type and quality in southwest Florida. Note desiccation of the cypress trees caused by regional drainage canals excavated during the mid–twentieth century.

Mapping. National land cover information is available through the United States Geological Survey (http://edcwww.cr.usgs.gov/programs/lccp/). A 30-meter resolution National Land Cover Dataset (NLCD) is available in digital format. The planned 31-volume compact disc (CD) set contains 21 categories of land cover information across the lower 48 states. Large-scale (e.g., 1:1,200) photographs can facilitate more detailed vegetation mapping. Color infrared photographs are especially effective for distinguishing subtle differences in vegetation health and vigor. Final classifications of vegetation communities are usually confirmed by visiting the site (Figure 6-2). A chloropleth map can show the locations of the site's major vegetation types (Figure 6-3). On sites with remnant natural areas, consideration should be given to mapping significant distributions of invasive exotic species. A map of these locations can be used in developing a plan for eradicating invasive exotic species and restoring native communities. Depending on the land use program and the site's context, restoration of wetlands, prairies, and/or woodlands also may be desired. Attribute information on soils, hydrology, and vegetation can help in identifying the most suitable locations for these eradication and restoration activities.

Global positioning systems (GPS) provide another way to map vegetation communities. With a handheld GPS receiver, a botanist or other individual who can identify the local flora walks the site and digitally records the boundaries of each major plant community. Taking a color aerial photograph into the field can help orient the

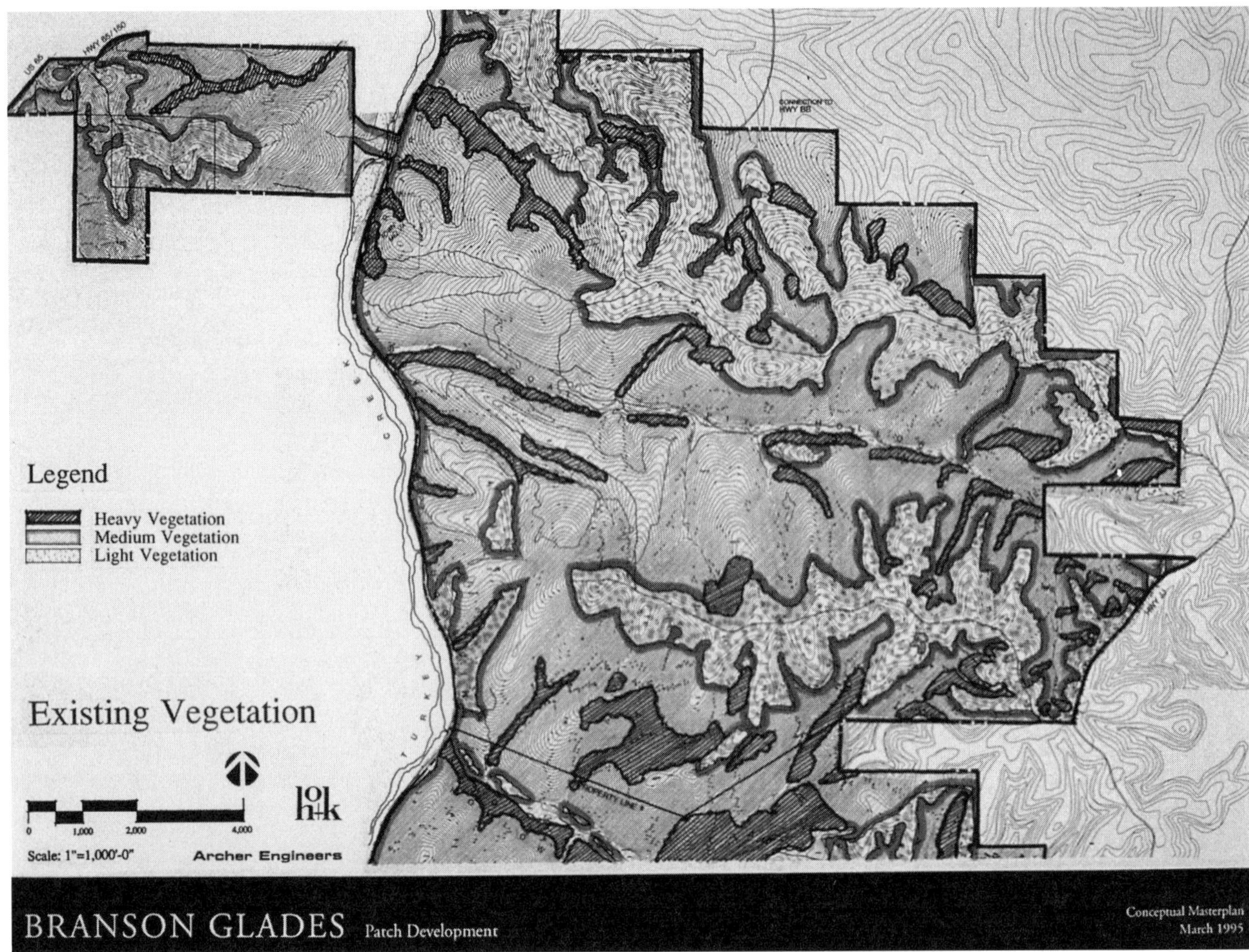

Figure 6-3 Chloropleth map showing three densities of vegetative cover. *Source:* The HOK Planning Group.

analyst and make the digital mapping process more efficient. Some plant communities have evolved under a fire regime. Fire history can also be mapped (Figure 6-4).

Specimen Trees

Trees on a site are assets that can yield multiple ecological and social benefits. Trees provide shade and can reduce heating and cooling costs of nearby buildings. Trees also can increase the economic value of real estate by providing a significant amenity. The International Society of Arboriculture, a nonprofit organization dedicated to research and education, identifies four factors to consider in evaluating the economic value of trees (Perry, 1999):

- tree size
- tree species (hardy, well adapted species are worth most)
- tree condition or health (e.g., roots, trunk, branches, leaves)
- tree location (functional and aesthetic values)

Trees serve various design functions that benefit people. For example, they provide shade, screen undesirable views, and serve as wind breaks. Trees also have aesthetic value. For example, they may provide a focal point or visual amenity. Consequently, a

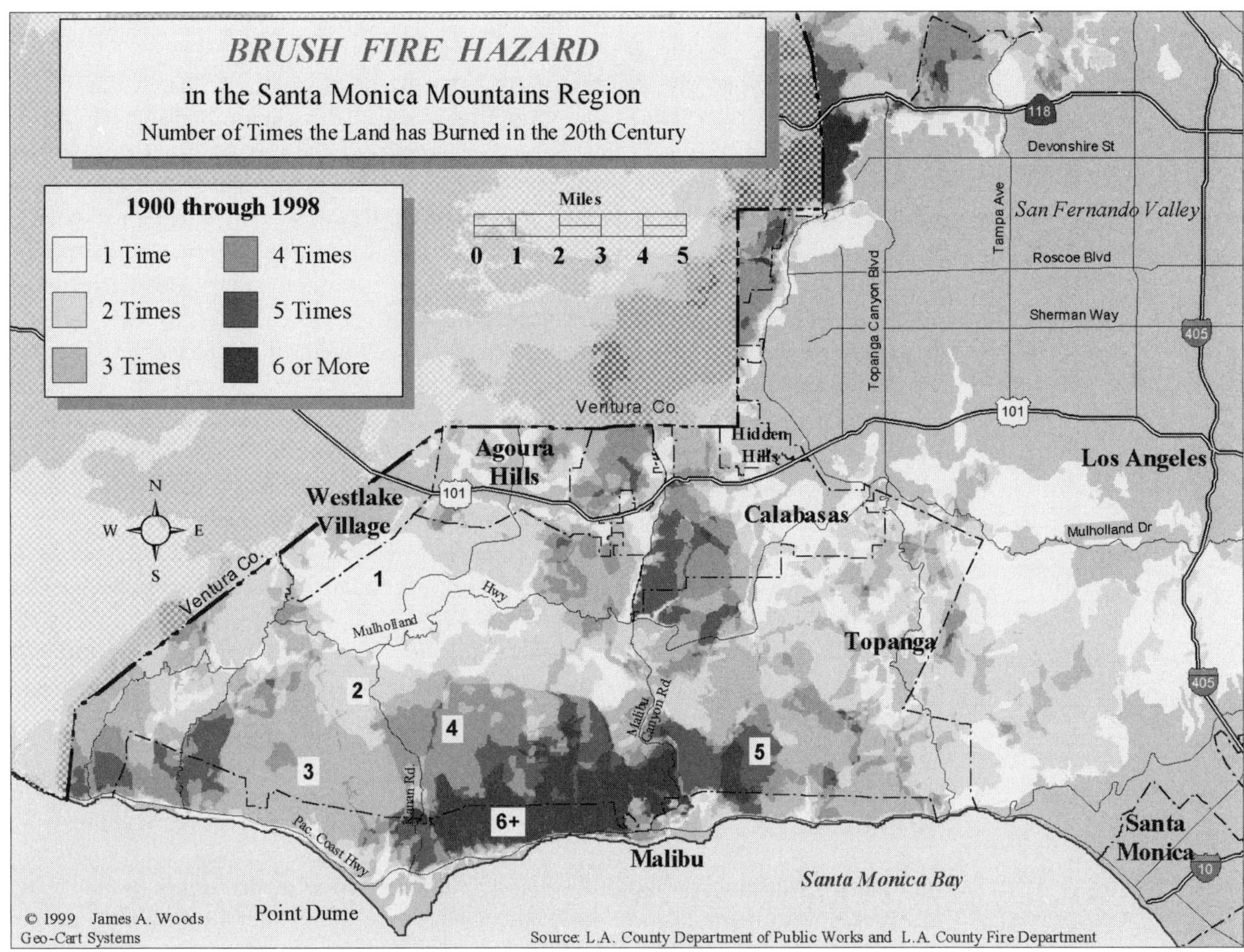

Figure 6-4 Chloropleth map of fire frequency in the Santa Monica mountains of California. Map categories reflect the number of times the land has burned. *Source:* © 1999 James A. Woods.

tree standing alone is usually worth more—from an economic perspective—than one that is growing in a group.

During the construction of buildings, infrastructure, and other site elements, existing trees on a site require protection. Common, yet easily avoided, construction damage may kill trees outright or lead to their slow demise. Typical construction impacts include soil compaction of the root zone, scraping the bark from trunks and branches, and grading (i.e., cutting or filling) of the root zone. Generally, construction disturbances should not occur within the "drip line" of a tree's canopy. Yet the shade of a tall tree is probably one of the favorite spots for construction workers to park trucks, bulldozers, and other machinery. These machines compact the soil over the roots and damage soil structure by reducing the air spaces within the soil. Tree protection measures usually include fencing around all major trees to prevent damage during construction. Municipalities may have ordinances that require the protection of trees during the construction and development process.

Mapping. Significant trees on the site should be mapped to ensure that as many trees as possible are protected. The information included on these inventories commonly include size, species, and location. Tree size is measured by the diameter of the trunk at breast height (dbh). Typical site surveys include an inventory of trees larger than a specified size (e.g., four inches dbh).

WILDLIFE

Populations of most wildlife species are naturally discontinuous. That is, the entire population consists of groups of subpopulations, called metapopulations. For example, separated wooded patches may be home to colonies of birds, mammals, and other animals. Local-scale extinctions of metapopulations are not unusual, and often are a natural part of ecosystem dynamics. It is essential, however, that the area in which a local extinction occurs remains viable as a habitat for future colonization and repopulation of the decimated metapopulation. This is a natural process involving local extinctions, migration and colonization, and reproduction. Of course, if the habitat is destroyed or degraded, or made inaccessible by intervening barriers, then the geographic range of the species is permanently reduced.

There are many benefits of conserving wildlife habitats within our built environments. Songbirds bring satisfaction to avid bird-watchers and casual observers alike. Many species of birds are prolific consumers of insects. Habitat protection is perhaps the most effective method of protecting endangered and threatened species.

Mapping. The intent of the federal Endangered Species Act (ESA) is to prevent local as well as regional extinctions of species. Maps of endangered and threatened species in the United States are prepared by the U.S. Fish and Wildlife Service. The maps do not show local distributions, but they do indicate the geographic range where individuals of these species are likely to be present. Site level data on wildlife distributions can be acquired through field studies by qualified biologists.

SUMMARY

As scientists learn more about the structure and function of landscapes, national, state, and local governments are increasingly involved in evaluating the environmental impacts of proposals for land development. The general public is also gaining a greater awareness of the linkages between environmental quality and human health and welfare. Heightened concern for environmental quality has led to increasing demands for accountability — and therefore documentation — from the land development industry.

Mapping a site's key biological attributes is one part of the site inventory (Table 6-1). Which attributes to map and evaluate depends, as with physical and cultural attributes, on the future uses of the site. Land development should "fit" the site. This will help protect the ecological integrity of the site during and after the plan's implementation. Vegetation and wildlife can give a new development a sense of place.

TABLE 6-1 Selected biological factors to consider in land use planning.

Sub-category	*Attribute*	*Land Use Significance*
Vegetation	Plant communities	Stormwater filtering and infiltration Wildlife habitat Microclimate moderation Fire hazards
	Specimen trees	Visual amenity Microclimate moderation Wildlife habitat
Wildlife	Endangered and threatened species	Development restrictions

CHAPTER

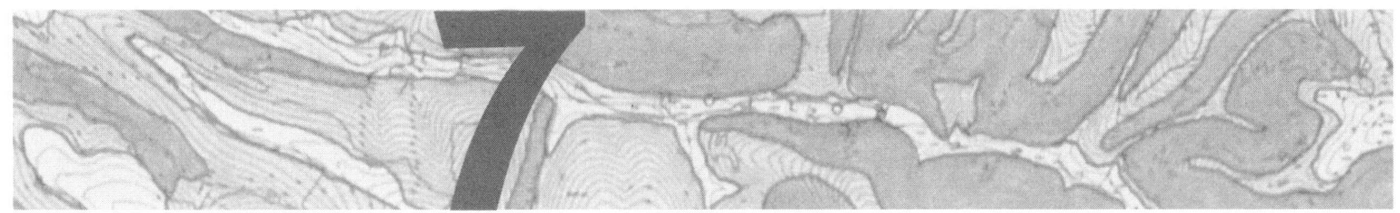

7 Site Inventory: Cultural Attributes

> The concept of public welfare is broad and inclusive...the values it represents are spiritual as well as physical, aesthetic as well as monetary. It is within the power of the legislature to determine that the community should be beautiful as well as healthy, spacious as well as clean.
>
> —William O. Douglas, U.S. Supreme Court Justice
> *Berman v. Parker*, 1954

INTRODUCTION

All land use changes occur within a cultural context. In this book, cultural context refers to the historical, legal, aesthetic, and other socially significant attributes associated with land and landscapes. In a classic essay on landscape perception, D. W. Meinig (1979) identifies ten possible ways in which knowledge, experience, and values influence our perceptions of land and landscapes (Table 7-1). All of these perspectives are rational, but each one is a product of the unique "lens" with which each of us views the world.

Landscape cultural attributes can have a pronounced effect on a site's future land uses. Maintaining, or creating, a "sense of place" hinges on understanding and

TABLE 7-1 Ten perceptions of landscape meaning.

Landscape As...	*Associated Concepts*
Nature	Fundamental Enduring
Habitat	Adaptation Resources
Artifact	Platform Utilitarian
System	Dynamic Equilibrium
Problem	Flaw Challenge
Wealth	Property Opportunity
Ideology	Values Ideas
History	Chronology Legacy
Place	Locality Experience
Aesthetic	Scenery Beauty

Source: Adapted from: D. W. Meinig, 1979.

responding to site context (Hough, 1990, Beatley and Manning, 1997). A sense of place is strengthened by using forms and materials that are common in the region or local area. Indigenous construction materials include locally quarried stone and collected boulders. Native and naturalized plant species also contribute to a site's identity. Therefore, development that "fits" the site is adapted to the site's unique character. Site character is defined by landforms, drainage patterns, vegetation, and other biophysical and cultural attributes.

Cultural features—whether historical, aesthetic, legal, or perceptual—typically create opportunities and/or constraints for development. A cultural resource assessment, not unlike an assessment of biophysical attributes, involves the inventory and analysis of these various cultural factors (Table 7-2). The built environment is a com-

TABLE 7-2 Selected cultural factors to consider in land use planning.

Category	*Attribute*	*Land Use Significance*
Legal	Political boundaries Land use incentives Land use regulations Easements & deed restrictions	Permitting and review process Land costs, development costs Permitted uses and densities Locations of permitted uses
Historic	Significant buildings	Amenities, development restrictions
Infrastructure	Streets Utilities	Site access Construction costs
Buildings	Massing (height, width), and articulation (fenestration)	Visual quality, sense of place
Context	Land use	Visual quality Potential nuisances (noise, odors)

plex array of buildings, streets, and other structures that has evolved incrementally, resulting in a mosaic of elements that vary widely in age and origin. Development sites may be remnant open spaces within, or adjacent to, a matrix of buildings and urban infrastructure. A systematic approach to selecting cultural attributes is particularly important with projects on difficult sites or with complex programs.

LAND USE AND TENURE

A site inventory must consider the legal context for land planning and design decisions. Yet legal context varies widely at the local, the state or regional, and especially the national scale. Moreover, laws and policies change over time. The approach taken in this book is (1) to focus on major concepts and principles (i.e., endangered species protection, stormwater management), and (2) to provide some examples of major laws, policies, and permitting procedures from the United States. One limitation of this approach, of course, is that the legal context in the United States may be quite different from that in Australia, Britain, Canada, New Zealand, or other nations. However, each nation's development regulations address many of the same themes—namely, the protection of the environment and public health, safety, and welfare.

Fee simple purchase of land is the acquisition—for money or some other compensation—of the title to a land parcel. Land ownership, or tenure, entails both rights and responsibilities. In the United States, land use controls are intended to protect public health, safety, and welfare. The "bundle" of rights accompanying a property depend upon the parcel's location and physical, biological, and cultural attributes. Regulations that exceed these basic protective functions have been challenged in the courts—and upheld—as property "takings" (Bosselman and Callies, 1972). When regulations go beyond legitimate protective functions, the courts have ordered the regulating government to provide "just compensation" to the affected landowner.

Development rights also may be restricted in ways other than government land use regulations. Easements and deed restrictions, for example, are created for many different purposes. An easement may ensure access to a property that is accessible only by crossing another property. Easements that allow emergency vehicle access or utility maintenance vehicle access are also common. Covenants, deed restrictions, and other easements are often created for conservation purposes. Scenic easements, for example, can limit the scope and character of land development. These easements are typically held in the public trust. The purchase of development rights can keep land undeveloped for either a limited or a defined period of time. Transfer of development rights is a less common legal tool for shifting development from conservation areas to other areas more suitable for development.

Prior land use on a site may influence development suitability in a variety of ways. Knowledge that a site was previously used for industrial or commercial uses, for example, could indicate that chemicals and other toxic wastes remain on the site, either above or below ground. Prior agricultural uses may suggest other site problems. Historically, farming in the United States was often practiced with little concern for soil conservation and management. Consequently, many farms were subjected to soil erosion and extensive topsoil losses.

Mapping. Land tenure information is typically stored in publicly accessible databases. These records may include a certified survey map of the parcel boundaries, a history of land ownership, and any deed restrictions or covenants associated with the property. Digital mapping of parcel data is becoming increasingly common. Digital records identify the boundaries of all parcels, in addition to the attributes associated with each parcel. Collectively, these maps and associated "metadata" comprise a *cadastre.* There has been rapid growth in the development of digital map databases within North America, Europe, Australia, and other parts of the world. Many of these databases are available commercially or, in some cases, through government departments or agencies. One company in the United States, for example, sells digital topographic data models that are viewable as either two- or three-dimensional images (www.delorme.com). This company also offers detailed digital maps of streets, trails, unique natural features, and historic sites. Other digital data, such as vertical and oblique color infrared aerial photographs, are increasingly available for downloading through government sources (e.g., federal Upper Midwest Environmental Sciences Center, www.umesc.usgs.gov). The vertical photographs, in particular, provide a relatively detailed source of land use and land cover data.

LAND USE REGULATION

Federal and State Regulations

Government regulations influence land development directly and indirectly. Although land use control is often considered a local government issue, cumulative land use changes often have regional and even national implications. Consequently, federal and state laws and policies have been enacted to protect environmental quality and preserve historic and other cultural resources. For example, the National Environmental Policy Act (1969) was the first in a lengthy list of major federal legislation with broad influences on land use in the United States. In addition, several other federal laws and polices are designed to protect cultural resources or enhance quality of life. The Americans with Disabilities Act (ADA), for example, also has important site development implications that are addressed in later chapters of this book.

Federal regulations typically establish standards that are implemented at the state and local levels. The National Coastal Zone Management (CZM) Program (http://www.ocrm.nos.noaa.gov/czm/national.html), for example, is a voluntary partnership between the federal government and U.S. coastal states and territories. Authorized by the Coastal Zone Management Act, the purpose of the program is to (United States National Oceanic and Atmospheric Agency, 2000b):

1. preserve, protect, develop, and where possible, restore and enhance the resources of the Nation's coastal zone for this and succeeding generations;
2. encourage and assist the states to exercise effectively their responsibilities in the coastal zone to achieve wise use of land and water resources of the coastal zone, giving full consideration to ecological, cultural, historic, and esthetic values as well as the needs for compatible economic development;
3. encourage the preparation of special area management plans to provide increased specificity in protecting significant natural resources, reasonable coastal-dependent economic growth, improved protection of life and property in hazardous areas, and improved predictability in governmental decision-making;

4. encourage the participation, cooperation, and coordination of the public, federal, state, local, interstate and regional agencies, and governments affecting the coastal zone.

The Coastal Nonpoint Pollution Control Program is an important component of coastal management in the United States. This program requires states and territories with approved coastal zone management programs to develop and implement methods for coastal nonpoint pollution control. Techniques to limit the addition of pollution to coastal waters have been developed by the EPA for five source categories of nonpoint pollution: agricultural runoff, urban runoff, forestry runoff, marinas, and hydromodification.

As populations continue to increase, and the built environment covers an increasingly larger portion of the United States, state-level growth management programs are becoming more common (Gale, 1992). Yet other government policies in the United States facilitate land development in a variety of ways. Government policies create incentives that influence not only the location but also the type of land development (Nivola, 1999).

Local Regulations

In the United States, the power to regulate land use is granted to local governments through state-level enabling legislation. Land use regulations are a subset of "police powers" for protecting the public health, safety, morals, and welfare. Local governments control land use and influence the pace, location, and character of new development in several ways. In conjunction with comprehensive land use planning, zoning codes control development patterns within the community. Zoning is a common form of land use control at the local level. A zoning map may have hundreds of districts in which certain uses are permitted and other uses are prohibited (Figure 7-1). Local land use controls also include subdivision ordinances, stormwater management ordinances, and landscaping ordinances. The subdivision of one or more parcels of land into several smaller parcels is a key step in many land development projects. Subdivisions for future residential uses are very common. Subdivision ordinances typically set minimum requirements for parcel size, and these ordinances may also limit the number and location of curb cuts, or street access points, allowed to a property. They often establish building setbacks from adjacent properties.

Legal constraints that could affect the uses of a site should be documented. Legal issues that should be investigated for each site include (White, 1983; Garvin, 1996):

- zoning classification (permitted land uses and densities)
- easements, covenants, and other deed restrictions
- government agencies with jurisdiction over the property
- building placement requirements (required front-, back-, and side-yard setbacks)
- allowable buildable area
- building height and bulk restrictions
- parking requirements
- open space requirements

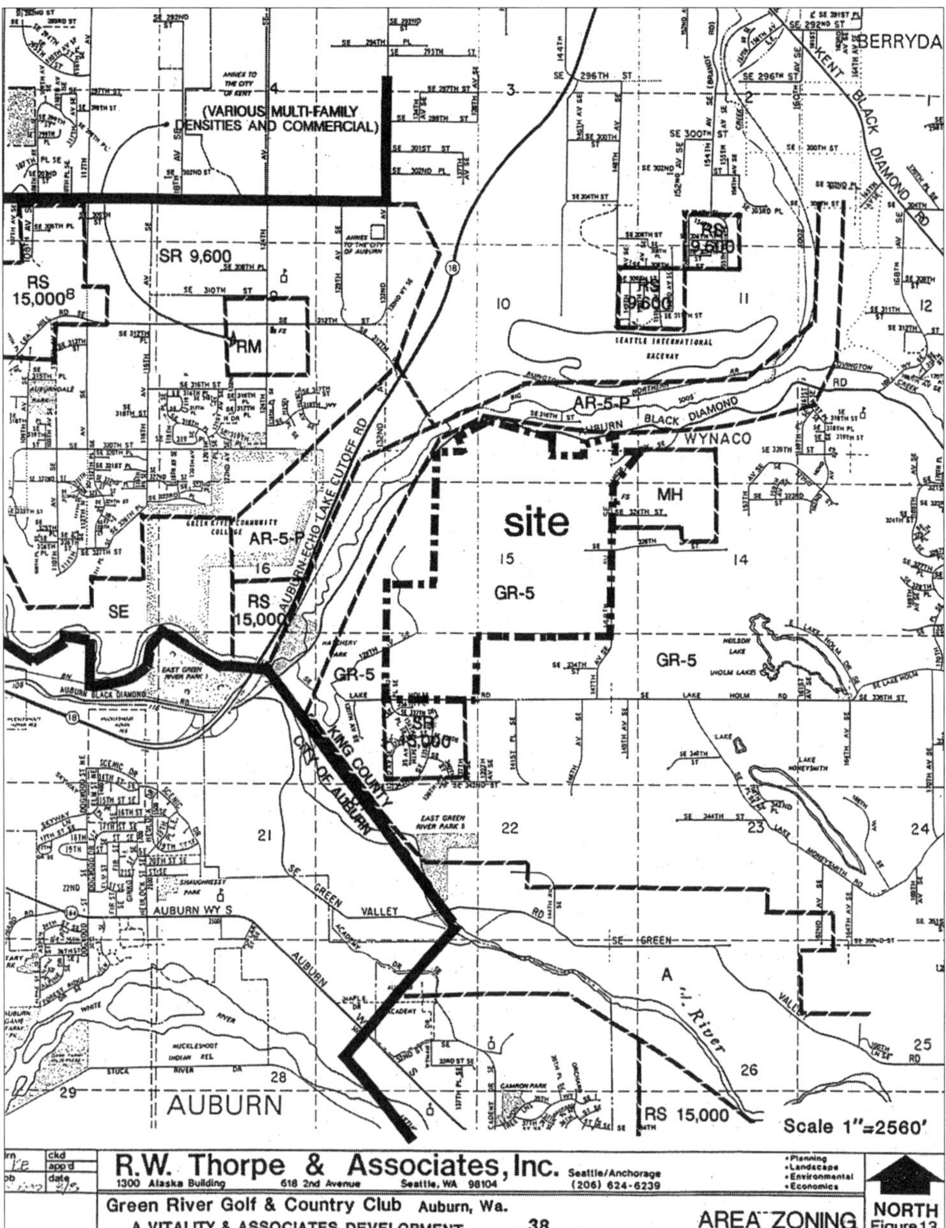

Figure 7-1 Zoning map for the area surrounding a site planned for a new golf course community near Seattle, Washington. *Source:* R. W. Thorpe and Associates.

- stormwater management and erosion control requirements
- landscaping requirements

Local zoning codes allow variances from the code requirements under certain conditions. Increasingly common forms of zoning variance are the planned unit development (PUD). These rezoning districts may be permitted to facilitate large, mixed-use land development projects. PUD provisions usually allow for the consolidation of multiple parcels into a single master-planned project. This provides greater flexibility in meeting the overall density and land use requirements for the site as a whole, rather than for each of the site's individual parcels. Design review is an increasingly common part of the land use regulatory process, particularly as municipalities rely more heavily on performance standards. To withstand possible legal challenges, design standards and the process for reviewing and approving designs must be clear and unambiguous.

PUBLIC INFRASTRUCTURE

The built environment is a vast array of structures and systems. The spatial organization and articulation of the built environment influences environmental quality, land value, and the costs of delivering public services. The public—and in many cases private—infrastructure includes stormwater sewerage systems, sanitary sewerage systems, and potable water supply systems. The depth, location, and type of utility systems and structures present on the site and adjacent to the site are useful pieces of information in planning future uses of the site. Plans to develop, or redevelop, a site that has existing structures and utility systems must ensure that the new systems are compatible with the old.

Circulation

Understanding existing circulation patterns is an important part of the site inventory process. Many mistakes have been made in site planning and architectural design because established pedestrian and vehicle circulation patterns were either ignored or poorly understood. The effects of proposed development on existing—and future—circulation patterns must be considered. When these steps are not taken, the result for pedestrians can be inconvenience at best and, at worst, safety hazards.

Circulation systems, especially on urban and suburban sites, are frequently designed for pedestrians, bicyclists, and motor vehicles. On-site circulation systems must be internally well organized, and they must be linked to off-site circulation systems. Land planners usually have leeway in determining how and where pedestrians enter a site, so existing patterns should be taken into account. Failure to anticipate "desire lines" between existing and/or proposed entrances to the site, to buildings, or to other elements, may create pedestrian–vehicle conflicts.

Mapping. Nearby land uses can have either positive or negative impacts on the proposed uses of the site. In assessing a site's land use context, attributes that might be documented include:

- land use type (e.g., residential, commercial, industrial)
- land use intensity (e.g., dwelling units per acre/hectare, vehicle traffic)

Existing and projected traffic volumes on adjacent streets and highways can be estimated and mapped. Existing and potential conflicts between vehicles and pedestrians also should be identified. The location of adjacent streets, driveways, drop-off zones, service areas, and parking lots is contextual information that typically influences the spatial organization of the developed site. Different circulation systems (pedestrians, bicycles, vehicles) and volumes can be portrayed graphically by varying the width, color, and texture of the arrows (Figure 7-2).

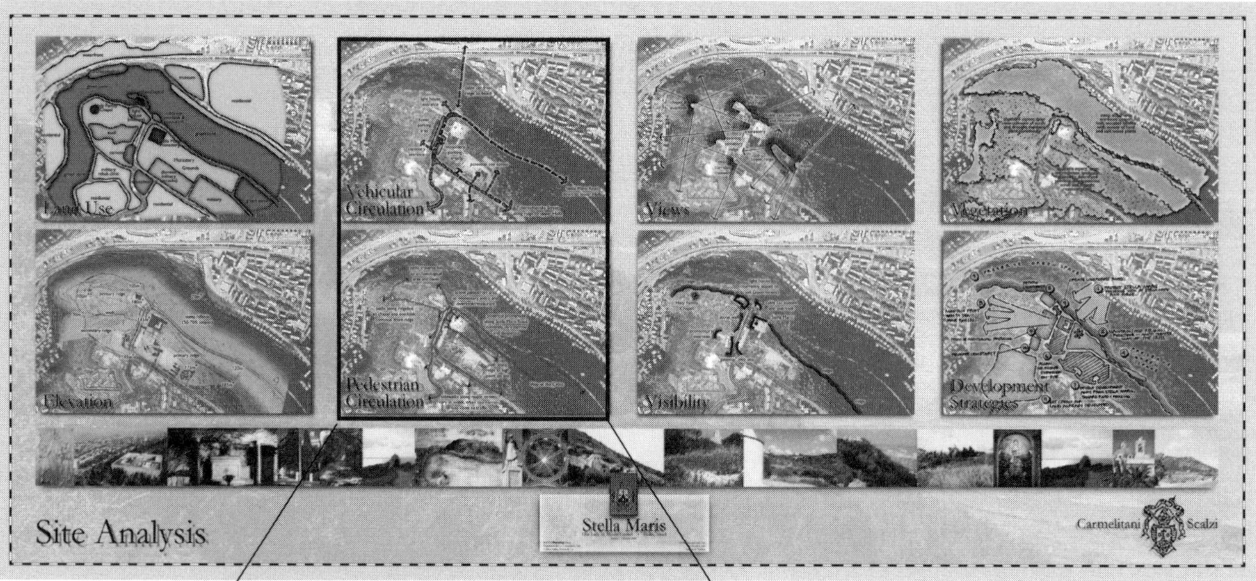

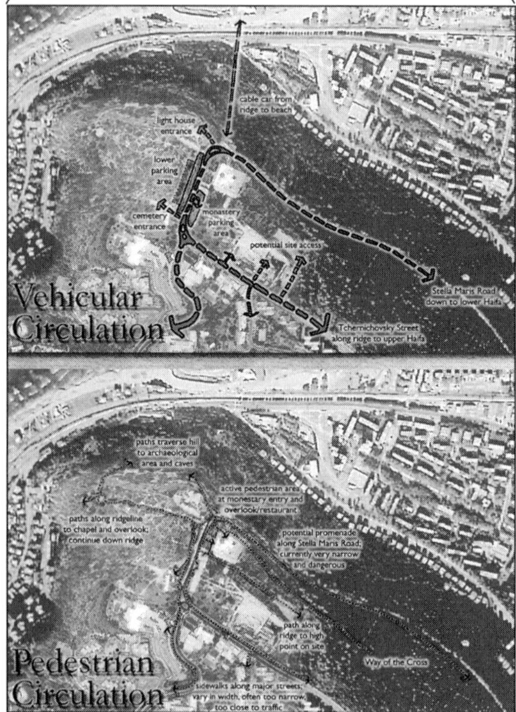

Figure 7-2 Existing vehicle and pedestrian circulation patterns near the Stella Maris monastery in Haifa, Israel. *Source:* The HOK Planning Group.

Utilities

Infrastructure is conventionally thought of as streets, bridges, and sewer systems. But utilities serving a site may also include other networks for the distribution of energy and potable water, and for communications. Other utility systems serve sites by removing stormwater and sanitary wastes. New utility systems often account for a significant share of a site's development costs. In the site inventory, it is important to understand where the public utility systems are—and how connections to these systems will be made (Figure 7-3).

Mapping. A site utility inventory should at least include the locations and sizes of the utility systems, if they exist on or adjacent to the site:

- stormwater sewer
- sanitary sewer
- potable water
- electricity
- natural gas
- telephone
- television cable

Open space is an integral element of community infrastructure. Undeveloped open spaces may be visual amenities that create opportunities for both passive and active recreation. Open spaces may also perform essential ecological functions that have direct benefits to society. Perhaps the most important function of these open spaces—especially if part of an integrated open space system—is to provide space for stormwater management. Water in the landscape may run off to surface waters, infiltrate into the ground, or return to the atmosphere through evaporation. Aquifers and other groundwater—the result of precipitation in the past (even thousands of years ago)—also provide a source of water for streams and lakes in some landscapes.

Figure 7-3 Sanitary sewer service to the site of a land development project in the state of Washington. *Source:* R. W. Thorpe and Associates.

BUILDINGS

The massing and placement of buildings in a city, village, or other settlement contribute to the character of the neighborhood. The design context of a site must be understood if the new development is to make a positive contribution to the area's visual quality. The following are ten common design attributes of buildings in traditional commercial districts (Pregliasco, 1988, p.15):

- height
- width
- setback
- proportion of openings
- horizontal rhythms
- roof form
- materials
- color
- sidewalk coverings
- signs

These attributes are typically documented with photographs, annotated elevations and sections, and maps.

Mapping. The relationship between mass and space on a site and its surroundings can be assessed through a *figure ground* analysis. This is a graphic method of visualizing the building patterns on a site and within the site's adjacent areas (Figure 7-4). This involves mapping just two elements: (1) buildings, and (2) the spaces between the buildings. The pattern of solids and voids reveals a site's sense of enclosure or openness of the urban texture surrounding the site. This can be useful in determining not

Figure 7-4 Figure ground diagram showing building "footprints" superimposed on a vertical aerial photograph. Figure ground diagrams effectively simplify urban texture. This technique facilitates a visual assessment of this important contextual attribute. *Source:* The HOK Planning Group.

only the location of any new buildings, but also each building's "footprint." An orthophoto has the geometric qualities of a map. The relief displacement of a standard vertical aerial photograph has been removed so that the ground features in an orthophoto are displayed in their true ground position. This property allows direct measurement of distance, areas, and positions. Orthophotos may also display cultural features that are omitted on other available maps. Land cover information on digital orthophotos can be used to create site base maps, figure ground maps, and other attribute maps of the site and its context.

HISTORIC RESOURCES

Cultural resource assessments inventory the location, quality, and historic significance of buildings and other human-made elements, as well as prior land uses (Figure 7-5). Historic resources include bridges, buildings, walls, signs, and many other significant structures or elements built in previous eras. In the United States, the National Historic

Figure 7-5 Historic timeline showing major historic and cultural events occurring within the region of a greenway planning project near St. Louis, Missouri. *Source:* The HOK Planning Group.

Preservation Act (NHPA) affords legal protection to buildings, bridges, and other structures registered on the list of nationally significant historic resources. Programs and policies aimed at protecting and restoring historic resources also exist at the state and local levels.

The criteria for designating the historic significance of a structure or site include age, quality, rarity, and representativeness. The style of architecture and the significance of the historic resource in comparison to other similar buildings in the state or region are important factors to consider in a site inventory.

Mapping. Sanborn maps are detailed city maps that were originally created for the fire insurance industry in the United States. These maps are developed through field surveys, and they provide detailed information on building "footprints," heights, construction materials, uses, and other building attributes (Sanborn, 1999). Sanborn maps are commercially available as georeferenced vector or raster GIS data layers. Additionally, more than 750,000 Sanborn maps have been donated to the United States Library of Congress (Sanborn, 1999).

Other historic resources that might be mapped include historic districts, churches, houses, fountains, bridges, and monuments. Historic areas may be mapped as "overlay districts," with special local land use controls. These maps are available from local planning agencies. In inventories of cultural resources, historic districts may be mapped to illustrate the site's cultural context (Figure 7-6). The architectural resources within historic districts also may be mapped (Figure 7-7).

PERCEPTUAL QUALITY

Maslow's (1954) hierarchy of human needs suggests that basic needs must be satisfied before higher-level secondary and tertiary needs can be satisfied. Physical safety and security—along with food, clothing, and shelter—are the most basic needs in the hierarchy. Human perceptions of a site's safety and security vary among individuals of different age, gender, and other demographic attributes. Our ability to see, smell, taste, touch, and hear give us access to extensive information about our surroundings. Medical researchers are just beginning to understand the powerful linkages between mind and physical well-being. Human perception of land-based amenities—and disamenities—involves at least three senses: hearing, sight, and smell. Consequently, visual quality, sound quality, and air quality are relevant in land planning and design. The significance of these different attributes depends on the site and its context, of course, but also on the program. Perceptions of a site are formed primarily, however, through the sense of sight. A visual resource assessment is concerned with both visibility and visual quality.

Visibility

A site's context plays an important role in land planning and design. Land use on adjacent sites can influence, in several different ways, the suitability of a site for a development or redevelopment program. Adjacent land uses may affect a site through sights, noises, odors, and other perceptible impacts. The distance around a site that is relevant to how the site will be used in the future varies, of course, with what can be seen from the site. The identification of viewsheds, or areas visible from specific locations on the

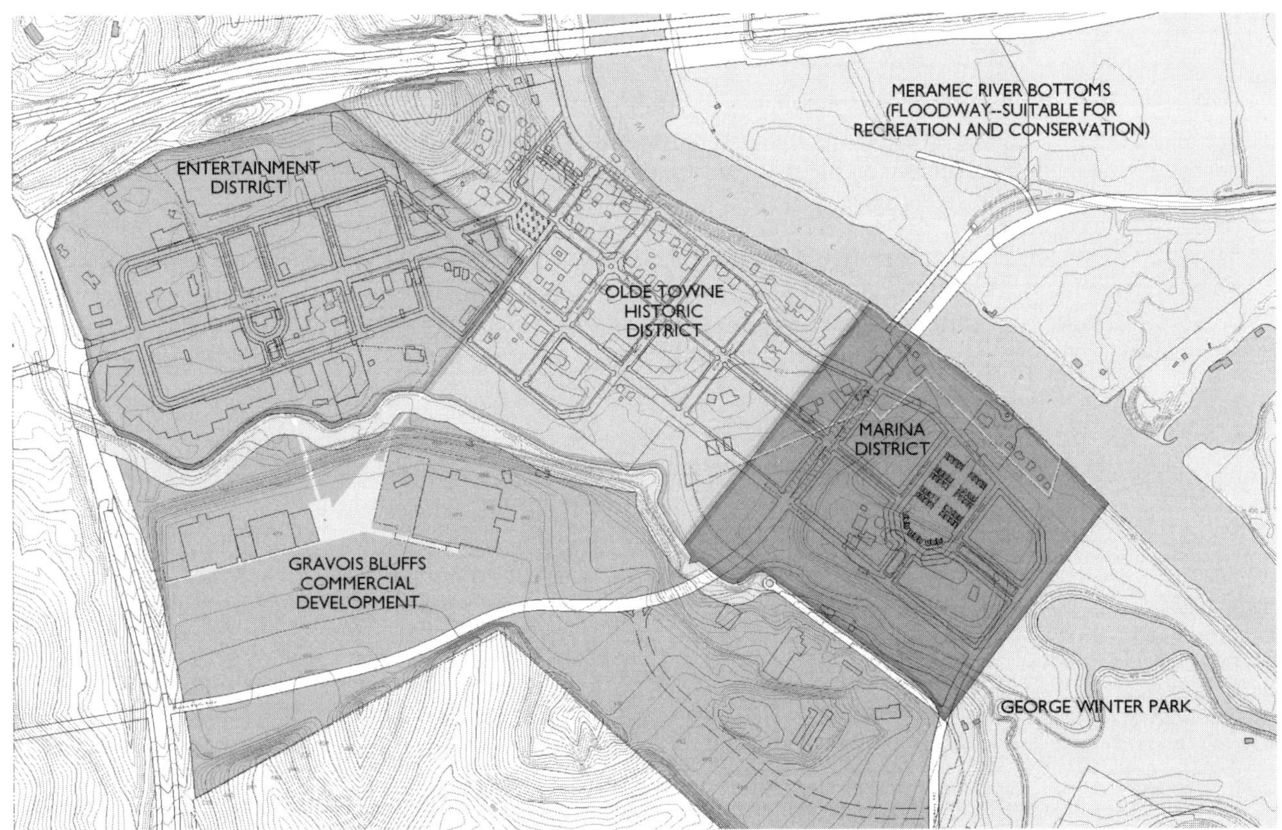

Figure 7-6 Inventories of cultural attributes include mapping of visually and functionally distinct urban districts. This map shows six districts, including one historic district in Fenton, Missouri. *Source:* The HOK Planning Group.

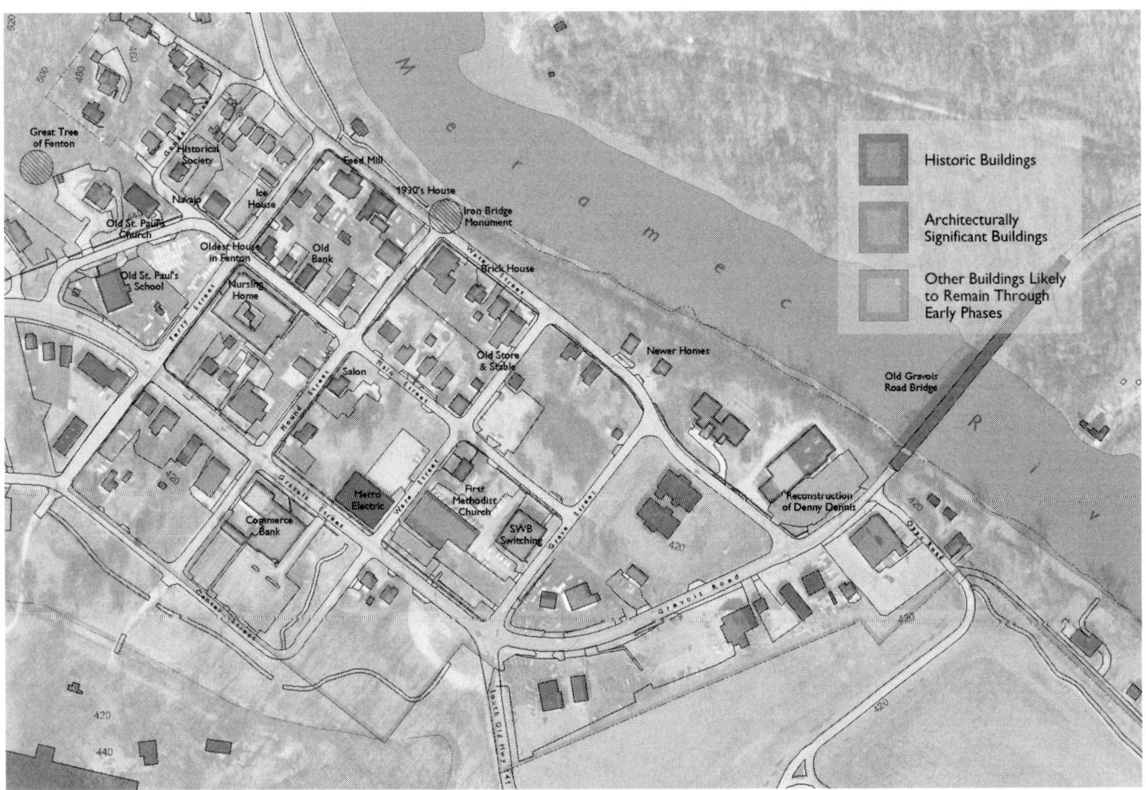

Figure 7-7 Map of historic and architecturally significant buildings within the Olde Towne district of Fenton, Missouri. Three classes of building significance are identified. *Source:* The HOK Planning Group.

ground, is amenable to automation within a GIS. Identifying viewsheds from topographic data alone becomes more complex, of course, when trees and tall shrubs are present to block views. In temperate climates, viewsheds may vary seasonally, too, if the vegetation is deciduous and the leaves are dropped in autumn.

Mapping. A visibility (or viewshed) map graphically shows what locations can be seen from an individual viewing point. A "frequency seen" map characterizes the visibility of locations from two or more viewing points (Computer Terrain Mapping, 1997). Within a GIS, this map can be created by overlaying a series of one-point viewshed maps. A value of "1" is assigned to the visible areas on each layer, and areas that are not visible are assigned a value of "0." The viewshed maps are combined through a polygon overlay process, and the attribute values for all layers are summed. For example, when five viewshed maps are combined, the "frequency seen" or "visibility" values on the output layer could range from zero (locations that are not visible from any of the five viewing points) to five (locations that are visible from all five viewing points). Each visibility class would be depicted with a single color and/or texture.

At the site scale, an inventory of site views should be labeled to identify what can be seen within each view (Figure 7-8). The most common seasonal influence on visibility to and from a site is vegetation. Deciduous trees and shrubs may form an effec-

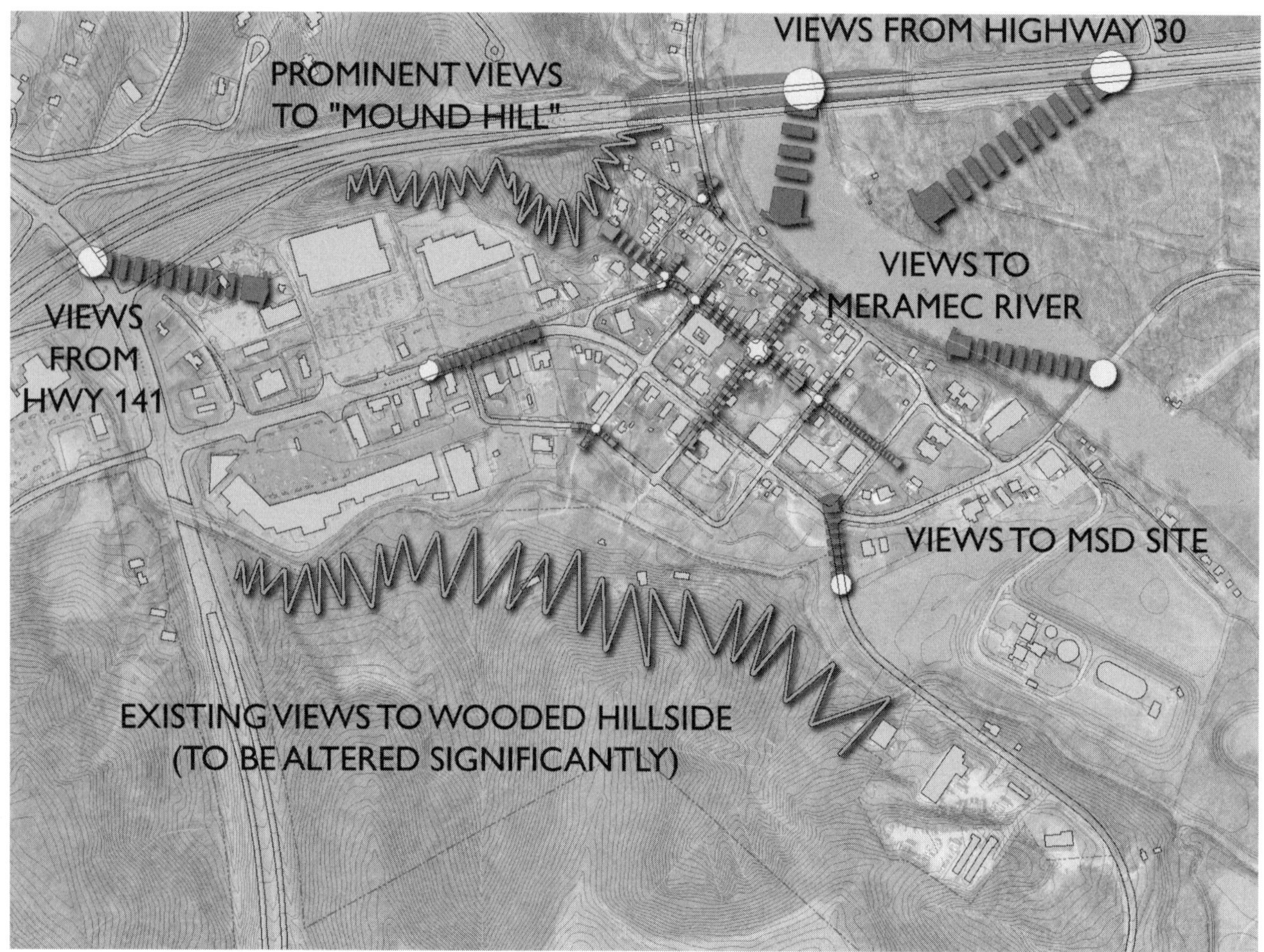

Figure 7-8 Inventory of important views from—and to—a prospective development site in Fenton, Missouri. *Source:* The HOK Planning Group

tive screen during the time of the year in which the plants are in leaf, but during the remaining weeks and months, the leafless plants may provide very little screening of views. The visibility of off-site features may be as important, on some projects, as visibility to on-site features. A site that is heavily forested yet relatively flat, for example, limits views on and off the site. In contrast, in landscapes with long, unobstructed views—as in mountainous terrain or on the open plains—the visible distance from the site can be substantial.

Visual Quality

Visual quality plays an important role in land planning decisions. Two approaches, or paradigms, have been utilized in assessing landscape visual quality. The objectivist approach assumes visual quality (or lack thereof) is an inherent landscape attribute, whereas the subjectivist approach assumes that visual quality is merely in the eyes of the beholder (Lothian, 1999). Although it is true that conceptions of beauty are influenced by culture and experience, the only real significance of this distinction is in the approach that is taken to assess visual quality.

The objectivist approach relies on experts in landscape aesthetics. Evaluations by experts take into account an area's scenic qualities, or visible characteristics, which include form, proportion, line, color, and texture. The subjectivist approach shuns evaluations by trained experts in design or aesthetics. Instead, this approach typically assembles a representative, often randomly selected, group of individuals who provide their assessments of scenic quality. Typically, these assessments or preferences are elicited for a carefully selected set of photographic scenes. A related approach is to provide cameras to the selected individuals and ask them to photograph scenes that they particularly like or dislike.

Kevin Lynch (1960), in *The Image of the City,* proposed a typology of structural elements to explain how people form cognitive maps, or mental images, of the built environment. The five functional elements identified, with examples of each, are:

- edges (e.g., shorelines, roads, and hedgerows)
- paths (e.g., streets, walkways)
- districts (e.g., neighborhoods)
- nodes (e.g., entrances, plazas, street and walkway intersections)
- landmarks (e.g., unique buildings, structures, and natural features)

Views and vistas to natural and cultural features may be site amenities with social as well as economic value. Jakle (1987, p.11) focuses on tourism and sightseeing in writing about landscape visual assessment:

> Tourists come as strangers with accompanying needs to orient to new places. What they see is novel and it attracts attention accordingly. As they seek interest and pleasure in their visual surroundings, they are sensitive to those aspects of landscape, to those places, which portend interest and pleasure.

Visual resources can create, for tourists and for residents, memorable images of place. At the University of Washington in Seattle, for example, the campus layout responds to distant views of Mount Rainier, Washington. Although this mountain is many miles to the east, this prominent physical element serves as a campus landmark.

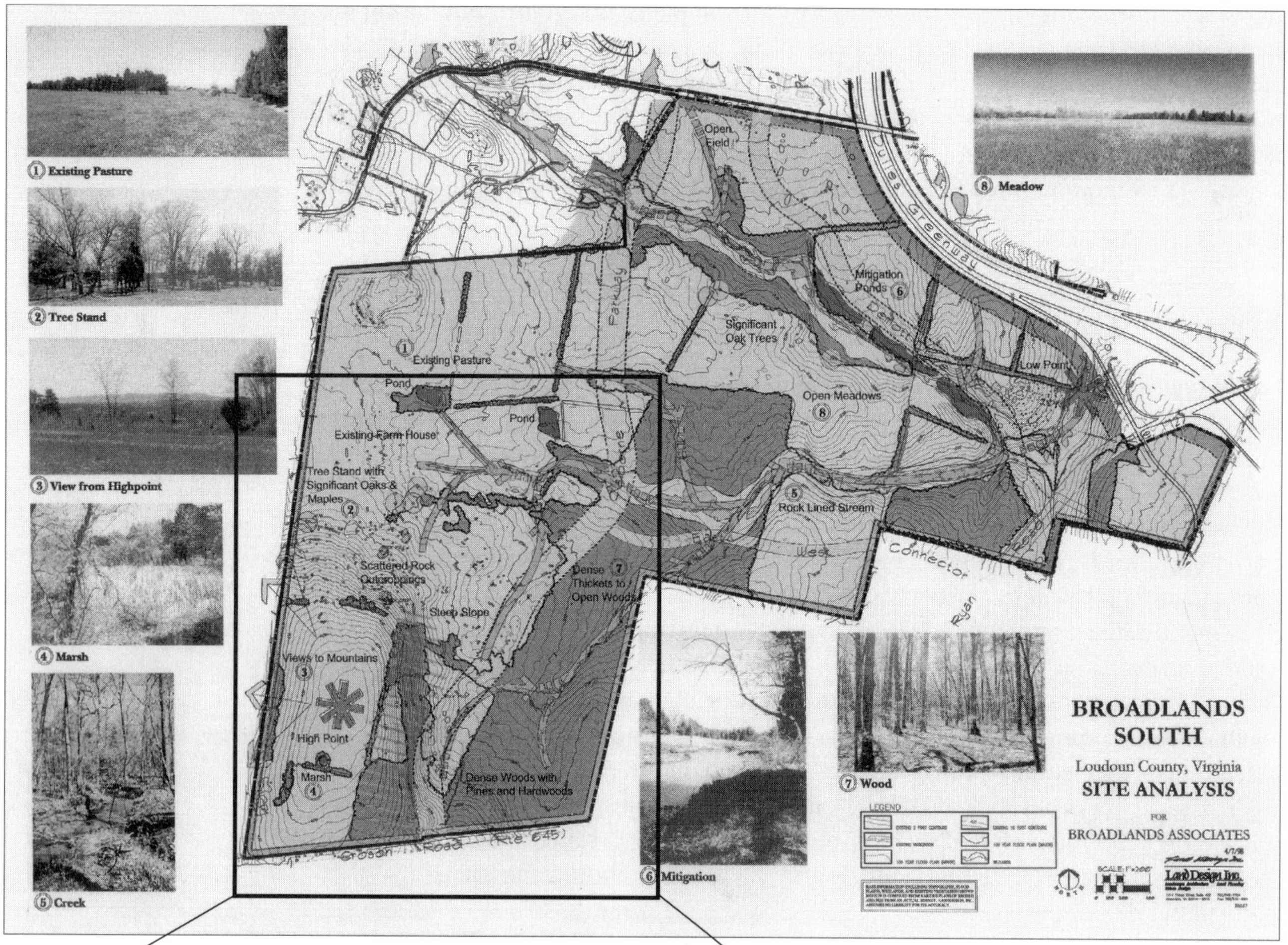

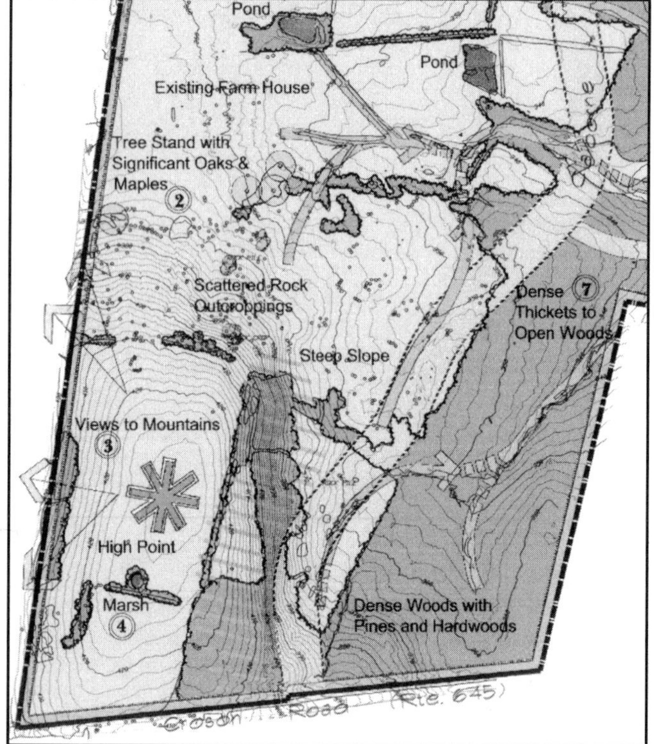

Figure 7-9 The visible context for a project extends well beyond the site's boundaries. *Source:* Land Design.

This visual linkage was strengthened by carefully preserving unobstructed sight lines between the mountain and several major campus open spaces.

Visual quality of the site itself, and the visible off-site features, can be important to the success of restoration and/or development projects. A commercial project is more likely to require good visibility to the site from adjacent streets, highways, and other off-site locations. Visibility is a form of advertising, and this site attribute is typically reflected in increased purchase prices or rental incomes.

Residential real estate, in contrast, often places a premium on seclusion and screening from off-site locations. Proximity to a nearby highway, for example, is usually an undesirable feature that can eliminate sites from consideration for residential development. The visibility of unsightly on- and off-site features is also important. A landfill, overhead wires, and industrial sites are elements that, for many people, degrade a landscape's visual quality.

Views to historically significant buildings, prominent mountains, or other landmarks are important site attributes because they convey a clear sense of place (Figure 7-9). Vertical elements, such as buildings, trees, and landforms, have a substantial influence on landscape character and visual quality. Particularly in hilly and mountainous landscapes, where tourism is an important component of the local or regional economy, the skyline is a significant visual resource. Protecting views and vistas to scenic resources may be a land use policy objective at the municipal and, in some cases, the state or province level. Restricting the heights of buildings in capitol cities are efforts to maintain the visual prominence of each city's capitol building—the symbol of the seat of government. This perceptual quality can be as important as any other attribute to the success of a development proposal or, if the proposal is successful, a completed project. This is particularly true if the project entails residential, commercial, or recreational uses.

Views and vistas, whether aesthetically positive or negative, are important attributes that can play an important role in the site inventory and analysis (Figure 7-10).

Mapping. Visual quality can be depicted on the basis of an area's biophysical and cultural distinctiveness. Distinctive biophysical features include rock outcrops, water bodies, wooded areas, and isolated specimen trees. Distinctive cultural features include both historical and contemporary elements such as cemeteries, stone walls, and ruins, as well as churches and farmsteads. A regional map of visual quality could be divided into a regular grid, and each grid cell rated for visual quality using one of four ordinal classes (Anderson, 1980):

- very unique
- unique
- frequent
- common

This approach also can be taken in documenting the visual quality of sites and other smaller areas. Moreover, the mapping units depicted on a map of visual quality do not need to be uniform in either size or shape. They can be modified to conform with the dimensions of the spaces and features in the landscape.

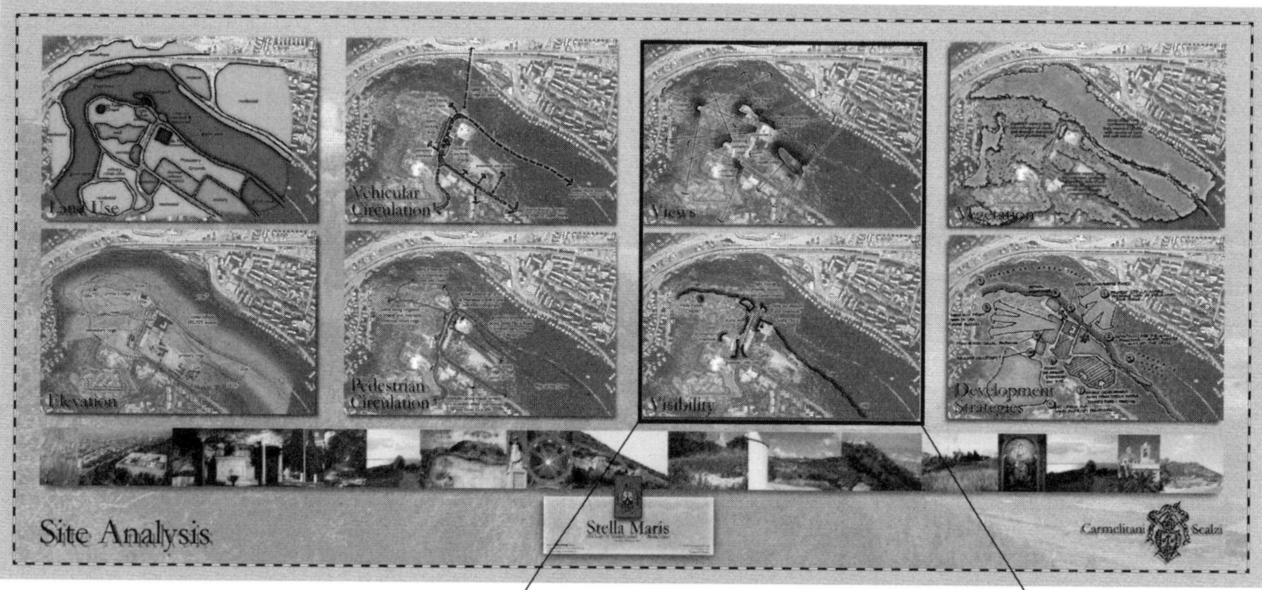

Figure 7-10 Composite set of site inventory maps. Individual maps depict views from the site and the site's visibility from surrounding areas (Haifa, Israel). *Source:* The HOK Planning Group.

Noise and Odors

A site's perceptual quality is affected not only by what people can see, but also by what they can hear and smell. Noise is an attribute that may vary on a daily or seasonal basis. It is an increasingly common nuisance within the built environment. Noise—or lack of noise—has a significant impact on perceptual quality and recreational experiences in outdoor environments. In *The End of Nature,* McKibbon (1989) suggests that a wilderness experience includes freedom from the noise of chain saws. Noise also has an impact on quality of life. Noise can be described in terms of intensity (perceived as loudness) and frequency (perceived as pitch). Both the intensity and the duration of noise exposure determine the potential for damage to the inner ear. Even sounds perceived as "comfortably" loud can be harmful (Rabinowitz, 2000). Sound intensity is measured as sound pressure level (SPL) on a logarithmic decibel (dB) scale. Permanent hearing loss can result from chronic noise exposures equal to an average of 85 dB(A) or higher for an eight-hour period (Morata et al., 1993). However, four hours of noise exposure at 88 dB is considered to provide the same noise "dose" as eight hours at 85 dB (Clark and Bohne, 1999). Common noise sources and loudness levels, measured in decibels (dB), are (Rabinowitz, 2000):

- Gunshot (140 to 170)
- Jet takeoff (140)
- Rock concert, chain saw (110 to 120)
- Diesel locomotive, stereo headphones (100)
- Motorcycle, lawn mower (90)
- Conversation (60)
- Whisper (30 to 40)

Prolonged noise damages the inner ear's hair cells that carry sound to the brain. Not only can noise pollution cause hearing loss, but too much noise also can lead to other human health and development problems. For example, loud noise can delay reading skills and language acquisition skills in children (Hendrick, 1997).

The federal Occupational Safety and Health Administration (OSHA) has set noise standards for the workplace. When noise in work environments is louder than 90 decibels for more than eight hours, employers must ensure that workers wear earplugs or other hearing protection. Hearing protection is recommended for anyone exposed to 85 decibels or higher, especially if the exposure is for a prolonged time.

Odors may be a major problem with sites near large industrial or agricultural operations. The direction of the prevailing breezes is particularly important for land development in the vicinity of these activities.

SUMMARY

Understanding a site's cultural context may involve collection and mapping of a diverse array of data. Legal factors often play an important role in limiting the range and intensities of permitted uses. Land use controls and other legal constraints typically have spatial dimensions that can be mapped. Historic resources may be present on or adjacent to a site, and may require special treatment. Visibility and visual quality play an increasingly important role in influencing land use preferences and real estate value, and these, too, must be addressed in the site inventory. Finally, cultural atrributes include the physical infrastructure of streets, utilities, and buildings. Depending on the land use program, any of these attributes can have a significant influence on how the site is ultimately designed and developed.

BOX 7-1 In Practice

Visual Resource Assessment

Oklahoma City, Oklahoma

Consultant
Edward D. Stone, Jr. and Associates
Fort Lauderdale, Florida

Project Goals
Assess the visual resources within several highway corridors, and determine the region's potential for scenic quality enhancement.

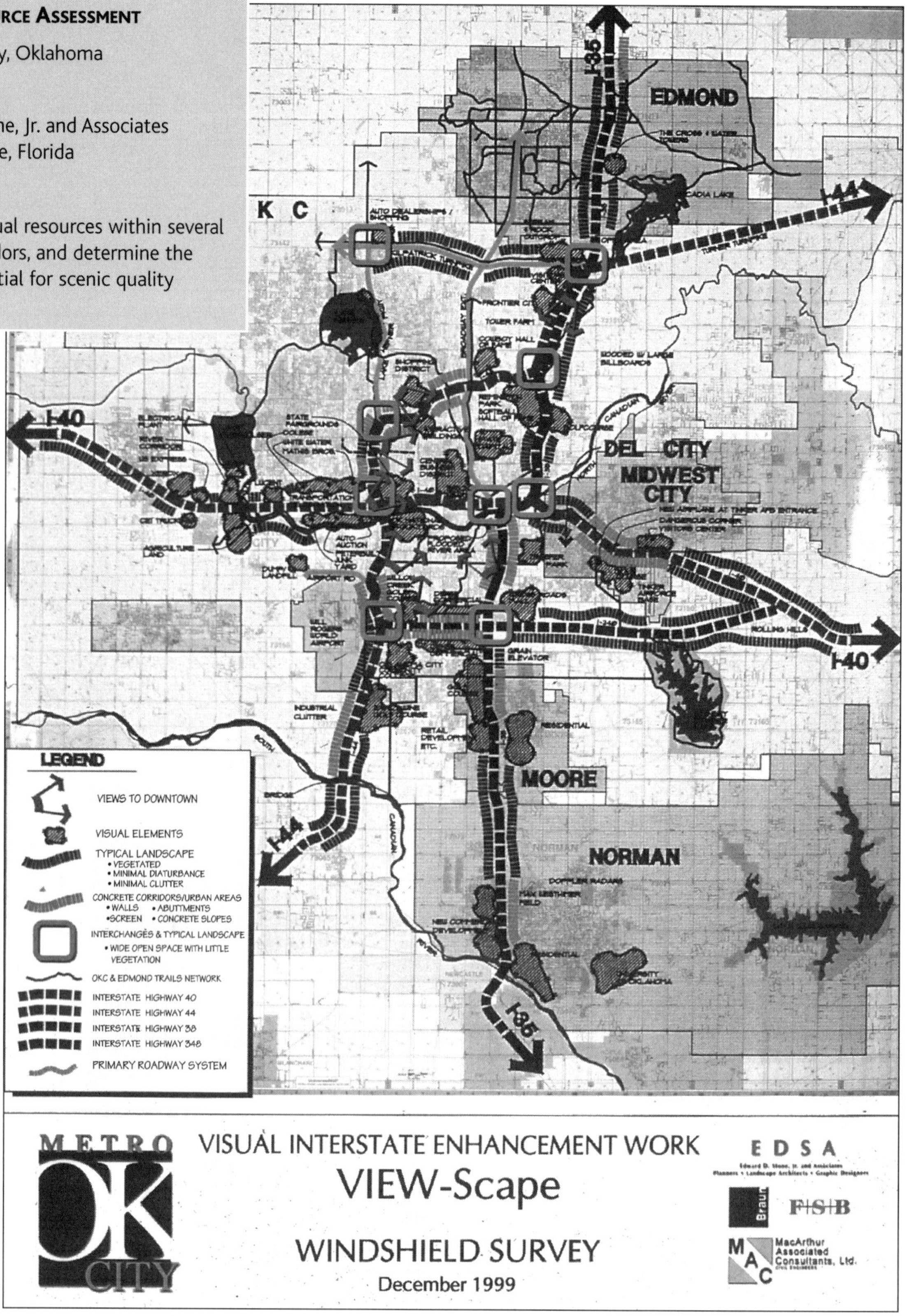

METRO OK CITY

VISUAL INTERSTATE ENHANCEMENT WORK

VIEW-Scape

WINDSHIELD SURVEY

December 1999

Figure B7-1 Windshield survey of views along 85 miles (130 km) of important highway corridors. *Source:* Edward D. Stone, Jr. and Associates.

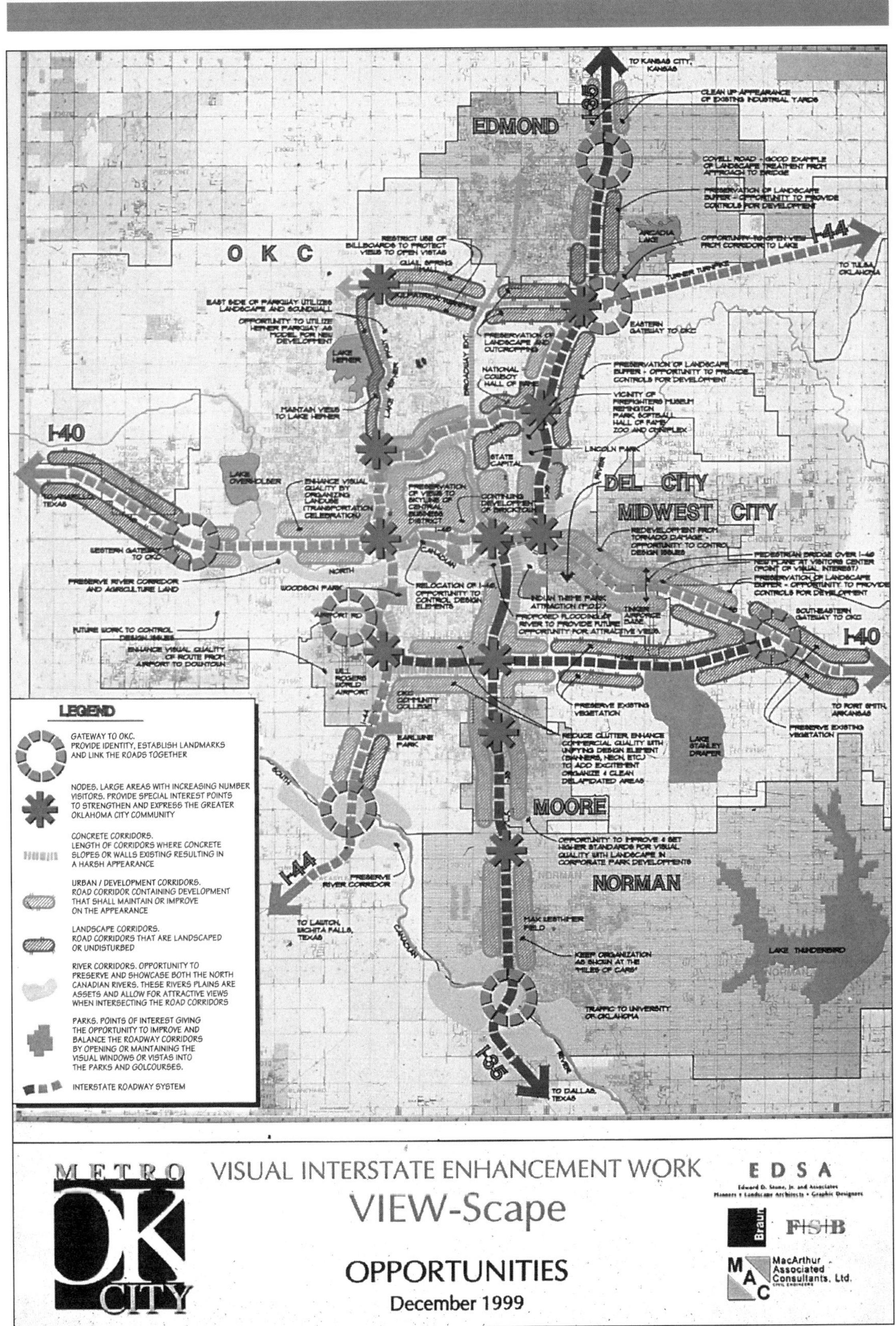

Figure B7-2 Opportunities for enhancing scenic quality within the areas visible from the major highway corridors. *Source:* Edward D. Stone, Jr. and Associates.

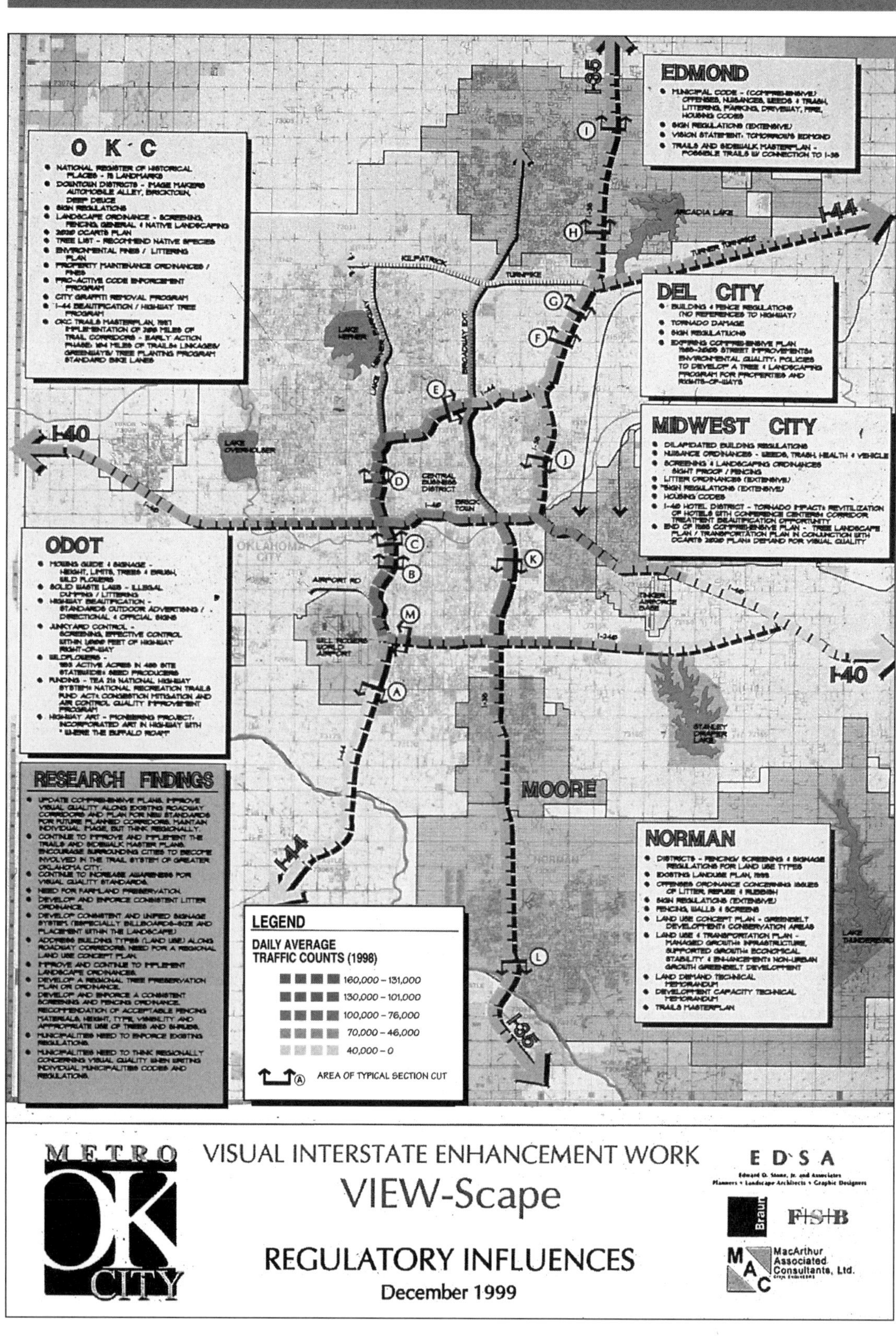

Figure B7-3 Influences of regulations on visual quality within the viewshed corridors. *Source:* Edward D. Stone, Jr. and Associates.

CHAPTER

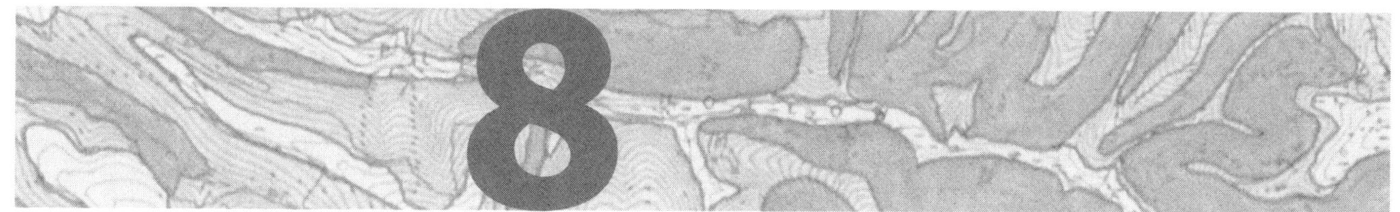

Site Analysis: Integration and Synthesis

Look and you will find it—what is unsought will go undetected.

—Sophocles

INTRODUCTION

A site analysis is a program-driven assessment of a site's physical, biological, and cultural attributes. The site analysis identifies the opportunities and constraints for a *specific* land use program. Therefore, a site analysis is a *diagnostic* process, and not just a matter of descriptive mapping. The attribute maps created in the site inventory provide the physical, biological, and cultural data needed for this program-specific analysis.

The amount of land on a site that is suitable for development is determined during the site analysis phase. Some parts of the site may be unsuitable for development because of inherent physiographic constraints. These constraints include shallow bedrock, steep slopes, and highly erodible soils. Other parts of the site may be suitable for development but relatively inaccessible. Lack of access to part of a site may be due to intervening site conditions, such as water and wetlands, or to property boundaries that preclude alternative access routes. These physical and legal barriers substantially increase the costs of extending roads and utilities to the isolated areas. Consequently, pockets of developable but inaccessible land, in addition to accessible but undevelopable areas, can make the original program objectives unfeasible. An overly ambitious set of program objectives is a common reason for revising the project program.

Selecting the appropriate approach to the site analysis depends on the site and the program. On relatively large sites, especially where built elements will cover a minor fraction of the parcel's surface area, land use suitability analysis may be an appropriate first step. Site inventory maps are the input data required for this analysis. Suitability maps are created for individual land uses or for clusters of similar uses. Suitability of the site for development may be expressed in several ways. Typically, suitability for development is interpreted to mean the site's suitability for the construction of roads and buildings. In more rural areas, site suitability may also consider the soil's capacity to accommodate on-site wastewater treatment systems — or specific agricultural uses, such as vineyards.

The suitability analysis can be further refined by dividing development — a broad land use category — into specific types. For example, if residential, commercial, or industrial uses are planned for a site, the suitability analysis may consider locational criteria that apply to each individual land use category. Locational criteria for each land use type must be identified, and then the relevant attribute layers analyzed for each set of criteria. Areas on the site that either meet or fail to meet the specified location criteria should be identified and mapped.

Development suitability is a function of a site's opportunities and constraints. Opportunities are favorable, suitable, or advantageous locations on the site. These areas have attributes that are either essential for a use to occur, or they facilitate access to the area where the use will occur. Constraints, however, are locations that are unsuitable or restricted for a particular use. Constraints exclude or prevent that use from occurring as desired, or they increase the difficulty or cost of putting the use at that particular location. Neutral areas are locations that are neither opportunities nor constraints.

Constraints may exist on the site itself, or in the area surrounding the site. Constraints may reduce site development potential or increase development costs. A constraint could be a project liability, particularly if it is a nuisance that will negatively impact the developable parts of the site. But development constraints can also be amenities that enhance a site's visual character (or sense of place) and increase the economic value of the land and future development. Although not mutually exclusive, several major types of development constraints are summarized in Table 8-1.

TABLE 8-1 Selected development constraints. Any location on a site could fall into one or more of these constraint categories.

Constraint	*Examples*
Ecological infrastructure	Aquifer recharge areas, wetlands, surface water, critical wildlife habitat
Health or safety hazards	Natural hazards (e.g., fault line, floodplain, landslide)
Physiographic barriers	Steep slopes, highly erodible soils, shallow bedrock
Natural resources	Prime farmland, sand and gravel deposits
Historic resources	Historic buildings and structures, archaeological sites
Legal restrictions	Wetland regulations, zoning codes, easements, deed restrictions
Visual amenities	Specimen trees, scenic views
Nuisances	Undesirable views, noises, or odors

Site constraints vary greatly among different combinations of site and land use program. Moreover, any particular land use may be limited by one or more site constraints. Therefore, the site analysis must be tailored to each unique combination of site and program. Traditional site analysis—as practiced by site planners such as Frederick Law Olmsted—is a synthetic analysis of all important site factors. Before overlay approaches to site analysis were developed, the site analyst walked the site and gathered information visually. This approach requires a significant amount of knowledge, skill, and experience. A modern variation of this method can take advantage of contemporary computing capacities. Site inventory maps and land use suitability maps may be considered in this step, along with any other useful sources of site data (Figure 8-1). The result of this process is typically a single map that presents the composite site analysis.

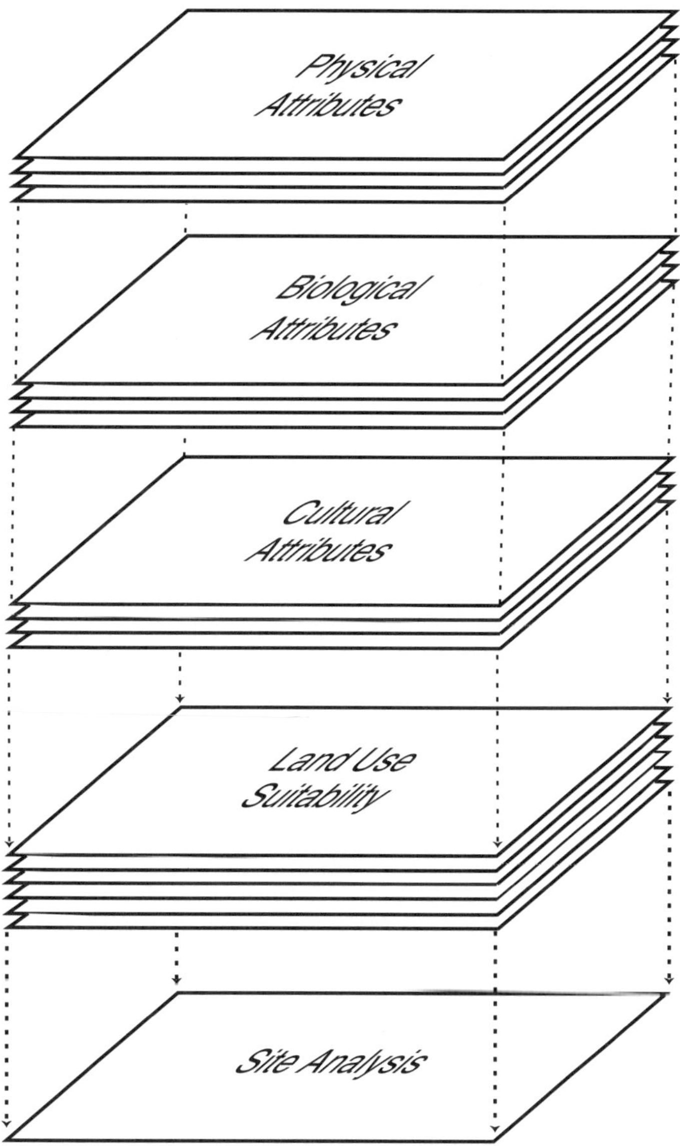

Figure 8-1 Diagram of the relationship between attribute mapping, land use suitability analysis, and site analysis.

SPATIAL ANALYSIS FUNDAMENTALS

Data Accuracy

Data accuracy is an issue that has received greater attention as applications of spatial information technologies have become more common. How accurate do data layers need to be? The answer to that question depends on the purpose for which the data will be used. A parcel boundary map, which is the basis for property transactions, must be highly accurate (e.g., within a few centimeters). Spatial data accuracy for other attribute data, such as slope gradient, can be less accurate, perhaps to within a few meters.

Single Attribute Analysis

In the book *Design With Nature,* McHarg (1969) advocated a land use planning process called "environmental determinism." This decision-making process relies on biophysical factors to drive land use allocation decisions. McHarg's book brought overlays, and overlay analysis, to the attention of land planners and environmental scientists. Geographic information system software is continually being refined, and these programs facilitate the analysis of single as well as multiple overlays, or attribute layers.

Partitioning

The analysis of a single attribute layer may have several objectives, but the primary objective usually is to find areas that meet a given condition. This condition, or conditions, could be locations on the site where attribute values are either:

- greater than a specified minimum (e.g., elevations at least 1 meter above sea level)
- less than a specified maximum (e.g., slopes less than 20 percent)
- within a specified range (e.g., slopes with southwestern, southern, or southeastern aspects)

A GIS database consists not only of maps, but also tables of data that are linked to the points, lines, and polygons on the maps. These tabular data values provide information about the location and attributes of each map unit. The analysis of an individual attribute layer, therefore, is a process of partitioning the spatial distribution of attribute values. When this partitioning occurs within a GIS, locations with the specified attribute conditions can be easily identified.

Buffering

Buffering is used to identify locations within a specified distance of one or more reference points, lines, or polygons (Figure 8-2). For example, buffering may be used to locate areas within a specified distance of:

1. natural resources requiring protection from development (e.g., wellheads, wetlands, habitat of legally protected species)
2. cultural resources requiring protection from development (e.g., historic buildings, battlefields)
3. hazards posing significant risks to human life and property

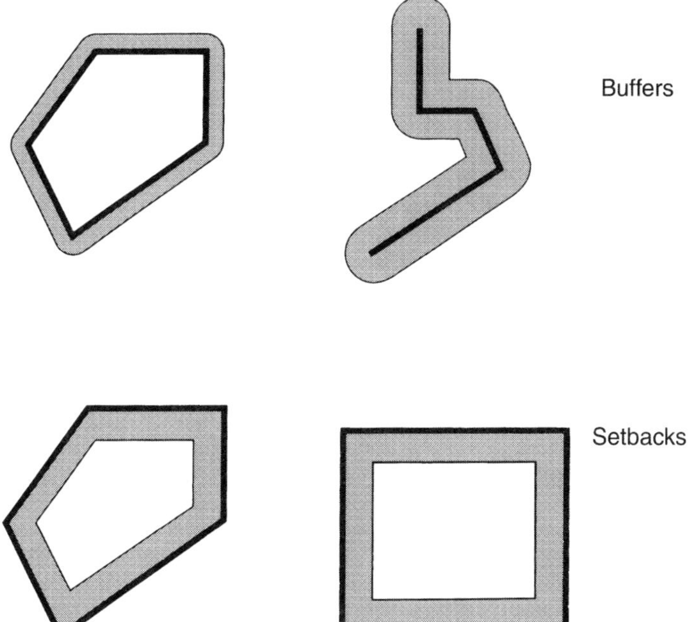

Figure 8-2 Diagram of buffers and setbacks within a GIS. *Source:* Chrisman, copyright © 1997, p. 142, Figure 6-1. Reprinted by permission of John Wiley & Sons, Inc.

The buffering distance can be easily changed and the area within the buffer zone quantified. Chrisman (1997) distinguishes between buffers and setbacks, but the only significant difference between these two is the direction (outward or inward) in which the new area is created.

Possible analyses of these buffer areas include the presence or absence of a single attribute condition (such as vegetation or soil type). In addition to simply indicating the presence or absence of some attribute value, the analyst may want to characterize the quality of a particular attribute. Buffering may be used to identify areas on a site that have the highest value for protecting—or even enhancing—environmental quality. A landscape's ecological infrastructure may include riparian corridors, wetlands, and other similar areas. Buffering might identify, for example, all areas within a specified distance of a stream. This resulting corridor could remain undeveloped and serve as a stormwater purification and infiltration area. Riparian vegetation cover can significantly limit erosion, sedimentation, and chemical pollution of aquatic ecosystems by filtering stormwater surface runoff. The buffer areas also facilitate groundwater infiltration. Other benefits of riparian buffers include the protection (or restoration) of terrestrial and aquatic habitat.

Multiple Attribute Analysis

Although complex spatial analyses are possible with GIS technology, a small number of analytical functions are most useful for land planning and design. The overlay approach to suitability analysis typically involves two or more attribute layers. The intersection and union analyses are two of the most common, and useful, algebraic functions for analyzing multiple attribute layers. For a comprehensive review of these GIS operations, see Chrisman (1997).

Union

The union of two sets of numbers yields a third set that contains each unique number in the two original sets.

{1, 3} Union {2, 3} = {1, 2, 3}

In a GIS, the union function identifies locations where any of the specified attributes occur. For example, the analyst might want to identify all areas that pose severe constraints for excavation and subsequent construction of building foundations. Attribute values that could hinder excavation or construction include shallow depth to water table and shallow depth to bedrock. In an overlay analysis using the union function, all site areas would be identified that meet either one or both of these conditions.

Intersection

The intersection of two sets of numbers yields a third set of numbers that are common to both original sets.

{1, 3} Intersection {2, 3} = {3}

This algebraic function is the conceptual basis for another important type of GIS overlay analysis. With multiple layers of attribute data, a GIS is capable of identifying locations where two or more attribute conditions are spatially coincident (overlap). An intersection might yield, for example, site locations with slopes of less than 20 percent and subsurface conditions suitable for the excavation of building foundations.

Other Combinations

Although modern information technologies provide powerful tools for spatial analysis, there is always a risk of pushing the data beyond the point where the resulting conclusions are valid. A GIS is capable of easily comparing "apples and oranges"—even when these comparisons are inappropriate and could lead to invalid conclusions (Hopkins, 1977; Chrisman, 1997). Weighting schemes, for example, are frequently used to assign priority values to various site attributes. The challenge in using weighting schemes is to identify reasonable weights that can be justified empirically.

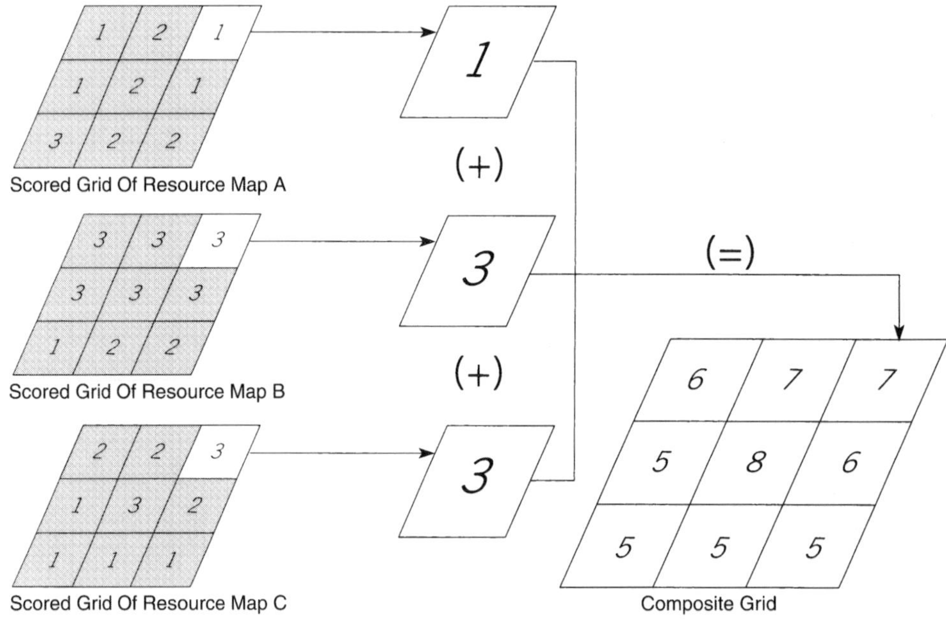

Figure 8-3 Overlay analysis using a linear combination approach. *Source:* Chrisman, copyright © 1997, p. 132, Figure 5-11. Reprinted by permission of John Wiley & Sons, Inc.

Although rules of thumb exist, applied research is needed to develop improved land use siting criteria.

Another concern involves the comparison of completely unrelated physical, biological, and cultural attributes. Although it is mathematically possible to weight each of these different attributes and arrive at an algebraic sum, the significance of the values may be highly questionable. For example, a site analyst may consider visual quality, slopes, and soil erodibility to be the most important attributes for a particular site and program. But how much weight should be placed on each of these potential land use constraints? One could assign, for example, a 15 percent weight to visual quality, 25 percent weight to soil erosiveness, and 60 percent weight to slopes. These are far from trivial decisions.

SITE DEVELOPMENT CAPACITY

Sustainable development, simply put, does not jeopardize the ability of future generations to meet their needs (World Commission on Environment and Development, 1987; Beatley and Manning, 1997). At the very least, therefore, sustainable development requires protection of: (1) ecological integrity and critical natural resources, and (2) our cultural heritage.

Land development, and postdevelopment land uses, can create significant off-site impacts, or externalities, that impose various economic and social costs on others. Yet development can be designed to minimize these impacts and mitigate damage to the environment and society. Rather than using technology and engineering expertise to overcome the intrinsic "difficulties" that a site poses for development, some locations should simply remain undeveloped. Developing in "difficult" natural areas tends to have the greatest hydrologic and ecological impacts. Refraining from developing in certain sensitive or unique areas can be easily justified from an environmental quality perspective, but this also can be supported on economic grounds. Protecting a site's significant natural and cultural resources can be profitable. Fortunately, the real estate development industry has begun to understand the linkage between environmental quality and economic value (Bookout, 1994).

> Good subdivision design involves much more than an engineer's efficient layout for streets and utilities. The most cost-efficient plan often is the rectangular grid layout that became popular in tract-home subdivisions in the 1940s and 1950s. However, the most profitable plan is one that takes advantage of the natural features on a site or provides other interesting features or focal points. (Peiser, 1992, p. 71)

Developing "with nature" is also fiscally prudent for the municipalities in which the development occurs. This approach helps protect public health, safety, and welfare from land-related hazards and reduces the costs of disaster relief after damage has been incurred.

Legal challenges to land use controls in the United States assert that the regulations amount to a "taking" of private property. These challenges generally have been unsuccessful, however, when it could be shown that the land use restrictions were based on measures of the site's intrinsic suitability, or capacity, for development. Determining a site's development capacity requires explicit knowledge of the site's physiographic and cultural constraints.

SUITABILITY ANALYSIS

Process

Suitability analysis, as defined by Steiner (1991, p. 132), is "the process of determining the fitness, or the appropriateness, of a given tract of land for a specified use." Suitability analysis, therefore, is (1) spatially explicit, and (2) program dependent.

A location that is suitable for a particular land use is one that can accommodate the proposed development with the minimum amount of inputs or resources. This concept of site suitability is similar to the U.S. Natural Resources Conservation Service (NRCS) definition for classifying the capability of soils for agriculture. Prime soils, for example, are those that require the fewest inputs for productive agriculture. Locations with prime soils require comparatively less irrigation, less fertilizers and pesticides, and less effort devoted to erosion control.

Most suitability analyses involve the analysis of several site attributes. If conducted within a GIS, with site inventory maps in digital format, suitability maps can be generated for each of the proposed land uses. Land use suitability analysis identifies and maps areas with different levels of development suitability. Suitability maps can be combined in a GIS to create—on a single map—a synoptic analysis of more than one land use class (Figure 8-4). In addition, statistics on the amount of site area in each suitability class can be derived from these maps.

A suitability analysis involves three discrete steps.

1. identify suitability criteria for each anticipated land use
2. collect and map the relevant site attribute data
3. identify the site locations with attribute values that meet the suitability criteria for the targeted land uses

Site attribute layers that are commonly used as input layers for suitability analyses include slopes, elevation, and vegetation type. The suitability criteria are the site conditions that are most desirable—or undesirable—for each land use type. If both suitable and unsuitable characteristics are identified, then a more informative suitability analysis is possible. The result of this analysis is a suitability map for each targeted land use. This map may be the product of either the union or intersection of two or more attribute maps. For example, the intersection of three attribute layers (slope, aspect, and soil drainage) could yield a map showing all locations on the site with slopes less than 20 percent, a southern aspect, and well-drained soils. Different levels of suitability for any given land use can be identified.

An important step in evaluating a site's suitability for specific uses is the selection of attributes and suitability criteria. Choosing appropriate attributes and sources of data are important decisions. In selecting data themes and data sources, several factors should be considered (Anderson, 1980; Pease and Sussman, 1994):

- Data requirements (e.g., for permitting applications to public agencies)
- Data relevance (e.g., data are current and relate to the suitability criteria for proposed uses)
- Data reliability (e.g., data are accurate in location and attribute classifications)
- Data availability (e.g., data exist at the needed scale, or can be affordably acquired)

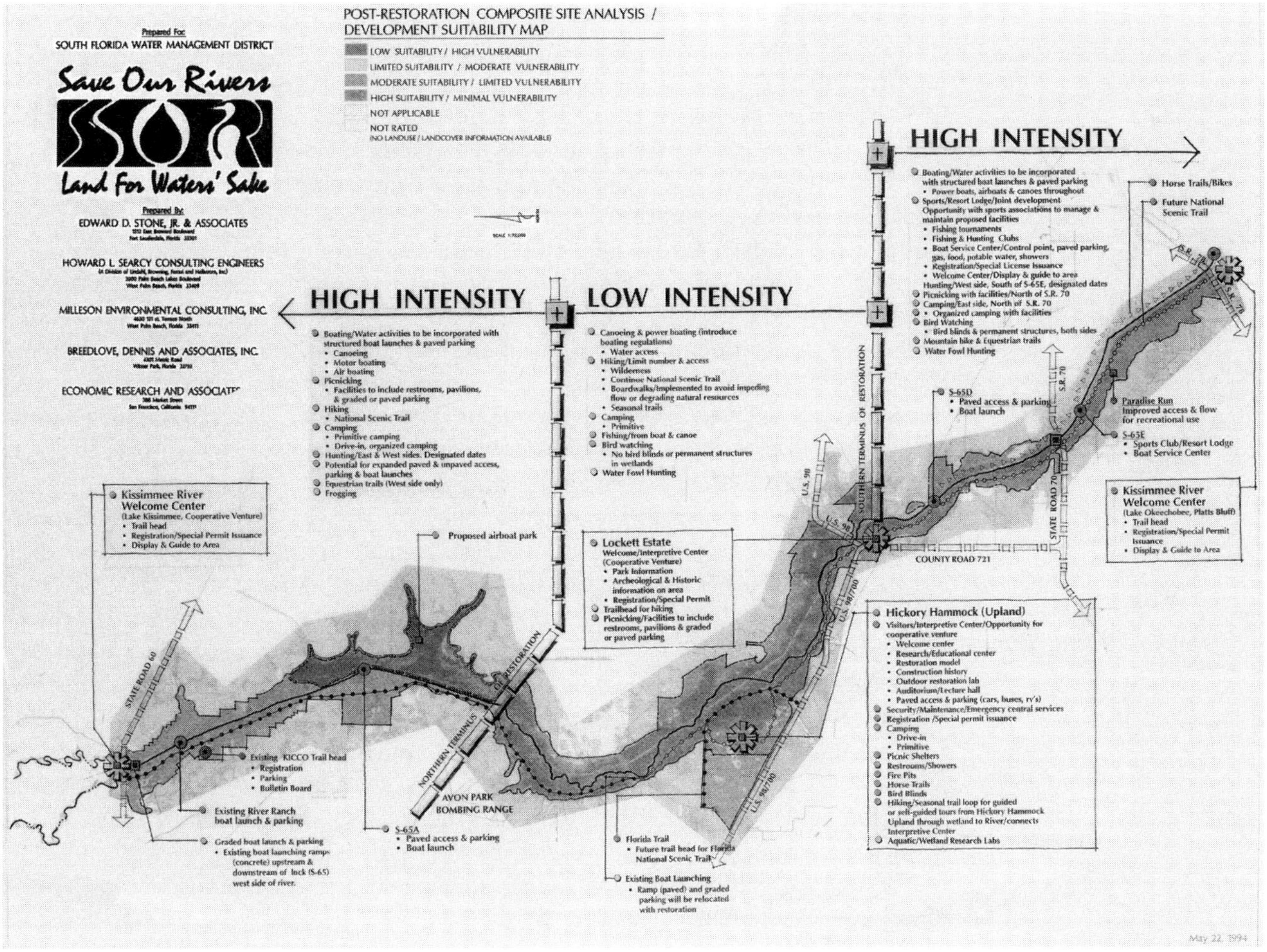

POST-RESTORATION COMPOSITE SITE ANALYSIS / DEVELOPMENT SUITABILITY MAP

- LOW SUITABILITY / HIGH VULNERABILITY
- LIMITED SUITABILITY / MODERATE VULNERABILITY
- MODERATE SUITABILITY / LIMITED VULNERABILITY
- HIGH SUITABILITY / MINIMAL VULNERABILITY
- NOT APPLICABLE
- NOT RATED (NO LANDUSE / LANDCOVER INFORMATION AVAILABLE)

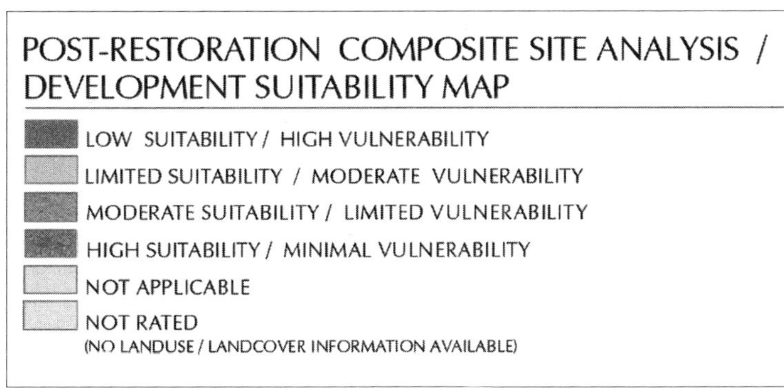

Figure 8-4 Composite site analysis/development suitability map for the restoration of one stretch of the channelized Kissimmee River in central Florida. The project area, analyzed with a GIS, is divided by intensity of future uses. *Source:* Edward D. Stone, Jr., and Associates.

The land evaluation and site assessment (LESA) system, developed by the U.S. Department of Agriculture, has been used by local and state governments to protect prime, unique, or locally important farmland from development (Steiner et al., 1994). The LESA system has been used in determining the boundaries of agricultural zoning districts, identifying farms that are eligible for purchase of development rights (PDR) and transfer of development rights (TDR), and other land use policy objectives (Malloy and Pressley, 1994).

One criticism of the LESA system, as it was being used in the early 1990s, is that it mixed two disparate policy concerns in one aggregate index (Pease and Sussman, 1994). The site assessment model lumped together agricultural productivity and potential for development. Given the objectives of the assessment, these two factors should have been evaluated separately. Although not unique to LESA, another potential problem of suitability analysis is data redundancy. The results of the analysis can be skewed, for example, if some constraints disproportionately influence the results because they are represented by multiple data themes (Pease and Sussman, 1994).

Suitability criteria for a given land use may vary substantially with differences in local and regional conditions. Universal development standards are impractical. Variations in climate, topography, and other landscape attributes preclude a "one size fits all" approach to development standards. For example, maximum feasible slope gradients for housing development will vary with local factors such as soil and geologic conditions, and climate. Locations with subfreezing winter temperatures are much more limiting because of the dangers that icy and slippery conditions create for pedestrians and vehicles. The steep street gradients in San Francisco, California, for example, would be undesirable in a city with snowstorms and freezing winter temperatures. San Francisco's street system—primarily a grid configuration imposed on a hilly landscape—has street gradients much higher than 20 percent, a common development standard. These steep grades would be impractical in cities with colder climates. Snowstorms and other freezing weather conditions would make streets and walkways slippery and dangerous.

A suitability analysis can also identify optimal locations for specific site activities or functions. For example, most land development projects require one or more vehicle entrances to the site. Site factors that might influence the selection of an entrance location include the vertical and horizontal alignment of adjacent roads, existing site amenities such as significant trees or landforms, and views from the site to the surrounding landscape. The suitability of potential locations for the new site entrance could be analyzed by assessing elevation, adjacent land use, and a variety of other attributes. Possible locations for the entrance could be ranked according to the suitability of each alternative location. This analysis could be portrayed by a map with four suitability classes (ordinal scale): no constraints, minor constraints, moderate constraints, and severe constraints. The map would graphically display the suitability of the site's perimeter for one or more vehicle entrances.

Suitability Criteria

Resource inventory maps created by state and federal governments can provide information about the locations of both natural and cultural resources and hazards. But these maps are typically not intended to be the sole source of information for site-level decision making. The boundaries of various mapped attributes, such as landslide hazards or flood hazards, are inexact and may be inaccurate by several meters. The Environmentally Critical Areas Policies and Regulations adopted in Seattle, Washington (USA), recognizes this limitation. These land use controls are linked to site attributes (Table 8-2) rather than to constraints maps:

> When specific actions are proposed in or adjacent to mapped critical areas, more detailed review may be required. Projects located within a mapped area could be exempted from the regulations if the applicant can demonstrate that the site does not, in fact, meet the definition of the critical area. Conversely, developments outside of the mapped area could be covered by the regulations if it is shown that the site does, in fact, meet the definition. (Marks, 1997, p. 231)

TABLE 8-2. Criteria for defining and mapping environmentally critical areas in Seattle, Washington.

Critical area	*Attributes*
Landslide hazards	Known landslide areas Slopes greater than 15 percent with specified geologic conditions Slopes greater than 40 percent Previously altered slopes greater than 40 percent
Liquefaction hazards	Identified by the U.S. Geologic Survey
Flood hazards	Areas on FEMA flood insurance maps
Abandoned solid waste landfills	Sites listed by the State Health Department Areas within 1000 feet of methane-producing landfills Sites identified by public or historical research
Toxic disposal sites	Sites listed by the State Health Department Sites discovered by historical research, site sampling, or during project review
Steep slopes	Areas over 40 percent slope
Riparian corridors	Class A Riparian corridors of year-round or salmonid water bodies Class B Intermittent streams without salmonids Buffers 100 feet from water body or 100 year floodplain (which ever is greater)
Wetlands	U.S. Fish and Wildlife Service inventory Areas that support a prevalence of vegetation typically adapted for saturated soil
Fish and wildlife habitat	Priority species habitat (identified by State Department of Wildlife) All water bodies providing migration corridors and habitat for fish, especially salmonids

Source: Adapted from Marks, 1997, Table 18.1.

The State Growth Management Act, passed in Washington State in 1990, requires local municipalities to adopt critical areas ordinances that protect wetlands, aquifer recharge areas (for potable water sources), fish and wildlife habitat conservation areas, frequently flooded areas, and geologically hazardous areas (Marks, 1997). The Environmentally Critical Areas Policies for Seattle states:

> The Critical Areas Ordinance should allow land to be developed in accordance with the constraints and opportunities provided by the land itself. All land is not the same. If a person purchases a parcel that is 80% wetland, it is significantly different than other types of property. The same is true with areas subject to landslides or floods. The owner purchased property that contained a wetland, or a landslide area, or a flood plain. The Critical Areas Ordinance should recognize that the reasonable development potential of such properties is less than the reasonable potential of unconstrained sites. The ordinance should permit development that makes use of a site's natural opportunities and that recognizes its natural constraints (quoted in Marks, 1997, pp. 230–231).

Taking a similar approach, a model ordinance for traditional neighborhood development (TND) includes explicit criteria for determining a site's potential building

TABLE 8-3. Constraints and ratios for calculating allowable development density (that is transferred to the developable portions of the site).

Ratio	*Site Constraint*
0.00	Street rights-of-way Floodways within 100-year floodplain
0.05	Wetlands and "very poorly drained" soils Bedrock at the surface Rock outcrops and boulder fields Utility easements for high-tension electrical transmission lines (greater than 69 kilovolts)
0.25	Slopes greater than 25 percent gradient
0.33	"Poorly drained" soils (in unsewered areas) Bedrock within 42 inches of the surface (in unsewered areas)
0.50	100-year floodplains (excluding floodways or wetlands within floodplains) Bedrock within 36 inches of the surface (in unsewered areas)
0.75	"Poorly drained" soils (in sewered areas) Bedrock within 42 inches of the surface (in sewered areas) Slopes between 15 percent and 25 percent gradients
1.00	Unconstrained land

Source: Adapted from Arendt, 1999, p. 100, Table III.B.2.1.

capacity for new housing development (Arendt, 1999). Several constraint categories, each with a different rating, are used to determine the number of dwelling units permitted on the developable areas of the site (Table 8-3). To determine a site's "total adjusted tract acreage," the area of land in each of the constraint categories is multiplied by the development ratio, and these values are summed (Arendt, 1999). This number (total adjusted tract acreage) is then multiplied by the allowable dwelling density in that zoning district. This results in the total number of dwellings (absent density bonuses) that can be built on the site.

Another similar, but broader, approach is described by Nelesson (1994). This method includes an extensive array of physical, biological, and cultural attributes that constitute development constraints. Constraints are categorized into three levels: highest, severe, and moderate. These categories of constraints, with associated ratings, are used to determine the permitted number of dwelling units on the portions of the site without constraints. In addition to the many site constraints listed in the TND model ordinance (Table 8-3), Nelesson (1994, pp. 116–117) also includes:

- Open water
- Aquifer recharge areas
- High levels of toxic waste
- Low levels of toxic contamination (with cleanup or treatment potential)
- Historic or archaeologic sites
- Class I and II agricultural soils (in an active farming community)
- Mature vegetation
- Major viewsheds
- Ridge tops

INTEGRATION AND SYNTHESIS

Site Context

Development sites in suburban and rural areas may be covered with either native or naturalized vegetation. These sites may be on land that has been used for agriculture, forestry, or mining. In these areas, soils may have been highly disturbed and native vegetation destroyed decades or even centuries earlier. Because these sites have never been developed, and they are relatively removed from other development, the analysis of these sites may consider primarily biophysical attributes. In contrast, sites in built-up urban areas would always warrant an additional set of concerns. Because of the more complex context of these sites, the site analysis must consider a wide array of social, or cultural, issues. These more urban sites tend to be comparatively smaller in size, however, so a composite, or integrated, analysis is not only feasible but necessary. The composite analysis communicates — on one drawing or map — all of the existing site and contextual conditions that are relevant to the proposed program.

Site Constraints (and Problems)

Site constraints are a function of the land uses for which the site is being evaluated. Site constraints are locations where the proposed development would be inappropriate or more complex and costly to design, gain necessary approvals, or construct. Building in difficult locations requires comparatively more time and money before, during, and after construction. Steep slopes, for example, are a significant constraint for many developed uses (Figure 8-5). Building foundations on steep slopes must be more complex — perhaps stepping down a hillside — and are therefore more costly to construct. In locations where site drainage is poor or where subsurface materials are unstable, additional design and construction effort is needed to ensure the building's structural integrity. The construction process itself is also more complicated if the site is more vulnerable to development impacts such as soil erosion, groundwater contamination, and the degradation of critical wildlife habitat. Acquiring permits for development on difficult sites is complicated by the potential environmental impacts of the construction process and the post-construction uses of the site. Consequently, development of difficult sites may be economically — or politically — unfeasible.

Building in harmony with intrinsic environmental patterns has been advocated by scientists and planners over the past two centuries. A landscape's ecological infrastructure includes open water, wetlands, aquifer recharge areas, and unique landforms. In Wisconsin, Philip Lewis, Jr., pioneered the concept of environmental corridors. These "e-ways" — representing ecology, education, and ethics — coincided with the location of water, ridge tops and steep slopes (Lewis, 1996). Earlier, in Illinois, Lewis found that most of the state's significant ecological and cultural resources were associated with these locations. Ignoring or discounting potential hazards can lead to expensive — even deadly — disasters. Natural hazards that may impact a site are often weather related. During periods of good weather, the dangers may be absent, but the danger is greatest when relatively infrequent, but severe, weather events occur. Earthquakes, hurricanes, and other natural hazards occur at infrequent intervals. The recurring nature of these events suggests, however, that it's not a question of if, but when, the event will occur.

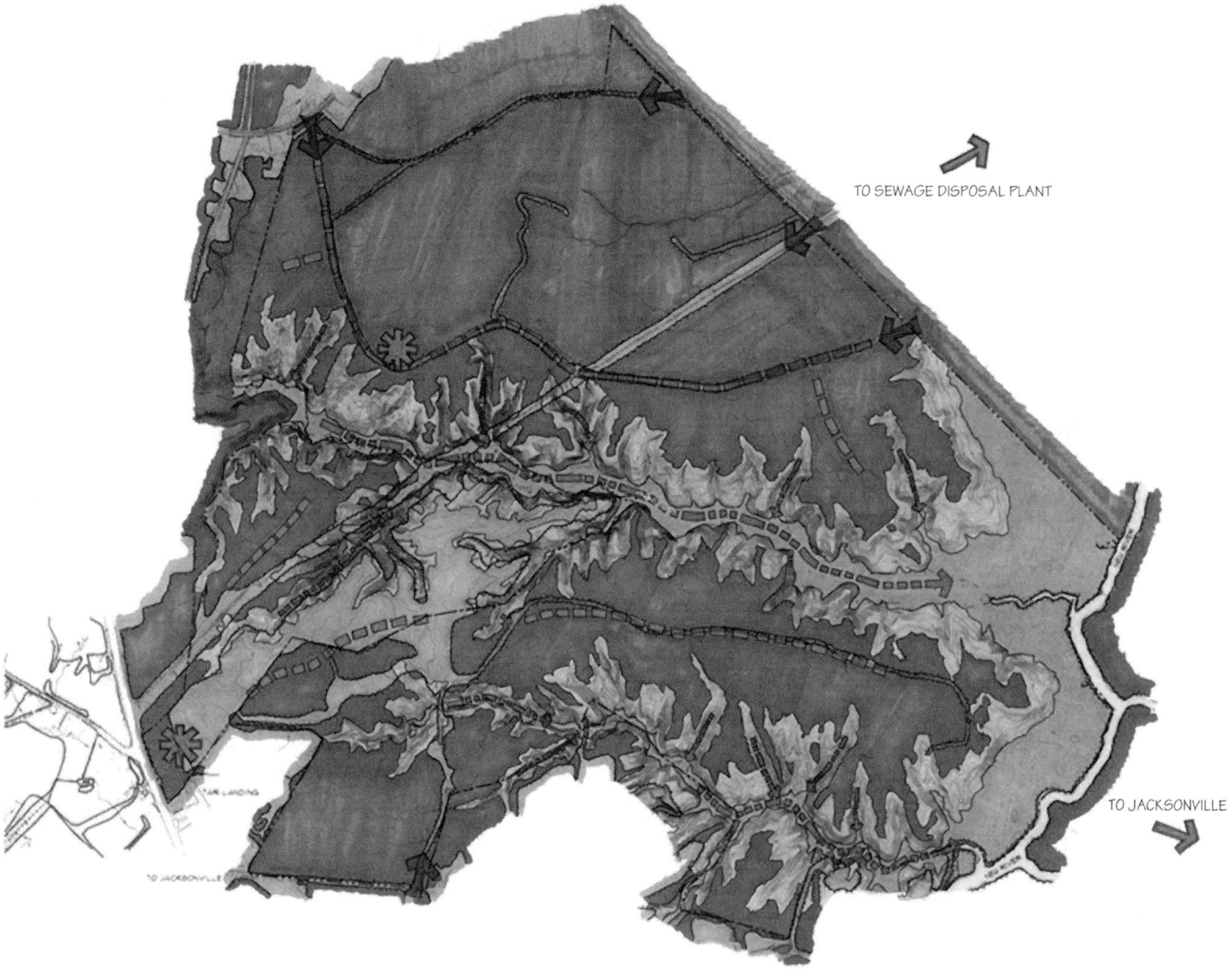

TO SEWAGE DISPOSAL PLANT

TO JACKSONVILLE

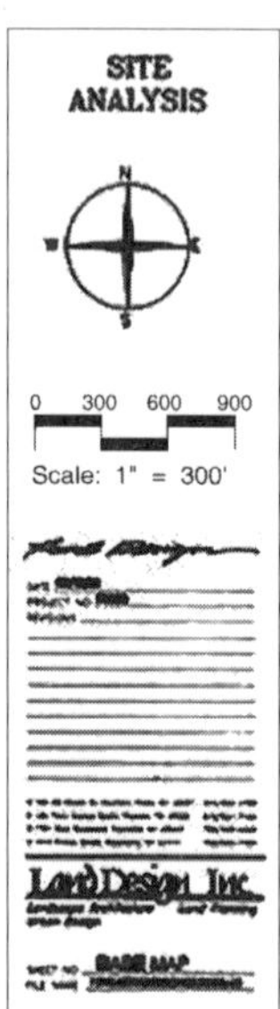

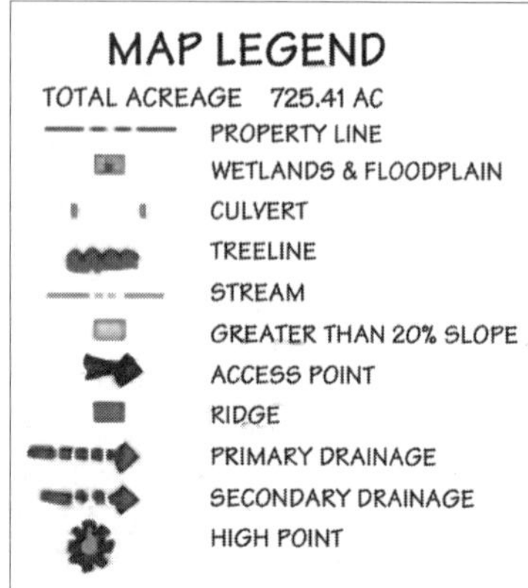

Figure 8-5 Site analysis clearly showing development constraints: drainage patterns, ridges, and areas with slope gradients greater than 20 percent. This analysis also identifies potential site access points to a future industrial park in Onslow County, North Carolina. *Source:* Land Design.

There is little that planners or builders can do to mitigate the effects of tornadoes, with winds of 300 miles per hour or more, on conventional wood-frame construction buildings. Hurricanes, in contrast, are weather events that raise significant land use planning implications. Hurricanes always form over water, so the risk they pose is greatest in coastal communities. Because hurricanes are long-lasting storms, their persistent rains typically saturate soils and exacerbate the threats of local flooding. Advances in building construction methods have reduced the risk of structural failures from storm wind loads. But a hurricane's main threat to life and property is the accompanying storm surge.

Storm surges associated with hurricanes may create walls of water that are at least several meters above normal high-tide elevations. Development in low-lying areas is especially vulnerable. Moreover, mean sea level could rise up to one meter over the next century as the earth's climate continues to warm (Mileti, 1999). That seemingly small increase could have devastating economic implications for real estate along many coastal areas. The least costly public policy option for managing this risk is to discourage development (and redevelopment) in these high-risk areas.

Snow, ice, and rain storms create other hazards. The 1993 floods of the upper Mississippi River demonstrated the destruction that can result when humans underestimate the forces of nature. Levees and dams—meant to channel and confine the river—were unable to contain the river during this flood season. The capacity of the upland areas to infiltrate stormwater runoff was reduced by the presence of buildings, roads, and other impervious surfaces. Flooding is exacerbated in landscapes where buildings, paving, and other impervious land cover substantially reduce the normal capacity of the land to retain and infiltrate stormwater. Earthquakes and volcanoes are also dangerous geological hazards. The shaking forces on buildings, bridges, utility lines, and other structures demand extraordinary design and construction to mitigate the risk. If the risk can be avoided or reduced significantly by not building in the most active areas (fault zones), then this is clearly the prudent course of action.

Urban and other built-up areas are complex environments. Site analyses, in this context, must examine much more than the site's physiographic conditions (Figure 8-6). A broad array of contextual information is needed to determine if new buildings and other site elements will be visually and functionally compatible with the surrounding cultural context. Urban structure, for example, is an important contextual element that may not be obvious from the ground, or even from an aerial photograph. The search for order and pattern within an urban context should be part of the inventory and analysis process. Patterns of mass and space, and the relationships between these basic urban building blocks, can be assessed with figure ground diagrams.

The assessment of context also involves identifying neighborhood and community spaces, and determining what activities and symbolic values are associated with those spaces. The spatial and temporal qualities of "place" are particularly relevant to urban in-fill projects. Jakle (1987, pp. 4–5) comments on these two dimensions of place:

> Certainly, places as behavioral settings have spatial context. They also, however, have temporal dimensions because they open and close at set points in time and thus function for set durations of time, often with cyclical regularity. They are occupied by people (usually a limited range of types), by activities (usually a limited set of general behaviors), and by a limited array of furnishings supportive of those behaviors.

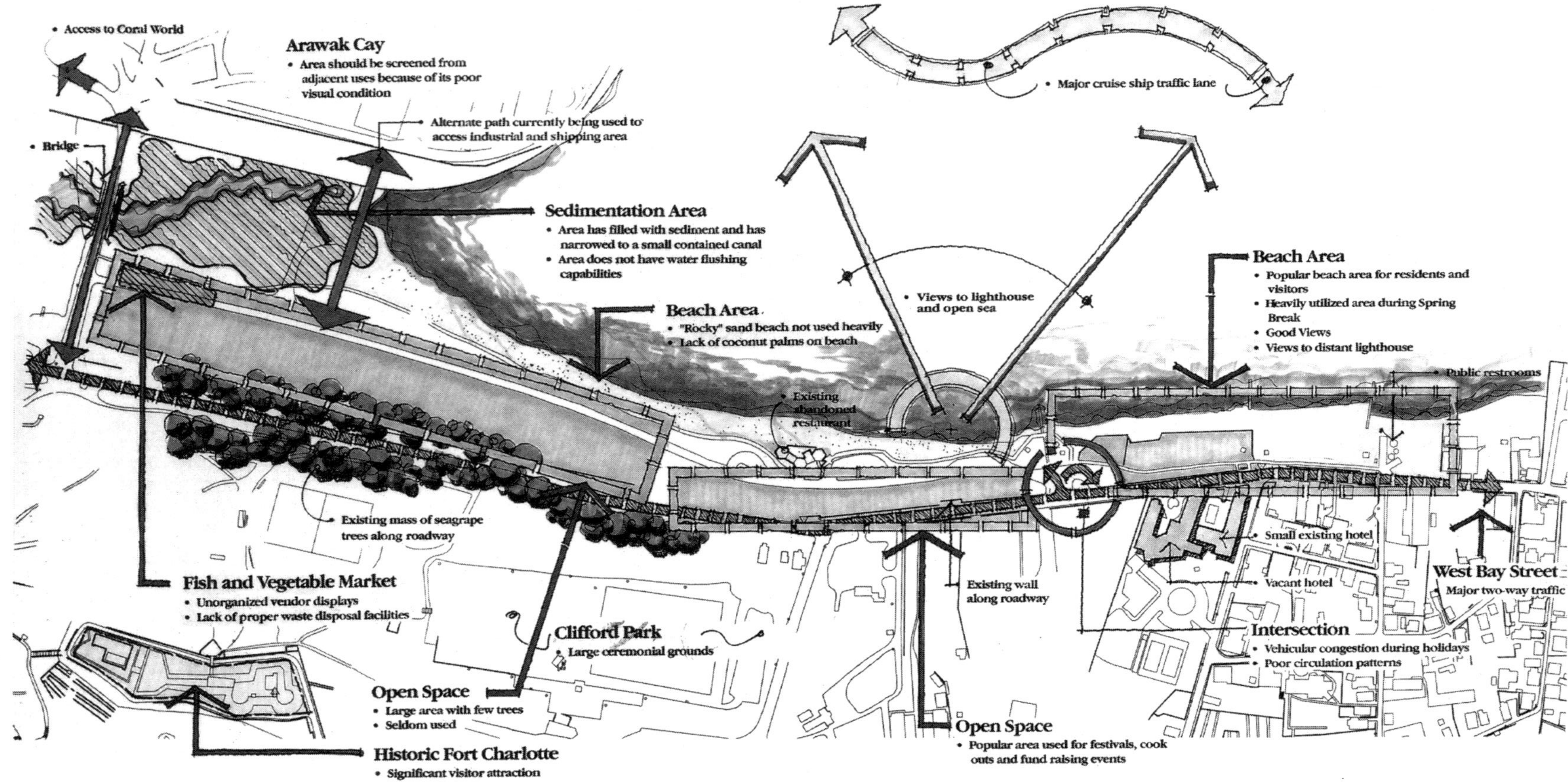

Figure 8-6 Site analysis showing prominent views, pedestrian–vehicle conflicts, local cultural amenities, and a variety of other site opportunities and constraints.
Source: Edward D. Stone, Jr., and Associates.

In urban environments, microclimate also can vary dramatically over short distances. Buildings can create outdoor areas that are relatively sheltered from the wind. In cooler climates, these pockets of calm air — especially if they have access to direct sunlight — can have much milder microclimates than other nearby windy or shaded sites. Exploiting these milder microclimates, or consciously creating them, provides valuable opportunities for outdoor uses of the urban environment.

Yet relatively harsh and uncomfortable microclimates also exist in urban areas. Tall buildings and groups of buildings may deflect or channel winds to create turbulent areas, or virtual "wind tunnels." A lack of solar radiation can also make outdoor spaces substantially colder than nearby areas with full exposure to the sun. Existing — or proposed — trees, buildings, and other structures on or near the site will cast shadows. Understanding these shadow patterns as they vary daily and seasonally is crucial to the site planning process. An urban site analysis, especially, should utilize sun and shade diagrams created during the site inventory.

Depending on the project program, other analyses of specific elements within an urban environment may be warranted. These analyses should assess both positive and negative features — before the conceptual design phase begins. An analysis of pedestrian circulation within, or surrounding, a development site would seek to identify potential entrance locations and existing scenic views. But the analysis should also identify problems, such as:

- lack of walkway connectivity (unfulfilled desire lines)
- inadequate capacity (congestion)
- conflicts among vehicles, bicycles, and pedestrians (safety hazards)
- lack of seating and other site furniture (amenities)

Similarly, an analysis of the architectural context for a downtown revitalization project would certainly seek to identify the positive attributes of the area's better designed buildings. But the analysis must also identify the existing problems or weaknesses of the area's architecture. These problems, which could be addressed in a comprehensive renovation and adaptive re-use program, include:

- large, unarticulated building facades
- facades covered with visually monotonous materials (e.g., concrete, concrete block)
- unbroken rooflines the entire length of the building
- insufficient maintenance

The analysis of urban streetscapes might also reveal a variety of potentially correctable problems. These include:

- lack of spatial enclosure
- poor-quality materials (e.g., paving, seating)
- lack of maintenance (e.g., curbs, walkways, plantings)
- no unifying design theme (e.g., materials, forms, proportions)
- insufficient or excessive lighting
- insufficient seating and other site furniture (e.g., signs, trash containers)

Site Opportunities (and Assets)

A site analysis focuses on more than just site constraints, although this alone is enough to justify a site analysis. Significant site assets also should be identified. Site assets have social, economic, ecological, and aesthetic value. These might include specimen trees or high points with views to natural features such as water or landforms, or to landmark buildings or other significant cultural features (Figures 8-7 and 8-8). These physical assets, if integrated within a development plan, can preserve a site's sense of place and enhance quality of life for future site users. Site amenities also include unique rock outcrops, and historic or culturally significant buildings and structures (Table 8-4). Protecting or enhancing cultural amenities can add value to a completed project and make it more desirable to site users. Another example of a site amenity would be a high point for a scenic overlook adjacent to water (Figure 8-9).

Efforts to protect, or enhance, a community's sense of place involve many small-scale design decisions concerning building size, massing, and placement. Sense of place is not only a result of the number and quality of buildings, it is also fundamentally influenced by the landforms, vegetation, and other tangible and intangible elements within the built environment. Development that does not respond to local site conditions — including the surrounding context — contributes to placelessness in contemporary landscapes. The transformation of pastoral landscapes — most significantly since the end of World War II — has resulted from the interplay of many social, economic, and technological factors. In part, land use changes have been influenced by the international flow of information and materials. Construction methods and materials, for example, have become more standardized.

Efforts to fit a program to a site reflect a design ethic that values both nature and culture. This contextual approach to land development attempts to create places that are "good neighbors" within the surrounding community (Box 8-1). The biophysical and cultural context for a development site encompasses local, community, and regional factors. Michael Hough (1990, p. 180) comments on the biophysical and cultural complexity of regional context:

> Regional identity is connected with the peculiar characteristics of a location.... It is what a place has when it somehow belongs to its location and nowhere else. It has to do, therefore, with two fundamental criteria: first, with the natural processes of the region or locality — what nature has put there; second, with social processes — what people have put there.

According to Hough (1990, p. 186):

> The protection of natural and cultural history — the reuse and integration of the old into the new without fanfare while avoiding the temptation to turn everything into a museum because it is old — lies at the heart of maintaining a continuing link with the past and with a place's identity.

TABLE 8-4 Selected amenities and resources that may be identified for protection or enhancement on a site analysis. (*Note:* some elements could be listed under more than one category.)

Visual Amenity	*Natural Resource*	*Cultural Resource*
Open water	Prime agricultural lands	Historic buildings and landmarks
Ridge tops and high points	Sand and gravel deposits	Archaeological sites
Specimen trees	Aquifer recharge areas	Scenic vistas
Native plant communities	Springs and seeps	

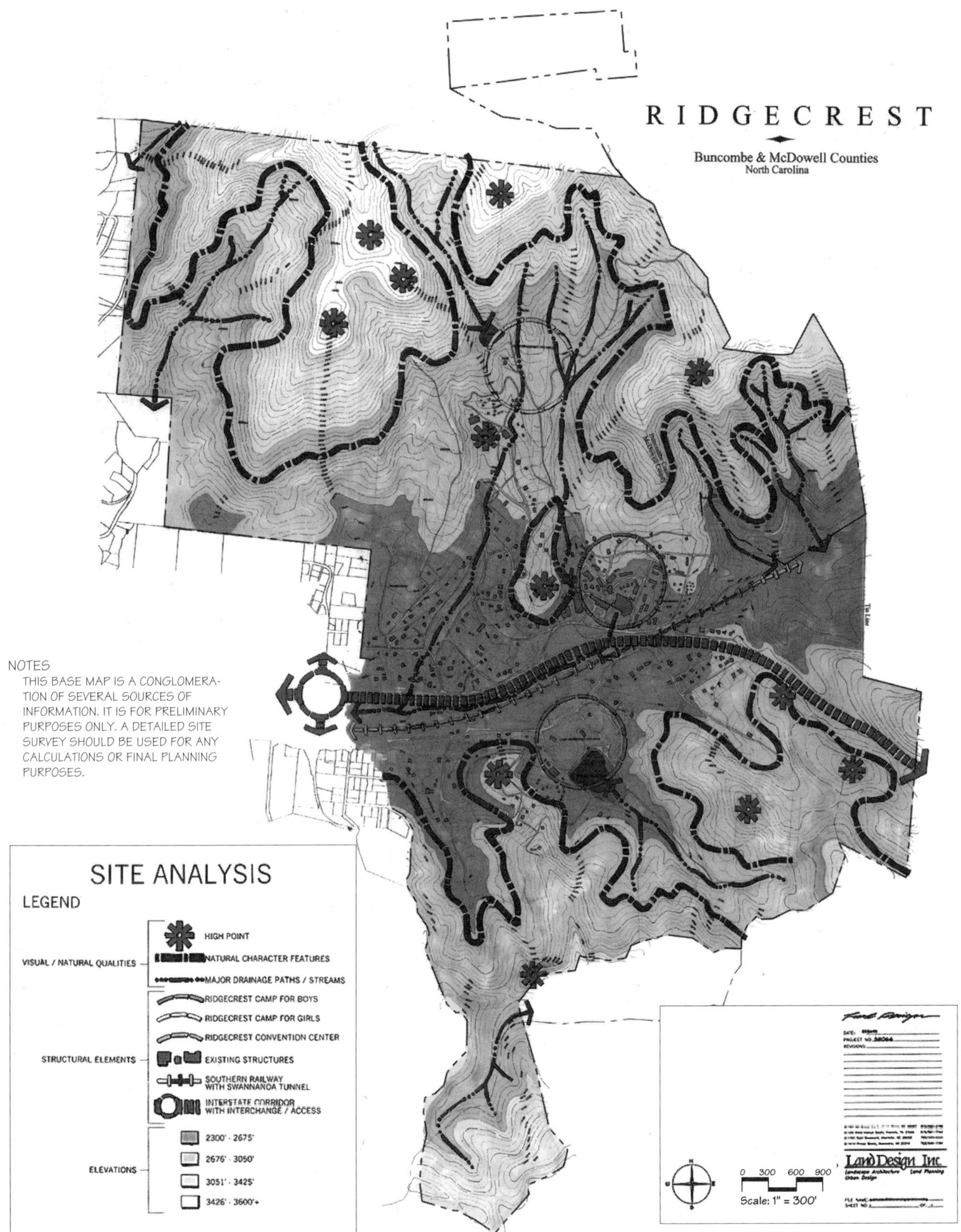

Figure 8-7 Site analysis showing major transportation corridors, drainage patterns, and site high points. The ridges and hilltops, which are clearly identified on the analysis, contribute to the site's visual quality. *Source:* Land Design.

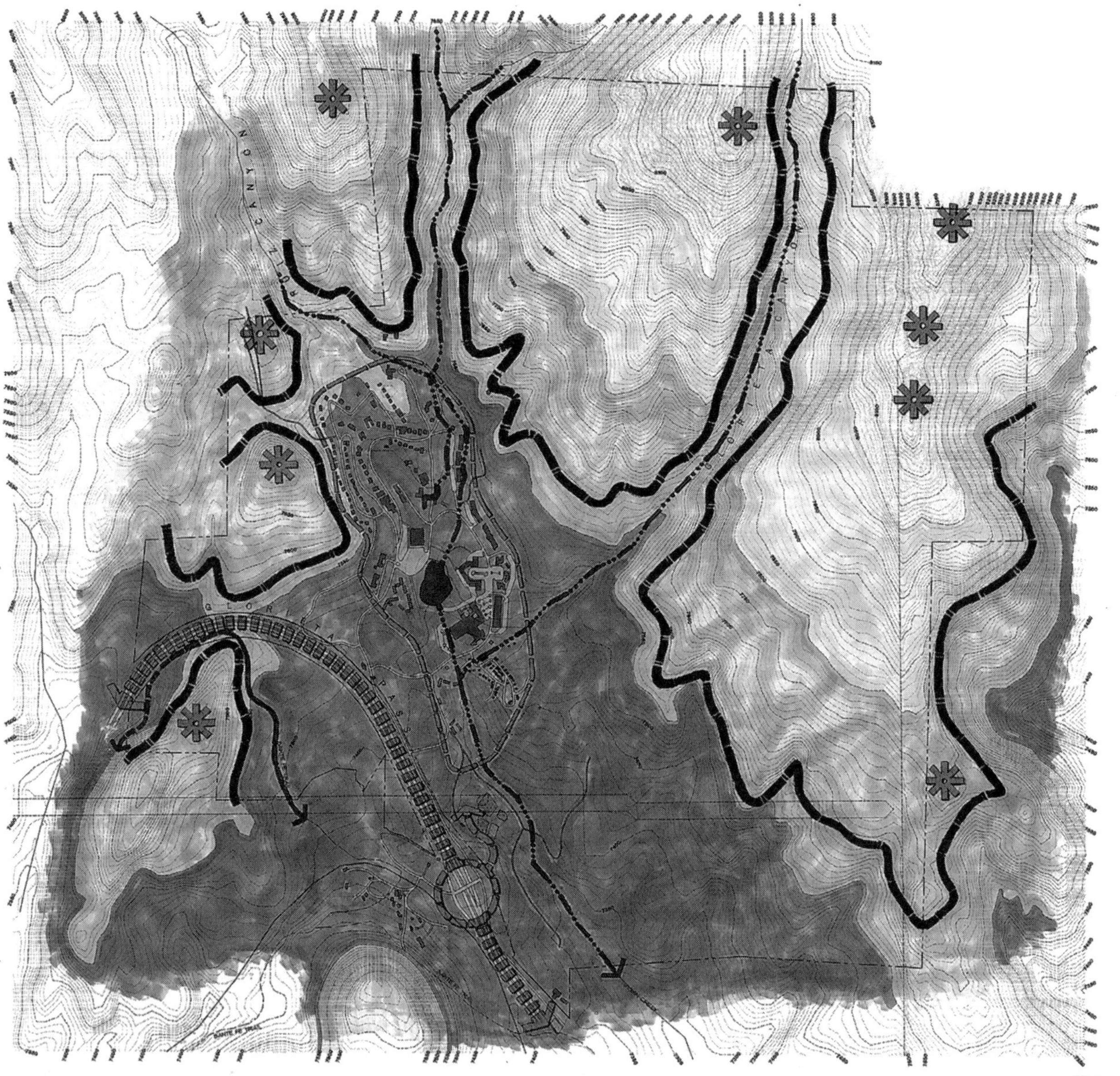

NOTES
THIS BASE MAP IS A CONGLOMERATION OF SEVERAL SOURCES OF INFORMATION. IT IS FOR PRELIMINARY PURPOSES ONLY. A DETAILED SITE SURVEY SHOULD BE USED FOR ANY CALCULATIONS OR FINAL PLANNING PURPOSES.

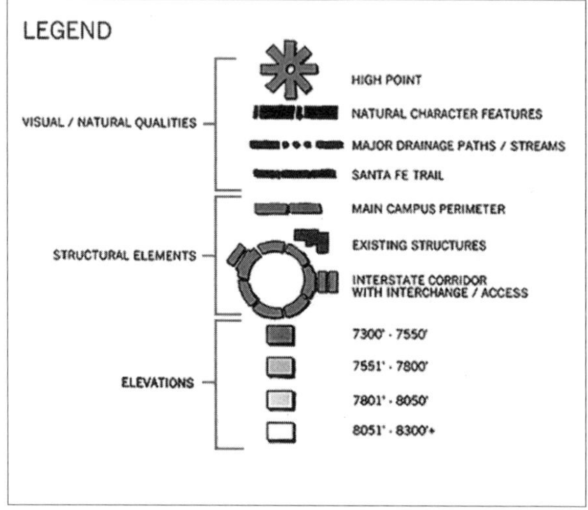

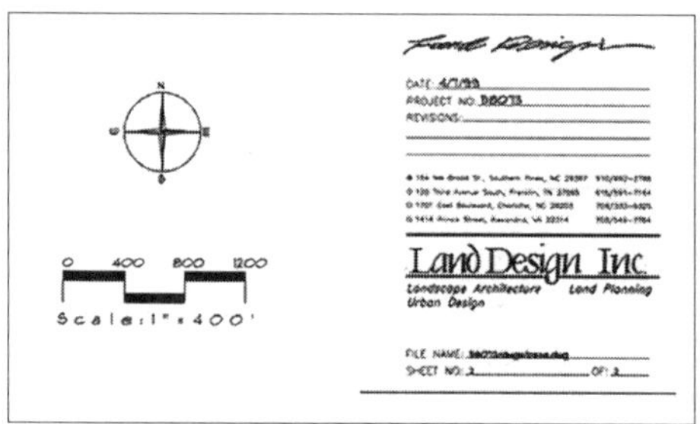

Figure 8-8 Site analysis showing high points, elevation ranges, drainage patterns, and other significant natural features. *Source:* Land Design.

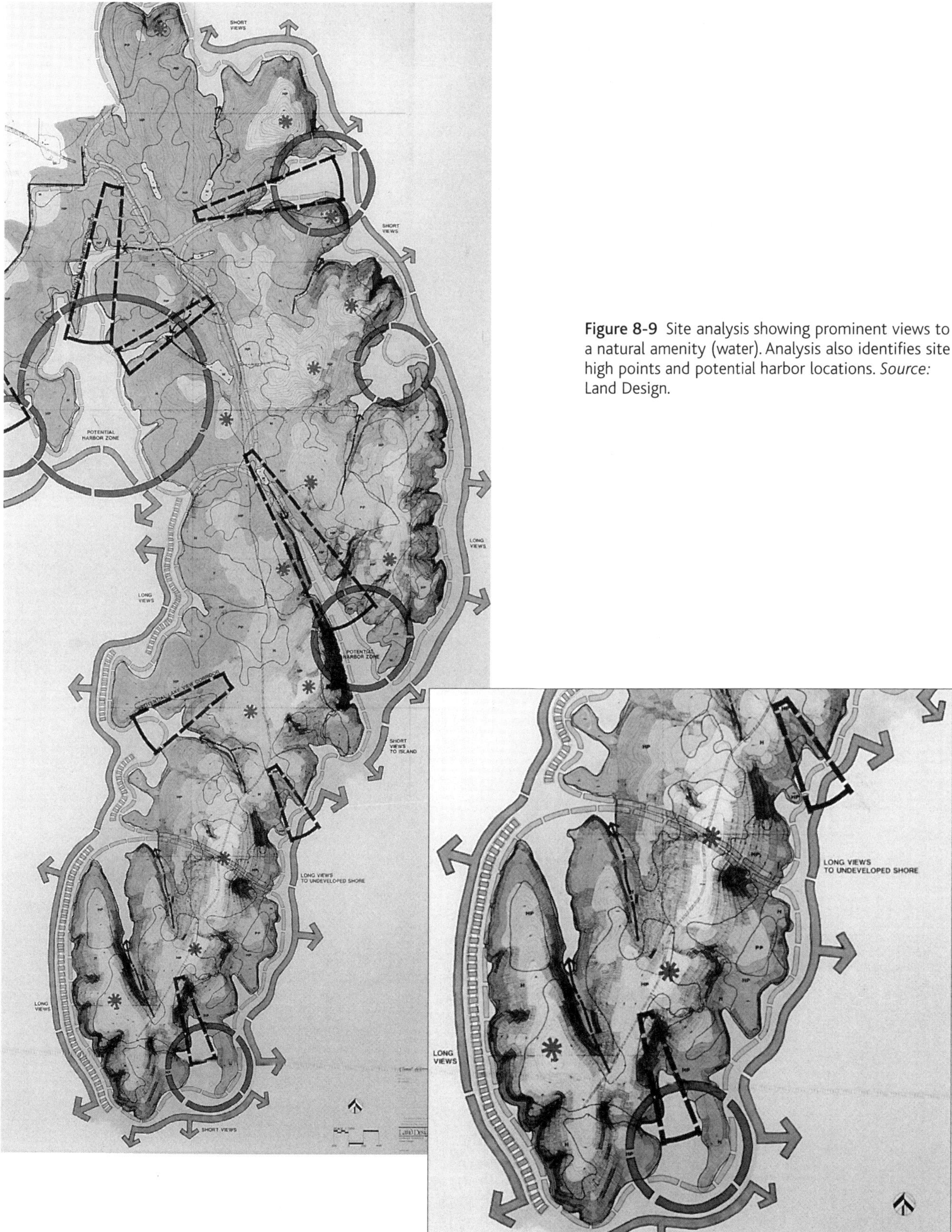

Figure 8-9 Site analysis showing prominent views to a natural amenity (water). Analysis also identifies site high points and potential harbor locations. *Source:* Land Design.

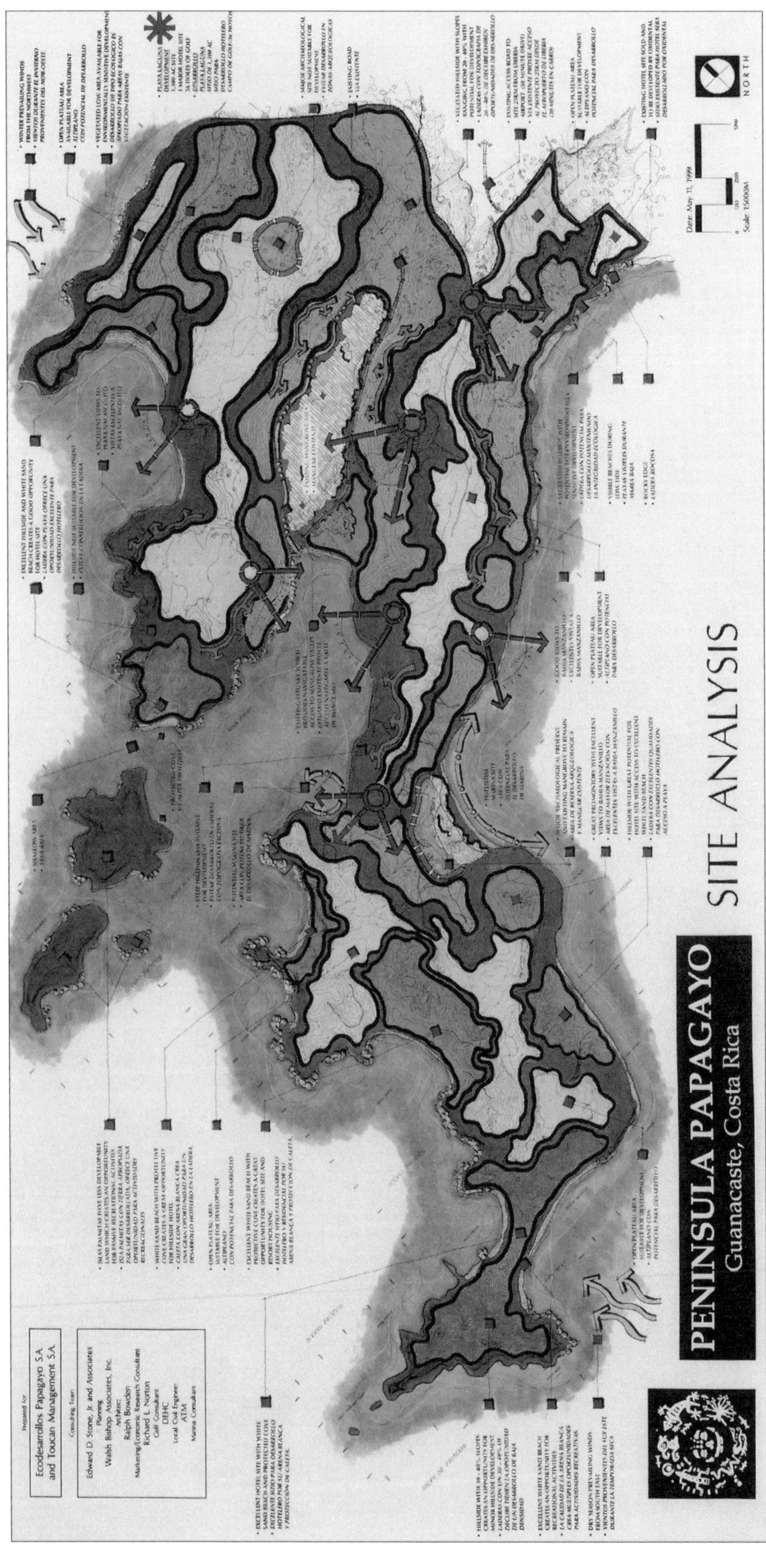
PENINSULA PAPAGAYO
Guanacaste, Costa Rica
SITE ANALYSIS
NORTH

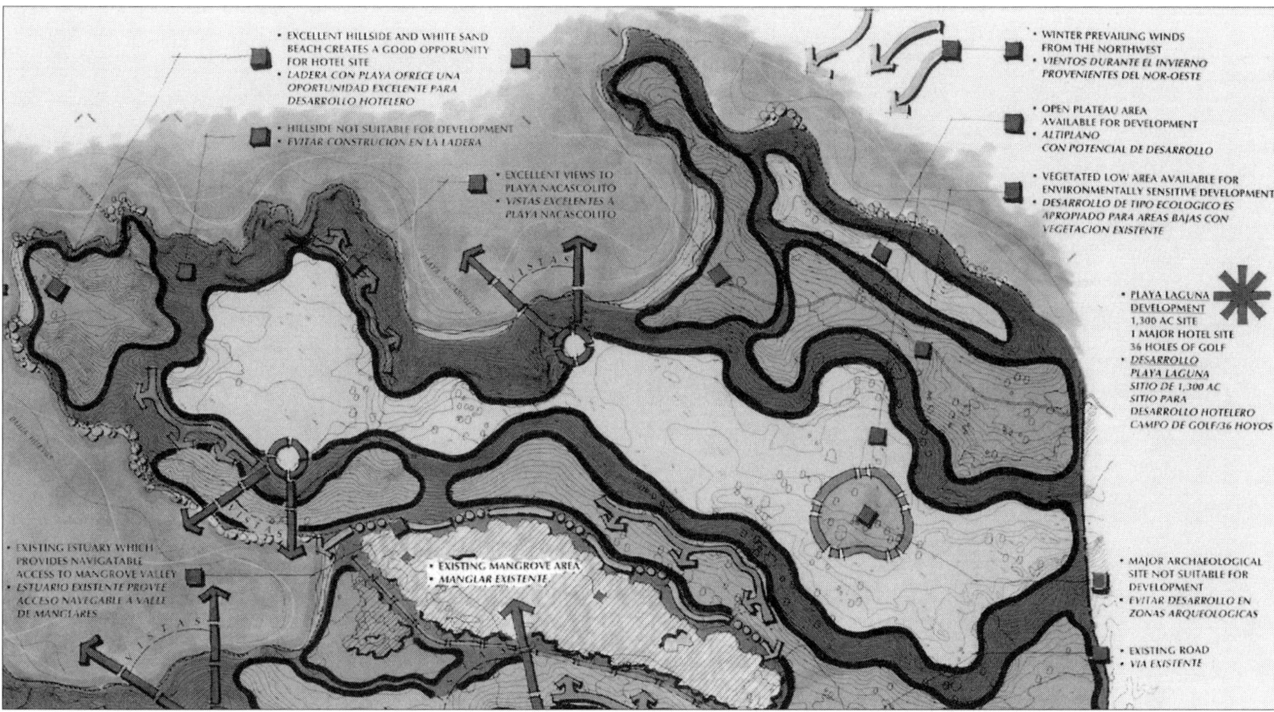

Figure 8-10 (opposite and above) Site analysis conveying the location's physical, biological, and cultural context. Extensive labels and notes help communicate important design determinants. *Source:* Edward D. Stone, Jr., and Associates.

Placelessness occurs when buildings are constructed and sites developed without adapting to the site's historical and environmental context. Natural landforms and native vegetation are important biophysical components on many sites. Older, architecturally significant buildings are important cultural components. Contemporary references to earlier design styles, construction methods, and construction materials can take into account—and create linkages to—the site's cultural history and existing environmental character (Figure 8-10).

Placelessness may also reflect a lack of attention to space making. Built environments contain streets, bridges, buildings, and other structures. Too often, little attention is given to the spatial organization of these elements, or to the refinement of outdoor spaces created by these structures. Improving the spatial qualities of cities requires the analysis of space as well as mass.

On urban sites especially, a unique set of social, cultural, and biophysical factors should be considered. Post-occupancy evaluation of outdoor spaces is particularly useful for urban sites (Cooper-Marcus and Francis, 1999). Analysis of existing outdoor environments includes the examination of how—and why—people use, or avoid, outdoor spaces. Our sense of hearing, sight, and smell are probably the three most important ways that we form impressions about the quality of the environment. Our perceptions of a site could be determined, for example, by views of utility lines and parking lots, and by noise from commercial operations or from traffic on nearby highways (Table 8-5). Environmental preferences drive our behavior concerning where we live, shop, work, and play. Amenities, as well as nuisances, play an important role in determining the desirability of a location for a particular use. Off-site factors, including both physical and legal conditions, may be significant design determinants (Figures 8-11 and 8-12).

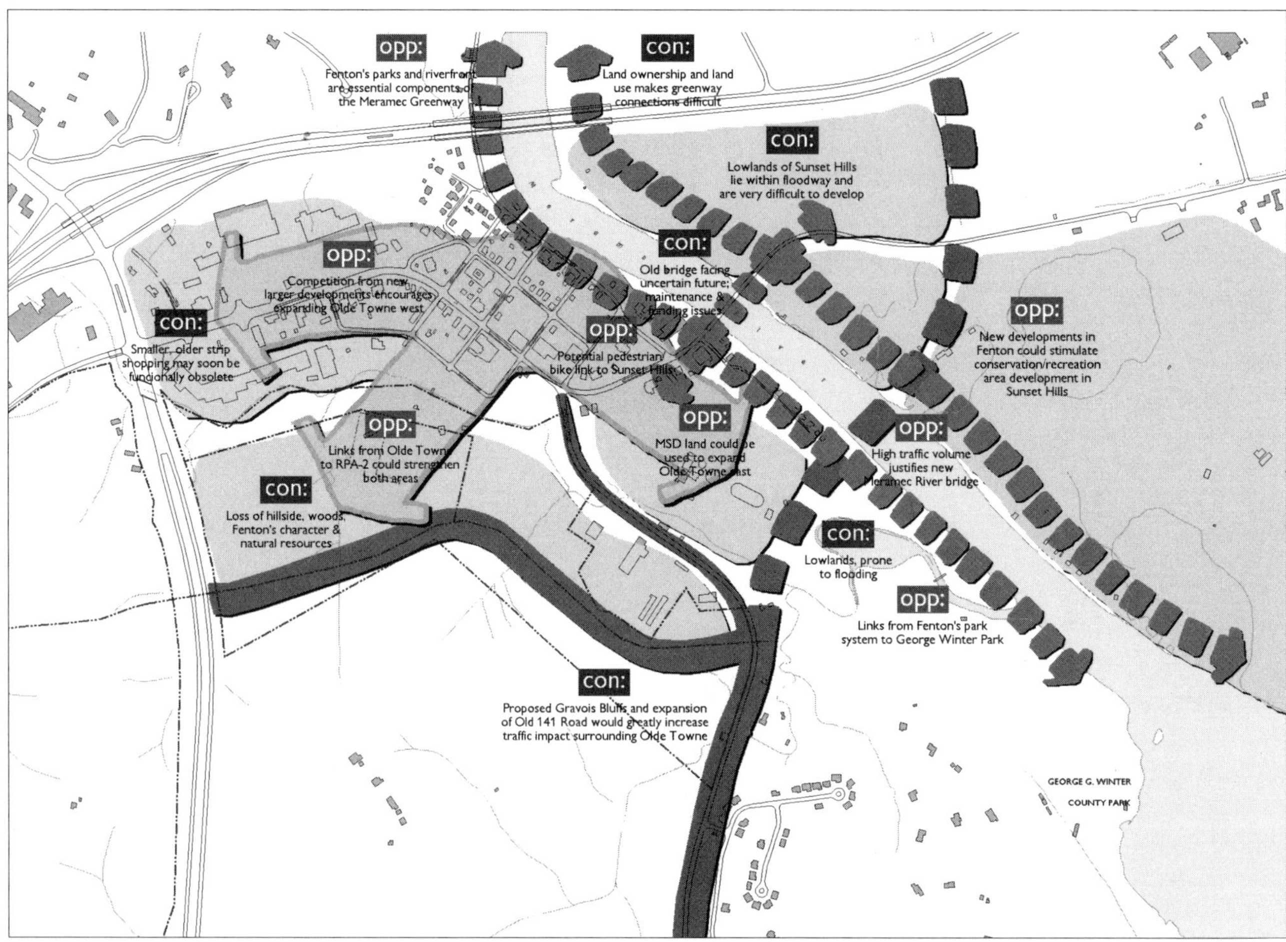

Figure 8-11 Opportunities and constraints diagram for the expansion of a historic village in Missouri. *Source:* The HOK Planning Group.

TABLE 8-5 Selected off-site contextual issues to consider in a site analysis.

Category	*Subcategory*	*Attributes*
Physical	Groundwater	Community wells
		Aquifer recharge areas
	Microclimate	Direction of prevailing breezes (summer)
		Direction of winter winds (storms)
		Direction of sunrise and sunset (summer and winter)
		Fog pockets
Biological	Endangered species	Significant habitats
		Landscape connectivity
	Architecture	Massing (e.g., height, width)
		Articulation (e.g., fenestration, materials)
Cultural	Vehicle circulation	Street pattern
		Traffic volume and speed
		Site accessib0ility
	Pedestrian circulation	Activity generators
		Desire lines
	Sensory impacts	Views
		Noises
		Odors
	Market	Competing developments
		Customer/stakeholder demographics

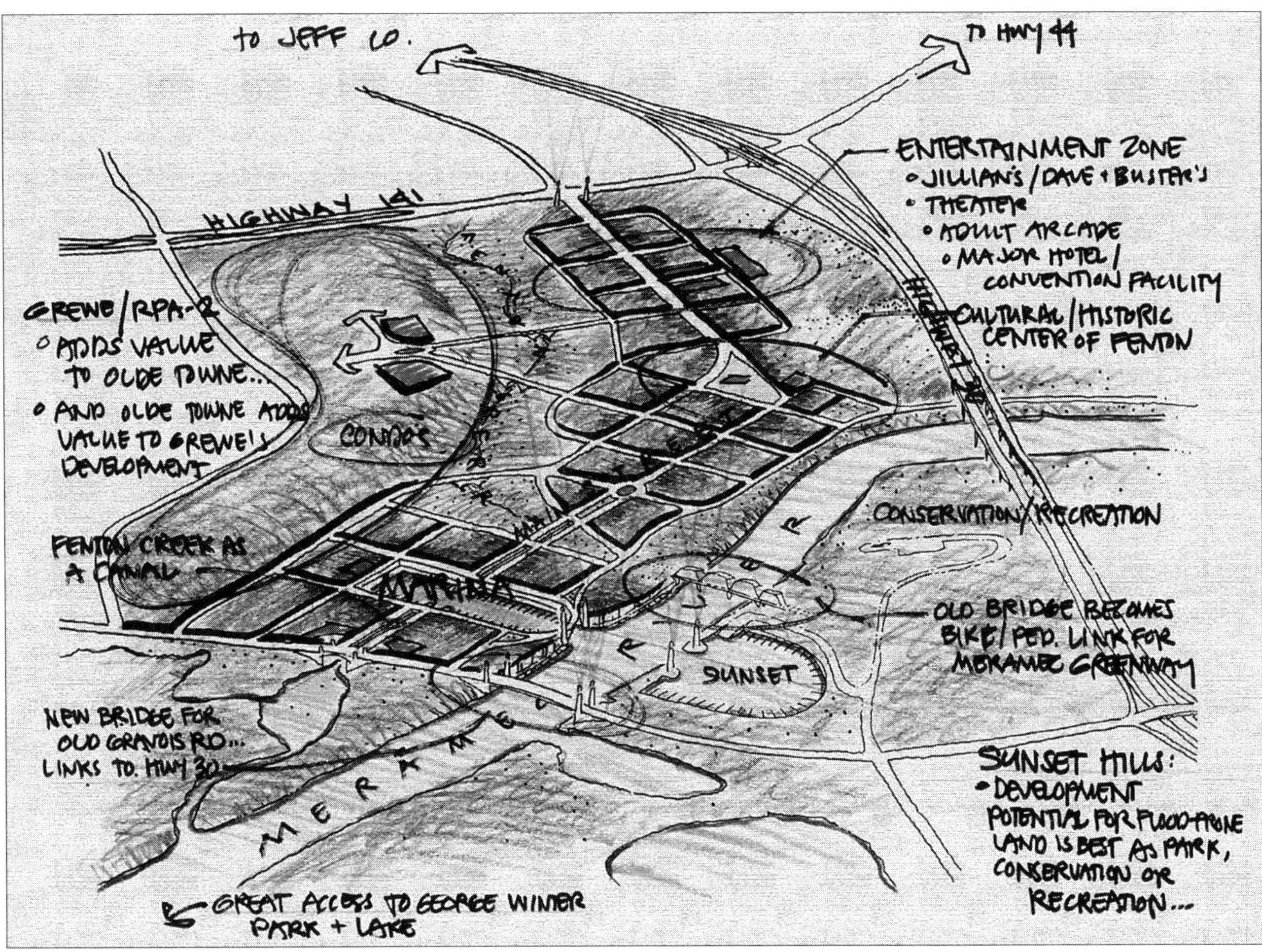

Figure 8-12 Aerial perspective urban analysis identifying important contextual design determinants. *Source:* The HOK Planning Group.

SUMMARY

Sustainable development requires the protection of landscape ecological integrity, critical natural resources, and our cultural heritage. But land development can result, both during and after construction, in significant impacts that degrade the environment and impose a variety of economic and social costs on others. With careful site and contextual analysis, development can be designed to minimize these impacts and mitigate damage to the environment and society. Rather than attempting to overcome the intrinsic "difficulties" that a site poses for development, some locations should simply remain undeveloped.

Variations in topography, hydrology, vegetation, and many other landscape attributes preclude a "one size fits all" approach to development. Development suitability is a function of a site's opportunities and constraints. A site's suitability for individual land uses can be effectively analyzed and mapped with a geographic information system. Other, more complex analyses are less amenable to automation using the currently available spatial information technologies. This older, more traditional form of site analysis results in a composite, or integrated, analysis. The composite site analysis attempts to summarize all of the existing site and contextual conditions that could substantially influence the spatial organization and articulation of the development program on the site.

BOX 8-1 In Practice

Community Planning and Farmland Preservation

South Livermore Valley, California

Land Planner
Wallace, Roberts & Todd, LLC
San Francisco

Background
South Livermore Valley is in California's rolling hills of Alameda County (Figure B8-1). This has been a grape-growing and wine-producing area since the 1880s. As in other communities across North America, however, rural residential development began significantly changing this landscape. Standard zoning codes and associated land use policies were unable to protect the Valley's rural character and viticulture industry. A participatory planning process, supported by a thorough analysis of the Valley's biophysical and cultural conditions, led to a new approach for guiding land use change within the Valley.

Planning Process
An advisory committee was formed, consisting of concerned citizens and representatives from local municipalities. The planning process, which began in 1987, ultimately resulted in the South Livermore Area Plan (City of Livermore, 1999). This plan sets the framework for development in a 14,000-acre (5,600-hectare) area. The two major goals of the plan are to reinforce and rejuvenate the Valley's wine-producing industry, and to preserve the area's rural character.

Plan and Policy Implementation
Three strategies for accomplishing the community's goals were adopted:

1. *Specific Plan*. This land use plan targets new growth within seven distinct and noncontiguous subareas along six miles of Livermore's southern border (Figure B8-2). The total area allocated for new development is about 1500 acres (600 hectares), or about 1/10 of the entire planning area. Constraints maps and composite site analyses helped the planning team determine the preferred character and location of all new development (Figure B8-3 and B8-4).

   > A "specific plan" is a mechanism made available to local governments by the State of California. It is essentially a planning and regulatory tool intended to implement a city or county general plan through policies, programs and regulations. In the case of Livermore, it provides a fine-grain resolution to questions about how, where, and what development can take place—including detailed design guidelines to ensure consistency with the community's character—as well as establishes the means by which agricultural and natural resources are conserved. (Hammond and Roberts, 1999, p. 16)

2. *Incentives*. The plan creates a density bonus to encourage compact development, while also protecting and enhancing the Valley's agricultural activities. One new residential unit is allowed for each 100 acres (40 hectares), but four additional residential units are allowed if 90% of the 100 acres is legally protected in perpetuity (with agricultural easements) and these 90 acres (36 hectares) are planted with orchards or vineyards. Unlike many other agricultural uses, orchards and vineyards are economically viable in smaller areas.

3. *Implementation*. A nonprofit land trust, funded through development fees ($10,000 per unit), manages the agricultural easements required by the plan. The land trust also buys additional easements to help achieve the plan's agricultural preservation goals.

Design Features
The plan attempts to reduce the visual impact of new development on the Valley's rural, agricultural character (Figure B8-4). The plan also seeks to maximize open space amenities, including an extensive hiking trail network (Figure B8-5), which will benefit residents of both existing and new developments. Standards and guidelines require that development patterns, details, and materials enhance the Valley's historic wine country character (Figure B8-6). This is accomplished through the development of narrow, tree-lined streets with drainage swales (rather than curbs and gutters), short blocks, and traditional styles of architecture (Figure B8-7).

Figure B8-1 The aesthetic character of this California landscape is defined by hills and vineyards. *Source:* Wallace Roberts & Todd, LLC.

Figure B8-2 Oblique aerial photo with development boundaries delineated. *Source:* Wallace Roberts & Todd, LLC.

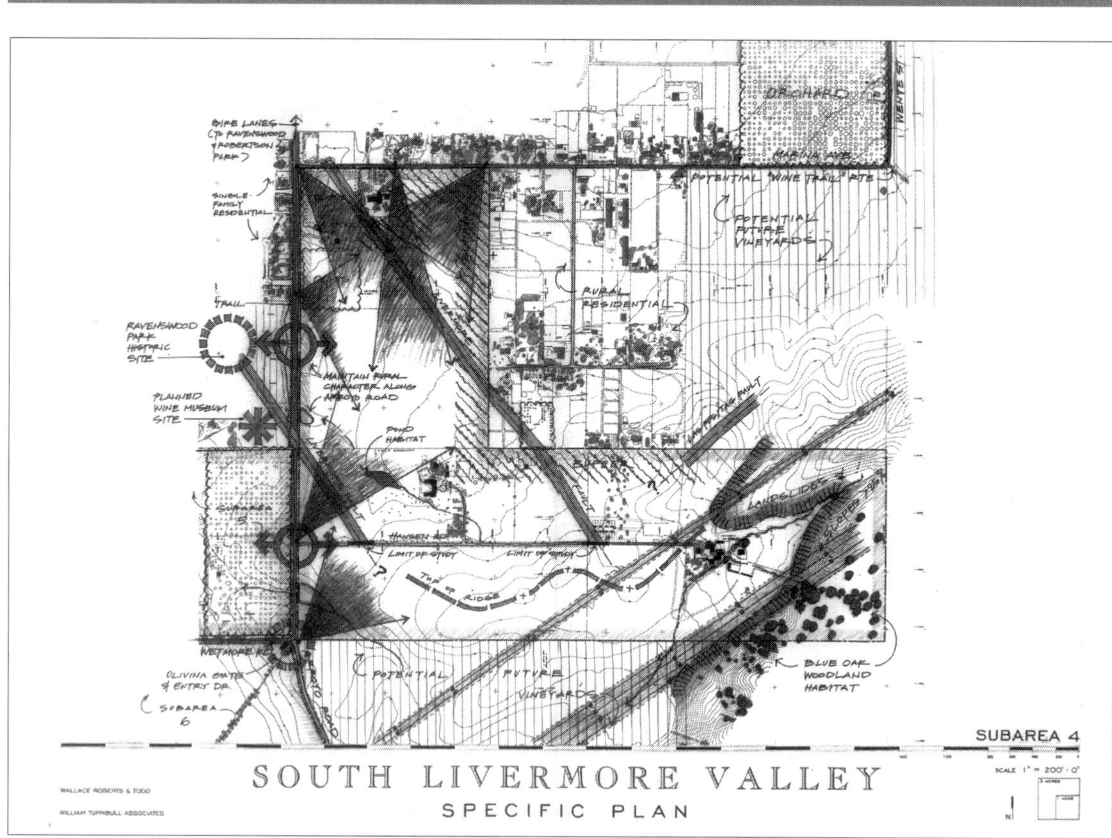

Figure B8-3 Site analysis for one of the seven development subareas. *Source:* Wallace Roberts & Todd, LLC.

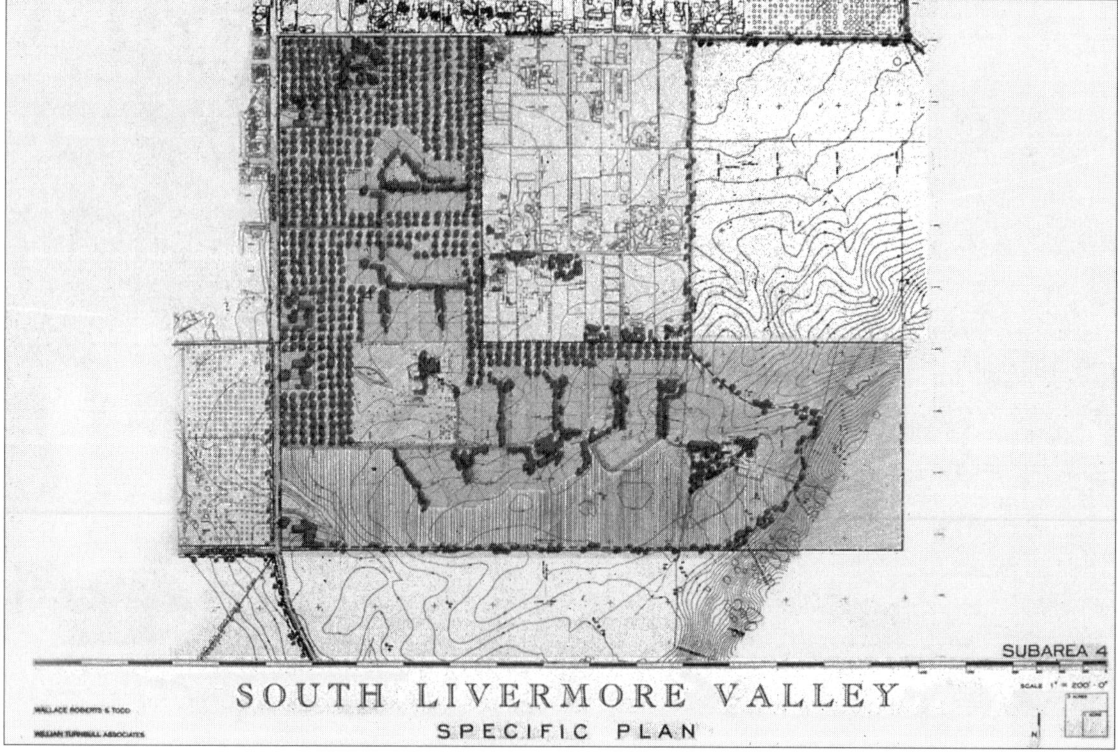

Figure B8-4 Land use plan for the development subarea shown in Figure B8-3. *Source:* Wallace Roberts & Todd, LLC.

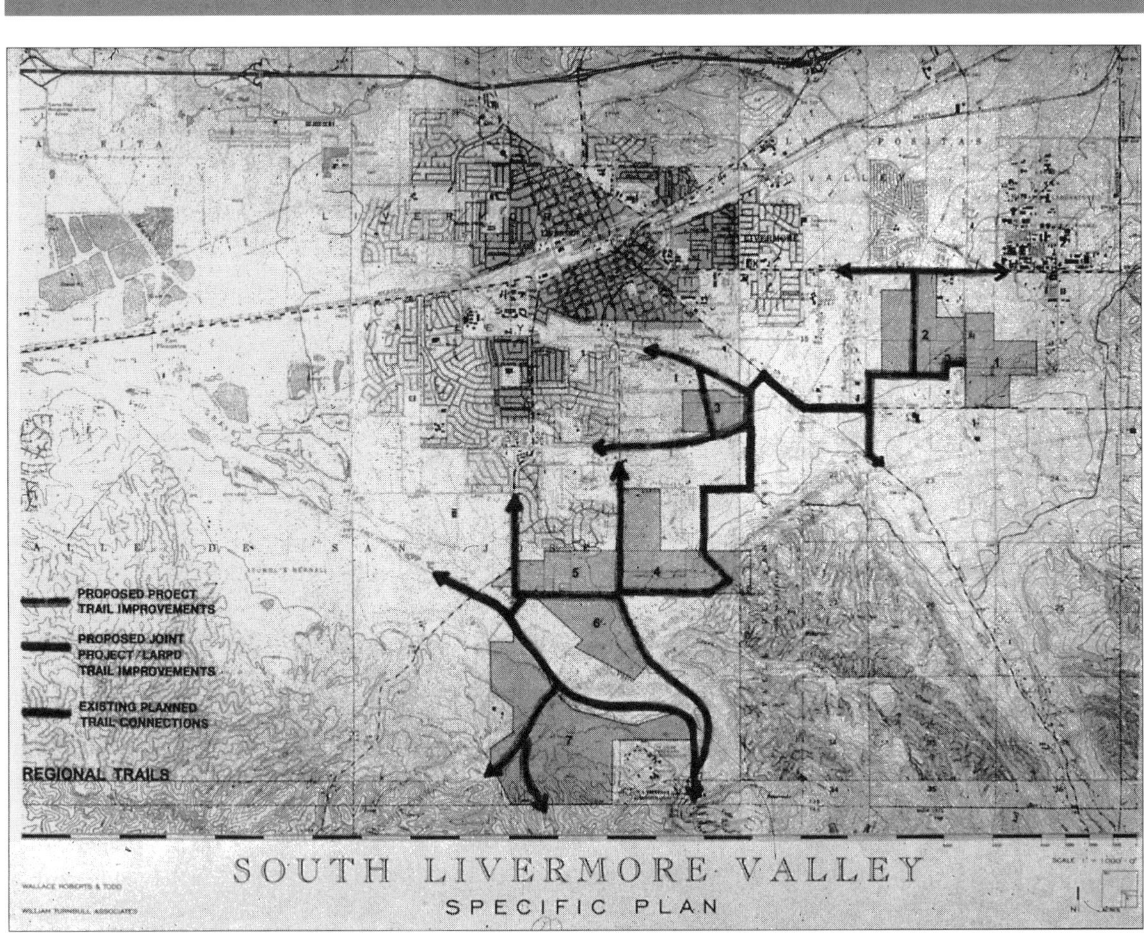

Figure B8-5 Community trails plan, also showing the seven development subareas. *Source:* Wallace Roberts & Todd, LLC.

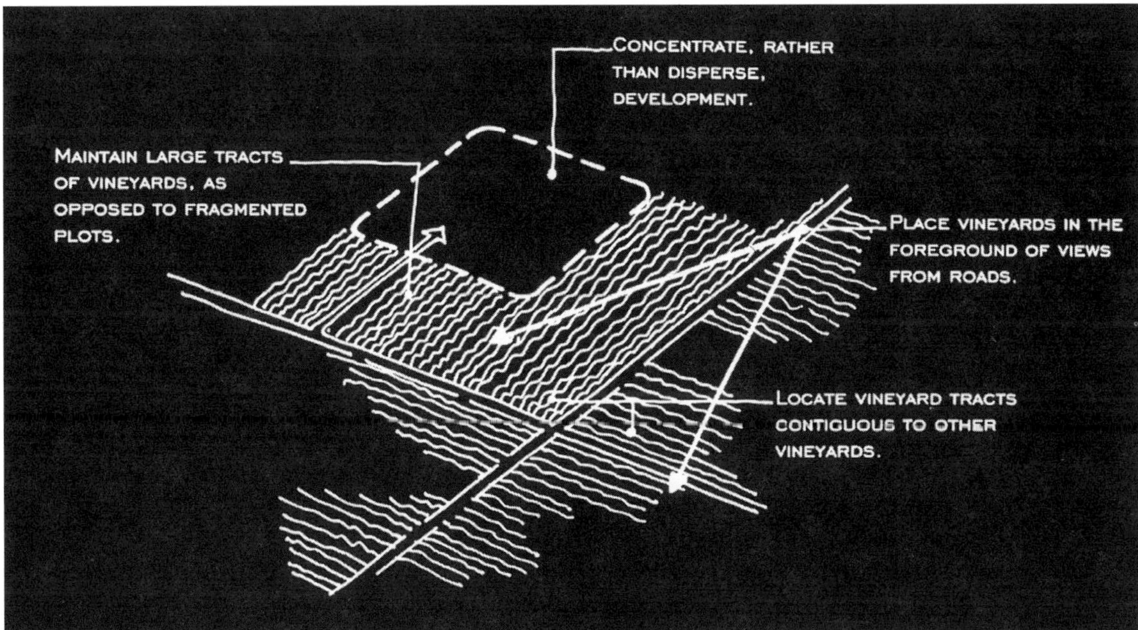

Figure B8-6 Site development design guidelines shown on an aerial perspective sketch of a future commercial site. *Source:* Wallace Roberts & Todd, LLC.

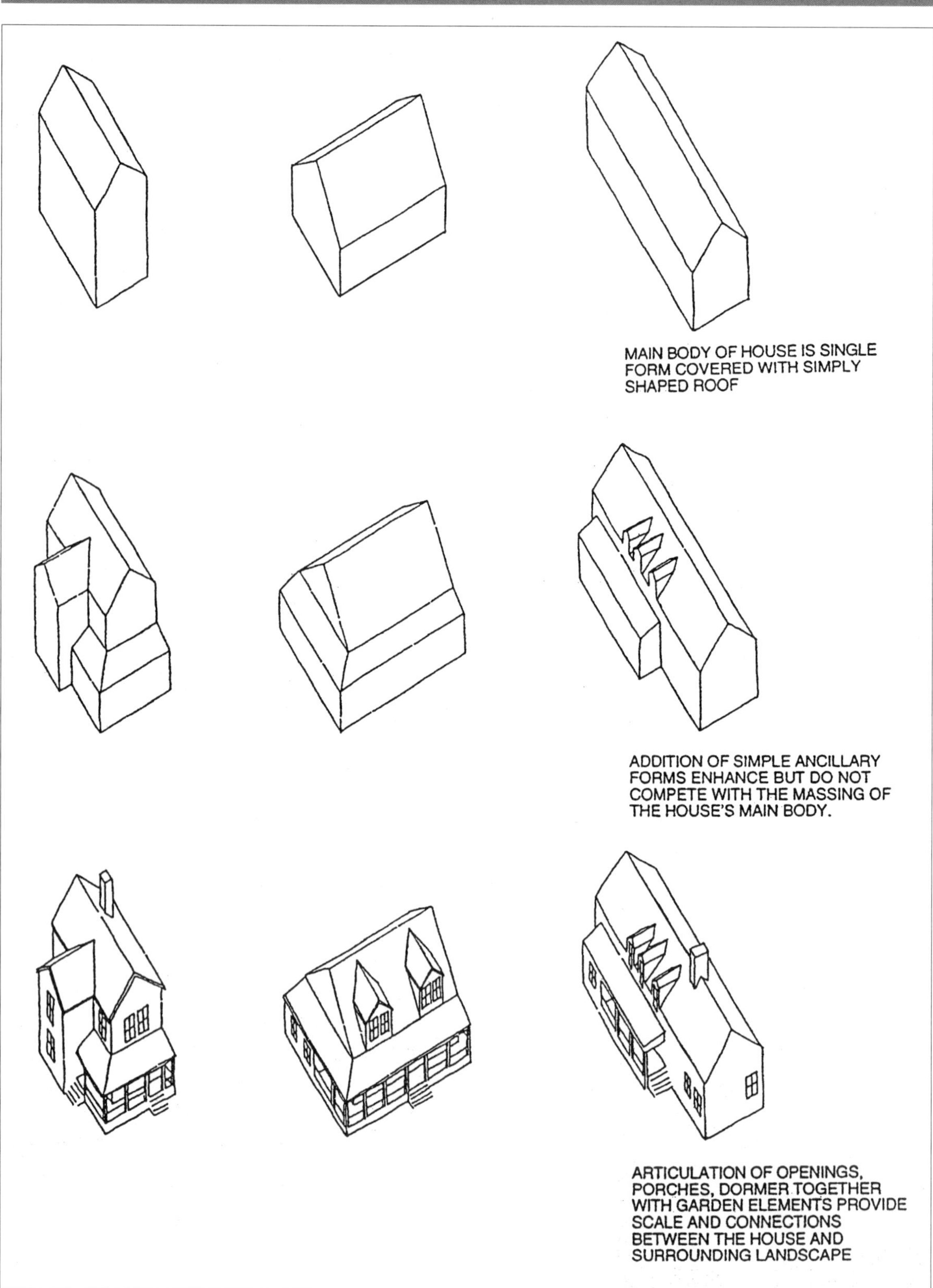

Figure B8-7 Design guidelines illustration showing examples of desired building massing and facade articulation. *Source:* Wallace Roberts & Todd, LLC, with Turnbull Griffin Haesloop Architects.

PART IV

DESIGN AND IMPLEMENTATION

PART IV

DESIGN AND IMPLEMENTATION

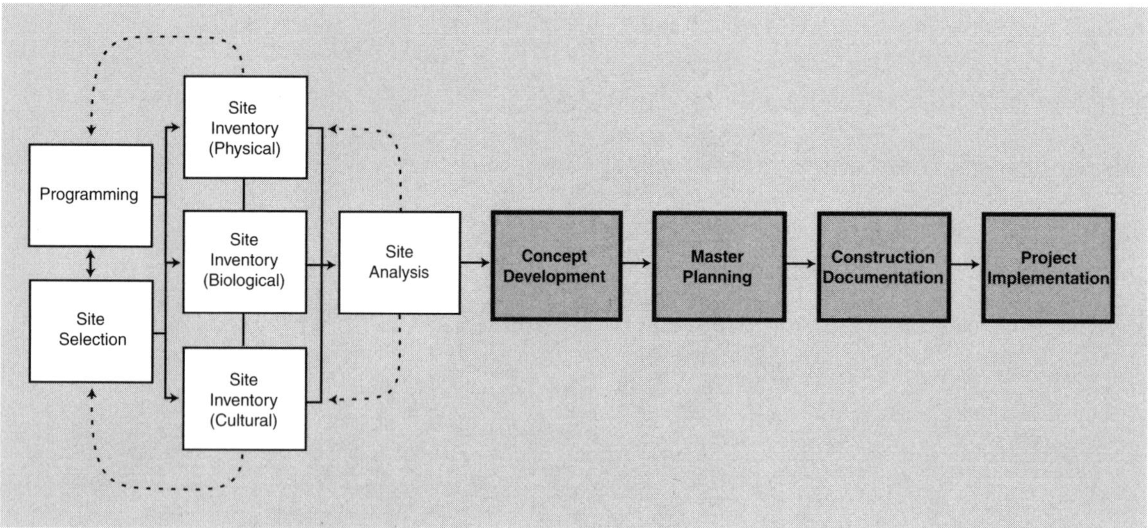

This final section of the book has two chapters. These chapters address the form-giving aspects of land planning and design. This process begins with the spatial organization of the proposed buildings and other improvements on the site. Concept development, covered in Chapter 9, addresses the spatial organization of the site. Subsequent design development involves the spatial articulation of the site. This process, covered in Chapter 10, entails the detailed design of buildings, circulation systems, and other program elements.

CHAPTER

9 Concept Development

INTRODUCTION

The concept development phase of the land planning process follows the program-specific site analysis. Concept development begins with the spatial allocation, or organization, of the proposed land uses on the site (Table 9-1). The conceptual land use plan, or concept diagram, is the spatial framework for subsequent detailed design. Yet concept development is frequently an iterative process. This is the time to explore alternative spatial arrangements of the proposed land use program (Figure 9-1). Revision is an inherent part of the effort to fit the land use program to the site.

Exploring alternative spatial configurations of a proposed development program does not require a major investment in time and effort. Yet this is a critically important phase of the land planning and design process. The conceptual organization of the site's programmed uses is the foundation for subsequent, more detailed, design decisions. Consequently, the conceptual land use plan—establishing the spatial framework for future site development—has significant economic, social, and aesthetic implications.

"Smart growth," "new urbanism," and other similar terms encompass a broad-based effort to correct problems associated with urban growth and development since World War II. Improving on previous development patterns requires close attention to physical design, or the spatial organization and articulation of the built environment. Low-impact development does not jeopardize the health, safety, and welfare of current

TABLE 9-1 Examples of proposed and existing elements that can be conveyed graphically on a conceptual land use plan.

Category	*Specific Elements*
Open space	Active recreation areas Passive recreation areas Nature conservation areas
Vehicle circulation	Street hierarchy Site entrances Parking lots
Pedestrian circulation	Site and building entrances Plazas Pedestrian crosswalks
Other circulation	Bikeways Light railways
Buildings	Residential Commercial Industrial Public
Utilities	Electric transmission lines Water distribution lines Sanitary collection lines
Views	Prominent views from the site Prominent views to the site

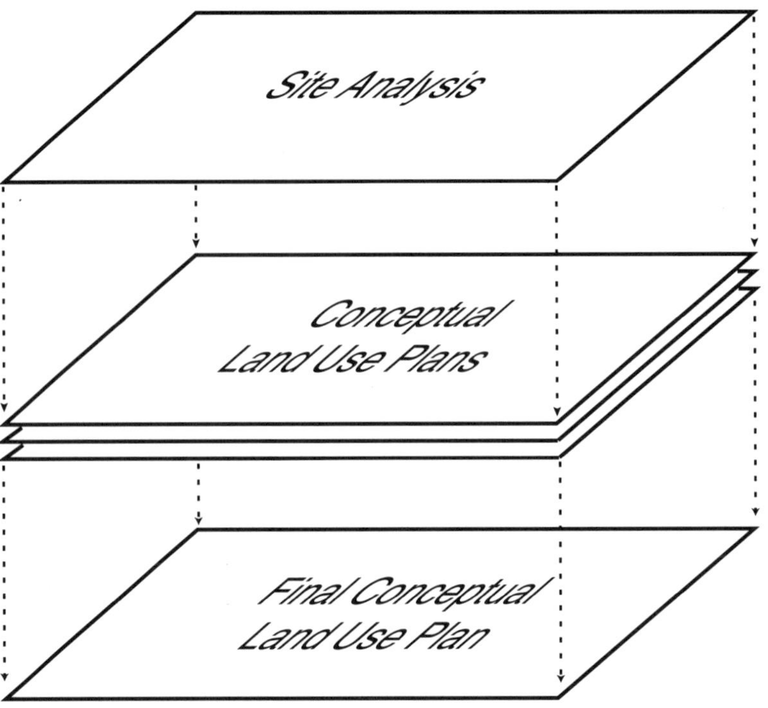

Figure 9-1 Alternative concept plans can be developed from a single site analysis.

or future generations. It also attempts to minimize nonrenewable energy use and protect key natural and cultural resources. In addition, low-impact, or sustainable, development should not shift the costs of public services and infrastructure to other members of the community.

The characteristics of a sustainable and livable neighborhood or community include (Daniels, 1999; Kunstler, 1998; Western Australian Planning Commission, 2000):

- mixed, and integrated, uses (i.e., housing, shops, workplaces, schools, parks, and civic facilities)
- diversity of housing types and prices
- compact development to minimize infrastructure costs and limit environmental impacts
- open space systems that protect site natural resources and provide recreational opportunities
- a center that combines commercial, civic, and cultural uses
- site and architectural design that enriches public open spaces, especially streetscapes, and creates neighborhoods with a clear sense of identity
- multimodal transportation infrastructure (i.e., pedestrian, bicycle, mass transit, private vehicles)

With any land development or restoration project, there are many possible design solutions. When the program is complex, the number of possible solutions may seem limitless. Yet the site analysis—which identifies the site's opportunities and constraints for the given land use program—reveals spatial patterns on the site that limit the number of feasible solutions. The sites with the most character, resulting from both natural and cultural features, are often the most likely to produce a plan that "fits" the site. Conversely, it typically is more difficult to plan for a site that has few, if any, significant biophysical or cultural features. In these situations, there may be no obvious site conditions—or design determinants—to influence the spatial organization of proposed activities and structures. The absence of significant site features or constraints permits a much wider range of feasible design solutions, and this lack of site character can make it more difficult to create a strong sense of place.

Research suggests that creativity, encompassing the ability to produce unique yet appropriate solutions, can be nurtured through education and training (Kvashney, 1982). The creative problem-solving process, as summarized by Kvashney (1982, p. 107), involves five activities:

1. fact-finding
2. problem-finding
3. idea-finding
4. solution-finding
5. acceptance-finding

Each of these activities corresponds to one or more phases of the land planning and design process. Fact-finding occurs in the programming and inventory phases. Problem-finding occurs in the site analysis phase. Idea-finding takes place during concept development. Solution- and acceptance-finding occur during design development and implementation. In this context, the land planner's objective is to find appropriate land use solutions to "problems" posed by the program and the site.

BASIC PROJECT COMPONENTS

Open Space

Most developed sites incorporate paved and unpaved open space. Too often, however, development proposals pay little attention to the size, location, and character of the open space. Yet open space systems serve many important functions. Open space systems can be the spatial framework around which buildings and other infrastructure are organized. An interconnected open space network can perform a myriad of valuable functions. Open space systems facilitate stormwater management, protect scarce wildlife habitat, and add visual amenity. Open space systems can also provide opportunities for recreation and leisure, reduce life and property risks from hazards, and serve as organizing elements that define neighborhoods, promote way-finding, and strengthen site character and identity.

Strategically located open space systems can be designed to protect the landscape's ecological structure and function (Ahern, 1991). Landscape corridors, for example, serve several important ecological functions (Dramstad et al., 1996):

- habitat (for upland species, and refuge for floodplain species displaced by flooding or lateral channel migration)
- conduit (for individual upland animals)
- filter (remove dissolved-substance inputs from overland stormwater runoff)
- source (food and cover)
- sink (during flooding, absorb floodwaters and trap sediment)

The width, and type connectivity, of land cover within corridors are the primary factors that influence corridor functions. Protecting these, and other, strategically located areas can help mitigate a development's hydrologic and ecological impacts (Forman, 1995; Dramstad et al., 1996). Critical areas — both large areas and linking corridors — can become integral elements of a community's open space infrastructure (Stenberg et al., 1997).

Natural and cultural features add value to a development, and should be integrated where possible. Prominent views to nearby natural or cultural features should be maintained. Providing pedestrian access to interconnected open space systems is also important. Recommended design standards for conservation subdivisions typically suggest that at least half of the site should remain in undeveloped open space. Open space standards for traditional neighborhood subdivisions are 65 to 75 percent of the site in unsewered rural areas and 40 to 50 percent in serviced infill areas (Arendt, 1999).

Land development that integrates open space is a feature of the contemporary "links-style" golf course communities. The most visually interesting courses, which also appear to "fit" well into the existing landscape, utilize natural drainage patterns as golf course hazards (Figure 9-2). In cases where the natural drainage patterns and vegetative cover have been substantially disturbed, restoration may be considered. This environmentally responsive approach to golf course architecture reduces the costs of construction and long-term maintenance, protects critical hydrological processes and habitats, and creates a unique and memorable playing experience for golfers. By locating the golf course's highly maintained tees, greens, and fairways in areas that preserve the inherent character of the site, multiple economic, ecological, and aesthetic benefits are realized.

Figure 9 2 Conceptual land use plan for the Soos Creek Golf Club and Estates, developed by OB Sports near Seattle, Washington. The housing arrangement maximizes adjacency to nearby the golf course amenity. *Source:* R. W. Thorpe and Associates.

Stormwater Management

Stormwater management is an important public policy issue. Because stormwater runoff can have important on-site and off-site impacts, the proposed stormwater management system should be addressed during the concept development process.

Depending on the context and size of the site, three basic approaches to stormwater management can be considered:

- open (surface) systems
- closed (subsurface) systems
- hybrid systems (combination of open and closed systems)

Open systems accommodate stormwater runoff above ground. A surface system may include grassed swales, detention/retention basins, and ponds. Closed systems, in contrast, accommodate stormwater runoff with below ground catch basins, drop inlets, and a network of underground pipes. In highly urban or built-up areas, closed systems are unavoidable. Sites are too small and impervious surfaces too large to detain and infiltrate all stormwater on-site. But this infrastructure is expensive to construct. Moreover, closed systems convey stormwater off the site—often to a municipal stormwater drainage system that drains directly into local lakes, rivers, or other water bodies. Because urban and suburban runoff transport a variety of chemicals—from lawns, streets, and parking lots, for example—this runoff has detrimental impacts on local aquatic ecosystems.

Locating the proposed surface drainage and infiltration system at the concept planning phase is important for two reasons. First, buildings and circulation systems should be located outside of this open space network. This can reduce flooding hazards and minimize the potential for property damage from flooding. Second, accommodating stormwater runoff within a contiguous open space system will eliminate construction costs associated with subsurface stormwater drainage infrastructure.

Whenever feasible, development should not be located in areas that conflict with major surface drainage patterns. An undeveloped open space drainage network provides an opportunity to reduce the effective impervious surface area (EISA) of a developed site. Impervious surfaces include rooftops, streets and parking lots, and other paved or compacted areas. Groundwater infiltration on a site can be increased by interrupting the stormwater runoff with surfaces that are pervious and conducive to infiltration and groundwater recharge. The spatial configuration of open spaces on a site can, therefore, have a significant effect on stormwater management.

A common requirement of stormwater ordinances is that runoff leaving the developed site must not exceed the volume of stormwater runoff leaving the site under predevelopment conditions. Achieving this standard, while substantially increasing the site's total impervious surface area, requires careful site design and stormwater management system engineering.

Low-impact development minimizes local hydrologic impacts by facilitating stormwater infiltration and groundwater recharge, removing waterborne pollutants, and maintaining other important hydrologic functions. Conventional engineering approaches to stormwater management typically result in concrete-lined ditches, large retention and/or detention basins, and other "end-of-pipe" solutions. A small-scale, multifaceted, bioengineering approach to stormwater management is ecologically superior, less expensive to build and maintain, and often more attractive and natural looking.

Three strategies for minimizing land development's hydrologic impacts are (Prince George's County, 2000):

- avoid development of the hydrological infrastructure (e.g., streams and their buffers, floodplains, wetlands, steep slopes, high-permeability soils, and woodlands)

- control stormwater at the source (e.g., minimize and mitigate land development impacts at, or near, the site disturbance)
- use simple, small, nonstructural methods (e.g., grassed swales and shallow basins with gentle side slopes, "rain" gardens planted with native or naturalized vegetation)

Identifying and mapping the hydrologic infrastructure is a crucial step in stormwater management. Barring other constraints, this delimits the areas of a site that are least suitable for development. Micromanagement techniques rely on multiple ways of controlling stormwater at, or near, the source of the runoff. Specific land planning strategies, or best management practices (BMP), include (Prince George's County, 2000):

- limit site clearing and soil disturbance to the areas required for building footprints, construction access, material storage, and safety setbacks
- disconnect impervious surfaces to increase infiltration and reduce runoff
- disperse drainage from roofs and other large impervious surfaces to lengthen flow paths and encourage slow, shallow runoff over vegetated, pervious surfaces
- protect existing native trees, shrubs, grasses, and forbs

Sending rooftop runoff over a pervious surface before it reaches an impervious surface can decrease the annual runoff volume from residential development sites by as much as 50 percent (Kwon, 2000). Clustering development also reduces impervious cover and lowers construction costs for streets and other infrastructure.

Circulation Systems

Circulation systems may be designed for motor vehicles, pedestrians, bicycles, and, where appropriate, water taxis, ferries, light rail, or other less common forms of transportation. These systems may convey both people and materials. Circulation systems are essential elements of most conceptual land use plans. These systems should be distinguished, during concept development, by type of use—such as vehicles, pedestrians, or bicycles. Circulation systems are typically designed as hierarchical systems. A street hierarchy, for example, can facilitate efficient movement within a community. Three types of streets are commonly associated with individual land development projects. Ranging from the highest level to the lowest level, these are:

- arterial streets (connect neighborhoods and districts)
- collector streets (usually do not provide direct access to single-family lots)
- minor streets (provide direct access to individual parcels)

Generally, the horizontal configuration of circulation systems may be a combination of one or more basic patterns:

- linear
- loop
- grid
- radial
- spiral

Each of these configurations may best serve a specific kind of land use or activity. Linear walkway systems, for example, are commonly used for recreational corridors. They may roughly parallel natural features such as streams, rivers, or oceanfront. They may be curvilinear, zigzag, or straight. Street grid patterns are common in denser urban areas. Advantages of the grid include ease of orientation and flexibility in vehicle movement. In suburban locations, particularly where the primary land use is residential, loops and cul-de-sacs are common. Although cul-de-sacs reduce circulation options and make wayfinding more difficult, this pattern has two significant positive features. First, the loop and cul-de-sac pattern requires substantially (as much as 25 percent) less paving than a grid system (Prince George's County, 2000). This pattern also can result in large, linear, and connected open spaces that provide good locations for walkways, bike trails, and associated recreational activities.

A spiral configuration may be appropriate for climbing a hill or mountain where steep slopes preclude movement directly up the fall line. Spiral systems are appropriate for ceremonial walkways—particularly when those walkways are descending or ascending toward a special destination. Sculpture gardens, memorials, and other contemplative outdoor sanctuaries commonly employ this configuration. In many land planning and design projects, the circulation systems are a combination of two or more basic spatial configurations.

Several functional issues should be considered in conceptually designing the site's circulation systems. Access to the site is a fundamental consideration (Figure 9-3). This, of course, requires an understanding of the site's context—specifically, other existing circulation systems for vehicles, pedestrians, bicycles, or other forms of transportation. Once the location for access to the site is identified, the entry and arrival sequence to significant destinations on the site must be considered.

Buildings and Utilities

Each site's biophysical and cultural context can—and, many would argue, *should*—play a fundamental role in the design of the built environment. Exceptional works of architecture and landscape architecture achieve this objective in simple yet often elegant ways. Many notable examples of architectural and landscape architectural design receive recognition because the buildings or other structures are designed in response to the unique conditions of the site. These elements are organized and articulated in ways that would be inappropriate on any other sites.

Frank Lloyd Wright's Falling Water is a building that not only fits its site well, but the building's form actually mimics the cascading effect of the streambed. Another example of site-driven architecture is the collaboration of Venturi and Halprin on Sea Ranch. The windblown conditions of the northern California coastal landscape were major design determinants. Outdoor spaces, as well as the arrangement of buildings, vegetation, and berms, were all influenced by concern for the local microclimate.

The amount of detail shown on a conceptual land use plan depends largely on the size of the area being considered. For example, a conceptual land use plan for a 2,000-acre (800-hectare) site might show only general land use categories, such as residential, commercial, and industrial. Or, within the residential category, the plan might identify areas where certain housing densities will be located. These densities are typically expressed as dwelling units per acre or hectare. The concept plan for a project of this size might be drawn at a scale of 1:4,800 (1 inch = 400 feet) or smaller. In contrast, a conceptual land use plan for a 10-acre (4-hectare) site might provide much

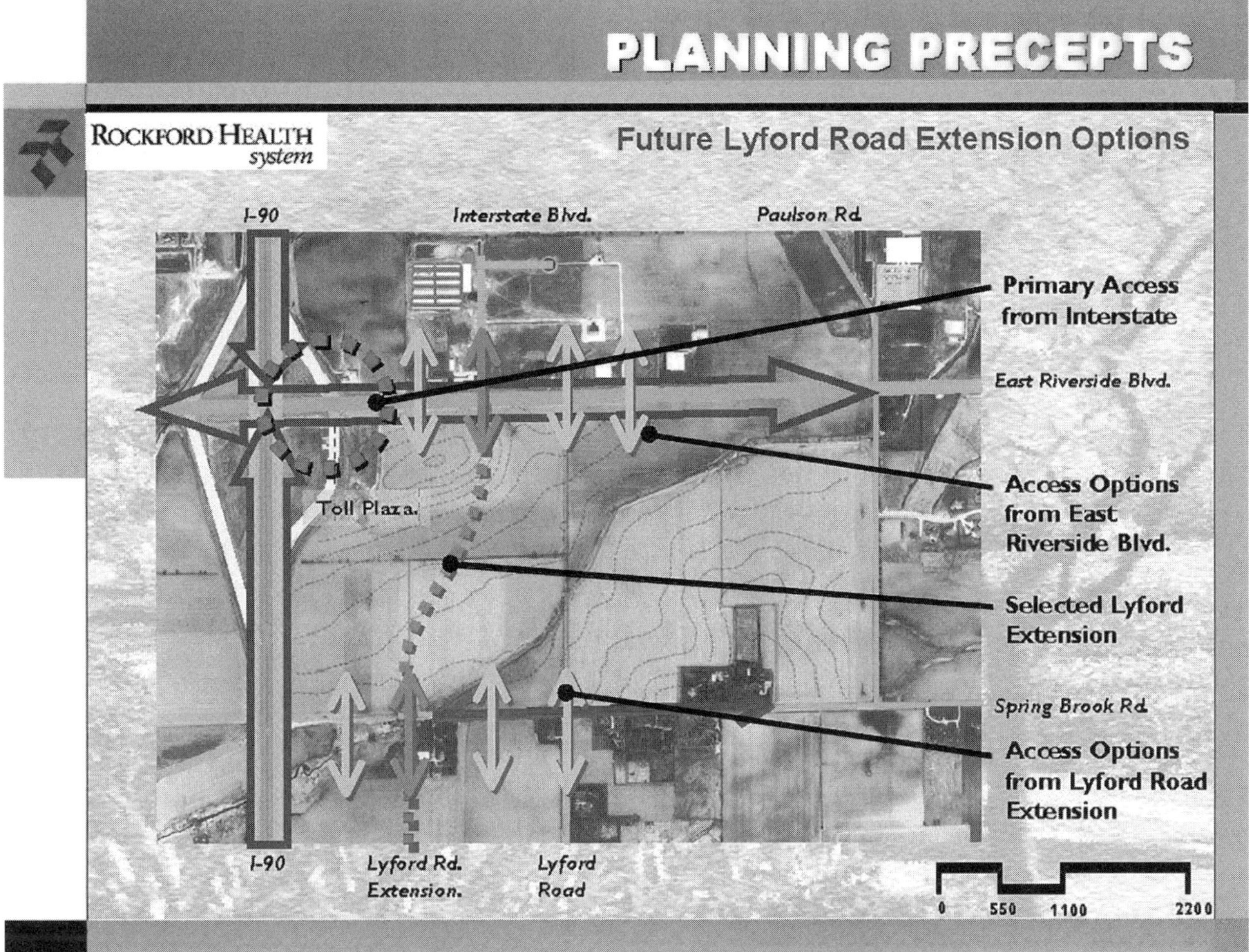

Figure 9-3 Vehicle circulation concept diagram showing potential access locations. *Source:* The Hok Planning Group.

more detailed information about the proposed development. It could, for example, suggest the preferred locations for individual buildings and building entrances. This concept plan might be drawn at a scale of 1:480 (1 inch = 40 feet). The level of development detail that can be shown on a conceptual land use plan is largely determined by the scale of the drawing.

Utility systems on a site provide a variety of basic services to buildings and other structures, and are important components of a site's infrastructure. These systems physically connect individual buildings with off-site facilities. Site outputs, such as sanitary waste, is removed from the buildings and either treated on-site or collected at an off-site treatment facility. Site inputs, such as water and electricity, are delivered to the site. Other utility linkages may include gas, electric, telephone, and television cable. This infrastructure may be shown on a concept plan if the site is particularly small, and in an urban or suburban context.

Site Boundaries

The periphery, or edge, of the property is particularly important. Significant contextual elements may influence the spatial organization of the programmed activities. Potential conflicts might exist between on-site and off-site uses or features, and these

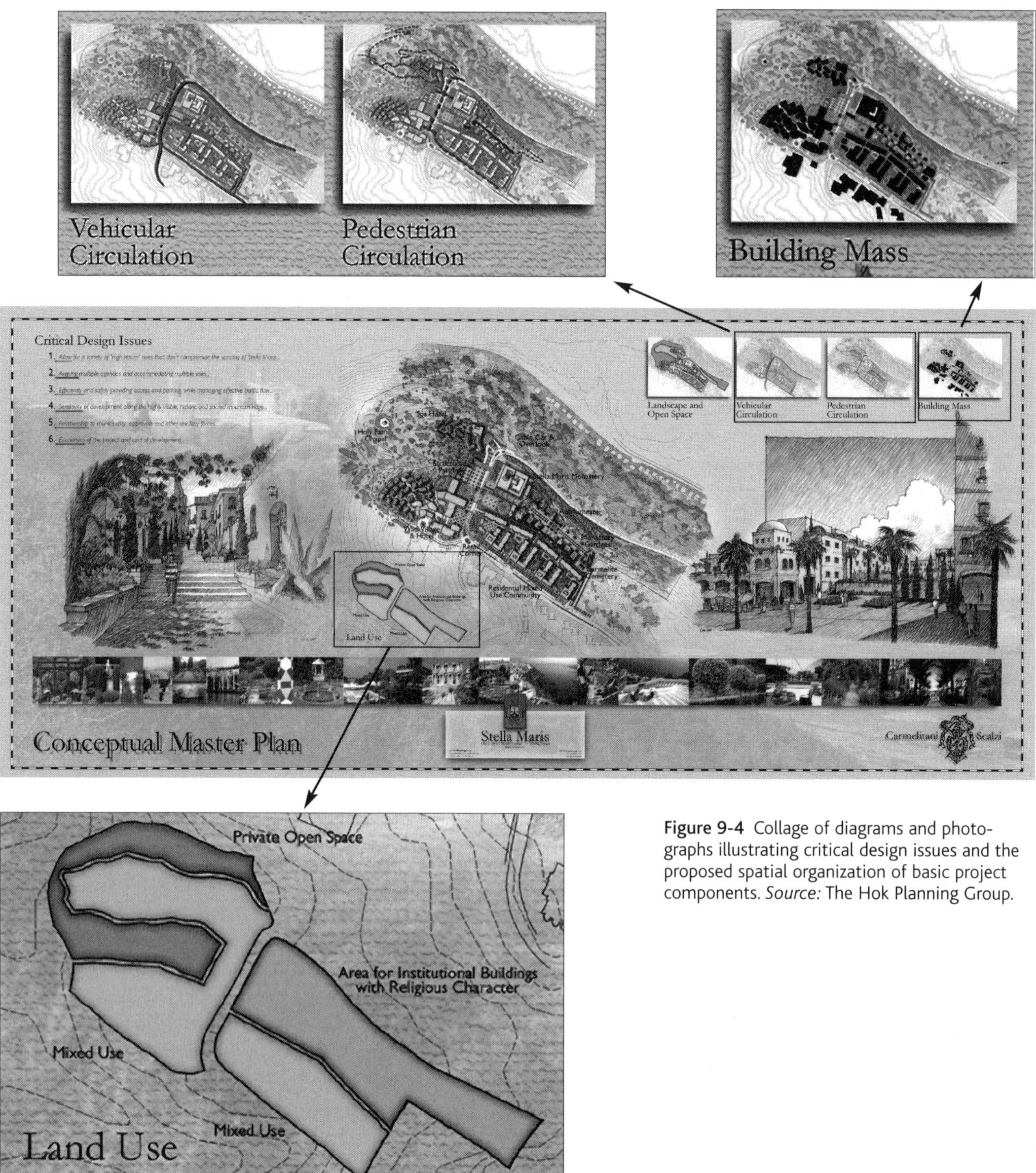

Figure 9-4 Collage of diagrams and photographs illustrating critical design issues and the proposed spatial organization of basic project components. *Source:* The Hok Planning Group.

conditions should be addressed at the concept development phase. These off-site conditions may be incompatible uses, such as a busy highway, that impact the site with noise, odors, and undesirable views. When conflicts do exist, the organization of uses on the site should mitigate those conflicts. Uses that are less sensitive to negative impacts can be sited nearer to those impacts than other, more sensitive, uses. Buffers or screens also may be needed, and these should be shown diagrammatically on the concept plan. At this phase, however, the materials that will buffer or screen do not need to be specified. The selection of the materials occurs later in the design process.

Movement of water and wildlife typically occurs at spatial scales that transcend the boundaries of most land development sites. Ecological linkages between the site and the surrounding landscape can be, to a significant extent, achieved through undeveloped open spaces. These open space systems not only have ecological value, but they may also provide a variety of recreational and educational opportunities.

CONCEPT PLANS

Concept diagrams, functional diagrams, or bubble diagrams convey fundamental information about the spatial organization of the proposed land uses on the site (Table 9-1). These plans may also include information on the functional relationships among various plan elements. Also known as conceptual land use plans, these diagrams may provide information about the site's biophysical and cultural context and significant existing site elements that will be protected and integrated into the proposed land development project (Figure 9-4).

Functional diagrams or conceptual land use plans are preliminary designs. Proposed land uses for the site are organized on the diagram, but this plan is not highly articulated. The concept plan is spatially explicit, yet information regarding the dimensions of streets, buildings, and other site elements — as well as the types of materials needed to build these structures — is not typically conveyed during the concept planning phase. This more detailed design occurs during the subsequent phases of design development and construction documentation.

Communicating information about the intended project is an important task of the land planning and design team. Information needed for the public review of large development projects typically includes resource inventory maps, a composite site analysis, and plans and summary tables of the proposed land uses. Alternative conceptual land use plans can be created for each project. This practice is particularly useful in generating input from stakeholders. In addition to increasing the prospects for an optimum solution, this demonstrates flexibility, and provides evidence that the planning team does not have a predetermined solution.

Graphic communication is essential in efforts to visualize land use futures. The symbols used on functional diagrams or conceptual land use plans are essentially the same as those used on site analysis maps. Typically, information is conveyed with three geometric forms: polygons (areas), lines, and points. These symbols convey different kinds of land information.

Kevin Lynch developed a useful typology for explaining urban structure from a cognitive perspective. Appearing in *Image of the City* (Lynch, 1960), the typology comprised five categories of elements that shape human perceptions of cities and other physical environments. These elements are: districts, edges, paths, nodes, and landmarks. This typology is a useful framework for organizing and communicating conceptual land use plan information.

Areas (Bubbles)

The spatial organization of the site's new uses and structures is determined during the concept development phase. But the opportunities and constraints identified in the site

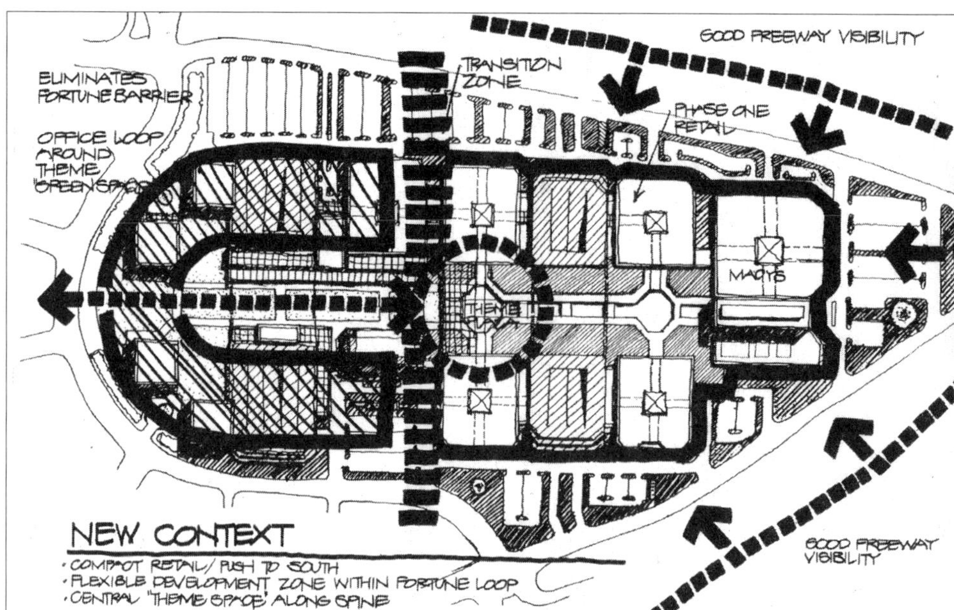

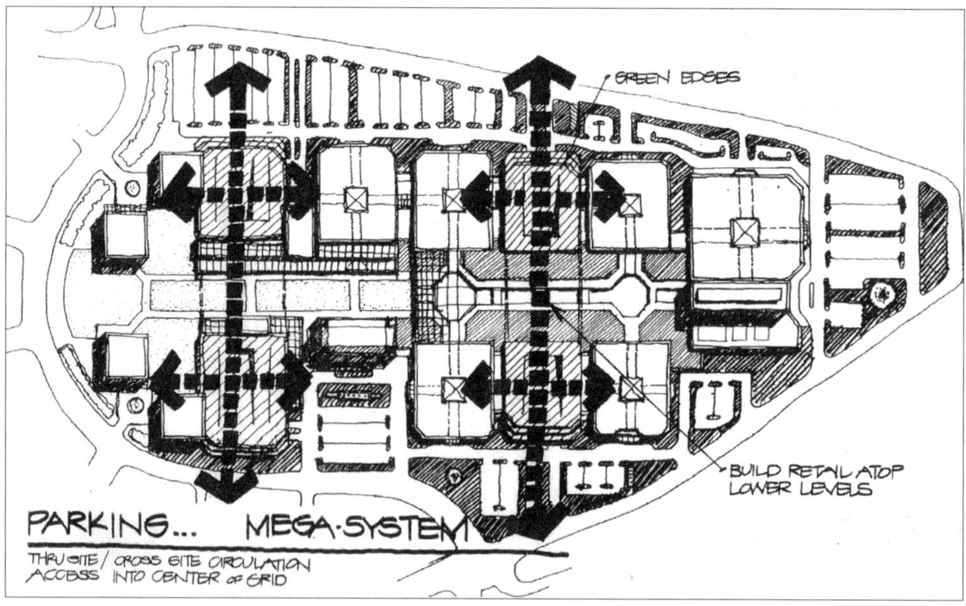

Figure 9-5 Concept diagrams showing proposed uses and important spatial relationships. The central axis for this development project is a bold and effective organizing element. *Source:* The HOK Planning Group.

analysis determine the spatial "envelope" where the proposed elements are located. The conceptual land use plan depicts in the simplest of terms the important site conditions and proposed changes to the site. Major uses of the site are typically portrayed diagrammatically as areas, polygons, or "bubbles." These areas may include, for example, residential, commercial, or industrial uses. As the conceptual land use plan is refined, these land use bubbles are further subdivided to show building locations and minor circulation patterns. As the planning process moves further into the design development phase, these bubbles are then subdivided into smaller areas, and eventually each one is designed in detail.

In addition to showing the locations of proposed uses, conceptual land use plans also show the areas that will not be developed. Undeveloped areas typically become key components of the site's open space system. These areas typically include:

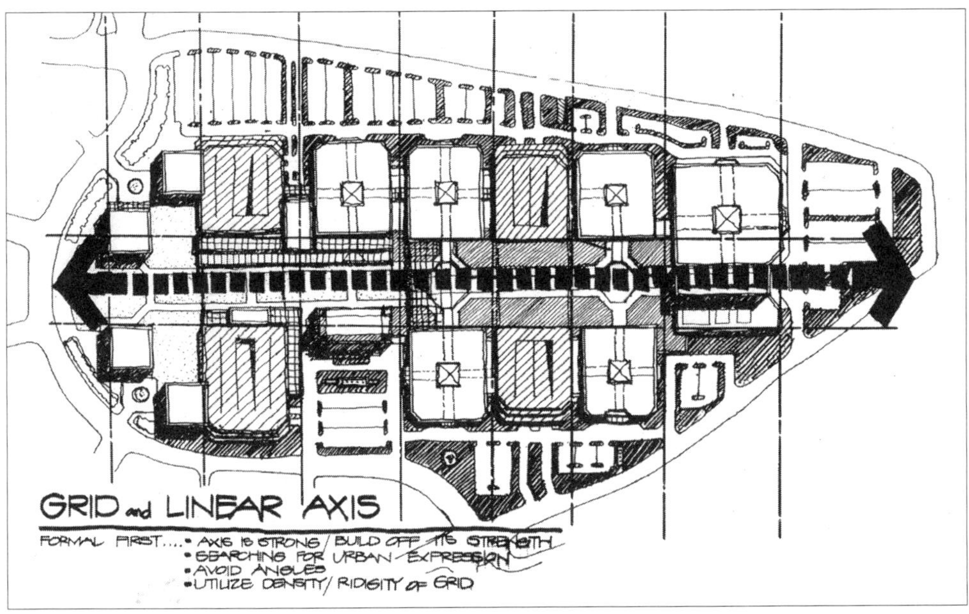

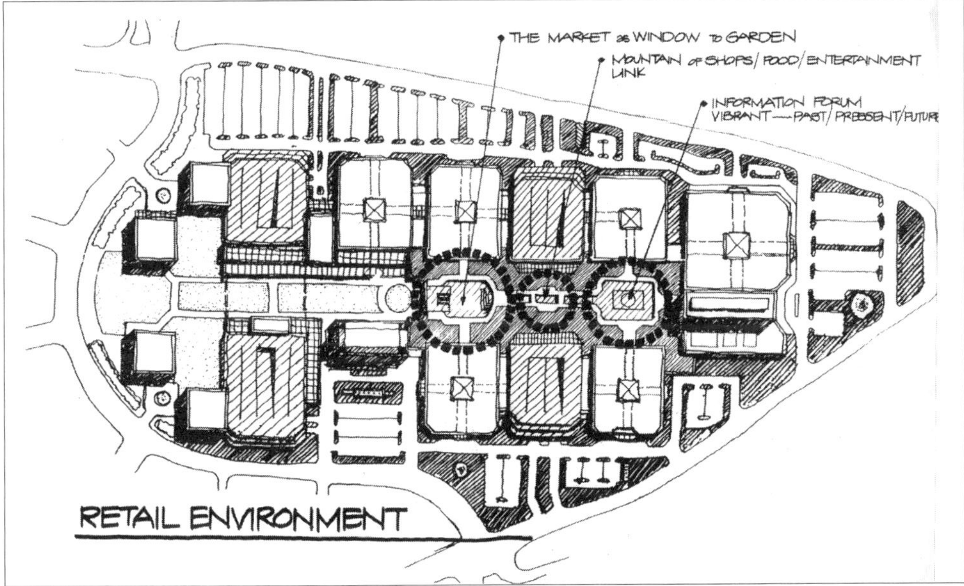

- open surface waters
- wetlands
- steep slopes
- highly erodible soils
- other significant natural features

Lines (Arrows)

The desired relationships among programmed uses may be both functional and visual. Functional relationships can be portrayed graphically as arrows on the concept plan (Figure 9-5). Desired views between locations on the site or between locations on and off the site also may be identified on a conceptual land use plan. Conversely, screening of views may be warranted, and this design objective should be portrayed graphically, particularly on large-scale plans for small sites.

The Capitol area in Washington D.C., for example, is replete with significant buildings and national monuments that are strategically placed in a geometric configuration. The axial relationships — and visual linkages — between these prominent landmarks create interlocking "shafts of space" that contribute to a cohesive urban milieu. This urban design concept is well illustrated in the classic book *Design of Cities*, by Edmund Bacon (1974). A concept plan can help explain intended functional or visual relationships among existing and proposed site uses.

Other linear elements on a concept plan may represent:

- circulation systems (e.g., pedestrian, bicycle, and vehicles)
- stormwater surface drainage patterns
- utility lines (above ground and subsurface)
- views (favorable and unfavorable)
- edges (e.g., abrupt changes in topography)

Colors, textures, widths, and styles of lines and arrows help distinguish these disparate types of site information. Annotations, or notes, are also useful in conveying information about the intended functional and visual relationships between the proposed land uses.

Points (Nodes)

In addition to areas (bubbles) and lines (arrows), the conceptual land use plan may also identify points (nodes) at the locations of significant site features. Off-site nodes and landmarks may be key elements of the surrounding biophysical and cultural context. Nodes can be portrayed graphically as points. These plan elements include:

- entrances
- intersections of pedestrian and vehicle circulation systems
- high points, view points, or scenic overlooks

Landmarks are also portrayed as points, and these plan elements include:

- specimen trees
- bridges
- monuments
- unique buildings

Nodes are typically locations that warrant special design treatment. Entrances to the site or to buildings, and major intersections of the pedestrian circulation system, are examples of locations where plazas or special seating areas could be developed. Other significant design objectives related to circulation include establishing gateways and creating a sense of arrival. The entrance driveway to a new building might be located, for example, on-axis with the proposed building or some other significant existing feature. This visual "anchor" could be a large specimen tree, or it could be a prominent off-site landform.

Protecting significant existing site features lends a unique character — or sense of place — to a developed site. These features potentially enhance the development's economic value by making the completed project more competitive in the marketplace. The protection of intrinsic environmental and cultural features also has social and ecological benefits.

CONCEPT EVALUATION

As the urban or built-up area of communities and regions increase — and populations continue to grow — undeveloped spaces are bound to become more valuable. These islands of undeveloped space typically increase in economic value, and this is why land is often bought as a speculative investment. But these undeveloped sites have become increasingly important ecologically and hydrologically. Increasing concern for environmental quality has led to greater involvement by local governments and citizens in land planning, design, and management.

Public officials and interested stakeholders are frequently involved in evaluating development proposals. This review process often includes stakeholders in the community who have little or no formal design training. The criteria for evaluating development plans will vary among different project types, project sites, and applicable land use regulations. Yet several potential impacts on the public should be considered when evaluating any development proposal. These include:

- infrastructure costs
- public service costs
- traffic generation
- stormwater runoff (quantity and quality)
- pedestrian circulation (safety and convenience)
- visual impacts

A fundamental goal of sustainable development, or "smart growth," is the protection of functional linkages among ecosystems that are on and adjacent to development sites. Yet Carol Franklin (1997), a principal of the firm Andropogan, writes:

> Sustainable design must go beyond the modest goal of minimizing site destruction to one of facilitating site recovery by reestablishing the processes necessary to sustain natural systems. This approach is not "naturalistic landscaping" or "preserving endangered species" but the preservation, restoration, and creation of self-sustaining, living environments.

The United Nations World Commission on Environment and Development (1987, p.8) defines sustainable development as:

> ...development that meets the needs of the present generation without compromising the ability of future generations to meet their own needs.

The costs — or impacts — of a proposed development can be estimated from the conceptual land use plan. This information is the basis for plan refinement, public approvals and permitting, and financing.

The strengths and weaknesses of alternative concept plans also can be evaluated and compared quantitatively. Statistics that summarize the existing site conditions and the proposed development are essential in evaluating the merits of any land use plan. The area and percent of total site area within different land use categories can be easily quantified. The percentage of a site covered by impervious surfaces, for example, is a key environmental indicator of potential hydrologic impact (Arnold and Gibbons, 1996). Count data, such as the number of specimen trees or the volume of stormwater runoff leaving the site, also can be quantified. Graphical and statistical summaries of these data can facilitate land development or conservation scenarios. Descriptive statistics about a proposed development facilitates review and revision by planning team members, and it also enables informed review by public planning staff, elected officials, and other interested stakeholders. The comparison of alternative concept plans can be useful in developing a final plan that combines the best features of each preliminary concept alternative.

SUMMARY

Land planning is a very challenging activity, because there are so many possible alternatives — or permutations — for arranging programmed elements on the site. The site inventory and analysis identify the relevant physiographic and cultural factors. These opportunities and constraints — or design determinants — provide the spatial framework for fitting the program to the site. When sites have significant assets and/or constraints, a systematic and analytical approach to concept development is essential. This deliberate approach is capable of producing defensible land use decisions and, ultimately, higher-quality built environments.

BOX 9-1 In Practice

COMMUNITY PLANNING

Indian Trace
Broward County, Florida

Owner/Developer
Arvida Corporation, Miami, Florida

Traffic Engineer/Economist:
Wilbur Smith and Associates, Miami, Florida

Engineer
Gee and Jenson, West Palm Beach, Florida

Land Planner
Environmental Planning & Design (EPD), Miami Lakes, Florida

Overview
This new town project was planned for 10,000 acres (4,000 hectares) along the western edge of a large, urbanized, and rapidly growing metropolitan area along the southeastern coast of Florida. Indian Trace is a planned unit development (PUD) designed to ultimately accommodate about 100,000 residents. A two-year research, analysis, and planning effort culminated in the conceptual master plan summarized here. The process involved many local, State, and Federal agencies, citizen groups, and a wide array of leading planners, engineers, economists, and ecologists. The projected build-out period for this new town is forty years.

Site Analysis
The 16-square-mile (41-square-kilometer) site is bounded by four major existing or proposed highways. To the north and west of these highways are protected Everglades Conservation Areas. Long-range projections of population and land use were provided by the Broward County Area Planning Board and the County Planning and Zoning Department. The site, the local environs, and the larger region were all examined during the site inventory and analysis.

The analysis of a site topographic survey and aerial photographs was supplemented by field investigations of soil, water, vegetation, and wildlife. More than thirty "eco-determinant" maps were created to define the site's ecological context and long-range constraints and possibilities. These maps addressed climate (Figure B9-1), hydrology (Figure B9-2), and a wide variety of other biophysical attributes. Vegetation on this site includes an abundance of invasive exotic species (i.e., Melaleuca, Brazilian Pepper, Australian Pine). No endangered animal species were found. Relatively shallow groundwater, low site elevations in relation to mean sea level (MSL), and abundant seasonal rainfall were important land use constraints.

Significant cultural factors that influenced the conceptual land use plan included the locations of various public facilities and infrastructure. Regional transportation systems, schools, public safety and medical facilities, and overall land use patterns were considered, along with many other cultural attributes. For each of these elements, existing conditions as well as community and regional plans for the future were assessed.

Design Features

1. *Open Space.* An extensive open space system defines neighborhoods and provides recreational and visual amenities (Figure B9-3). In addition to the lakes, waterways, and wetlands ("blueways"), the plan also creates a diverse array of upland green space. Together, the water areas and the green spaces create a clearly defined framework for future development.

2. *Water.* The water resources management plan is designed to prevent flooding, protect water quality, replenish underground reserves, and develop surface water storage areas as community amenities (Figure B9-4). Approximately 3,000 acres (1,200 hectares) are allocated to lakes, waterways, and other water storage areas. Stormwater runoff will be filtered by grassed swales and buffer strips adjacent to lakes and waterways. The normal water elevation in the lakes will be 4.0 feet above mean sea level. During rainy periods, discharge to the South New River Canal will occur, at a limited rate, when the system reaches 5.0 feet above MSL.

3. *Neighborhoods.* Residential population on the site will be distributed as a gradient from low density in the southwest to medium densities in the northeast. Neighborhoods will vary in shapes and sizes to accommodate a variety of housing types, ranging from semirural "villages" to apartment complexes with urban densities (Figure B9-5). Average housing density will be 4.08 dwelling units per gross acre (0.4 hectare). Neighborhood gathering places, focal points, and recreation activities are designed to be within easy walking or biking distances of residents. Commercial and civic uses are planned for neighborhood centers. In addition, all of the schools, major cultural facilities, and commercial districts are strategically located in proximity to at least two neighborhoods.

4. *Circulation.* The plan's multimodal transportation network includes a regional public transit node and a hierarchy of freeways, arterial parkways, collector roads, and local streets (Figure B9-6). The plan also includes separate bus lanes, mini-transit routes, and an extensive walking and biking trail system. Two-lane roads designed for low speeds and limited traffic volumes will be common in many neighborhoods. Limited building frontage will be allowed along major parkways and collector roads. The right-of-way for parkways will accommodate walkways and bicycle paths. Utility lines for water distribution and wastewater collection will parallel the site's network of major roads and streets (Figure B9-7).

5. *Recreation.* Upon completion, the new town will contain more than 20 acres (8 hectares) of recreational land for each 1,000 residents. These recreational areas include several school/neighborhood parks, five larger urban parks, one regional park, and two golf courses (Figure B9-8).

6. *Community Center.* A planned Community Center will accommodate civic, cultural, and commercial uses, along with a regional transit terminal. Industrial uses planned for areas outside of the community center include a regional goods distribution center and assorted research-oriented light industry.

Source: Environmental Planning & Design (EPD).

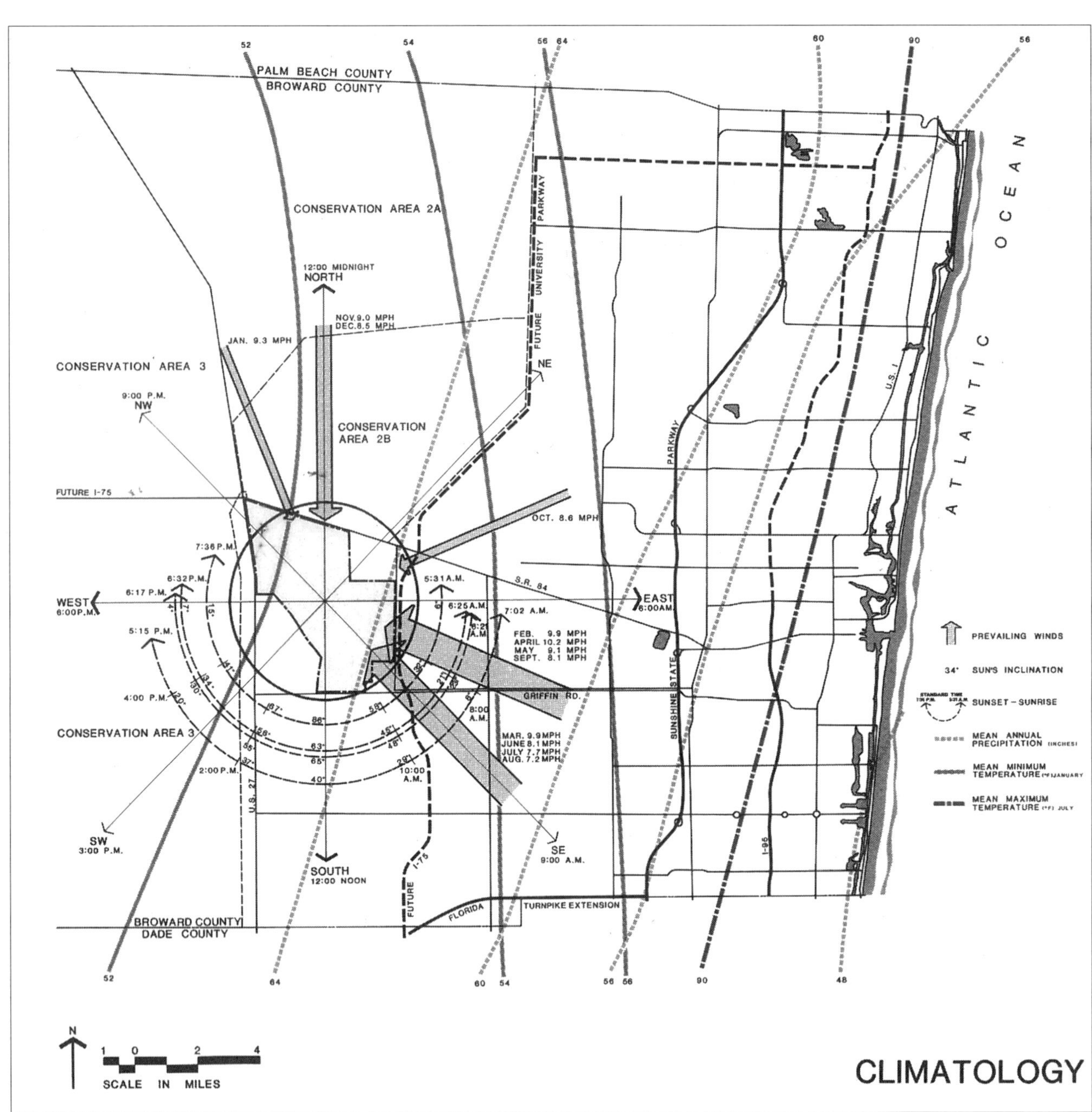

Figure B9-1 Map of climatic factors influencing the site. This map shows the direction of winter winds, average seasonal precipitation, seasonal times of sunrise and sunset, and average seasonal temperatures. *Source:* Environmental Planning & Design.

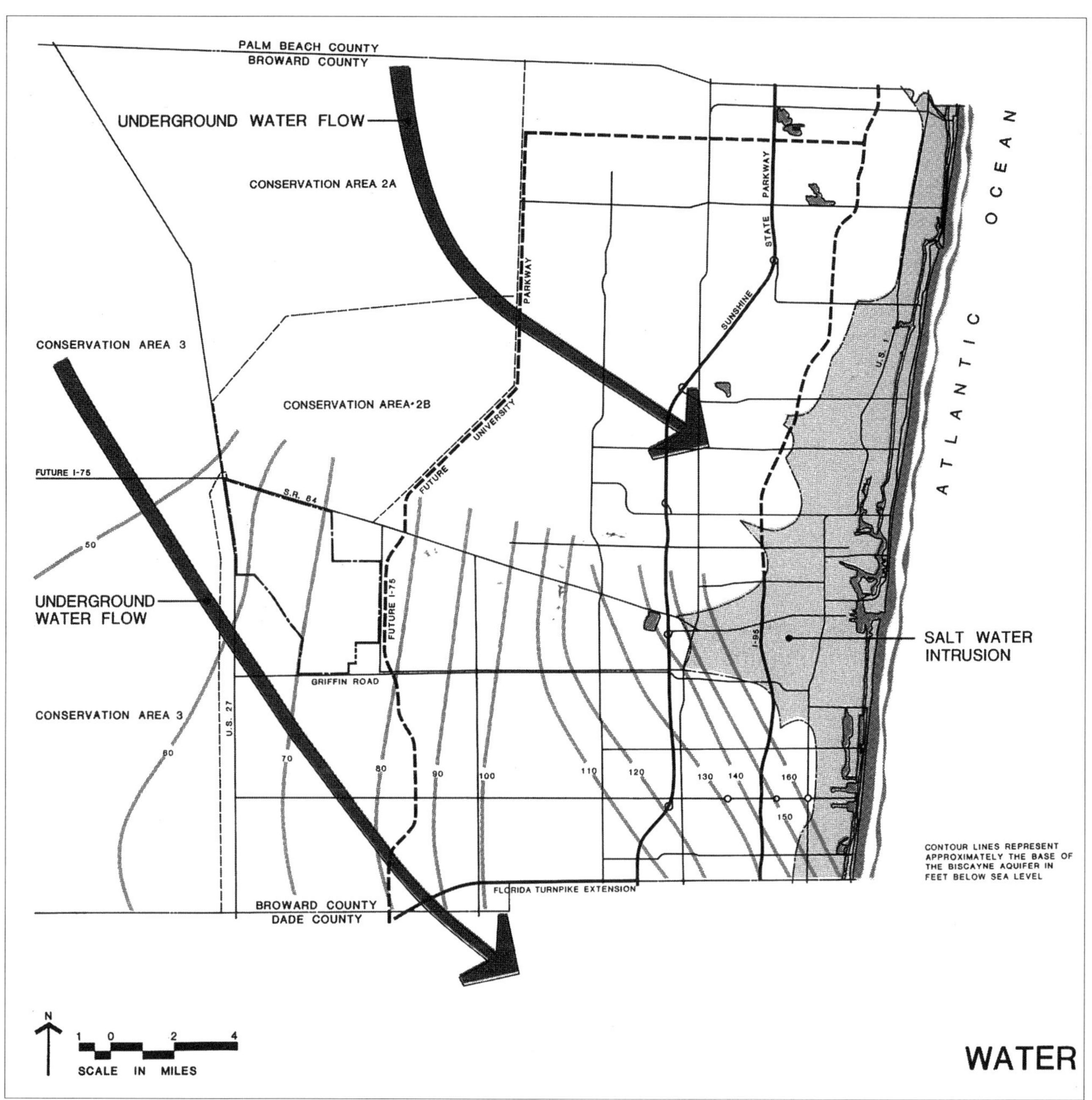

Figure B9-2 Map of groundwater showing locations of salt water intrusion, aquifer depths, and direction of groundwater flow.
Source: Environmental Planning & Design.

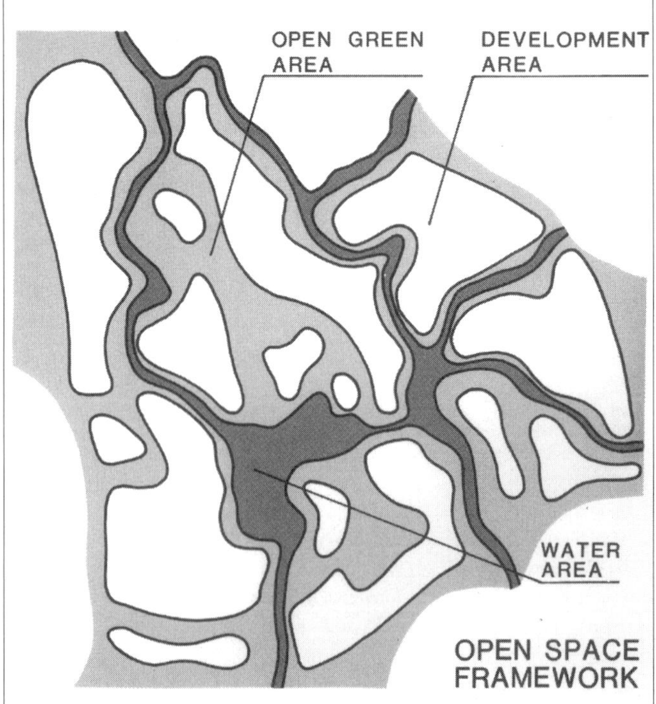

Figure B9-3 Conceptual diagram of the proposed open space system, providing the spatial framework for future development. *Source:* Environmental Planning & Design.

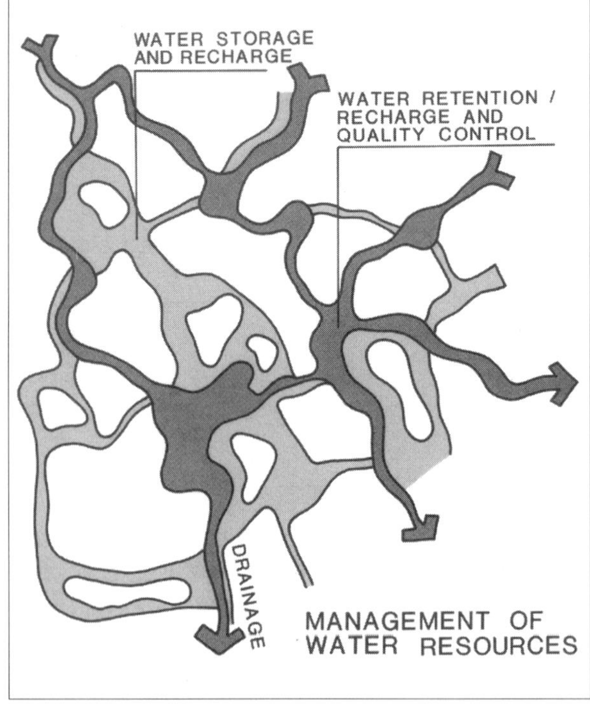

Figure B9-4 Conceptual diagram of the water resources management plan. *Source:* Environmental Planning & Design.

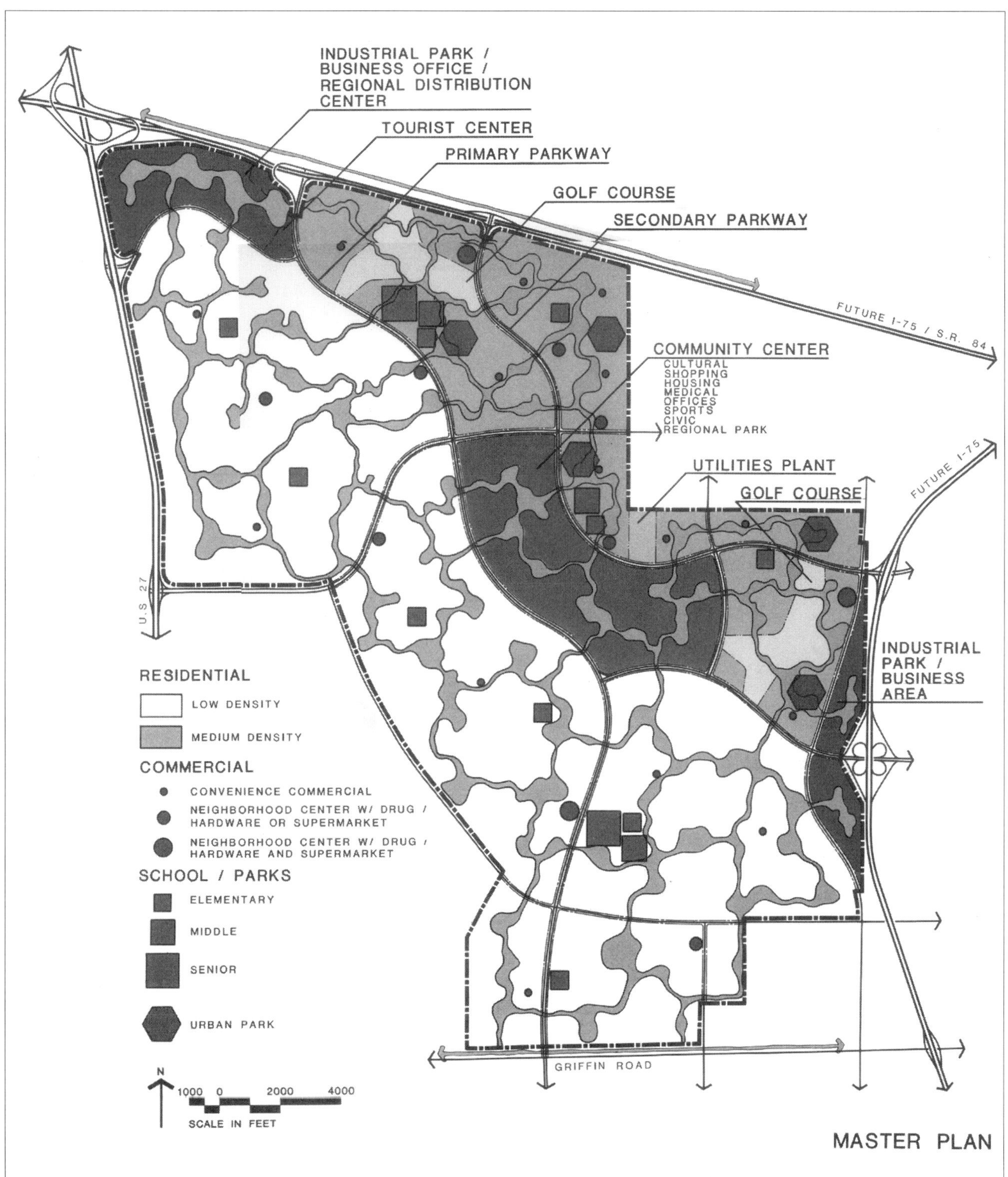

Figure B9-5 Conceptual land use plan for the entire site. *Source:* Environmental Planning & Design.

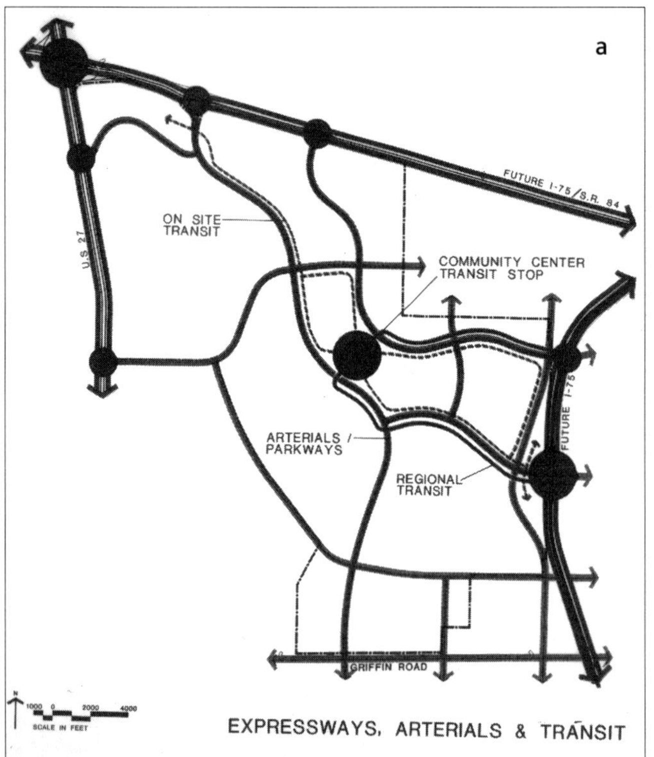

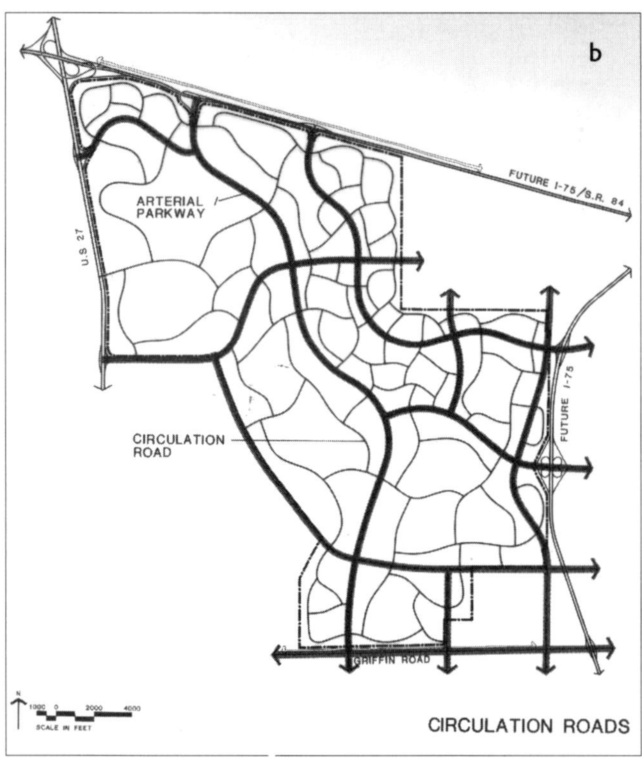

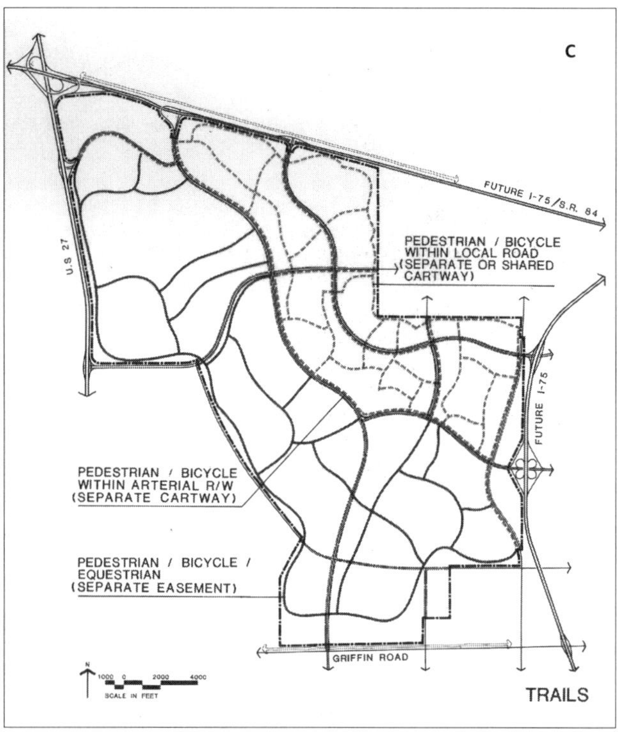

Figure B9-6 (a–c) Conceptual diagram of the proposed circulation system. A hierarchy of components includes arterial highways, public transit stops, local streets, walkways and bike paths. *Source:* Environmental Planning & Design.

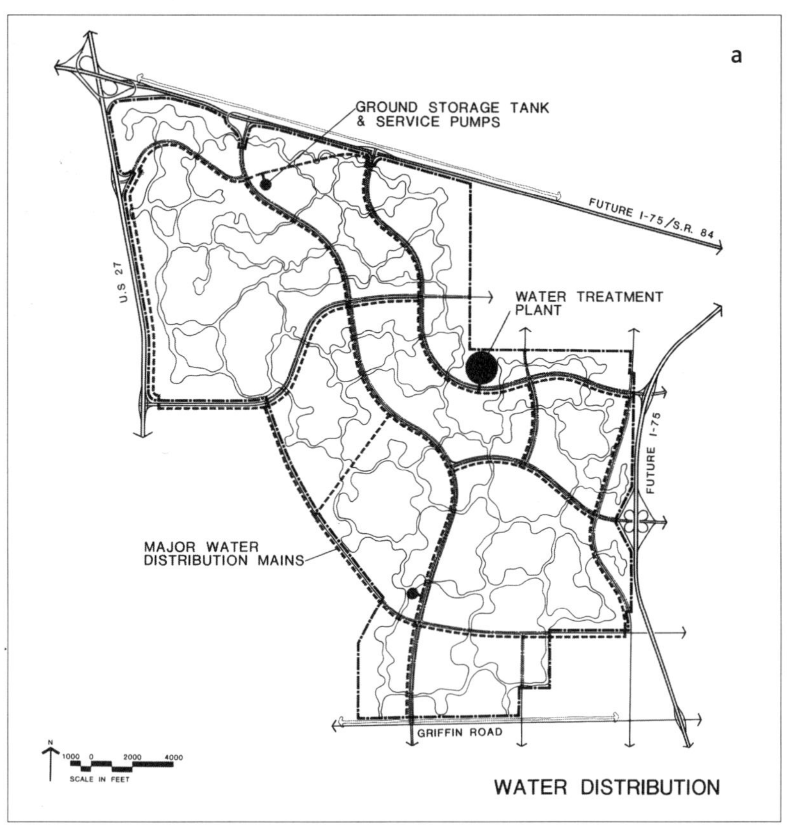

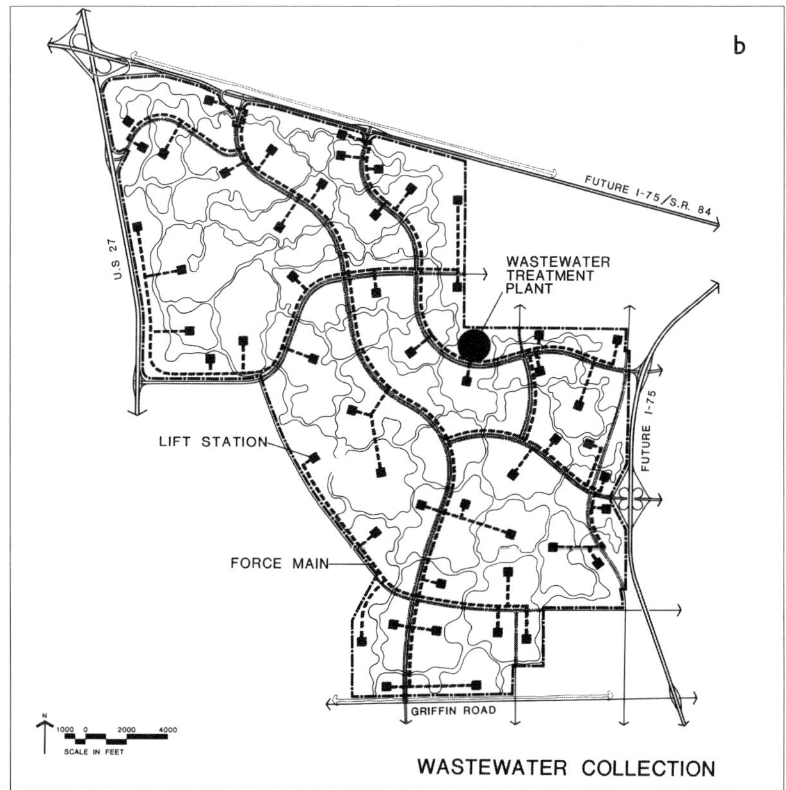

Figure B9-7 (a–b) Conceptual diagrams of proposed water distribution and wastewater collection systems. *Source:* Environmental Planning & Design.

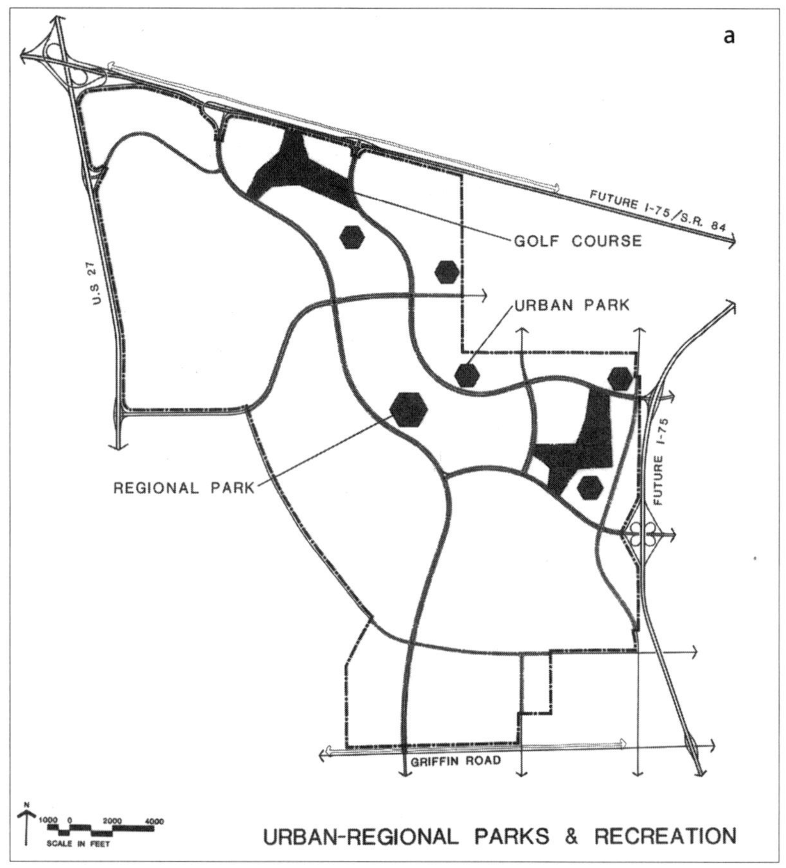

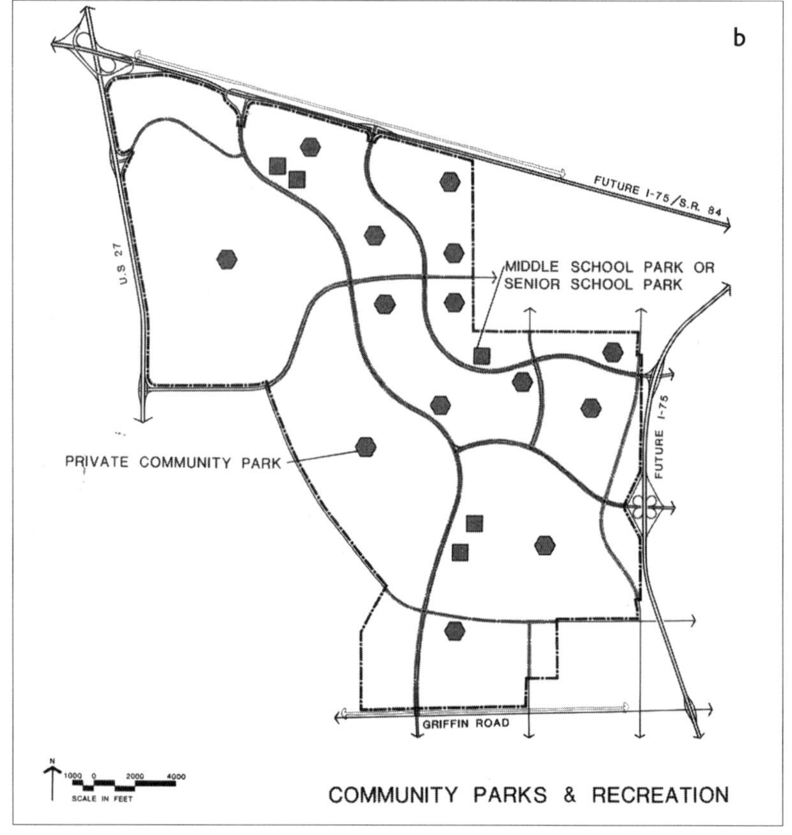

Figure B9-8 (a–d) Conceptual diagrams of the proposed recreation, parks, and open space systems. The hierarchy of open spaces spans a range of spatial scales: regional/urban, community, and neighborhood. *Source:* Environmental Planning & Design.

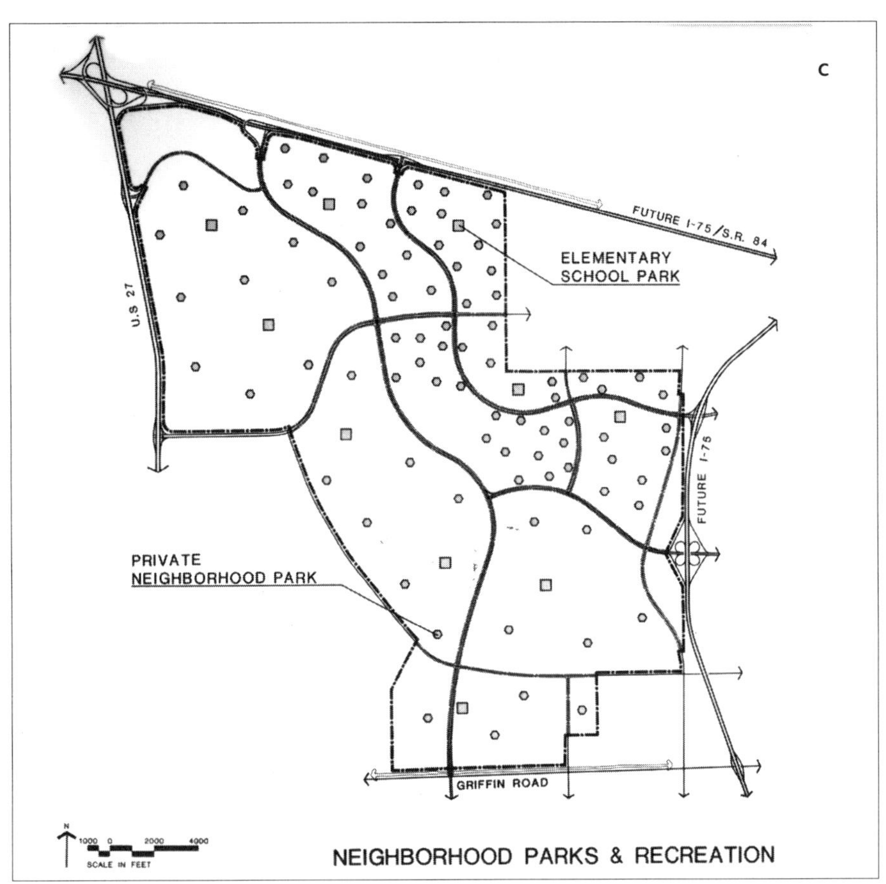
c
FUTURE I-75/S.R. 84
ELEMENTARY SCHOOL PARK
U.S 27
FUTURE I-75
PRIVATE NEIGHBORHOOD PARK
GRIFFIN ROAD
N
1000 0 2000 4000
SCALE IN FEET
NEIGHBORHOOD PARKS & RECREATION

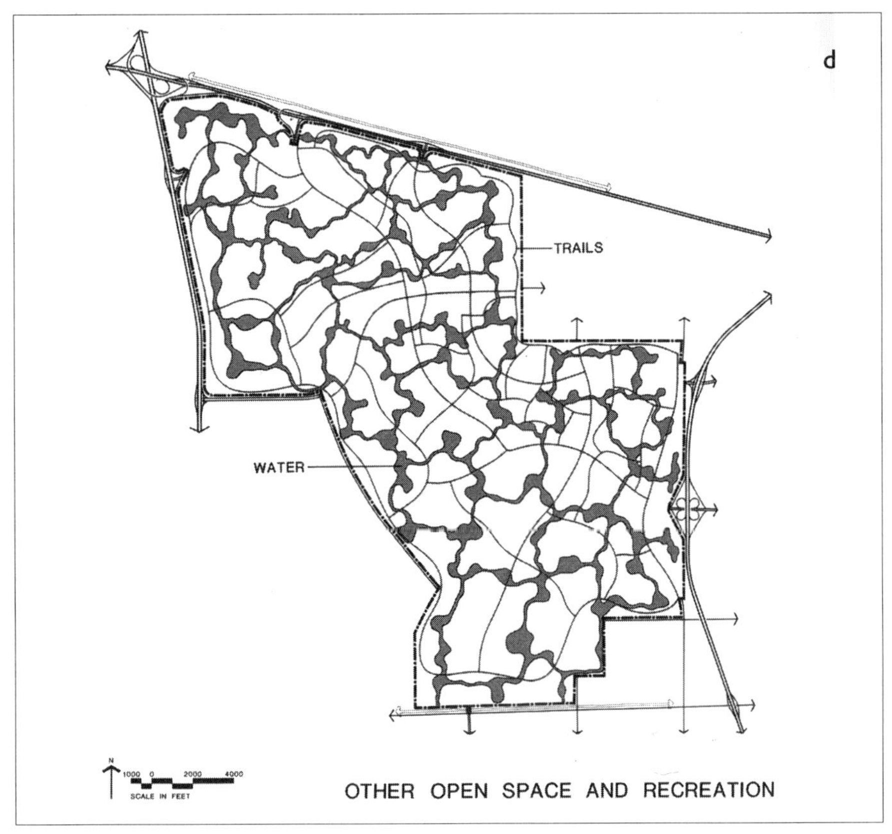
d
TRAILS
WATER
N
1000 0 2000 4000
SCALE IN FEET
OTHER OPEN SPACE AND RECREATION

CHAPTER

10 Design Development and Implementation

INTRODUCTION

A common misconception among the general public is that design is merely a matter of aesthetics. In a land development context, design of the built environment is expressed at multiple spatial scales. One level of design determines the spatial organization of buildings, circulation systems, open spaces, and other site elements (Figures 10-1 and 10-2). A more detailed level of design involves the articulation of each individual site element (Figure 10-3). These broad- and fine-scale design decisions determine whether or not the development will adequately serve its intended uses, how it will impact environmental quality, and what effects it will have on human comfort and safety. The site's organization and articulation also determine how much the development will cost to build, and what its value will be, in monetary terms, upon completion.

The land planning and design process is a problem-solving endeavor. For each land development or restoration project, the unique combination of site and program creates a unique set of location-specific design problems. There are often dozens of ways to solve these problems. Different design solutions may be satisfactory, on a purely functional level, but they may have significant environmental impacts. The most successful solutions are not only functional but also aesthetically pleasing and environmentally benign.

Figure 10-1 Diagrams illustrate an important design feature: open space hierarchy comprising public, semipublic, and private space. *Source:* The HOK Planning Group.

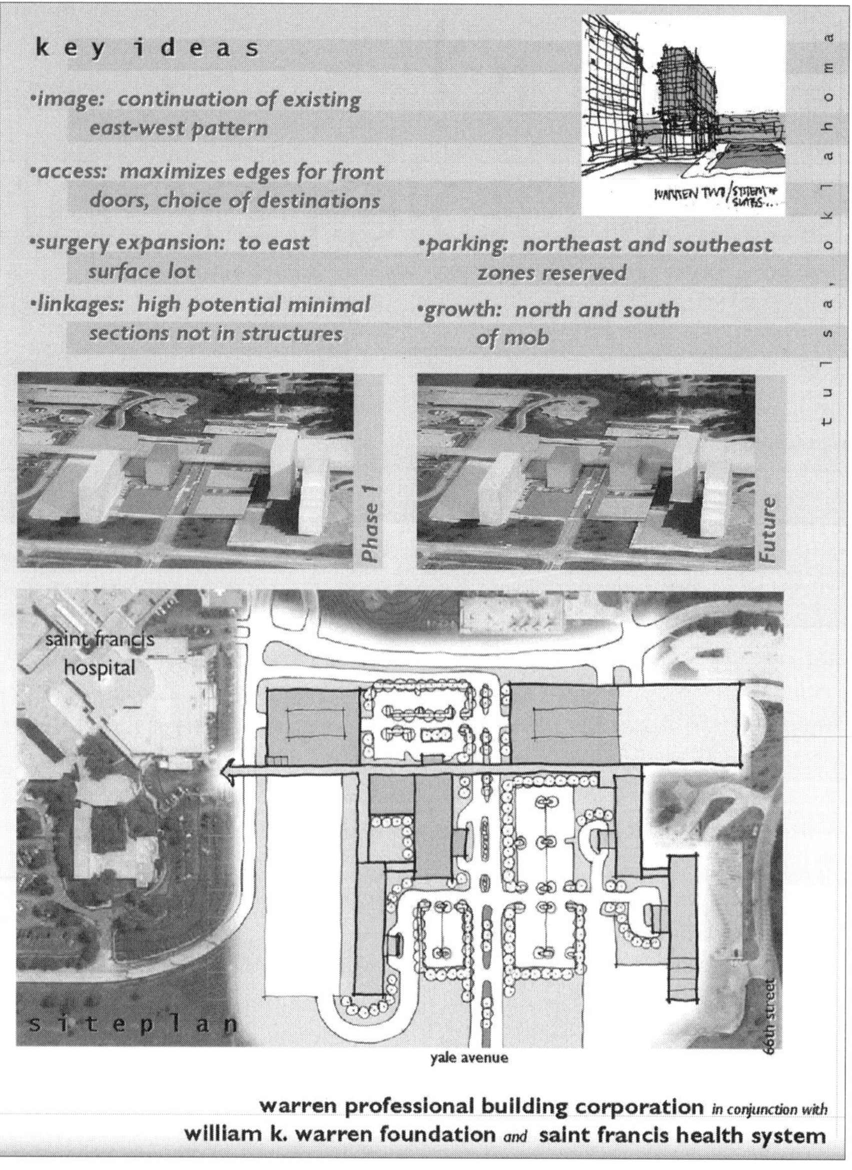

Figure 10-2 Key design objectives for the site's spatial organization are communicated on this project phasing diagram. *Source:* The HOK Planning Group.

Figure 10-3 Design character studies for a subtropical waterfront resort. *Source:* Edward D. Stone, Jr., and

The conceptual land use plan, or concept plan, spatially organizes the proposed site uses. Subsequent design development leads to a master plan or site plan that is a spatially explicit representation of future site conditions. Detailed information about the dimensions of structures and other site elements, and the materials used to build these structures, are subsequently conveyed in the construction drawings (Figure 10-4).

Site planning projects can be organized into a typology, based on one key program attribute. The three basic types of projects are those with: (1) no buildings, (2) one building, or (3) two or more buildings. Projects with no buildings include parks, greenways, and other areas designed for active and/or passive recreation (Figure 10-5). Nature conservation areas and nature interpretation centers also fit under this category. Projects with a single building are perhaps the most common type of site planning. Projects with several buildings are usually the most complex type of site planning (Figure 10-6). Ideally, the design of the building and the design of the site are integrally linked. The arrival and entry sequence to a building, for example, can be a carefully controlled series of movements from off the site to inside the building. Also, the footprint of a building can be adapted to fit the site (Figure 10-7). Hilly sites, for example, may lead to the design of a building in which the foundation, and even the floors of the building, step down the hillside. Concern for indoor–outdoor relationships can have a substantial influence on both architectural and site design.

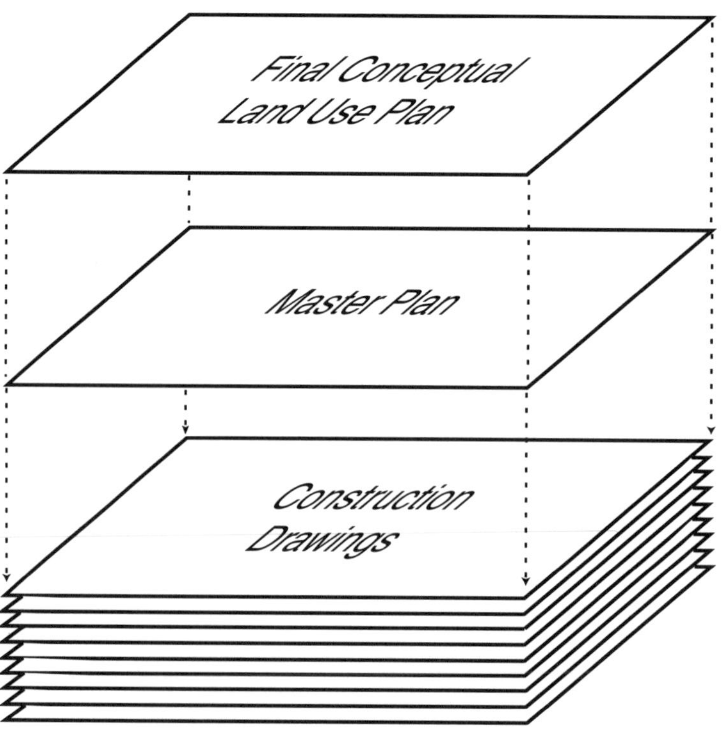

Figure 10-4 The final conceptual land use plan provides a spatial framework for developing the site's master plan. The master plan refines the concept plan and serves as the basis for more detailed construction drawings.

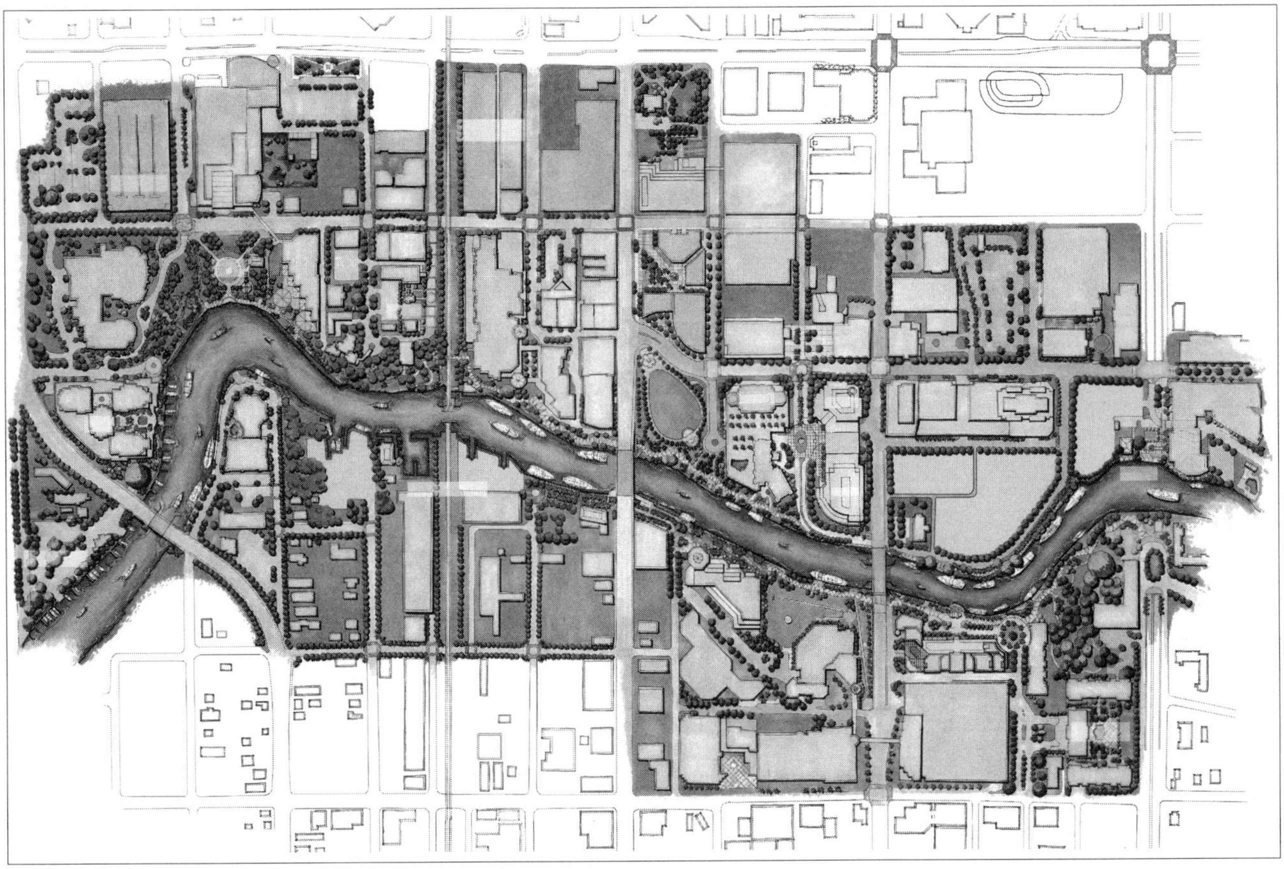

Figure 10-5 Master plan showing a recreational corridor within an urban context (River Walk, Fort Lauderdale, Florida). *Source:* Edward D. Stone, Jr., and Associates.

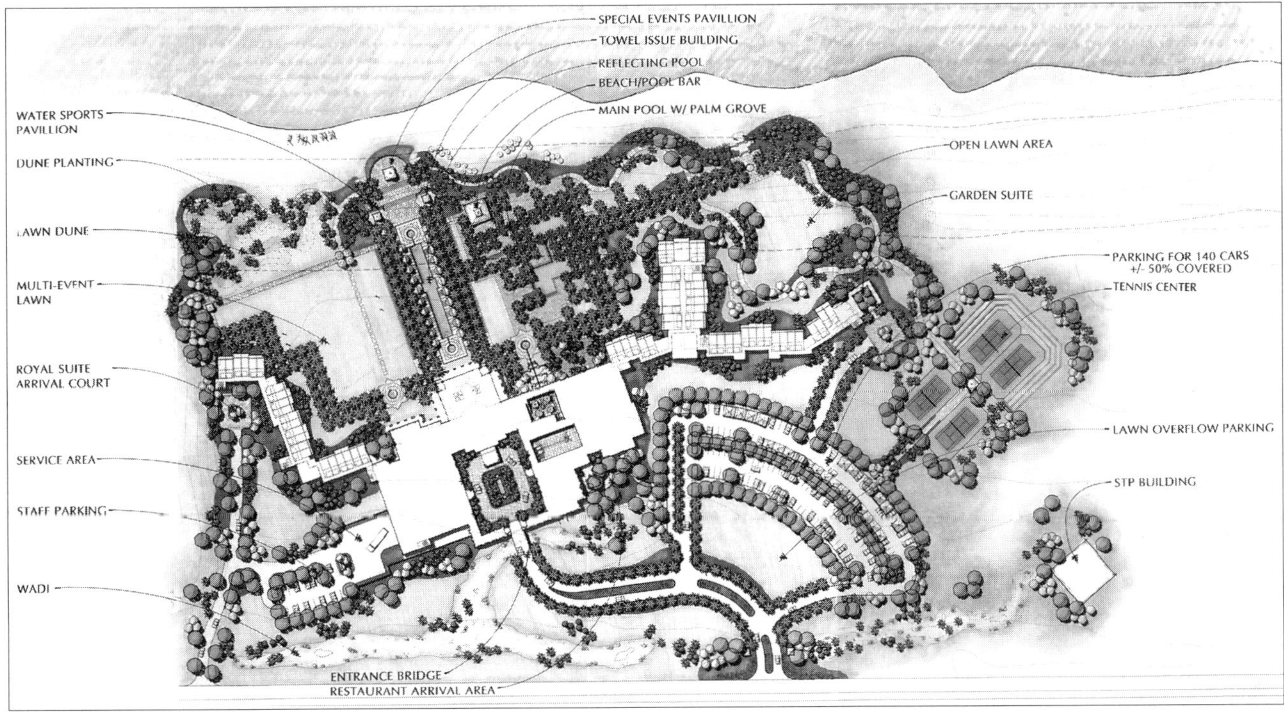

Figure 10-6 A clear entry and arrival sequence is provided to the site's main building. *Source:* Edward D. Stone, Jr., and Associates.

Figure 10-7 Master plan for a resort project with buildings sited to maximize scenic views and other amenity values. A table organizes useful information about the site's proposed development. *Source:* Edward D. Stone, Jr., and Associates.

DESIGN CHALLENGES

Site plans must first and foremost satisfy the basic functional and regulatory requirements presented by the program, the site, and applicable laws and public policies. Local zoning ordinances, for example, might require the construction of thirty parking spaces, including three spaces for the physically disabled. A local stormwater ordinance might require that stormwater leaving the site must not exceed the volume of water leaving under predevelopment conditions. Poorly designed site plans may create persistent deficiencies that inconvenience site users, increase their exposure to safety risks, and negatively impact environmental quality. It is beyond the scope of this book to summarize the many design principles that influence decisions about the organization and articulation of the built environment. Instead, this section will address three specific issues that are often raised in criticisms of land development projects. These three issues, which are directly influenced by design decisions, are: pedestrian circulation, ecological integrity, and visual quality.

Pedestrian Circulation

Pedestrians often face conflicts with vehicles that could be avoided through better design of site circulation systems (Figure 10-8). Pedestrian–vehicle conflicts are a common problem where automobiles are the dominant form of transportation. Pedestrians may even be relegated to using vehicle circulation systems (e.g., streets, parking lots) to get to their desired destinations. Pedestrian circulation systems should be designed to incorporate the following principles:

- efficiency (avoids redundancy, duplication, or excess pavement)
- capacity (accommodates anticipated traffic)
- connectivity (continuous walkways, with minimum interruptions, link common destinations)
- separation from incompatible circulation systems (avoids pedestrian–vehicle conflicts, vehicle-related fumes and noises)
- orientation (facilitates way finding and a sense of arrival and entry)
- amenities (provides seating, lighting, and other site furnishings)

Clients, government officials, and other stakeholders evaluate development proposals with various criteria. Pedestrian circulation should be a high priority in the review process.

Ecological Integrity

Environmental quality is influenced by the spatial patterns of land development. For example, the arrangement of streets, buildings, and other elements influences the ability of fauna to move within the landscape for food, water, and the completion of life cycles that require different habitat types. The spatial structure of the built environment also affects the movement of water, nutrients, and sediment. Poorly managed stormwater runoff may degrade surface waters and contribute to local flooding.

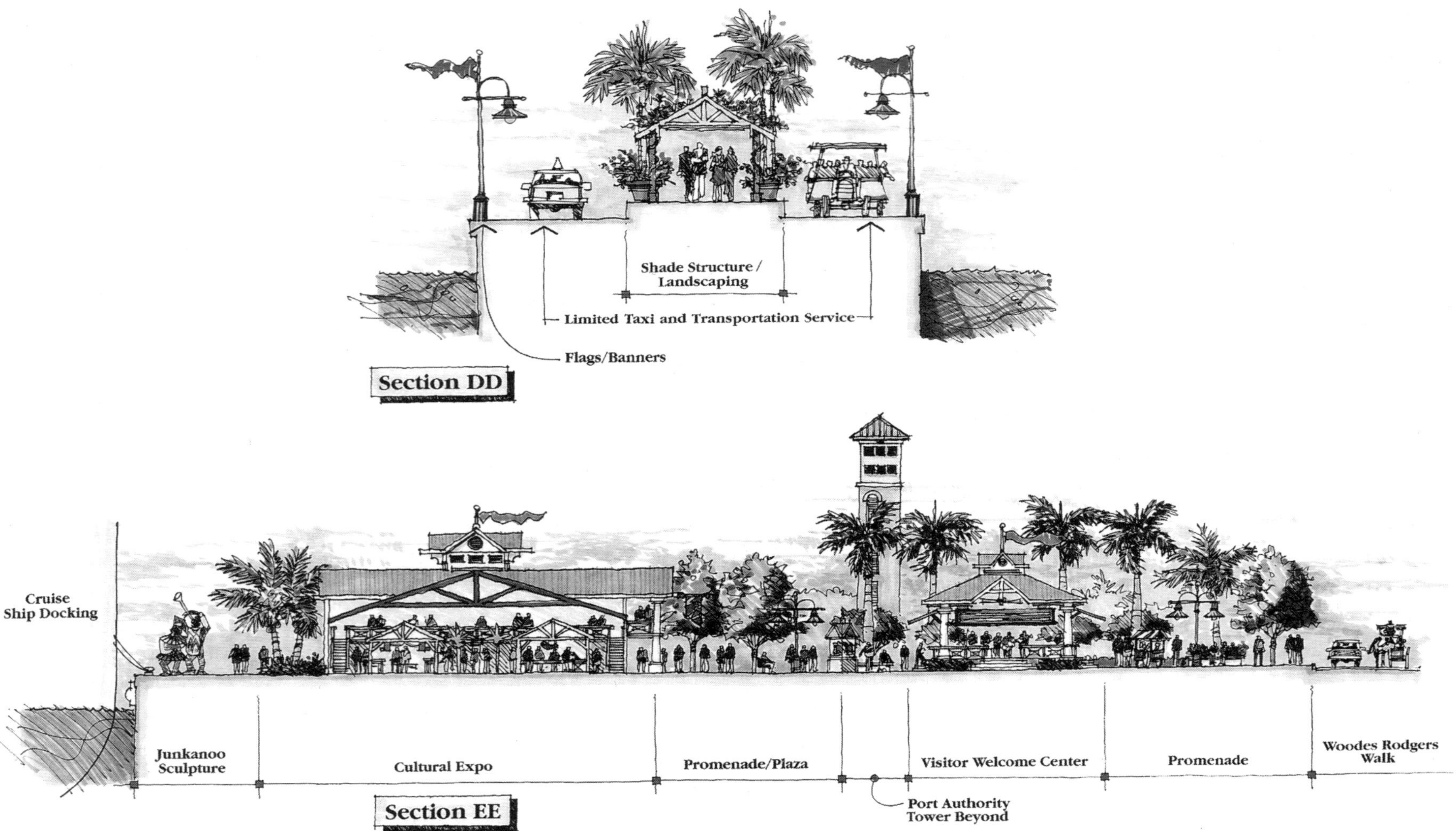

Figure 10-8 Section DD of a proposed pier communicates an important design principle: separate incompatible vehicle and pedestrian circulation systems.
Source: Edward D. Stone, Jr., and Associates.

Water *quality* in developed, and developing, areas may be compromised by four kinds of pollution:

- thermal pollution (e.g., runoff with elevated temperatures)
- sedimentation (e.g., sand, silt, clay)
- chemical pollution (e.g., hydrocarbons, heavy metals, fertilizers, pesticides)
- pathogens (e.g., bacteria, viruses)

Land development can also change the distribution, or *quantity*, of water within a watershed. Groundwater depletion, for example, occurs when groundwater pumping is not balanced by groundwater recharge. The result of this imbalance is a slow but steady "mining" of groundwater resources.

Effective stormwater management on construction sites controls erosion, retains the majority of sediments on the site, and facilitates runoff retention and infiltration. Sediment discharges from construction sites can be many times greater than the discharges from undeveloped areas. Moreover, heavy metals, nutrients, and other pollutants can attach to sediments carried by stormwater runoff. Nonpoint source pollution controls attempt to reduce and mitigate the impacts of urban runoff both during and after construction. State and local governments in the United States, for example, are taking a more proactive role in regulating development impacts. An increasingly common requirement is that peak runoff rates, average runoff volumes, and average annual total suspended solid (TSS) loadings be maintained at levels that do not exceed predevelopment levels (U.S. Environmental Protection Agency, 1993).

Erosion control is based on two main concepts (U.S. Environmental Protection Agency, 1993): disturb the smallest area of land possible for the shortest period of time, and stabilize disturbed soils to prevent erosion from occurring. Primary erosion control methods for construction sites include (U.S. Environmental Protection Agency, 1993):

- Schedule clearing and grading to avoid periods of highest erosion potential (spring thaw) and favor periods of the year with lowest erosion potential (dry season).
- Stage land disturbance activities to expose only the area currently under construction. As soon as the grading and construction in an area are complete, the area should be stabilized with seeding, sodding, and, on steeper slopes, matting or mulching.
- Restrict clearing to the areas essential for construction. The proposed land disturbance limits should be physically marked off to ensure that only the required land area is cleared. Fencing should be used to protect tree root systems from cutting, filling, and compaction caused by heavy equipment.
- Locate potential nonpoint pollution sources (e.g., material stockpiles, borrow areas, construction access roads) away from steep slopes, highly erodible soils, and areas that drain directly into sensitive water bodies. Cover or stabilize topsoil stockpiles.
- Divert runoff away from exposed areas or newly seeded slopes. Construct benches, terraces, or ditches at regular intervals to intercept runoff.
- Minimize the length and steepness of slopes. Use retaining walls to decrease the steepness of a slope and reduce runoff velocity.
- Stabilize drainage channels with erosion-resistant lining (e.g., grass, sod, riprap). Add check dams in swales or channels to reduce the runoff velocity.

Erosion controls also can reduce the size and cost of sediment control structures. Sediment controls capture sediment that is transported in stormwater runoff. Detention (gravitational settling) and filtration are the main techniques for removing sediment from runoff. Construction site sediment controls include (U.S. Environmental Protection Agency, 1993):

- Sediment basins for drainage areas between 5 and 100 acres (2 and 40 hectares)
- Sediment traps in drainageways for drainage areas less than 5 acres (2 hectares)
- Filter fabric fencing where there is sheet flow from drainage areas less than 0.5 acre (0.2 hectare)
- Straw bale barriers where there is sheet flow from drainage areas less than 0.25 acre (0.1 hectare)
- Drain inlet protection traps (using filter fabric, straw bales, gravel, or sand bags)
- Vegetated filter strips where there is low-velocity sheet flow

In addition, construction entrances should be placed in locations where equipment will be less likely to track mud and other sediment off the site. A pad of gravel, over filter fabric, at the construction entrance can help dislodge the mud and other debris picked up by the tires of construction vehicles.

Vegetation performs many important ecological and aesthetic functions in the built environment (Table 10-1 and Figure 10-9). Vegetated buffer zones, for example, can protect critical environmental areas from contaminated runoff and also facilitate infiltration and groundwater recharge. Native and naturalized plant materials can significantly reduce both planting costs and maintenance costs for irrigation, mowing or pruning, and pest control. In the midwestern United States, for example, maintaining irrigated turfgrass costs as much as six times more than the cost of maintaining native prairie or wetland communities (Applied Ecological Services, 2000).

TABLE 10-1 Selected uses of plants in the built environment.

Objective	*Specific use*
Architectural design	Defining (enclosing) space Creating linkages between buildings or spaces Controlling or directing circulation Marking the location of an entrance
Environmental engineering	Controlling erosion Slowing and filtering stormwater runoff Intercepting and facilitating stormwater infiltration
Microclimate amelioration	Reducing wind velocity Shading solar radiation
Aesthetic enhancement	Screening undesirable views Framing desirable views or focal points Softening building corners and walls
Ecological integrity	Creating wildlife habitat (food, cover, and shelter) Providing corridors for wildlife movement Improving air quality

Source: Booth, 1983; Brooks, 1994.

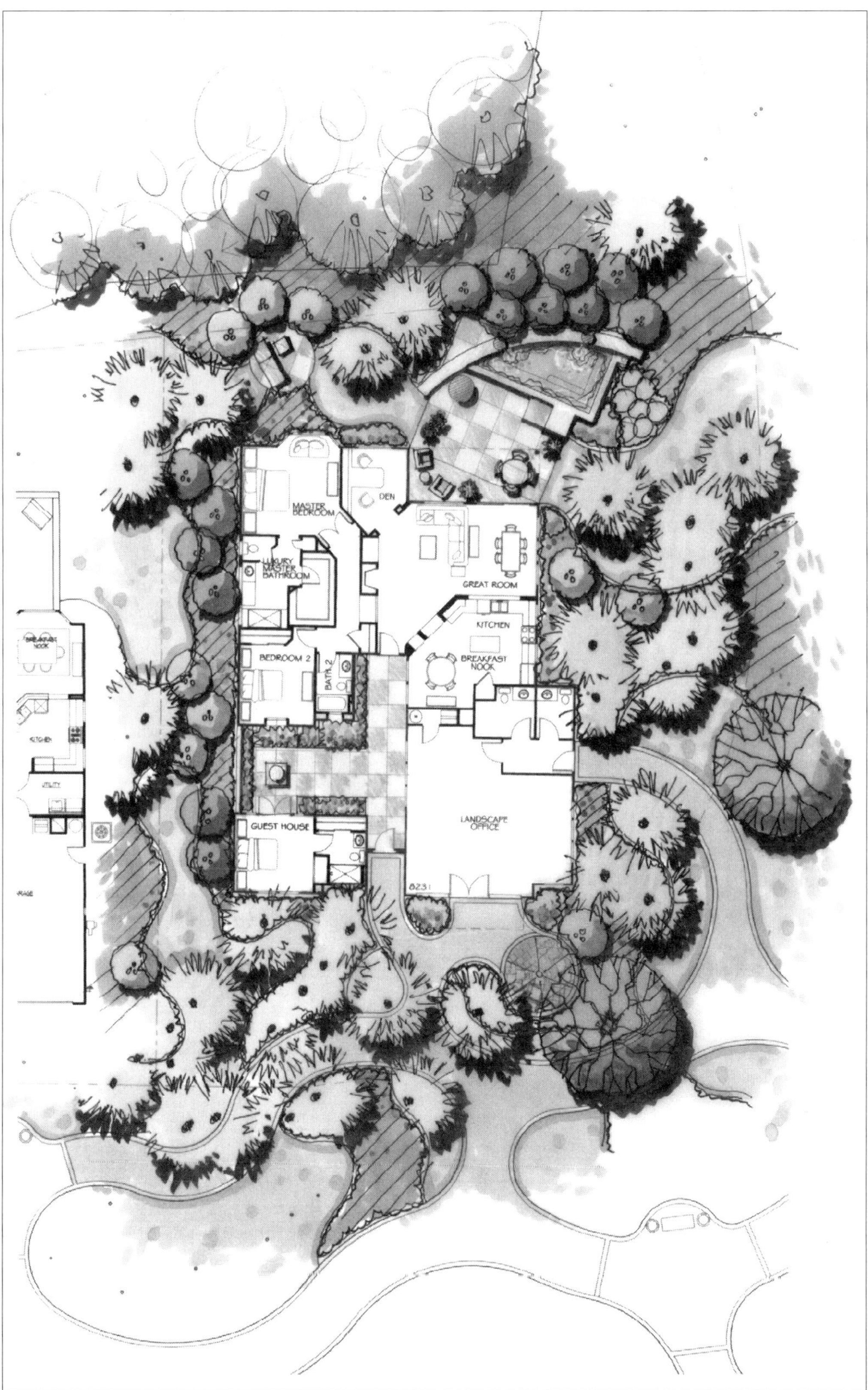

Figure 10-9 Site plan showing landscape/building relationships for a new single-family residence. Trees and shrubs define outdoor spaces, provide shade, screen views, and perform a variety of other design functions. *Source:* Edward D. Stone, Jr., and Associates.

Visual Quality

Space—whether inside buildings or outside within the landscape—is defined by a ground plane, a vertical plane, and an overhead plane. In the outdoor environment, these three planes can be defined by buildings, landforms, plants, and many other physical elements. The functions performed by the ground, vertical, and overhead planes are summarized in Table 10-2. Visual quality in the built environment depends, in part, on the size and shape of the space. Visual quality is also a function of the forms and the materials employed. These may be visually unifying, visually chaotic, or somewhere in between. Unity, balance, and emphasis are three fundamental aesthetic principles that help guide the design of the built environment. Many different design fields—automobile design, furniture design, and others—share these basic design principles. Unity is achieved through the repetition of elements with similar visible attributes. Unity can be achieved, for example, by repeating similar forms, textures, or colors (Figure 10-10). Unity implies wholeness, internal coherence, and compatibility with the surroundings. Designs may be internally consistent but in visual conflict with the surroundings.

An urban site, for example, may be surrounded by a rich visual context of buildings, walls, street furniture, pavement, and vegetation. Each of these elements has visible attributes that contribute to the character, or identity, of the built environment. On urban infill projects, choices of construction materials are driven by several factors, including material durability, cost, and appearance. Which materials are used, and how they are combined, determines to a large extent if the project is visually unified and balanced, and if it fits in with its surroundings. Balance, in this context, refers to the "weight" associated with color, form, texture, and other visible attributes of the built environment. Balance is often achieved by using an axis to organize buildings and spaces within the landscape (Figure 10-11).

What is appropriate or inappropriate for a particular site is a matter of judgment, but this evaluation should consider the purpose of the project and the nature of the surrounding context.

TABLE 10-2 Selected design functions of the three basic spatial components.

Plane	*Design Function*
Ground	Separation Orientation Enclosure Linkage
Vertical	Screening Enclosure Background Direction Transition Framing Buffering
Overhead	Screening Enclosure Shading Protection

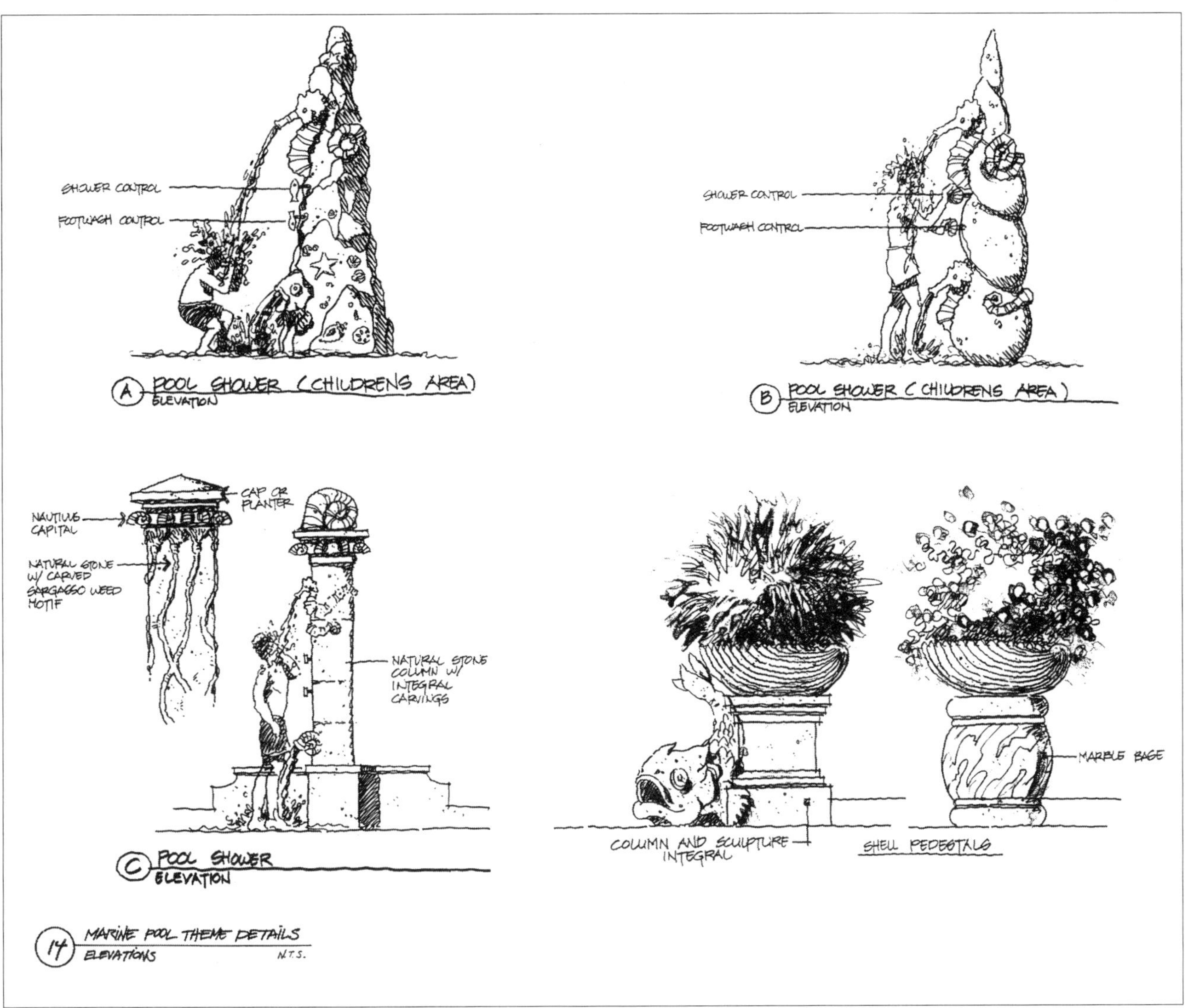

Figure 10-10 Character studies depicting a unifying design theme for features of a waterfront resort. *Source:* Edward D. Stone, Jr., and Associates.

Compatibility with the site's context can be achieved by choosing similar materials, proportions, and forms. The National Mainstreet Center (1995), for example, identifies ten design attributes that contribute to a visually unified downtown commercial district. These attributes, which are typically considered in the design of urban infill projects, are:

- Building height
- Building width
- Building proportion (height-to-width ratio)
- Relationship to street (i.e., setback)
- Roof and cornice forms
- Composition (organization of facade parts)
- Rhythm (windows)
- Proportions of openings (height-to-width ratio, wall-to-window ratio)
- Materials
- Color

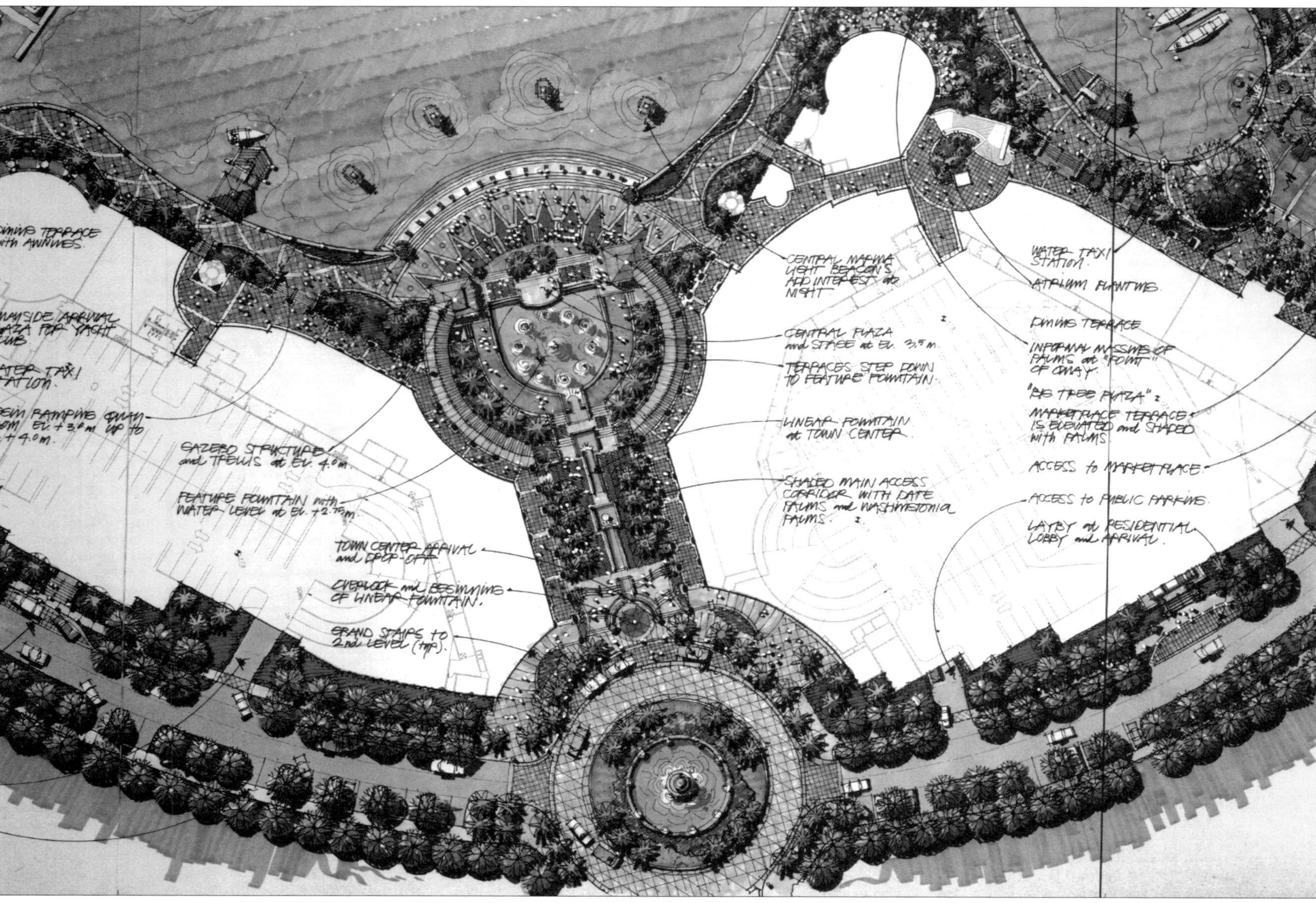

Figure 10-11 Detailed master plan provides useful information about the site's context and the proposed design. A balanced and unified outdoor environment is created, in part, by the repeated use of similar forms and materials. Note the bilateral symmetry along the project's central axis. *Source:* Edward D. Stone, Jr., and Associates.

In some cases, a new building should be different from the surrounding buildings. This is especially appropriate for buildings that will serve prominent civic functions. These buildings, which often become landmarks because of their special purpose and unique appearance, include schools, libraries, and hospitals. Emphasis, the third major aesthetic principle, is established when a building or other design element stands out from other adjacent or nearby elements. Visual hierarchies can be created by manipulating the arrangement of visible characteristics of each design element. These characteristics include: size, shape, placement, and surface attributes (e.g., color, texture).

PERMITTING AND APPROVALS

Regulatory Authority

Federal, State, and local governments in the United States are divided into three branches, each of which has specific functions:

- legislative branch (writes and enacts laws)
- executive branch (administers laws)
- judicial branch (interprets laws)

The legislative branch at the local government level consists of a city council that writes and enacts local laws (ordinances or codes). Although these elected officials are the final authorities for the regulation of land within the city's jurisdiction, they typically are advised by a planning commission of local citizens appointed by the mayor, the head of the executive branch (Owen, 1994). Many cities have a planning department, also in the executive branch, with a staff that prepares and administers the planning ordinances and policies. Cities may also have an advisory board or commission charged with design review of development proposals (Goodman and Freund, 1968; Hinshaw, 1995).

Land Use Controls

A fundamental goal of local government is to protect the public interest (Table 10-3). Municipalities may try to accomplish this goal in four ways (Chapin and Kaiser, 1985):

- public investment (e.g., transportation and utility system infrastructure, parks and open space)
- regulations (e.g., zoning and subdivision ordinances, building codes)
- incentives and disincentives (e.g., preferential taxation, zoning bonuses)
- land use planning (e.g., comprehensive plan, capital improvements plan)

Collectively, these plans and policies determine if, when, where, and how land development will occur.

In the United States, local land use policies and regulations include comprehensive plans, zoning codes, subdivision ordinances, and building codes (Owen, 1994). Comprehensive plans are community level land use plans that provide a "vision" for

TABLE 10-3 The public interest is protected, or promoted, through a variety of public actions and policies.

Objective	*Examples of related public policies*
Health and safety	Protection from hazards and excessive noise Provision of adequate ventilation and daylight Provision of recreational opportunities
Convenience and efficiency	Regulation of transportation Regulation of land use patterns and intensities Incentives for energy conservation
Environmental quality	Protection of air quality Protection of water quality Protection of endangered and threatened species
Social equity and social choice	Assurance of equal access to education, recreation, and medical care Assurance of equal participation in political decision making
Amenity	Protection of visual quality Stabilization of property values

Source: Adapted, in part, from Chapin and Kaiser, 1985.

orderly growth and development, typically over a twenty- to thirty-year period. In many communities, visual quality is important to local tourist economies — as well as to local residents' quality of life. Preventing the degradation of scenic resources is a legitimate objective of local land use planning.

Subdivision Ordinances

Land development in the United States often involves the subdivision of one parcel of land into two or more smaller parcels. This is especially common when land is developed for single-family housing. The subdivision of land is a legal process requiring subdivision plat approval. This process generally begins with a pre-application meeting where the developer and planning staff discuss the proposed development and relevant legal requirements. Later, the preliminary plat is submitted for review. If approved, the developer must construct the improvements specified in the preliminary plat within a specified time period. The final plat records the legal boundaries of individual parcels, public easements, streets, and street rights-of-way (Owen, 1994). Upon approval, the final plat is recorded with the local register of deeds (or other appropriate land records office).

Zoning Ordinances

Zoning ordinances specify the land use types and intensities allowed within each zone, or district, within the municipality's jurisdiction. Zoning districts are mapped and the primary development districts are typically designated with a letter (indicating land use type) and a number (indicating land use intensity). An "R-3" district, for example, allows residential development at a medium density (e.g., multifamily attached dwellings). Development within each district must adhere to a specific set of design standards (e.g., minimums, maximums). Design standards may limit the percentage of the site covered by a new building, the building's floor area ratio (FAR), and the building's height and bulk. Other design standards influence the location of buildings on the site by specifying minimum lot sizes and required building setbacks from property lines. Additional design attributes that may be influenced by zoning standards include the location and dimensions of streets, parking lots, and signs. A "variance" may be requested if, due to unusual circumstances, compliance with the zoning requirements would pose a hardship on the land owner. Other "nonconforming" uses may be permitted with "conditional use permits." A zoning change may be granted if it would benefit the general welfare of the community, and if the change would be consistent with the objectives of the comprehensive plan (Owen, 1994).

Special "overlay" zoning districts may impose additional development standards, or they may allow greater flexibility in the interpretation of the existing standards. In historical districts, for example, design options are restricted in order to promote the preservation and restoration of buildings with historical significance. Other special districts may require new construction to conform to a specific architectural style. These special zoning districts are often intended to maintain (or create) a unique identity of a neighborhood, commercial district, or other urban area. "Performance zoning" provides greater design flexibility in meeting the community objectives specified in the comprehensive plan. "Incentive zoning" is also used to further the public interest. Incentive zoning in urban core areas encourages development that incorporates public amenities like parks, atriums, plazas, or second-story skywalks (Garvin, 1996).

Environmental Impact Assessments

If a project is expected to have "significant" environmental impacts, an environmental impact statement (EIS) must be prepared to explain the adverse impacts and describe the steps that will be taken to mitigate these impacts (Owen, 1994). Compliance with State or federal Environmental Policy Acts is required if, for example, the project has State or federal funding. State and federal agencies may become involved in reviewing a development proposal if certain natural or cultural resources might be impacted. For example, a proposal that could impact an endangered species would involve the federal Fish and Wildlife Service. Under the Endangered Species Act (ESA), it is unlawful to take, harm, or harass a species listed as endangered or threatened. "Take" includes actions that pursue, hunt, shoot, wound, kill, trap, capture, or collect. "Harm" and "harass" include actions that modify or degrade habitats to the point that the changes significantly impair essential behavioral patterns.

Building Codes

Building codes are concerned with the structural integrity of buildings subjected to various stresses, or loads, from occupants, seismic activity, wind and snow, and from the building's own weight (Owen, 1994). Building codes also address other health and safety issues associated with building design, including fire safety, plumbing, electrical power, and sanitation. Published national design and construction standards, such as the Uniform Building Code (UBC), are often adopted by municipalities and supplemented with local standards (Owen, 1994).

The Review Process

Public scrutiny of development proposals is likely to increase as population continues to grow, urbanized areas expand, and more is learned about the impacts of land development on environmental quality and community health, safety, and welfare. The development review and permitting process in the United States may take several months or, in some cases, years. It typically involves negotiation between the municipal planning staff and the consultants hired by the land owner.

The approval and permitting process also provides opportunities for the general public to review and comment on development proposals. Confusion about a development proposal, or its potential impacts on the environment and community, can jeopardize the success of a project requiring public hearings. In the often adversarial setting of the public review process, misconceptions can easily develop. Consequently, a project's success may depend heavily on effective communication with diverse audiences.

Land development proposals often generate opposition from neighbors, nonprofit advocacy groups, and other stakeholders. Project approval may hinge on successful communication of the steps that will be taken to avoid or mitigate negative development impacts. To protect public health, safety, and welfare, municipalities may impose conditions for the approval of a development proposal. Exactions, for example, are payments of money or land, in lieu of fees, to compensate municipalities for the costs of offsite improvements to public infrastructure—particularly transportation and utility systems. Necessary improvements may include widening street intersections, adding traffic signals, and extending water distribution or sanitary sewer lines. These impact fees also may be used for improved fire and police protection, new schools, or purchases of land for parks and playgrounds (Altshuler and Gomez Ibanez, 1993).

Legal challenges to land use regulations typically address either questions of "due process" or questions of "constitutionality" (Owen, 1994). Due process challenges may assert that the city council did not comply with the city's own ordinances. Constitutionality challenges assert that one or more of the city's ordinances are in conflict with the Fifth Amendment of the United States Constitution. The court may determine, for example, that the restrictions denied the property owner "reasonable" economic use of the land. This would then constitute a "taking" of private property for public use, and it would warrant "just compensation." In evaluating these claims, the courts take into consideration many factors, including the property's inherent suitability for the proposed uses.

Graphic Communication

Steinitz (1979) has argued that defensible methods are needed for regional landscape planning. This same approach is needed with site-scale planning and design. Evidence supporting land planning and design decisions should be clearly communicated. Documenting a project's design determinants creates a more defensible design proposal. Just as attorneys build court cases before going to trial, land planning teams should routinely document the evidence that supports their land development proposals. Members of the general public must be able to evaluate how well a development plan "fits" the site. Typically, a site plan, alone, is insufficient documentation.

Computer-based visualization technology is rapidly advancing, and continued improvements are likely to facilitate increased participation by the general public in land planning and design decision making. Video simulations and computer-generated simulations of a development scenario may realistically portray the site after the intended development (Figure 10-12). Yet if the proposal is *inappropriate for the site*—or if the general public and other stakeholders believe this is so—the skillfully rendered proposals or computer simulations will probably fail to secure the plan's implementation.

Elevations and sections are used to explain intended vertical and horizontal relationships among buildings and other site elements (Figure 10-13). These drawings,

Figure 10-12 Proposal for a park entrance and sign. Visual quality of the surroundings is a major design determinant. *Source:* Land Design.

Figure 10-13 Design sections of the River Walk in Fort Lauderdale, Florida. *Source:* Edward D. Stone, Jr., and Associates.

Figure 10-14 Aerial perspective of a three-dimensional site model. *Source:* The HOK Planning Group.

with a near-ground-level vantage point, are effective at portraying certain spatial relationships among various plan components. Other drawings that may complete the set of traditional illustrative materials are axonometric and isometric drawings, and perspective renderings—either from an eye-level or a "bird's-eye" view. "Fly-through" imaging is now feasible using advanced CAD and GIS technologies. Simulation of proposed changes to a site may also involve modifications of photographs or video images, or the production of three-dimensional physical models (Figure 10-14). Computer-generated simulations are a more elusive goal, although the quality of simulations is improving as advanced computer technologies become more affordable.

PROJECT IMPLEMENTATION

Construction Documentation

Project implementation is a process of converting site development or restoration plans into reality. Typically, this requires construction documents, which consist of drawings and written specifications. Construction documents become part of the legally binding construction contract. These documents are also the basis for construction cost estimates prepared by the consultants and by the contractors who bid for the construction project.

Construction Drawings

Construction drawings include plans, sections, elevations, and details. The construction plans are the foundation for the construction document (CD) package. Four plans, in particular, provide essential site engineering and construction information:

Layout plan (horizontal control). Locates property lines, buildings, streets and parking areas, walkways, utility lines, and other site elements.

Grading plan (vertical control, stormwater management). Locates existing contours (dashed lines), proposed contours (solid lines) and proposed spot elevations at high points, low points, and pavement corners. Drainage swales and storm drain systems are also included.

Utilities plan (subsurface and surface utilities). Locates sanitary sewer systems, on-site wastewater disposal and treatment systems, drinking water distribution lines, electrical supply lines, television and telephone cables.

Planting plan (trees, shrubs, vines, and groundcover). Locates new plant materials, including the desired spacing among plants. Plant quantities, sizes, and root conditions are included in a table or schedule.

In many States, an erosion and sediment control plan (ESC) must be submitted before development permits can be issued (U.S. Environmental Protection Agency, 1993). Typically, an erosion and sediment control plan includes the following information (U.S. Environmental Protection Agency, 1993):

- Description of predominant soil types
- Site grading details, including existing and proposed contours
- Design details and locations for structural controls
- Provisions to preserve topsoil and limit disturbance
- Details of temporary and permanent stabilization measures
- Description of the construction sequence

This documentation also assures that the costs of these measures are considered in the contract bidding process. Depending on the project program and the existing site conditions, a demolition plan and an irrigation plan also may be needed. If the project for the site includes one or more buildings, a full set of construction plans, details, and specifications for each building would be included in the construction documentation.

Construction details may be plans, sections, or elevations. Before digital technology became widely used in design and planning offices, the construction documentation phase required as much as 50 percent of the consultant's fee on a typical site planning and design project. As electronic technology has become an integral tool in land planning and design, construction detailing has become more efficient. With the advent of CAD, construction details are now saved as digital files and modified as needed for site and project-specific requirements. Standardized construction details are now available on the Internet. As more construction details become available on the Internet, this database should reduce construction documentation from the largest to one of the smallest aspects of professional design services (Cook, 1999).

Construction Specifications

Construction specifications are text that supplements the construction drawings. Specifications include information that is most conveniently assembled in report form, rather than directly on the construction drawings. Construction specifications are written descriptions of the procedures and materials required in implementing a development or restoration project. They include information about the quality of materials, construction methods, and work safety requirements. Some of these requirements are based on industry or government standards, such as those of the American Society for Testing and Materials (ASTM). They also cover topics such as required insurance and bonding, as well as incentives for completing construction before the final completion date.

Implementation

Construction administration and construction supervision are important, but different, processes. Construction supervision is the responsibility of the general contractor and the various subcontractors. The contractors directly supervise the work, which may involve earthmoving, demolition of existing buildings, and the construction of new buildings, roads, and other site structures. The designers, whether architects, landscape architects, or engineers, typically work for the client, not the contractor. The consultants protect the owner's interests through contract administration. The administration of the contract ensures that the work is completed as specified in the construction documents.

SUMMARY

Government plays a fundamental role in shaping the growth and redevelopment of cities and regions. Yet the built environment expands incrementally, parcel by parcel. Land use regulations and other public policies seek to protect public health, safety, and welfare. Consequently, the public sector plays a major role in determining when and where land development will occur. As the close relationship between physical design and quality of the built environment is more widely recognized, land development proposals are becoming more closely scrutinized. Sophisticated, computer-based evaluations of the fiscal, social, and environmental impacts of land development scenarios are now feasible at the local government level (Klosterman, 1999).

Land development proposals must be defensible and justified with documentation. A development project should be expected to "fit" the site for which it is proposed, and the site inventory and analysis are crucial components of the supporting documentation. To be considered successful, a plan must satisfy program requirements, but it must also be responsive to the site's physical, biological, and cultural characteristics. Moreover, the plan should further, or at the very least not harm, the public interest. Evaluating whether or not a development proposal satisfies these, and other, criteria requires detailed information about the project's design. Therefore, the land development process typically requires a lengthy period of analysis, experimentation, and negotiation.

BOX 10-1 In Practice

Urban Infill

Northwestern Memorial Hospital
Chicago, Illinois

Owner/Developer
Northwestern University

Land Planner
The HOK Planning Group, St. Louis, Missouri

Architect
Ellerbe Becket, Minneapolis, Minnesota

Overview
Northwestern Memorial Hospital, in cooperation with Northwestern University and its medical school, commissioned the joint venture team of Ellerbe Becket / HOK to design a new inpatient pavilion and ambulatory care facility in downtown Chicago. Accommodating the dramatic growth in outpatient care while providing more cost-effective hospital operations, the new medical complex consolidates services previously housed in aging ambulatory facilities located throughout a six-block area. The new complex is more convenient for patients, physicians, employees, and visitors. Construction of the new hospital took place without disrupting patient care at the existing medical facilities on the site.

Site Analysis
The site for the medical center is in the heart of downtown Chicago, one of the largest cities in the United States. The planning process for this project included the identification and comparative analysis of three potential sites (Figure B10-1). Five different development options for these three sites were compared (Figure B10-2). Several criteria were evaluated in making the final site selection decision, including each site's effects on the medical center's cost, image, and growth potential. Access and parking were among the other important site selection criteria.

The site inventory and analysis addressed a wide variety of physical, social, and legal issues. These studies also spanned a wide range in scale. For example, studies of vehicle circulation addressed arrival and departure patterns within a radius of several miles or kilometers (Figure B10-3). Other studies of vehicle circulation and access focused on potential arrival and entry sequences within a city block or two of the medical center site (Figure B10-4). Other factors that were considered in the analysis included pedestrian circulation patterns, microclimate, visual character of the surrounding architecture, and land use regulations for the site.

The planning process for the new medical center also involved extensive negotiations with the building's future occupants, municipal planning staff, and other community stakeholders. For example, the project's programming phase involved verification of the current program (for existing facilities) as well as reprogramming specific components of the existing facilities. One of the spaces designated for reprogramming was the clinical laboratory. The design team chose to develop an on-site core lab, with the majority of the laboratory space located off-site. Community stakeholders also played a significant role in identifying issues that ultimately influenced the design of the medical center (Figure B10-5).

Design Features
The new medical complex includes a 526-bed, one-million-square-foot hospital and a one-million-square-foot ambulatory care facility. The ambulatory care facility includes offices and clinical space for the 400 physicians in the Northwestern Medical Faculty Foundation group practice and 200 additional staff physicians. Special features of the complex include 96 intensive-care-unit beds, all new diagnostic and treatment facilities, integration of inpatient and outpatient services, and parking facilities for 2,100 cars in a multistory parking structure.

The design of the medical center building reflects, in many ways, a sensitivity to context (Figure B10-6). For example, the key guiding principles for the placement and design of the Medical Center included:

- Reduce bulk by "stepping down" the building toward Lake Michigan
- Break up the "super-block" by creating separate towers
- Create ground-level east/west pedestrian "malls"
- Create a "gateway" to the Medical Center

These, and other, design decisions were made to achieve specific functional and/or aesthetic objectives. Two of these objectives were to reinforce the urban streetwall and to continue the Chicago tradition of designing buildings with distinctive tops.

A project of this complexity requires creativity, negotiation, and a willingness to be responsive to the concerns of community stakeholders. To provide greater flexibility in how the project was designed, the consultants gained a zoning amendment to reclassify the site as a planned development area (Figures B10-7 and B10-8). The conditions for rezoning included no net increase in density and a shift in building mass away from Lake Michigan. Other requirements included improvements to the local pedestrian and vehicle circulation systems (Figure B10-9).

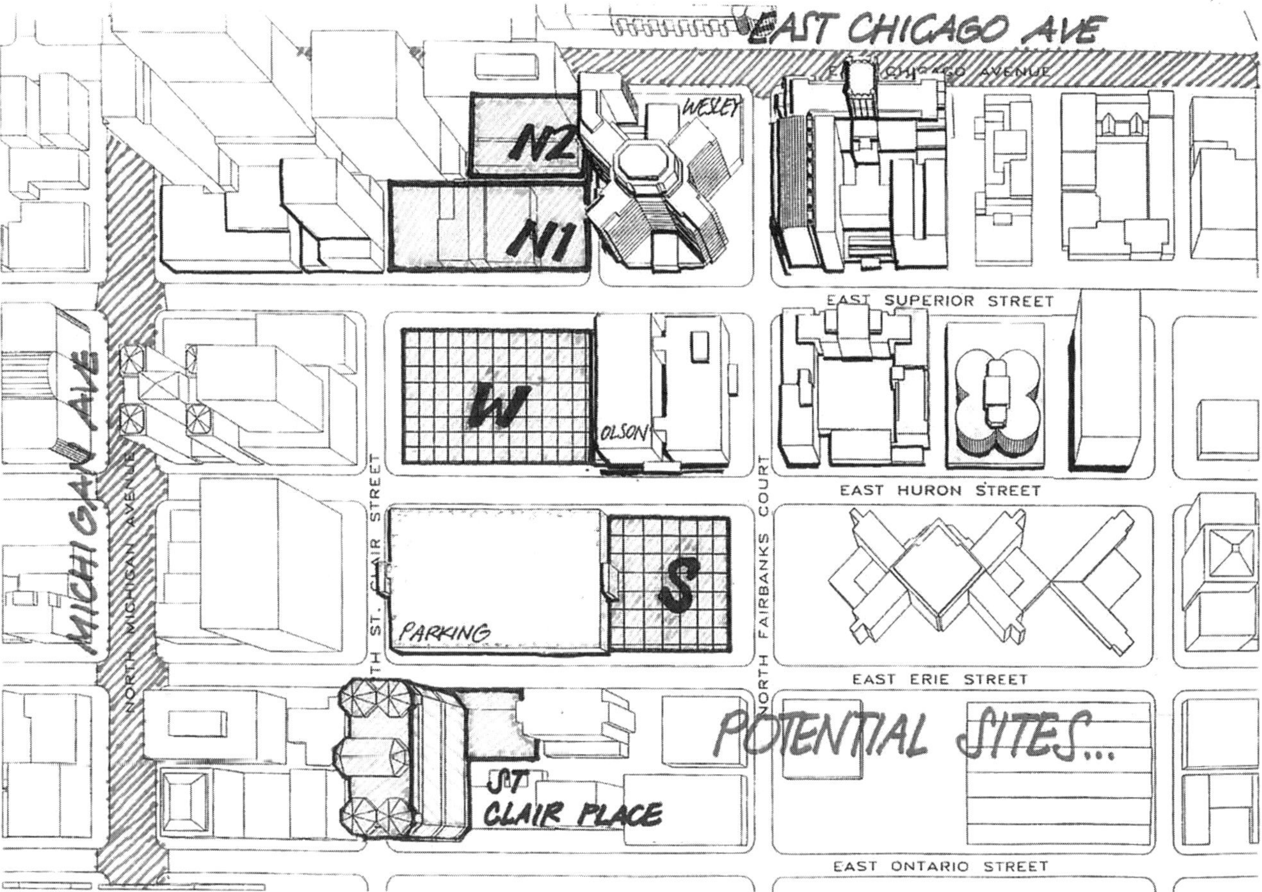

Figure B10-1 Map showing potential hospital sites. *Source:* The HOK Planning Group.

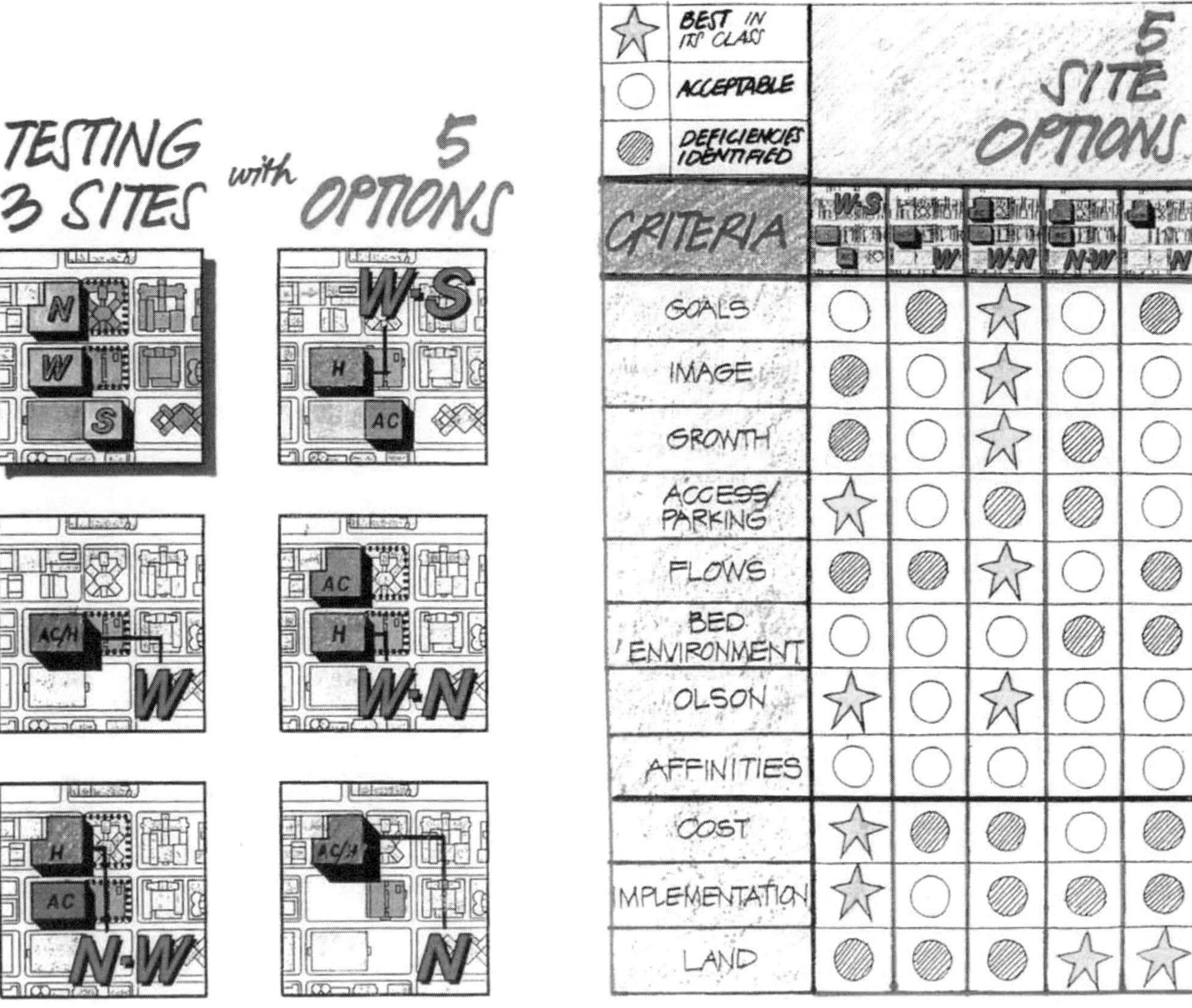

Figure B10-2 Matrix of site selection criteria. The matrix summarizes ratings for five site options and eleven selection criteria.
Source: The HOK Planning Group..

Site Analysis

ARRIVAL PATTERNS

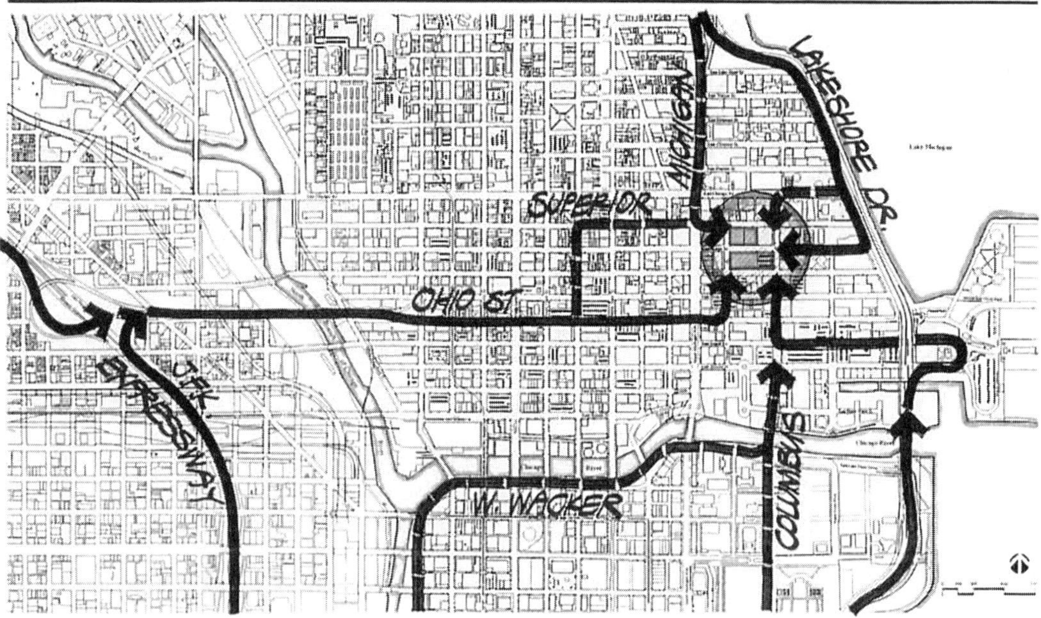

DEPARTURE PATTERNS

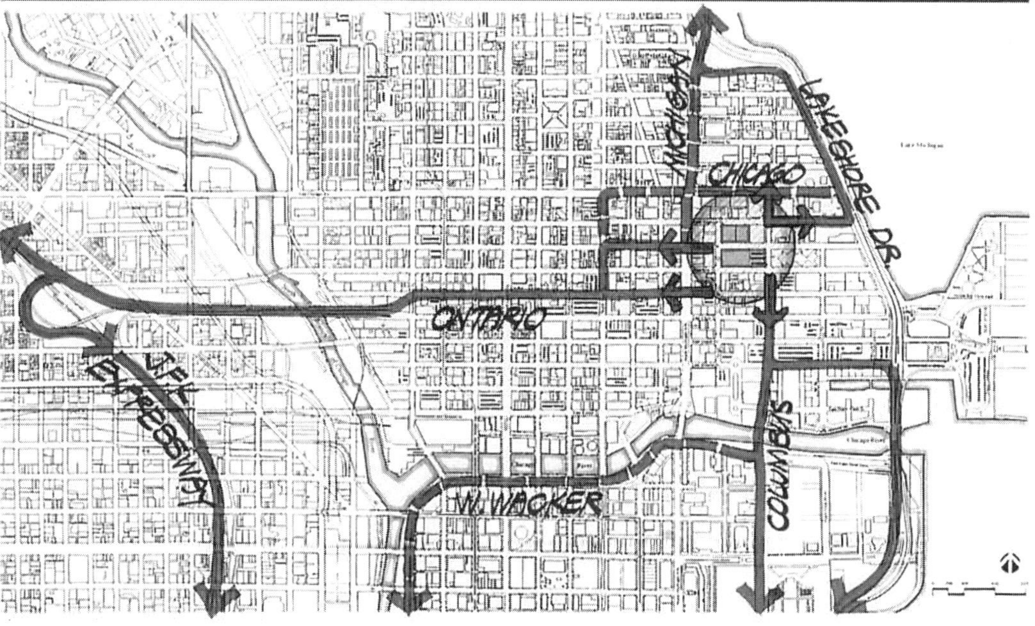

Ellerbe Becket/HOK

Site Analysis

October 1992

Figure B10-3 Inventory and assessment of vehicle arrival and departure patterns. *Source:* The HOK Planning Group.

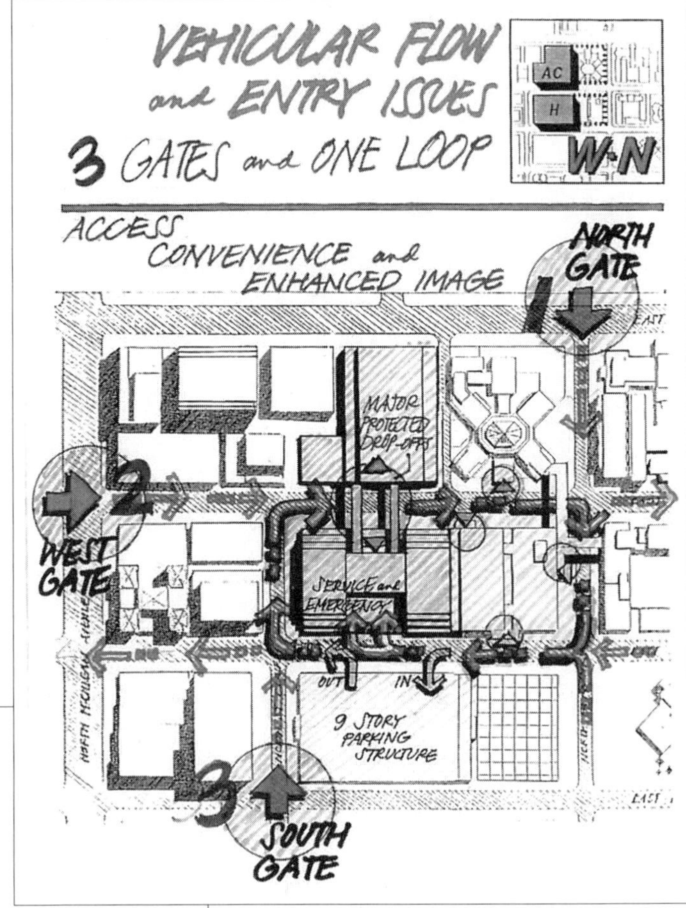

VIEW LOOKING SOUTH on FAIRBANKS

Figure B10-4 Diagram addressing vehicular circulation, entry, and parking issues. *Source:* The HOK Planning Group.

Community Input

ISSUES	INITIAL SUBMITTAL	NU/NMH DESIGN RESPONSE
BUILDING	Superblock	GOAL: Consolidate Services and Express the NMH Mission CONTEXTUALLY • Upper Level Setbacks ARTICULATE the ACC and Hospital...Higher Building Toward Michigan Ave. • Integrated Internally, but Visually Separated • Materials and Forms Similar to NU/NMH Campus
STREETSCAPE	No Setback	GOAL: Provide a Walkable Environment of Usable Open Space 10 Areas of Landscape Improvements: 1. 15' Setback @ St. Clair 2. 15' Setback @ Fairbanks 3. Create/Redevelop Setback @ VA 4. Redevelop Setback East of Health Science Bldg. with NU. 5. Pedestrian Way West of Health Science Bldg. 6. Pedestrian Way West of Erie/Fairbanks Garage 7. Landscape CTA Turnaround 8. Landscape West of Wesley 9. Contribute to Eli Schulman Park Development 10. Contribute to Lakeshore Park Development • NMH 9000 s.f. Open Space • Link to Michigan Ave. • Develop Streetscape that Exceeds City Requirements @ Huron and Erie • Open to the Community
EMERGENCY ROOM	Located at Erie and St. Clair	GOAL: Design Clear, Highly Accessible Entry Minimize Congestion at Street • Locate @ Erie and Fairbanks • All Vehicle Movements INSIDE Bldg. • Dedicated Ambulance/Police and Private Vehicle Parking Areas • Trauma and "Fast Track" Service

Ellerbe Becket/HOK 13-MAY-93

Figure B10-5 Community input on the planning and design of the proposed building, streetscape, and emergency room entrance. *Source:* The HOK Planning Group.

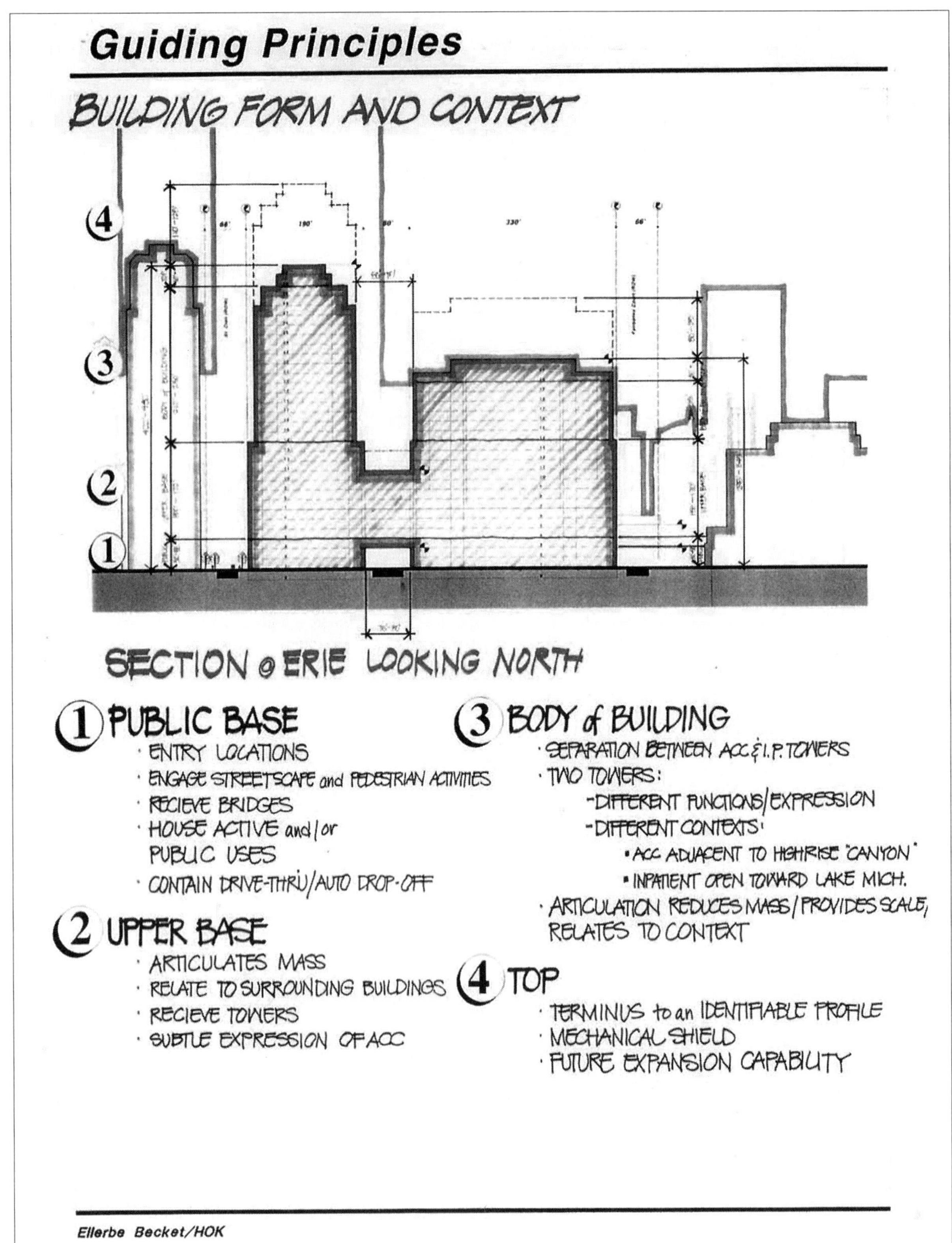

Figure B10-6 Design guidelines communicate seven main design principles for building massing. *Source:* The HOK Planning Group.

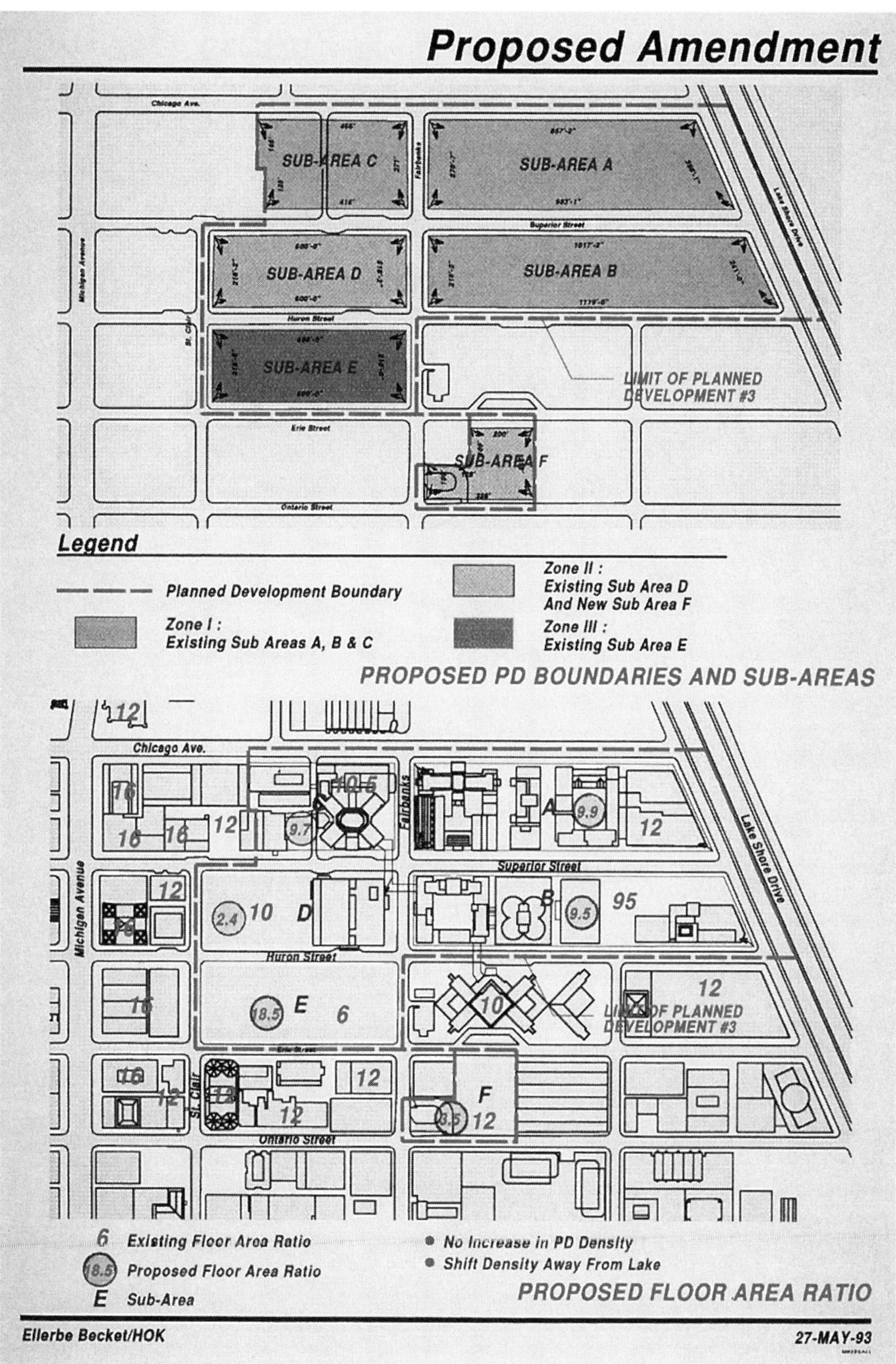

Figure B10-7 Proposed zoning amendment proposes a planned unit development (PUD). Floor area ratios are provided by subarea. *Source:* The HOK Planning Group.

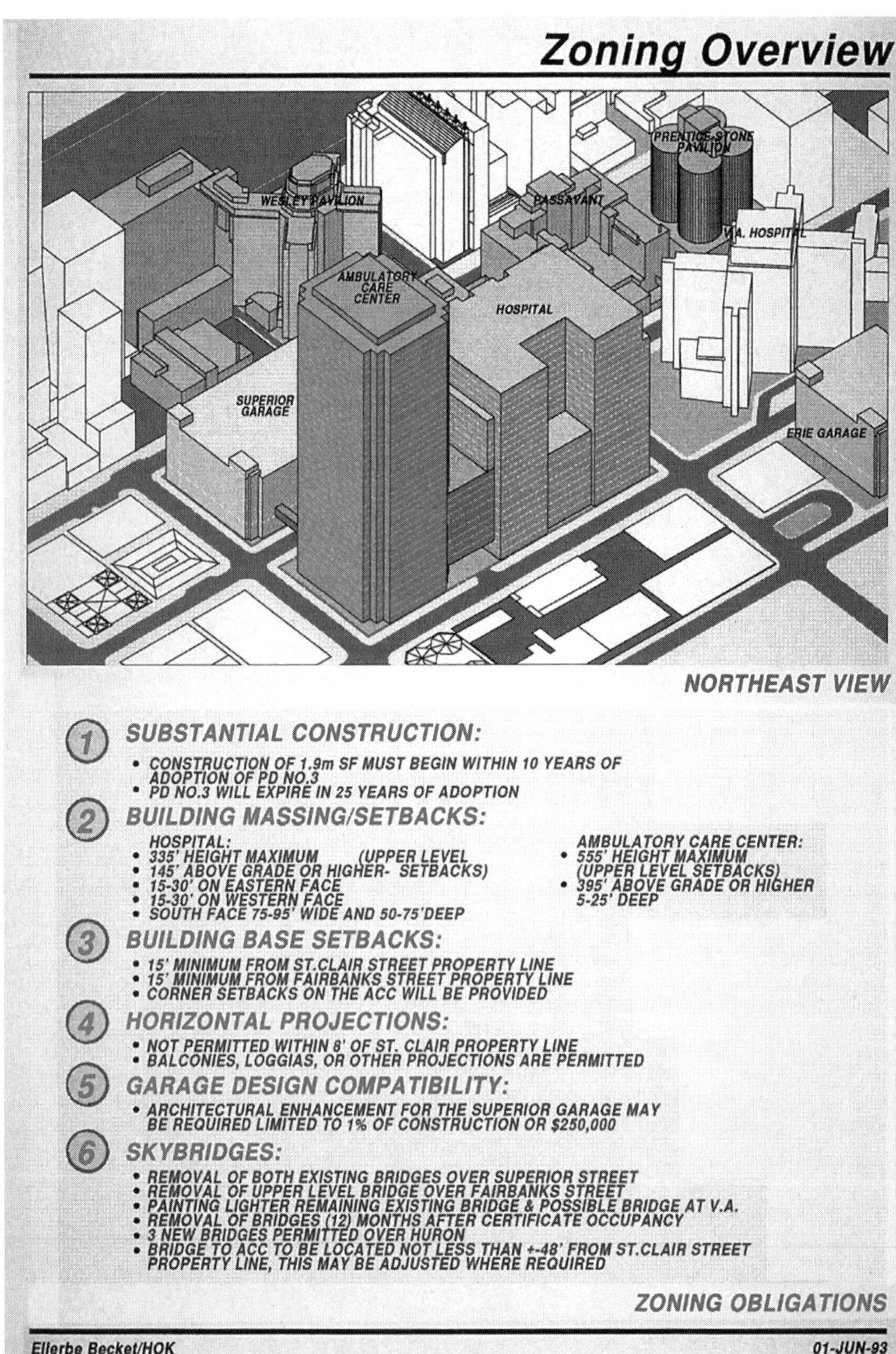

Figure B10-8 Summary table addressing seven categories of zoning issues. *Source:* The HOK Planning Group.

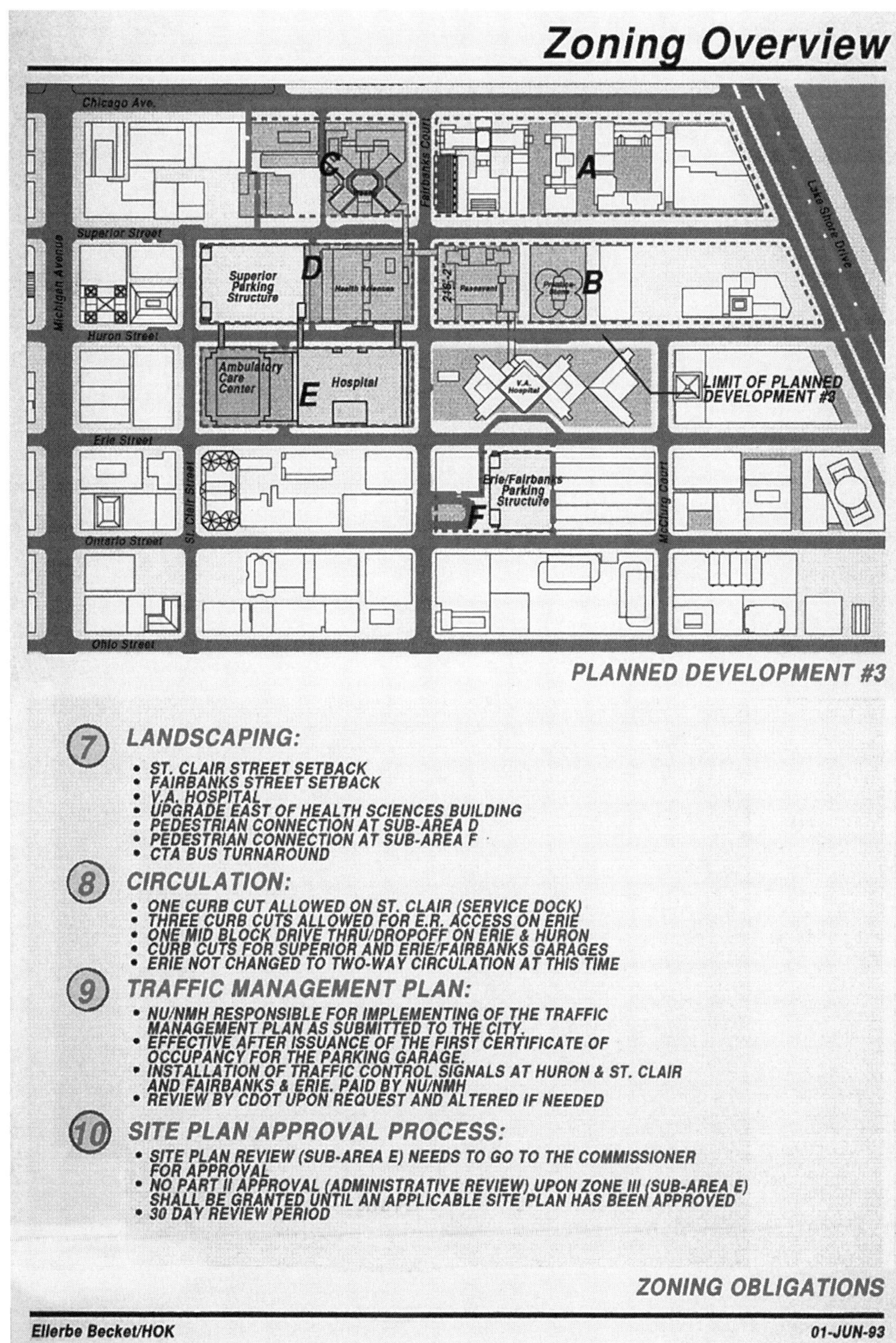

Figure B10-9 Summary table (continued) addressing three other zoning issues: landscaping, circulation, and the approval process. *Source:* The HOK Planning Group.

APPENDIX

Sources for Resources

INTRODUCTION

This Appendix includes a variety of interesting World Wide Web sites that were functional in the fall of 2000. This listing of resources is far from exhaustive. Included here is a, hopefully, representative and useful sample of the vast network of Web sites pertaining to land planning, development, and management.

FEDERAL AGENCIES (UNITED STATES)

Census Bureau - TIGER
Topologically Integrated Geographic Encoding and Referencing (TIGER) system
URL: http://www.census.gov/ftp/pub/geo/www/tiger/
Resources: digital database of geographic features such as roads, railroads, rivers, lakes, political boundaries, and census statistical boundaries for the entire United States.

Council on Environmental Quality (CEQ)
URL: http://ceq.eh.doe.gov/nepa/nepanet.htm
Resources: NEPAnet - information on where and how to file an environmental impact analysis; source of the National Environmental Policy Act and other federal legislation.

Environmental Protection Agency (EPA) - Office of Water
URL: http://www.epa.gov/OWOW/NPS/
Resources: information on low impact development and stormwater management practices; Online source of environmental legislation.

Fish and Wildlife Service (FWS)
URL: http://www.fws.gov/
Resources: national wetlands inventory maps and data; information on endangered species, ecosystem management, and other environmental programs.

Geological Survey (USGS)
URL: http://nsdi.usgs.gov/
Resources: USGS Geospatial Data Clearinghouse - an Online source of metadata and maps of topography and geology, biological resources, and water resources; Web links to other nodes of the National Spatial Data Infrastructure (NSDI).

National Climatic Data Center
National Oceanic and Atmospheric Administration (NOAA)
URL: http://www.ncdc.noaa.gov/
Resources: climate archives and statistical tables for weather observation stations nationwide; weather summaries for cities and states.

National Weather Service
National Oceanic and Atmospheric Administration (NOAA)
URL: http:/www.nws.noaa.gov/
Resources: statistics on fatalities, injuries, and damages caused by weather related hazards; general information on weather related topics.

FEDERAL SOURCES (INTERNATIONAL)

Centre for Topographic Information (Canada)
URL: http://maps.NRCan.gc.ca/main.html
Resources: archive of topographic maps (1:50,000 and 1:250,000 scale).

Environment Australia
URL: http://www.environment.gov.au/
Resources: Online databases for biodiversity, cultural heritage, marine and water, parks and reserves, and other resources; publications and Online courses on sustainability and environmental education; federal environmental and cultural heritage legislation.

National Air Photo Library (Canada)
URL: http://airphotos.nrcan.gc.ca/main.html
Resources: archive of over six million aerial photographs.

National Geospatial Data Framework (United Kingdom)
URL: http://www.ngdf.org.uk/
Resources: Online directory and clearinghouse for providers and users of geospatial data; standards for spatial data and metadata.

STATE SOURCES (UNITED STATES)

MassGIS
Office of Geographic and Environmental Information (Massachusetts)
URL: http://www.state.ma.us/mgis/
Resources: Online digital orthophotos; GIS metadata and datalayers for political boundaries, infrastructure, topography, coastal and marine features, demographics, and much more.

California Land Use Planning Information Network (LUPIN)
URL: http://www.ceres.ca.gov/planning/index.html
Resources: information on federal, state, and local land use regulations; technical information on various aspects of the built environment, including brownfields, infrastructure, planning and design, permitting, and pollution.

NON-PROFIT ORGANIZATIONS

Center for Liveable Communities
URL: http://www.lgc.org/clc/
Resources: bibliographies, studies, reports and model ordinances pertaining to pedestrian and transit oriented land use planning across the United States.

Center for Watershed Protection
URL: http://www.cwp.org/
Resources: information on effective techniques to protect and restore urban watersheds; assists local and state governments in developing effective urban stormwater and watershed protection programs.

Congress for the New Urbanism
URL: http://www.cnu.org/
Resources: news, events, and educational materials related to New Urbanism.

Cornell University Legal Information Institute - Land Use Library
URL: http://www.law.cornell.edu/topics/land_use.html
Resources: extensive database of federal, state, and local land use legislation and case law; links to other land use related websites.

Cyburbia - Planning Resource Directory
URL: http://cyburbia.ap.buffalo.edu/pairc/planning_resource_directory.html
Resources: clearinghouse for information on community development, environment, historic preservation, land use regulation, transportation, new urbanism, and much more.

Low Impact Development Center
URL: http://lowimpactdevelopment.org/
Resources: information on site design techniques to protect environmental quality by replicating preexisting hydrologic site conditions.

National Main Street Center
National Trust for Historic Preservation
URL: http://www.mainst.org/
Resources: books and other resources on urban revitalization and rehabilitating historic buildings.

Smart Growth Network
URL: http://www.smartgrowth.org/index2.html
Resources: bibliographies, reports, and other information on brownfield redevelopment, infill development, "green" building, and other Smart Growth issues.

U.S. Green Building Council (USGBC)
URL: http://usgbc.org/
Resources: information on energy and resource efficient building policies, programs, technologies, standards and design practices.

International Development Research Council (IDRC)
URL: http://www.sitenet.com/idrcnet/
Resources: commercial real estate news and management strategies; site selection database; Online bookstore.

National Association of Home Builders (NAHB)
URL: http://www.nahb.com/
Resources: project examples of traditional neighborhood development (TND), "green" building/cluster development, and urban infill development; news on trends in housing construction and costs.

Urban Land Institute (ULI)
URL: http://www.uli.org/indexJS.htm
Resources: books and other sources of information on urban planning, land use, and real estate development; project reference files summarize lessons learned, development challenges, and project data (including photos and site plans).

PROFESSIONAL ASSOCIATIONS

American Institute of Architects (AIA)
URL: http://www.earchitect.com/
Resources: Online catalog of books and reports on architectural design; news on government affairs, and other related issues; conference announcements.

American Real Estate and Urban Economics Association (AREUEA)
URL: http://www.areuea.org/
Resources: research and news on current and emerging real estate issues.

American Planning Association
URL: http://www.planning.org/
Resources: Online catalog of books and reports on community planning and development; conferences and educational opportunities; Online planning advisory service.

American Society of Landscape Architects (ASLA)
URL: http://www.asla.org/
Resources: Online catalog of books and reports on site planning and design; Online database of CAD details; news and conference announcements.

COMMERCIAL SITES

Environmental Systems Research Institute (ESRI)
URL: http://www.esri.com/
Resources: catalog of PC-based GIS and mapping software, including ARC/INFO and ArcView; Online book store; GIS news and conferences; GIS education and training opportunities.

GIS Data Depot
URL: http://www.gisdatadepot.com
Resources: Online clearinghouse for a wide range of biophysical and cultural GIS data for counties and states in the United States, and for other countries; source of GIS-related news and events.

SiteSeeker
URL: http://www.siteseeker.org/
Resources: Online database of available buildings and sites, research parks, and closed military bases.

Terraserver
URL: http://www.terraserver.com/
Resources: very high resolution (less than two meters) satellite imagery (panchromatic digital imagery is orthorectified and georeferenced).

Glossary

Accuracy: The closeness of observations, computations, or estimates to the true values or to values accepted as being true.

Aerial: Of, pertaining to, or occurring in the air or atmosphere.

Aerial Photograph, Oblique: An aerial photograph taken with the camera axis directed between the horizontal and the vertical: (1) *high oblique*—an oblique photograph in which the horizon is shown; (2) *low oblique*—an oblique photograph in which the horizon is not shown.

Aerial Photograph, Vertical: An aerial photograph made with the optical axis of the camera approximately perpendicular to the earth's surface and with the film as nearly horizontal as is practical.

Algorithm: A statement of the steps to be followed in the solution of a problem; an algorithm may be in the form of a word description, an explanatory note, or a labeled diagram or flowchart.

Alluvium: Any material deposited by running water; the soil material of floodplains and alluvial fans.

Altitude: Elevation above or below a reference datum; the datum is usually the mean sea level.

Analog: A form of data display in which values are shown in graphic form, such as curves.

Aquifer: Any subsurface material that holds a relatively large quantity of groundwater and is able to transmit that water readily.

Area: A generic term for a bounded, continuous, two-dimensional object that may or may not include its boundary.

Aspect: The horizontal direction in which a slope faces, commonly expressed as compass direction (e.g., North, Northeast) or degrees clockwise from North.

Attribute: A defined characteristic of an entity (for example, topographic slope).

Attribute Value: A specific quality or quantity assigned to an attribute (for example, 15 percent slope).

Band: A specific frequency or range of frequencies in the electromagnetic spectrum.

Baseflow: The portion of streamflow contributed by groundwater; it is a steady flow that is slow to change even during rainless periods.

Berm: A low, linear mound of earth and soil.

Buffer: (1) The zone around the perimeter of a wetland or lake where land use activities are limited in order to protect the water features; (2) a zone of a specified distance around any map feature in a GIS layer.

Cadastre: A parcel-based land information system.

Carrying Capacity: The level of development density or use an environment is able to support without suffering undesirable or irreversible degradation.

Characterization: The delineation or representation of the essential features or qualities existing at a site.

Chloropleth Map: A map comprised of areas of any size or shape representing qualitative phenomena (e.g., soil fertility) or quantitative phenomena (e.g., elevation); often has a mosaic appearance.

Climate: The general or representative conditions of the atmosphere at a place on earth.

Clustering: A land development concept in which buildings and infrastructure are grouped together, and large contiguous areas of open space remain undeveloped.

Coefficient of Runoff: A number given to a type of ground surface representing the proportion of rainfall converted to overland or surface flow.

Color-Infrared Film: Photographic film sensitive to energy in the visible and near-infrared wavelengths of the electromagnetic spectrum (usually from 0.4 to 0.9 mm).

Concentration Time: The time taken for a drop of rain falling on the perimeter of a drainage basin to pass through the basin to the outlet.

Constraint: Any feature or condition of the built or natural environment that poses an obstacle to proposed land uses.

Contour: An imaginary line on the ground, all points of which are at the same elevation above or below a specific datum.

Contour Interval: The difference in elevation between two adjacent contours.

Control Point: Any station in a horizontal or vertical control system that is identified on a photograph and used for correlating the data shown on the photograph.

Coordinate System: A reference system for uniquely defining the location of any point on earth.

Crown Diameter, Visible: The apparent diameter of a tree crown imaged on a vertical aerial photograph.

Data Set: A file or files that contain related geometric and attribute information; a collection of related data.

Datum: A reference system for measuring another attribute, such as horizontal or vertical location.

Decibel: A unit of measurement for the loudness of sound based on the pressure produced in air by a noise; denoted dB.

DEM (Digital Elevation Model): A topographic surface arranged in a data file as a set of regularly spaced x, y, z coordinates, where z represents elevation.

Design Storm: A rainstorm of a given intensity and frequency of recurrence, used as the basis for stormwater management.

Detention: A strategy used in stormwater management in which runoff is detained on-site to be released later at some prescribed rate.

Development Density: a measure of intensity of development or land use; defined, for example, on the basis of area covered by dwelling units, impervious surfaces, or building floor area.

Digitization: The process of converting a photograph, map, or other image into numerical format.

Discharge: The rate of water flow in a stream channel or from a site; measured as the volume of water passing through a cross-section of a stream or swale per unit of time, commonly expressed as cubic feet (or meters) per second.

Discharge Zone: An area where groundwater seepage and springs are concentrated.

Disturbance: An impact on the environment, such as forest clearing, characterized by physical or biological change.

DLG (Digital Line Graph): A digital representation of cartographic information; digital vectors converted from maps and related sources.

DOQ (Digital Orthophotoquadrangle): A digital image with the properties of an orthographic projection; derived from a digitized vertical aerial photograph so that image displacement caused by camera tilt and relief of terrain are removed, or rectified. Orthophotos combine the image characteristics of a photograph with the geometric qualities of a map.

Drainage Network: A system of stream channels usually connected in a hierarchical fashion.

Drainage Basin: The area that contributes runoff to a stream, river, or lake.

Easement: A right-of-way granted, but not dedicated, for limited use of private land for a public or quasi-public purpose.

Ecosystem: A group of organisms linked together by a flow of energy; also, a community of organisms and their environment.

Ecotone: The transition zone between two groups, or zones, of vegetation.

Electromagnetic Radiation (EMR): Energy propagated through space in the form of an advancing interaction between electric and magnetic fields. EMR is also called *electromagnetic energy.*

Elevation: Vertical distance from a datum point, such as mean sea level, to a point or object on the earth's surface; not to be confused with altitude, which refers to points or objects above the earth's surface.

Endangered Species: According to the U.S. Endangered species Act, a species in imminent danger of extinction in all or a significant portion of its range.

Environment: The aggregate conditions that affect the existence or development of properties intrinsic to a site.

Environmental Site Characterization: The delineation or representation of the essential features or qualities, including all of the conditions, influences, and circumstance, existing at a place or location designated for a specific use, function, or study.

Environmental Assessment: A preliminary study or review of a proposed action (project) and the influence it could have on the environment; often conducted to determine the need for more detailed environmental impact analysis.

Ephemeral Stream: A stream without baseflow; one that flows only during or after rainstorms or snowmelt events.

Erosion: The removal of rock debris by moving water, wind, or another agent; generally, the sculpting or wearing down of the land by erosional agents.

Eutrophication: The increase of biomass of a water body leading to infilling of the basin and the eventual disappearance of open water.

Evapotranspiration: The loss of water from the soil through evaporation and transpiration.

Feasibility Study: A type of planning aimed at identifying the most appropriate use of a site.

Filtration: A term generally applied to the removal of pollutants, such as sediment, with the passage of water through a soil, organic, and/or fabric medium.

Floodway Fringe: The zone designated by U.S. federal flood policy as the area in a river valley that would be lightly inundated by the hundred-year flood.

Floor Area: The area of all floors of a building or structure.

Footprint: Area covered by a building.

Geocoding: A coding process in which a digital map feature is assigned an attribute value (e.g., vertical or horizontal location).

Geographic Information System (GIS): A mapping system designed for analysis, planning, and management applications involving overlapping and complex distributional patterns. Two classes of GIS are *vector* and *raster.*

Geomorphology: A science that deals with the land and submarine relief features of the earth's surface, or the comparable features of a celestial body, and that seeks a genetic interpretation of them.

Georeference: To establish the relationship between coordinates on a planar map and real-world coordinates.

Geospatial Data: Information identifying the geographic location and characteristics of natural or constructed features and boundaries on the earth; geospatial data may be derived from, among other things, remote sensing, mapping, and surveying technologies.

Geostationary Satellite: A satellite so placed in orbit above the earth that it rotates with the earth and thus remains fixed over the same area.

Global Positioning System (GPS): The Navigation Satellite Timing and Ranging (NAVSTAR) GPS is a passive, satellite-based, navigation system operated and maintained by the Department of Defense (DOD).

Global Coordinate System: The network of east–west and north–south lines (parallels and meridians) used to measure locations on earth; this system uses degrees, minutes, and seconds as the units of measurement.

Gradient: The inclination or slope of the land; often applied to systems such as streams and highways.

Ground Truth (jargon): The term coined for data and information obtained on surface or subsurface features to aid in interpretation of remotely sensed data; *ground data* and *ground information* are the preferred terms.

Ground Resolution: The area on the terrain that is covered by the instantaneous field of view of a detector; ground resolution is determined by the altitude of the remote sensing system and the instantaneous field of view of the detector.

Ground Data: Data collected on the ground, and information derived therefrom, as an aid to the interpretation of remotely recorded surveys, such as airborne imagery; generally, this should be performed concurrently with the airborne surveys; data collected on weather, soils, and vegetation types and conditions are typical.

Groundwater: The mass of water that occupies the subsoil and upper bedrock zone; the water occupying the zone of saturation below the soil-water zone.

Habitat: The local environment from which an organism gains its resources; habitat is often variable in size, content, and location, changing with the phases in an organisms's life cycle.

Hardpan: A hardened soil layer characterized by the accumulation of colloids and ions.

Hazard Assessment: An evaluation of the dangers to land use and people from environmental threats such as floods, tornadoes, and earthquakes.

Horizon: A layer in the soil that originates from the differentiation of particles and chemicals due to moisture movement within the soil column.

Hydric Soil: Soil characterized by wet conditions, or saturation, most of the year; often organic in composition.

Hydrograph: A streamflow graph that shows the change in discharge over time, usually hours or days.

Hydrologic Cycle: The planet's water system, described by the movement of water from the oceans to the atmosphere to the continents and back to the sea.

Impervious Cover: Any hard surface material, such as asphalt or concrete, that limits stormwater infiltration and induces high runoff rates.

Infiltration Capacity: The rate at which a ground material takes in water through the surface; measured in inches or centimeters per minute or hour.

Infrared Image: An image acquired within the wavelength from about 0.7 mm to an indefinite upper boundary, sometimes set at 2.6 mm. Photographic infrared is 0.7 mm to about 2.6 mm; thermal infrared is between 2.6 mm and 13.5 mm.

Infrared Film: Photographic film capable of recording near-infrared radiation (just beyond the visible to a wavelength of 0.9 micrometer), but not capable of recording thermal infrared wavelengths.

Infrared Radiation: Mainly longwave radiation of wavelengths between 3.0–4.0 and 100 micrometers, but also includes near-infrared radiation, which occurs at wavelengths between 0.7 and 3.0–4.0 micrometers.

Isopleth Map: A map comprised of lines (isolines) that connect points of equal attribute value.

Lacustrine Wetland: A wetland associated with standing water bodies such as ponds, lakes, and reservoirs.

Land Cover: The materials such as vegetation and concrete that cover the ground. See also land use.

Land Use: The human activities occurring within an area of the landscape; for example, agricultural, industrial, and residential uses.

Layer: In a geographic information system, spatial data of a common type or theme.

Legend: An explanation of the symbols, colors, and styles used on a map or plan, usually in a box next to the map or plan.

Lithosphere: The solid part of the earth or other spatial body, distinguished from the atmosphere and the hydrosphere.

Lot: A parcel, tract, or area of land established by a plat or otherwise as permitted by law.

Lot Frontage: The portion of a lot adjacent to a street.

Magnetic Declination: The deviation in degrees east or west between magnetic north and true north.

Map: A graphical representation of a portion of the earth's surface, drawn to scale, on a specific projection, showing natural and manmade features.

Map Projection: An orderly system of lines on a plane representing a corresponding system of imaginary lines on a datum surface.

Metadata: "Data about data" describe the content, quality, condition, and other characteristics of data; for example, the date and source from which field data were collected.

Monochromatic: Pertaining to a single wavelength or, more commonly, to a narrow band of wavelengths.

Microclimate: The climate of small spaces, such as an inner city, a residential area, or a mountain valley.

Mitigation: A measure used to lessen the impact of an action on the natural or human environment.

Mitigation Banking: In wetland mitigation planning, the practice of building surplus acreage of compensation credits through replacement, enhancement, restoration, and/or preservation of wetlands.

Moraine: The material deposited directly by a glacier; also, the material (load) carried in or on a glacier; as landforms, moraines usually have hilly or rolling topography.

Mosaic: A term used in landscape ecology to describe the patchy character of habitat as a result of fragmentation through land use; an assemblage of overlapping aerial or space photographs or images whose edges have been matched to form a continuous pictorial representation of a portion of the earth's surface.

Nonpoint Source: Water pollution from a spatially diffuse source such as the atmosphere or agricultural land.

Palustrine Wetland: Wetlands associated with inland sites that are not dependent on stream, lake, or oceanic water.

Panchromatic: A term used for films that are sensitive to broadband (that is, the entire visible part of the electromagnetic spectrum).

Parent Material: The particulate material in which a soil forms; the two types of parent material are *residual* and *transported.*

Peak Discharge: The maximum flow of a stream or a river in response to an event such as a rainstorm, or over a period of time such as a year.

Percolation Rate: The rate at which water moves into soil through the walls of a test pit; used to determine soil suitability for wastewater disposal and treatment.

Percolation Test: A soil-permeability test performed in the field to determine the suitability of a material for wastewater disposal and treatment.

Permeability: The rate at which soil or rock transmits groundwater (or gravity water in the area above the water table).

Photogrammetry: The art or science of obtaining reliable measurements by means of photography.

Photosynthesis: The process by which green plants synthesize water and carbon dioxide and, with the energy from absorbed light, convert it into plant materials in the form of sugar and carbohydrates.

Physiography: A term from physical geography that is traditionally used to describe the composite character of the landscape over large regions.

Planned Unit Development (PUD): An area planned, developed, operated, and maintained as a single entity containing one or more structures and common areas; may include multiple land uses (e.g., commercial, residential).

Plat: A map or maps of a subdivision or site plan.

Point Source: Water pollution that emanates from a single source such as a sewage plant or stormwater outfall.

Projection: See *Map Projection*

PUD: See *Planned Unit Development*

Radiation: The process by which radiant (electromagnetic) energy is transmitted through free space; the term used to describe electromagnetic energy, as in infrared radiation or short-wave radiation.

Rainfall Intensity: The rate of rainfall measured in inches or centimeters of water deposited on the surface per hour or minute.

Rational Method: A method of computing the discharge from a small drainage basin in response to a given rainstorm; computation is based on the coefficient of runoff, rainfall intensity, and basin area.

Recharge Zone: An area where groundwater recharge is concentrated.

Recharge: The replenishment of groundwater with water from the surface.

Relief: The range of topographic elevation within a prescribed area.

Retention: A strategy used for stormwater management in which runoff is retained on-site in basins, underground, or released into the soil.

Right-of-Way: A strip of land occupied or intended to be occupied by a street, one or more walkways, utility lines, or other special uses.

Riparian Wetland: Wetlands that form on the edge of a water feature such as a lake or stream.

Riparian: The environment along the banks of a stream; often more broadly applied to the larger lowland corridor on the stream valley floor.

Risk Management: An area of planning that involves preparation and response to hazards such as floods, hurricanes, and toxic waste accidents.

Rubber Sheet: a procedure to adjust features of a digital GIS layer in a non-uniform manner; representing "from" and "to" locations are used to define the adjustment.

Runoff: The flow of water from the land as both surface and subsurface discharge; in the more restricted and common use, surface discharge in the form of overland flow and channel flow.

Scale: The relationship between a distance on a map, chart, or photograph and the corresponding distance on the earth.

Septic System: A sewage system that relies on a septic tank to store and/or treat wastewater; generally, an on-site (small-scale) sewage disposal system that depends on the soil for wastewater treatment.

Setback: The minimum distance that a structure or facility should be separated from an edge, such as a property line.

Siltation: The deposition of sediment in water due to soil erosion and stormwater runoff.

Soil Profile: The sequence of horizons, or layers, of a soil.

Solar Heating: The process of generating heat from absorbed solar radiation.

Solar Gain: The amount of solar radiation absorbed by a surface or setting in the landscape.

Solstice: The dates when the declination of the sun is at 23.27 degree north latitude (the Tropic of Cancer) and 23.27 degrees south latitude (Tropic of Capricorn)—June 21–22 and December 21–22, respectively.

Spatial Data: Data or information with implicit or explicit information about location.

Stream Order: the relative position, or rank, of a stream in a drainage network. Streams without tributaries, usually the small ones, are first-order; streams with two or more first-order tributaries are second-order, and so on.

Subdivision: The division of a lot, tract, or parcel of land into two or more lots, tracts, or parcels for sale or development.

Sun Angle: The angle formed between the beam of incoming solar radiation and a plane at the earth's surface.

Surge: A large and often destructive wave caused by intensive atmospheric pressure and strong winds.

Threatened Species: According to the U.S. Endangered Species Act, a species with a rapidly declining population that is likely to become endangered.

TIN: Triangulated irregular network. A surface representation derived from irregularly spaced points and breakline features. Each sample point has an x, y coordinate and a z (surface) value.

Topsoil: The uppermost layer of the soil, characterized by a high organic content.

Water Table: The upper boundary of the zone of groundwater. In fine-textured materials it is usually a transition zone rather than a boundary line. The configuration of the water table often approximates that of the overlying terrain.

Wellhead Protection: Land use planning and management to control contaminant sources in the area contributing recharge water to community wells.

Wetland: An area where the ground is permanently wet or wet most of the year and is occupied by water-loving (or tolerant) vegetation, such as cattails, mangrove, or cypress.

Zenith: For any location on earth, the point that is directly overhead to an observer.

This glossary was compiled, in part, from these sources:

Caliper Corporation. 1994–95. *Maptitude 3.0 User's Guide.* Caliper Corporation, Newton, Massachusetts.

Listokin, D., and C. Walker. 1989. *The Subdivision and Site Plan Handbook.* Center for Urban Policy Research, New Brunswick, New Jersey.

Marsh, W. M. 1998. *Landscape Planning,* 3rd ed. John Wiley & Sons, New York.

References

Abler, R., D. Janelle, A. Philbrick, and J. Sommer. 1975. *Human Geography in a Shrinking World.* Duxbury Press, North Scituate, Massachusetts.

Ahern, J. 1991. "Planning for an Extensive Open Space System: Linking Landscape Structure and Function," *Landscape and Urban Planning* 21: 131–145.

Altshuler, A. A., and J. A. Gomez-Ibanez. 1993. *Regulation for Revenue: The Political Economy of Land Use Exactions.* The Brookings Institution, Washington, D.C.

American Society of Civil Engineers. 1996. *Environmental Site Investigation Guidance Manual.* American Society of Civil Engineers, New York.

American Society of Golf Course Architects. 2000. *Handbook: New Development Steps.* [Online: http://www.golfdesign.org/regular/hand/dvlpmnt.htm]

Ammons, D. N., R. W. Campbell, and S. L. Somoza. 1992. *Selecting Prison Sites: State Processes, Site-Selection Criteria, and Local Initiatives.* Carl Vinson Institute of Government, The University of Georgia, Athens, Georgia.

Anderson, J. R., E. E. Hardy, J. T. Roach, and R. E. Witmer. 1976. "A Land Use and Land Cover Classification System for Use with Remote Sensor Data," Geological Survey Professional Paper 964. U.S. Government Printing Office, Washington, D.C.

Anderson, P. F. 1980. *Regional Landscape Analysis.* Environmental Design Press, Reston, Virginia.

Applied Ecological Services. 2000. *Cost of Native vs. Non-Native Species for Landscaping.* Unpublished fact sheet. Applied Ecological Services, Brodhead, Wisconsin.

Arendt, R. 1999. *Crossroads Hamlet, Village Town: Design Characteristics of Traditional Neighbor-hoods, Old and New.* Planning Advisory Service Report 487/488. American Planning Association, Chicago.

Arendt, R. 1999. *Growing Greener: Putting Conservation into Local Plans and Ordinances.* Island Press, Washington, D.C.

Arlinghaus, S. L., ed. 1994. *Practical Handbook of Digital Mapping: Terms and Concepts.* CRC Press, Boca Raton, Florida.

Arnold, C. L., Jr., and C. J. Gibbons. 1996. "Impervious Surface Coverage: The Emergence of a Key Environmental Indicator," *Journal of the American Planning Association,* 62(2): 243–258.

Bacon, E. 1974. *Design of Cities.* Penguin Books, New York.

Beatley, T., and K. Manning. 1997. *The Ecology of Place: Planning for Environment, Economy, and Community.* Island Press, Washington, D.C.

Beer, A. R. 1990. *Environmental Planning for Site Development.* E&F.N. Spon, London.

Bloom, A. L. 1978. *Geomorphology: A Systematic Analysis of Late Cenozoic Landforms.* Prentice-Hall, Inc., Englewood Cliffs, New Jersey.

Bookout, L. W. 1994. *Value by Design: Landscape, Site Planning, and Amenities.* The Urban Land Institute, Washington, D.C.

Booth, N. K. 1983. *Basic Elements of Landscape Architectural Design.* Waveland Press, Prospect Heights, Illinois.

Bosselman, F. P. and D. Callies. 1972. *The Quiet Revolution in Land Use Control. Prepared for the Council on Environmental Quality.* U.S. Government Printing Office, Washington, D.C.

Brooks, K. R. 1994. "Landscape Architecture: Process and Palette," pp. 221–230 in T. J. Bartuska and G. L. Young, eds., *The Built Environment: A Creative Inquiry into Design & Planning.* Crisp Publications, Inc., Menlo Park, California.

Broughton, J., and S. Apfelbaum. 1999. "Using Ecological Systems for Alternative Stormwater Management," *Land and Water* (Sept./Oct.):10–13.

Brown, C. R. and T. K. Scarborough. 1993. "Applying the Problem-Seeking Approach to Engineering Programming," pp. 47–64 in W. F. E. Preiser, ed., *Professional Practice in Facility Programming.* Van Nostrand Reinhold, New York.

Brown, R. D., and T. J. Gillespie. 1995. *Microclimatic Landscape Design.* John Wiley & Sons, New York.

Castle, G. H. III, ed. 1998. *GIS in Real Estate: Integrating, Analyzing, and Presenting Locational Information.* Appraisal Institute, Illinois.

Cathey, H. M. 1990. *USDA Plant Hardiness Zone Map.* USDA Miscellaneous Publication No. 1475. United States Department of Agriculture, Washington, D.C.

Chapin, F. S., Jr., and E. J. Kaiser. 1985. *Urban Land Use Planning,* 3rd ed. University of Illinois Press, Urbana, Illinois.

Chrisman, N. 1997. *Exploring Geographic Information Systems.* John Wiley & Sons, New York.

City of Livermore. 1999. *South Livermore Valley Specific Plan* (adopted November 17, 1997; Amended January 25, 1999). City of Livermore, Livermore, California.

CLARB, 1998. "Study of the Profession of Landscape Architecture Now Complete," *CLARB* (Council of Landscape Architecture Registration Boards) *News* 13:1–8.

Clark, W. W. and B. A. Bohne. 1999. "Effects of Noise on Hearing," *Journal of the American Medical Association* 281: 1658–1659.

Computer Terrain Mapping, 1997. *Visual Landform Analysis.* CTM, Inc., Boulder, Colorado. [Online: www.ctmap.com/ctm/landform.html]

Cooper-Marcus, C., and C. Francis, eds. 1998. *People Places: Design Guidelines for Urban Open Space,* 2nd ed. Van Nostrand Reinhold, New York.

Cowardin, L. M., V. Carter, F. C. Golet, and E. T. LaRoe. 1979. *Classification of Wetlands and Deepwater Habitats of the United States.* U.S. Department of the Interior, Fish and Wildlife Service Report FWS/OBS-79/31.

Dahl, T. E. 1990. *Wetland Losses in the United States 1780s to 1980s.* United States Department of Interior, Fish and Wildlife Service. U.S. Government Printing Office, Washington, D.C.

Daniels, T. 1999. *When City and Country Collide: Managing Growth in the Metropolitan* Fringe. Island Press, Washington, D.C.

Dean, A. O. 1997. "Listening to Landscape Architects: What Do They Think of Architects?" *Architectural Record* 8:44–49, 160.

deGroot, R. S. 1992. *Functions of Nature: Evaluation of Nature in Environmental Planning, Management and Decision Making.* Wolters-Nordhoff, The Netherlands.

Diamond, H. L., and P. F. Noonan. 1996. *Land Use in America.* Island Press, Washington, D.C.

Dramstad, W. E., J. D. Olson, and R. T. T. Forman. 1996. *Landscape Ecology Principles in Landscape Architecture and Land-Use Planning.* Island Press, Washington, D.C.

Fabos, J. G., G. T. Milde, and V. M. Weinmayr. 1968. *Frederick Law Olmsted, Sr.: Founder of Landscape Architecture in America.* The University of Massachusetts Press, Amherst, Massachusetts.

Ferguson, B. K. 1999. "The Alluvial History and Environmental Legacy of the Abandoned Scull Shoals Mill," *Landscape Journal* 18(2):147–156.

Fisher, H. T. 1982. *Mapping Information: The Graphic Display of Quantitative Information.* Abt Books, Cambridge, MA.

Forman, R. T. T., and M. Godron. 1986. *Landscape Ecology.* John Wiley & Sons, New York.

Forman, R. T. T. 1995. *Land Mosaics: the Ecology of Landscapes and Regions.* Cambridge University Press, New York.

Franklin, C. 1997. "Fostering Living Landscapes," in G. F. Thompson and F. R. Steiner, eds., *Ecological Design and Planning.* John Wiley & Sons, New York.

Gale, D. E. 1992. "Eight State-Sponsored Growth Management Programs: A Comparative Analysis," *Journal of the American Planning Association* 58: 425–439.

Garvin, A. 1996. *The American City: What Works, What Doesn't.* McGraw-Hill, New York.

Goldman, M. and F. D. Petross. 1993. "Planning for a Captive Audience: Approaches and Problems in Programming Correctional Facilities," pp. 357–380 in W. F. E. Preiser, ed., *Professional Practice in Facility Programming.* Van Nostrand Reinhold, New York.

Goodman, W. I., and E. C. Freund, eds. 1968. *Principles and Practice of Urban Planning.* International City Managers' Association. Washington, D.C.

Hammond, S. D. and M. Roberts. 1999. "Smart Growth Livermore: California Preserves Ag Lands through Careful Planning," *Government West* July/August: 15–17.

Haresign, D. T. 1999. "Is a Corporate Campus Right for Your Business?" *Site Selection* January: 1118–1120.

Hendrick, B. 1997. "Loud Noise Can Delay Language Skills in Children, Research Finds." *The Atlanta Journal,* May 8, 1997, p. 3G.

Hinshaw, M. L. 1995. *Design Review.* American Planning Association, Chicago, Illinois.

H. John Heinz Center for Science, Economics and the Environment. 2000. *The Hidden Costs of Coastal Hazards: Implications for Risk Assessment and Mitigation.* Island Press, Washington, D.C.

Hopkins, L. D. 1977. "Methods of Generating Land Suitability Maps: A Comparative Evaluation," *American Institute of Planners Journal.* 43: 386–400.

Hough, M. 1990. *Out of Place: Restoring Identity to the Regional Landscape.* Yale University Press, New Haven, Connecticut.

Hurn, Jeff. 1993. *Differential GPS Explained.* Trimble Navigation. Sunnyvale, California.

Jakle, J. 1987. *The Visual Elements of Landscape.* The University of Massachusetts Press, Amherst, Massachusetts.

Jenks, G. F. 1976. "Contemporary Statistical Maps—Evidence of Spatial and Graphic Ignorance," *The American Cartographer* 3(1):11–19.

Johnston, R. J. 1980. *Multivariate Statistical Analysis in Geography: A Printer on the General Linear Model. Longman Scientific and Technical,* Essex, England.

Joyce, M. D. 1982. *Site Investigation Practice.* E and F.N. Spon, London.

Kaplan, S. J., and E. Kivy-Rosenberg, eds. 1973. *Ecology and the Quality of Life.* Charles C. Thomas, Springfield, Illinois.

Klosterman, R.E. 1999. "The What If? Collaborative Planning Support System," *Environment and Planning B: Planning and Design.* 26: 393–408.

Kolm, K. E. 1996. "Conceptualization and Characterization of Ground-Water Systems Using Geographic Information Systems," pp.131–145 in V.H. Singhroy, D.D. Nebert, and A.I. Johnson, eds., *Remote Sensing and GIS for Site Characterization: Applications and Stands,* ASTM STP 1279. American Society of Testing and Materials, West Conshohocken, Pennsylvania.

Krasnow, P. C. 1998. *Correctional Facility Design and Detailing.* McGraw-Hill, New York.

Kunstler, J. H. 1993. *The Geography of Nowhere: the Rise and Decline of America's Man-Made Landscape.* Simon and Schuster, New York.

Kunstler, J. H. 1998. *Home From Nowhere: Remaking Our Everyday World for the 21st Century.* Touchstone, New York.

Kvashney, A. 1982. "Enhancing Creativity in Landscape Architectural Education," *Landscape Journal* 1(2):104–111.

Kwon, H.Y. 2000. *Better Site Design—An Assessment of the Better Site Design Principles for Communities Implementing the Chesapeake Bay Preservation Act.* Center for Watershed Protection, Ellicott City, Maryland.

LaGro, J. A., Jr. 1996. "Designing without Nature: Unsewered Residential Development in Rural Wisconsin," *Landscape and Urban Planning* 35: 1–9.

Lewis, P. H., Jr. 1996. *Tomorrow by Design: A Regional Design Process of Sustainability.* John Wiley and & Sons, New York.

Linn, M. W. 1993. *Drawing and Designing with Confidence: A Step-By-Step Guide.* Van Nostrand Reinhold, New York.

Listokin, D., and C. Walker. 1989. *The Subdivision and Site Plan Handbook.* Center for Urban Policy Research, New Brunswick, New Jersey.

Lothian, A. 1999. "Landscape and the Philosophy of Aesthetics: Is Landscape Quality Inherent in the Landscape or in the Eye of the Beholder?" *Landscape and Urban Planning* 44: 177–198.

Lynch, Kevin. 1960. *The Image of the City.* MIT Press, Cambridge, Massachusetts.

Lynch, K. 1971. *Site Planning,* 2nd ed. MIT Press, Cambridge, Massachusetts.

Malloy, N. B. and J. A. Pressley. 1994. "LESA: The Next Decade," pp. 262–273 in Steiner, F. R., J. R. Pease, and R. E. Coughlin, eds., *A Decade with LESA: The Evolution of Land Evaluation and Site Assessment.* The Soil and Water Conservation Society, Ankeney, Iowa.

Marks, C. 1997. "Seattle's Environmentally Critical Areas Policies," pp.227–240 in Miller, D., and G. De Roo, eds., *Urban Environmental Planning: Policies, Instruments and Methods in an International Perspective.* Ashgate, Brookfield, Vermont.

Marsh, W. M. 1998. *Landscape Planning: Environmental Applications,* 3rd ed. John Wiley & Sons, New York.

Maslow, A. H. 1954. *Motivation and Personality.* Harper, New York.

Maxwell, C. E. and D. R. Brown. 1993. "Porgramming Processes for Military Health Care Facilities," pp. 249–278 in W. F. E. Preiser, ed., *Professional Practice in Facility Programming.* Van Nostrand Reinhold, New York.

McHarg, I. L. 1969. *Design with Nature.* Published for the Natural History Press. Falcon Press, Philadelphia, Pennsylvania.

McKibbon. 1989. *The End of Nature.* Random House, New York.

Meinig, D. W., ed. 1979. *The Interpretation of Ordinary Landscapes.* Oxford University Press, New York.

Mileti, D. S. 1999. *Disasters by Design: A Reassessment of Natural Hazards in the United States.* Joseph Henry Press, Washington, D.C.

Miller, G. A. 1956. "The Magical Number Seven Plus or Minus Two: Some Limits on Our Capacity for Processing Information," *Psychological Review* 63:81–97.

Miller, P. A. 1997. "A Profession in Peril?" *Landscape Architecture* 87(8): 66–88.

Moore, D. G. 1999. "Tips for Siting New Plastics Plants," *Site Selection* pp.804–819.

Morata, T. C., D. E.Dunn, L. W. Kretschmer, G. K. Lemasters, and R. W. Keith.1993. "Effects of Occupational Exposures to Organic Solvents and Noise on Hearing," *Scand J Work Environ Health* 19: 245–254.

Muller, J. C. 1976. "Numbers of Classes and Chloropleth Pattern Characteristics," *The American Cartographer* 3(2):169–175.

Myers, N., 1979. *The Sinking Ark: A New Look at the Problem of Disappearing Species.* Pergamon Press, New York.

National Main Street Center. 1995. *Keeping Up Appearances.* National Trust for Historic Preservation, Washington, D.C.

Naveh, Z., and A. S. Lieberman. 1984. *Landscape Ecology: Theory and Application.* Springer-Verlag, New York.

Nelessen, A. C. 1994. *Visions for a New American Dream: Process, Principles, and an Ordinance to Plan and Design Small Communities,* 2nd ed. Planners Press, American Planning Association, Chicago, Illinois.

Nivola, P. S. 1999. *Laws of the Landscape: How Policies Shape Cities in Europe and America.* Brookings Institute, Washington, D.C.

Odum, E. P. 1959. *Fundamentals of Ecology,* 2nd ed. Saunders, Philadelphia, Pennsylvania.

Owen, M. S. 1994. "Urban Planning and Design," pp. 289–298 in T. J. Bartuska and G. L. Young, eds., *The Built Environment: A Creative Inquiry into Design & Planning.* Crisp Publications, Menlo Park, California.

Pease, J. R. and A. P. Sussman. 1994. "A Five-Point Approach for Evaluating LESA Models," pp. 94–105 in Steiner, F. R., J. R. Pease, and R. E. Coughlin, eds., *A Decade with LESA: The Evolution of Land Evaluation and Site Assessment.* The Soil and Water Conservation Society, Ankeney, Iowa.

Peiser, R. B. 1992. *Professional Real Estate Development.* Urban Land Institute, Washington, D.C.

Perry, E. 1999. *Trees and other Landscape Plants Have Great Monetary Value.* University of California Cooperative Extension, Modesto, California. [Online: http://www.cnr.berkeley.edu/ucce50/horticulture/6 hlt010.htm]

Pimentel, D., L. Lach, R. Zuniga, and D. Morrison. 2000. "Environmental and Economic Costs of Nonindigenous Species in the United States," *Bioscience* 50(1):53–65.

Platt, R. H. 1996. *Land Use and Society: Geography, Law, and Public Policy.* Island Press, Washington, D.C.

Pregliasco, J. 1988. *Developing Downtown Design Guidelines. California Main Street Program,* Department of Commerce, Sacramento.

Preiser, W. F. E., H. Z. Rabinowitz, and E. T. White. 1988. *Post-Occupancy Evaluation.* Van Nostrand Reinhold, New York.

Preiser, W. F. E. 1985. *Programming the Built Environment.* Van Nostrand Reinhold, New York.

Prince George's County. 2000. *Low-Impact Development: An Integrated Design Approach.* Prince George's County Department of Environmental Resources, Programs and Planning Division, Largo, Maryland.

Rabinowitz, P.M. 2000. "Noise Induced Hearing Loss," *American Family Physician* 61 (9): 2749–2757.

Robinson, A. H., J. L. Morrison, P. C. Muehrcke, A. J. Kimerling, and S. C. Guptill. 1995. *Elements of Cartography,* 6th ed. John Wiley and Sons, New York.

Russell, J. S. 1997. "How Design Hits the Bottom Line: An Overview of the 1997 Awards," *Architectural Record* (Oct.) :54–55.

Saaty, T. L., and L. Vargas. 1982. *The Logic of Priorities.* Kluver Nijhoff, Boston, Massachusetts.

Sanborn. 1999. *Traditional Mapping.* The Sanborn Map Company, Inc., Pelham, New York. [Online: http://www.sanbornmap.com]

Schulze, F. 1994. *Philip Johnson: Life and Work.* The University of Chicago Press, Chicago.

Schwartz, M. and C. Eichhorn. 1997. "Collaborative Decision Making: Using Multiattribute Utility Analysis to Involve Stakeholders in Resolution of Controversial Transportation Issues," *Transportation Research Record.* 1606: 142–148.

Siteseekers.org. Corporate Site Seekers Center. [Online: http://www.SiteSeeker.org]

Stein, K. D. 1997. "Good Design Is Good Business," *Architectural Records* (Oct.):54–55.

Steiner, F. 1991. *The Living Landscape: An Ecological Approach to Landscape Planning.* McGraw-Hill, New York.

Steiner, F. R., J. R. Pease, and R. E. Coughlin, eds. 1994. *A Decade with LESA: The Evolution of Land Evaluation and Site Assessment.* Soil and Water Conservation Society, Ankeny, Iowa.

Steintiz, C. 1979. *Defensible Processes for Regional Landscape Design.* Landscape Architecture Technical Information Series (LATIS). American Society of Landscape Architects, washington, D.C.

Stenberg, K. J., K. O. Richter, D. McNamara, and L. Vicknair. 1997. "A Wildlife Habitat Network for Community Planning Using GIS Technology," pp. 241–254 in Miller, D. and G. De Roo, eds., *Urban Environmental Planning: Policies, Instruments and Methods in an International Perspective.* Ashgate, Brookfield, Vermont.

Talarico, W. 1998. "Evaluating Hidden Site Conditions," *Architectural Record* (May):247–250, 390–392.

The Right Site, 2000. Easy Analytic Software, Inc. Vineland, New Jersey. [Online: http://www.easidemographics.com]

Tiner, R. W. 1997. "Technical Aspects of Wetlands Wetland Definitions and Classifications in the United States," in *National Water Summary on Wetland Resources,* United States Geological Survey Water Supply Paper 2425. [Online: http://www.nwi.fws.gov/bha/]

Tusler, W. H., F. Zilm, J. T. Hannon, and M. A. Newman. 1993. "Programming: The Third Dimension," pp. 227–247 in W. F. E. Preiser, ed., *Professional Practice in Facility Programming,* Van Nostrand Reinhold, New York.

United States Department of Agriculture. 1990. *USDA Plant Hardiness Zone Map.* USDA Miscellaneous Publication No. 1475.

United States Environmental Protection Agency. 1993. *Guidance Specifying Management Measures for Sources of Nonpoint Pollution in Coastal Waters.* EPA840B93001c. January 1993 (Revised January 21, 1997). [Online: http://www.epa.gov/OWOW/NPS/MMGI/index.html]

United States Geological Survey. 2000. National Geologic Map Database. [Online: http://ngmsvr.wr.usgs.gov/ngmdb/]

United States National Oceanic and Atmospheric Agency. 2000a. *Heat Wave.* National Weather Service Internet Weather Source. Revised: June 27, 2000. [Online: http://weather.noaa.gov/weather/hwave. html]

United States National Oceanic and Atmospheric Agency. 2000b. *Coastal Zone Management Act of 1972* (as amended through P.L. 104150, The Coastal Zone Protection Act of 1996). Revised: April 05, 2000. [Online: http://www.ocrm.nos.noaa.gov/czm/czm_act.html]

Venturi, R., D. Scott Brown, and S. Izenour. 1972. *Learning from Las Vegas: the Forgotten Symbolism of Architectural Form,* rev. ed. MIT Press, Cambridge, Massachusetts.

Way, D. S. 1978. *Terrain Analysis: A Guide to Site Selection Using Aerial Photographic Interpretation,* 2nd ed. Dowden, Hutchinson & Ross, Stroudsburg, Pennsylvania.

Wester, L. M. 1990. *Design Communication for Landscape Architects.* Van Nostrand Reinhold. New York:

Western Australian Planning Commission. 2000. *Liveable Neighborhoods,* 2nd ed. Western Australian Planning Commission, Perth, Australia.

White, E. T. 1983. *Site Analysis: Diagraming Information for Architectural Design.* Architectural Media, Tucson, Arizona.

Whyte. W. H. 1980. *The Social Life of Small Urban Spaces.* Conservation Foundation, Washington, D.C.

Wilcove, D. S., D. Rothstein, J. Dubow, A. Phillips, and E. Losos. 1998. "Quantifying Threats to Imperiled Species in the United States," *BioScience* 48: 607–615.

Wilson, E. O., ed. 1988. *Biodiversity.* National Academy Press, Washington, D.C..

World Commission on Environment and Development. 1987. *Our Common Future.* Oxford University Press, Oxford, UK.

Yeang, K. 1995. *Designing with Nature: The Ecological Basis for Architectural Design.* McGraw-Hill, New York.

Zeisel, J. and M. A. Maxwell. 1993. "Programming Office Space: Adaptive Re-Use of the H-E-B Arsenal Headquarters," pp.153–184 in W. F. E. Preiser, ed., *Professional Practice in Facility Programming.* Van Nostrand Reinhold, New York.

Index